Third Edition

SECONDARY SCHOOL CURRICULUM IMPROVEMENT

Meeting Challenges of the Times

J. LLOYD TRUMP
National Association of Secondary School Principals

DELMAS F. MILLER
West Virginia University

ALLYN AND BACON, INC.
Boston   London   Sydney   Toronto

Previous editions were published under the title *Secondary School Curriculum Improvement: Challenges, Humanism, Accountability,* Copyright © 1973, 1968 by Allyn and Bacon, Inc.

79-4597
Library of Congress Cataloging in Publication Data

Trump, J. Lloyd, 1908–
 Secondary school curriculum improvement.

 Includes bibliographical references and index.
 1. Education, Secondary—Curriculum. 2. Curriculum change. I. Miller, Delmas F., joint author.
 II. Title.
 LB1607.T7   1979   373.1'9   79–348
 ISBN 0–205–06600–3

Printed in the United States of America.

Contents

III DEVELOPMENTS THAT CUT ACROSS CURRICULUM AREAS   275

Introduction

Turmoil has always affected schools, especially in countries like the United States where the public speaks freely and school people invite opinions. Teachers and principals are expected to have ideas about the curriculum. They also encourage their students to participate in curriculum development.

Some writers today believe schools are a disaster. Many students apparently believe that considerable portions of today's curriculum are not relevant to helping them cope with today's problems and developments. Some teachers, administrators, parents, and others are uncertain about how to improve schools.

This book focuses on curriculum practitioners. Its targets include teachers in middle schools and junior and senior high schools who keep the curriculum in motion as they seek constantly to develop the maximum potential of each individual student. The principals and supervisors who work with those teachers and students also constitute a signficant audience—so do persons who work in state education departments and others who teach and study in universities.

Our aim is to provide materials that will stimulate college and university students at all levels, as well as educational practitioners, to examine their own thinking about the curriculum and to develop plans to transfer their ideas into school programs that they can accept and manage.

To set the record straight, we indicate what the book is *not*. We have not made a compilation either of various philosophies of curriculum or a lengthy list of current practices in schools, although both these topics are treated to help readers understand and appreciate present needs and developments. We have not assembled extensive references on philosophical statements or reports of research. Anyone interested in such a bibliography may utilize such guides as *Education Index*, the *Encyclopedia of Educational Research*, and other references found in most education libraries.

We take relatively strong positions on many issues. We believe deeply in these points of view or we would not express them. In fact, that is why we have written this book. We believe that readers also need to establish their own defensible positions—that is our goal for you.

Every chapter has suggestions for curriculum improvement. Recent developments in the subject areas are highlighted. Three new chapters treat some emphases that seem especially important today.

Secondary school curriculum improvement is more crucial now than ever before. We believe this book will help teachers and those who work with them to make beneficial changes in the schools where they work. That locale is where improvement can produce immediate positive results.

We think basic changes in curriculum and other aspects of schooling are necessary; however, we see no reason for panic. On the other hand, we believe that constructive efforts to improve programs are imperative. Decisions have to be made. We want to help people make wise choices.

This third edition finds the secondary school curriculum buffeted by many of the same pressures that existed in 1968 when the first edition was written. However, some forces are different now. Then student activism was at its height, especially in universities, but it was also reflected in secondary schools. Since the curriculum is at the heart of the program, there were pronounced protests against what schools were teaching. Many schools altered their programs to make them more responsive to student interests.

As the curriculum and other aspects of the schools became more flexible, criticisms about responsibility became more rampant. When the second edition of this book appeared in 1973, the word *accountability* was being heard frequently from critics of school programs.

Simultaneously, a number of proposals were made for comprehensive reforms in secondary education, including proposals for developing alternative schools and reducing the compulsory attendance age.

The content in Parts I, IV, V, and VI represents in part further development of ideas expressed by J. Lloyd Trump in *Focus on Change—Guide to Better Schools*, published by Rand McNally & Company in 1960. Articles by the same author on similar topics also have appeared in a number of educational journals and in a 1977 book, *A School For Everyone*, published by the National Association of Secondary School Principals.

Increasingly, educators recognize the necessity of improving all aspects of the school program simultaneously. Curriculum is more than content. Where teaching and learning occur, the variety of strategies, the evaluation methods, the differentiated staffs that produce changed roles of teachers and learners, and how a school uses time, spaces, numbers in student and teacher groups, and money all affect educational quality. Innovations in one area are nullified by failures to change other program aspects because all are interdependent.

Most of the foregoing pressures still exist. However, some new ones are on the scene. Declining birth rates are reducing school enrollments; in fact, some schools have closed. Population mobility changes the situation from place to place. The impact of strikes, unemployment, inflation, and difficult problems in international relations have increased during this period.

School programs reflect the times. The combination of student unrest and other factors that distract from schooling produce dissatisfactions. One result is that student performance on a number of norm-based instruments is less satisfactory than in the past. Do secondary school programs prepare students adequately for these examinations? Other outcomes include poor attendance, tendency to leave school earlier, and changes in young people's attitudes and mores. Are schools less attractive now? Most students spend more time watching television and engaging in recreational activities than doing homework and other school-related activities.

At the same time, teacher organizations are increasingly militant. Strikes are now common, not only in cities but also in wealthy suburban areas. Teachers are demanding higher salaries and better working conditions. Seldom is curriculum improvement an issue.

Recently, we completed an eight-year Model Schools Project, sometimes called Schools of Tomorrow, that involved a considerable number of schools. This revision reflects some ideas and procedures from that project.

JLT
DFM

I
Meeting Old and New Challenges

1

What Are Your Present Beliefs about the Curriculum?

No matter who you are — university student, teacher, supervisor, parent, or someone else concerned about better schools — you rightly have an interest in *what* schools teach and the *methods* used.

Are you and your ideas about a school program keeping up with the times? Are you prepared to help colleagues and students engage in constructive efforts to improve themselves and the society in which they exist? People still argue about whether schools should reflect the times or try to create a better world. History is on the side of the first point of view. But many people hope to reach the second goal.

How will you cope with the critics of your school's program? How will you change schools? How will you make the schools more humane? How will you make schools more accountable for what the program does to students and teachers?

Many questions affecting curriculum development divide professional workers in schools and universities. Parents, board of education members, and persons outside the schools also discuss these matters. Although research findings are available to help resolve some of the issues, others require more investigation. However, with or without evidence (but we hope with thoughtful consideration), every middle, junior high, and senior high school staff and the clientele they serve will resolve each issue one way or another — and you should have a part in these decisions.

Are schools too permissive or too rigid in the learning environments they provide for students and teachers? Should the curriculum resolve conflicts in society such as whether to preserve the environment or enhance technology and economic growth; preserve the older mores or go along with the freedoms in sexuality, dress, and conduct; stress cooperation more and competition less; and many other issues? What is the relative importance of sensory experiences in schools and conceptual knowledge? Have affective learnings in the curriculum been neglected by an overemphasis on cognitive and skills developments?

This chapter lists and explains twenty issues that are among those that will be discussed more fully in later chapters. At the end of each explanation you are asked to make a decision. After you have read and considered the subsequent material, you may change your mind. Answering the questions now, however, will help you to understand the nature of the secondary school curriculum better. Regardless of your present situation — student, teacher, administrator, supervisor, or someone outside the immediate professional field of education — your opinion is important, because you, along with other experts, will help to formulate the curriculum.

So, we ask you to think carefully about the twenty issues that follow. Of course, you may add others if you wish. At the end of the chapter you can check your understanding of the nature of curriculum with the definition we provide.

SOME ISSUES IN CURRICULUM DEVELOPMENT

1 Who Shall Determine What Is Relevant Curriculum Content for Secondary Schools?

An increased mobility of students pushes secondary education toward a national curriculum. The increased use of such mass communications media as television, radio, newspapers and magazines, standard textbooks, and programmed instruction underscore the need. Many persons recognize the importance of common denominators in the curriculum content of all secondary students in the United States. Increasingly the question is asked, Should persons in Bangor, Maine; Jackson, Mississippi; Portland, Oregon; or Farmer City, Illinois, be taught different facts, concepts, and skills in United States history? Curriculum programs aimed at national audiences are being developed by university professors and school teachers with foundation, commercial, and federal government support.

Other persons argue that the trend away from local curriculum development is unfortunate — that local initiative and interest are lost as national agencies and groups take over more and more responsibility for curriculum development.

Between the extreme positions are those who accept the advisability of a national curriculum for the basic education required for all citizens while preferring that the local school retain control over regional content and the "elective" subjects or "depth education" aspects of the curriculum wherein individual teacher and student interests and talents are manifest. Such persons point out that teaching methods and expenditures for special supplies and equipment tend to be localized. They emphasize that state governments and local districts have effectively resolved conflicts in the past.

What do you believe about this issue? (See Chapter 2 and Part II.)

2   What Rights and Responsibilities Do Students Have Insofar as the Curriculum Is Concerned?

One basic issue related to the question is how to balance student rights with responsibilities to the school in particular and to society in general. Historically, society has established schools to maintain an existing social order. As the mores change, the curriculum changes also, but never vice versa. Does it matter that some groups in society are better organized or otherwise more powerful than others? As a protection against such potential influences, should students have more rights to determine what subjects they study in schools?

A closely related issue involves teachers' rights to determine the curriculum. Teachers are more mature than students and may have better judgment about the importance of a subject. In addition, teachers certainly have a vested interest in the schools. If certain subjects are not required of all students, the teacher of these subjects may no longer be needed; in other words, they will lose their positions. Do they have a right to defend their vested interests?

If students were to control the curriculum, the question then is, which students? Students vary in interests, talents, socioeconomic backgrounds, goals in life, and many other areas. Should a particular group that constitutes a majority in the school control the lives of other students, or should they be able to do so?

What should be the effects on the curriculum of the rapidly changing mores relating to social behavior and careers of girls and women in our society? Their participation in interscholastic athletics is now more prevalent. More careers are open. Behavioral changes are natural results of these and other developments. Although we believe many of these changes are long overdue, other people have different points of view.

Students tend to follow fads. If they were to control the curriculum, there would be less stability in the school program. On the other hand, today's curriculum may be too stable.

What are your thoughts about the foregoing issues?

3 Shall the Professionals in Schools Resist the Pressures for Curricular Reforms that Originate Outside the System?

Slogans such as "back to the basics," "increase discipline," "eliminate frills," "improve accountability," and "earlier graduation or school leaving" are more commonplace today than when we developed the first and second editions of this book. Should school personnel ignore, respond negatively, or act aggressively in responding to such comments? After all, the public supports the schools; they have a right to express opinions. Are the complaints justified? Do the tests that indicate declines in literacy, computation skills, and the ability to express ideas and otherwise communicate accurately measure outcomes from schooling that are essential for everyone in today's society? Some studies show that many so-called illiterates hold professional and managerial jobs with relatively high salaries.

Which is more important: performance on tests of basic skills or the ability to get along with other persons, to be creative, and the like? Are such outcomes dichotomies or does one result depend on another?

Should curriculum goals emphasize changing attitudes as well as providing skills and memorizing facts? Who should determine *what facts* — curriculum specialists or laypeople such as parents, corporation executives, labor union officials, taxpayer association members, and journalists?

Is curriculum improvement actually limited by factors outside the control of professional educators? Some people blame existing problems in schools on working mothers, absent fathers, large poverty-stricken families, and other specified groups; or on television, permissiveness, disenchantment with the world as it is, changing values, and a host of other factors.

The basic question is whether the school curriculum should aim to change society or continue to reflect the existing mores and try to live with the situations. Are schools really helpless in the face of all these factors that seem to limit progress?

What are your reactions to these questions about external pressures on the curriculum?

4   How Shall the Curriculum Content Be Organized?

Throughout the centuries, curriculum developers have organized human knowledge in a variety of ways. Traditionally, the secondary schools in this country have taught such subjects as English, social studies or social sciences (history, geography, civics, economics, etc.), science (botany, zoology, physics, chemistry, etc.), mathematics (algebra, geometry, etc.), music, art, agriculture, auto mechanics, and so on, as discrete subjects. (We use that organization of curriculum content in this book in chapters 4 through 14.) Those who favor this approach to content point out that it eases the transition from secondary school to university, since universities follow similar patterns. The vocational goals also are stated in subject-matter terms: an engineer needs to know science and mathematics in addition to other professional skills; a writer needs to specialize in English; an attorney needs basic education in the social sciences. Those who favor discrete subjects point out that integration and correlation of content occurs in the mind of the learner as he or she calls on what has been learned in the various subject disciplines.

Other curriculum authorities prefer to structure content according to life experiences and needs, contending that every experience requires knowledge in many subjects. For example, preparing for effective home and family living requires understanding not only home economics, but also mathematics, social studies, English, fine and practical arts, sciences, health and physical education, and, in fact, every other curricular area. Understanding the concept of *democracy* also requires the study of many subject disciplines. Curriculum writers urge "core," "integrated," "broad fields," and other combinations of subject content.

An alternative to the two extremes might be the use of the discrete subject-matter approach in the basic education required of all students and the integrated subject-matter approach in the depth education programs that the school sponsors as a part of the independent study program; or you could argue a converse arrangement. (Basic education, depth education and independent study are discussed in chapters 2 and 20.)

What is your opinion about the organization of curriculum content?

5 Shall Curriculum Flexibility Be Encouraged Through New Mini-courses or May Similar Outcomes Be Attained Through Conventional Programs?

The mini-course approach to curriculum reform involves the further development of what were formerly called units in a subject field. The difference between the conventional units and mini-courses is that the mini-courses are entities in themselves. A student completes as many of these mini-courses as his or her interests warrant.

Since completion of these mini-courses is not tied into the conventional 180-day concept of regular courses, this approach provides more flexibility through a variety of offerings, wider types of experiences, and fewer restrictions on time. More provisions for individual differences are provided since a student may select a course for two, six, twelve, or some other number of weeks of instruction instead of being required to take a course for a minimum of one semester or an entire year.

Ideas for mini-courses may originate from either students or teachers. Surveys of student interests and needs suggest some titles. Teachers develop mini-courses in relation to their own special interests and competences, something that conventional programs fail to consider when standard courses of study are created, usually by persons outside the school. Thus, the content of mini-courses may be more relevant to today's students.

Opponents of mini-courses point out the great amount of work that has gone into the development of conventional semester- or year-long courses. Also, they may believe that mini-courses tend to concentrate on brief spans of knowledge and skills and omit important developments in the affective areas of learning. The mini-courses are not particularly related to each other, in contrast to the logical development that goes into conventional courses. A student who takes a series of mini-courses instead of a standard curriculum may miss important topics or skills.

What do you believe about mini-courses? Does the flexibility that such courses provide outweigh the potential gains from massive curriculum restructuring?

6 Shall Affective Education Be Given More Attention in Secondary School Curriculum Improvement or Is the Present Major Emphasis on Cognitive and Skills Outcomes More Defensible?

Affective education relates to such outcomes as the development of values, self-awareness, cooperation, compromise, sensitivity, and mental health.

The skills of affective education probably determine the character of a human being much better than what the individual knows and can do, the cognitive and skills areas. Mental health therefore needs to be as much a part of the curriculum as mathematics, reading, and history. According to some classifications, the whole area of social relationships falls in the affective domain, although others view it as a separate entity.

Most school programs today emphasize cognitive and skills outcomes because these objectives are easier both to teach and to evaluate. If schools already have difficulties in teaching basic skills and basic knowledge, why should they attempt to teach and measure outcomes in the affective areas? Schools already have too much to cover.

Moreover, if curriculum improvement is sorely needed in skills and knowledge, why should those efforts be complicated further by emphasizing the affective areas? The curriculum needs to concentrate on improving present programs rather than assuming also the complex area of affective education, which some educators think terrifying, to say the least.

How would you resolve this issue? As you study secondary school curriculum improvement, do you want to pay more attention to affective education?

7 Who Shall Operate Programs of Work Experience Education?

Should junior and senior high schools deal mainly with academically oriented youths and leave work experience programs to federal agencies or to industry? (See Chapter 14.) Another aspect of the issue concerns the acceptance of the idea of the comprehensive high school as opposed to separate academic and vocational schools. A third is whether vocational schools should be operated by federal agencies rather than by local or area administrations.

Not all youths profit from a totally academic or school-building-centered educational program. Some of these young people drop out of school, and others stay reluctantly, with limited gains. During the 1930s, the National Youth Administration and the Civilian Conservation Corps, federally supported and operated work experience programs, apparently met the needs of a great many students. Many schools today engage in work programs to a limited degree (for example, in distributive education), but such efforts reach relatively few students. Both federal and state agencies emphasize *career education*. They often propose work experience programs similar in many respects to those of the 1930s. Also, more funds for vocational education are proposed. Why did these earlier programs fail to become integral parts of the curriculum for all students?

Other curriculum questions revolve around the need for such specialized courses as *business* English, *shop* mathematics, or *pre-engineering* science. Should basic education be the same for all students, work-bound or college-bound, with adaptations made at the level of electives or depth education?

How would you resolve such questions and on what basis?

8   Shall More or Less Emphasis Be Placed on Extraclass (Cocurricular) Activities?

Today's emphasis on extra homework for the regular school subjects cuts into the time for athletics, clubs, social activities, publications, and other school activities. Nationally televised programs do the same. Is the need for extraclass activities diminishing? Most teachers enjoy working with students in extraclass activities, but some object to this "extra work" for a variety of reasons.

Should the school turn over these activities to various youth-serving agencies in the community? Many educators argue strongly against that solution, pointing out that the extraclass program complements the other curriculum services to students. They object to the pressures placed on students by persons and agencies outside the school who may not visualize the total needs of individual students.

An alternate solution of the problem is to recognize extraclass activities as an integral part of the curriculum. This solution requires changes in school schedules, assignment of teachers, school records and reports, and similar matters.

How would you resolve the issue? (See Chapter 17.) What activities, if any, would you add or subtract? Is the real question related to the quality of extracurricular activities?

9   How Shall Students Be Grouped for Instruction?

Most schools conduct instruction in a given subject in a self-contained classroom, with one teacher responsible for twenty-five to thirty-five students. Sometimes these classes are divided into subgroups on the basis of ability or achievement. When there is more than one section of a given subject, the entire class may be grouped on the basis of ability or past achievement. The issue, however, is not necessarily homogeneous versus heterogeneous ability or achievement grouping. Other grouping plans are also being demonstrated in schools.

Some schools vary the size and composition of groups, depending on the purposes and content of instruction and the needs of individual students. The issue is whether to organize classes of twenty-five with heterogeneous or homogeneous grouping or to use a combination of independent study, large-group instruction, and small-group discussion — three terms that are discussed in Chapters 20, 21, and 22, respectively.

What kinds of groups do you prefer? Will they be the same for all subjects?

10   To What Extent Shall Individual Programming of Students Be Encouraged?

As students mature and receive more education, the individual differences among them increase. How much of a student's day should be spent in classes required of everyone and how much of the day should be spent in work that is particularly interesting and appropriate for the individual? Are the "required-elective" system and the conventional school schedule for curriculum organization superior to a system of "basic depth" education (see Chapter 24) and flexible scheduling (see Chapter 25)?

The present system of programming and scheduling has evolved over many years as a systematic way to measure subject credits, graduation requirements, teacher and student class loads, and a variety of other administrative arrangements. The system is widely accepted and understood by students, parents, and teachers. But what about the relationships between quantity and quality?

The main question is, Can individual differences among youths be served adequately in a conventionally organized curriculum or are basic changes needed? The alternatives to the two extreme points of view involve the variety of rationalized changes presented in Parts IV and V.

How do you answer the foregoing questions? What are the bases for your present opinions?

11   Are School Programs Too Permissive or Too Rigid in the Learning and Teaching Environments They Provide for Students and Teachers?

The terms *open* and *closed* are used to describe schools. Students in some open schools can study where they want with no required attendance. Teachers and administrators hold them responsible for performance and passing tests and other measures of productivity. The closed environment aims to keep all students in classrooms for specified periods with emphasis on attendance and control. Educational progressives advocate the open school; the conservatives believe in the closed philosophy. Similar beliefs divide the students and their parents. School principals and their assistants find themselves in the middle of a hot controversy.

How would you resolve this dilemma?

12 Shall the Common A, B, C, D, F System for Evaluating Pupil Achievement Be Replaced by a P, F (Pass, Fail) System or by More Comprehensive Schemes That Record Each Student's Progress in Completing Specified Segments in Various Sequences of Learnings, Describe Special Projects Completed, and Appraise Other Selected Outcomes, Especially in the Affective Domain?

Two basic issues actually are involved. One question is whether the school shall recognize and formalize *failure* in the final appraisal and reporting system or whether it will only report the student's progress or lack of it. The other issue is whether the school shall collect and report much more data than single letter grades, including P and F, describe. Shall specific competences be listed and measured as prerequisites for completing courses or school? Since the reporting system influences pupil goals and parental aspirations, the issue is basic. Of course, a related issue concerns the degree to which the school's evaluation system emphasizes competition among students vis-à-vis a competition with his or her own past record. All these matters are discussed in Chapter 33.

What are your ideas about the grading system?

13 Shall Schools Abandon the Carnegie Unit or Similar Measures of Learning in Favor of Performance-based Criteria That Do Not Involve Standard Time Modules?

The conventional method for recording pupil progress through the school program and for graduation is to give credit for a course when a pupil spends 200 to 250 minutes per week for 18 weeks (0.5 credit) or 36 weeks (1 unit), having earned at least the minimum passing grade — typically D—. The proposed alternative is to give the credit whenever a student passes the tests and does whatever else is required in an acceptable manner, regardless of how long he or she requires. The latter alternative is basic to the continuous-progress, or ungraded, concept that individualized learning emphasizes (see Chapter 24). Yet universities require definite numbers of units for entrance and so do many high schools in accepting pupils from other schools or for determining who receives a diploma.

How might this issue be resolved?

14 Shall the Curriculum Typically Provided for Grades 12 and 13 Be Changed?

Is it possible to bridge the gap between high school and college without unnecessary repetitiveness? Can universities provide information that students actually need when they enter higher education?

Recently, a group of educators representative of all parts of the country recommended that the present twelfth grade be located in colleges so that students who wanted to take certain courses could take them during their first year of higher education. Conversely, higher education has been criticized by some persons who believe that the first year of college is too much like high school. Many concepts and much information that students had already obtained in their high schools were repeated. Some professors thought that the high schools had not done an adequate job; therefore, many facts needed repetition.

Since it is cheaper for students and their parents when students remain at home rather than to go away to a university, would it be better to provide much of the first year of the university as elective courses in the local high school? Should universities be expected to give entering freshmen placement examinations so they would not have to repeat certain university courses? Will transition between secondary school and universities always remain relatively unplanned?

Do you believe that the twelfth grade belongs in high school or in college? Or do you have a better idea to bridge the gaps between the two institutions?

15 Shall All Students Be Expected to Remain in the Secondary School Six Years?

A three-year junior high school (grades 7, 8, and 9) followed by a three-year senior high school (grades 10, 11, and 12), or a six-year school (grades 7 through 12), is the commonly accepted organization of secondary education in the United States. Because of their high ability and high motivation, some students are able to complete this program and pass examinations satisfactorily in less than six years. However, they may be kept productively busy for the six-year period through the provision of enrichment materials.

Shall there be more rapid acceleration through the schools or shall there be more enrichment of subject matter at each grade level, the amount of extra work being based on individual differences? Another suggested alternative is to eliminate annual promotions and to ungrade the schools so that each student may progress at her or his own rate of speed. (These ideas are discussed further in Chapter 24.) These decisions, of course, affect articulation with the elementary school and with the freshman year of college.

Related to this issue is the question of admitting what are now regarded as elementary-age pupils to secondary education in a "middle school." This school may include pupils formerly enrolled in the fifth grade and some advanced fourth-graders. Television and other mass media produce more sophisticated and informed children. Should the new secondary school serve learners eight or more years? How do the number of years affect the curriculum?

16   Shall the Present Arrangements for Educating Youth Be Replaced by Completely Different Programs and Procedures or Can Present Schools be Modified to Accommodate the Proposals That Critics Are Making?

Because most schools either ignore community resources or else use them only minimally or incorrectly, some writers urge the use of "schools without walls." That arrangement calls for schools in warehouses, office buildings, or abandoned stores that serve only as headquarters while most learning is in community agencies, institutions, offices, museums, and factories. The alternative is individualized, flexible scheduling and a variety of curricular changes (see Chapters 25, 27, and 30).

One more example is to abolish credential requirements for teachers and principals because present preparation programs produce so many educators who oppose change and do not relate well to the people and problems in the "real world." These critics would replace principals with experts on social change drawn from industry and other fields outside education. Similarly, laypeople would be recruited as teachers, with a preparation program completely different from the present teacher education curricula.

Are such alternatives better than what schools can provide?

**17   To What Extent Shall Schools Attempt
      to Supplement the Work of Parents,
      Society in General, and Social Agencies?**

The locations of some schools produces de facto segregation of pupils
along racial, religious, or national lines. Some persons argue that such a
distribution affects curriculum adversely. They argue that students
should be transferred from one area to another to create a more balanced distribution, busing the children if necessary. Others argue that
the fault is with housing regulations or social mores and that the school
should not do what society itself has not done.

Parents should provide sex education in the home, according to
some persons. Others point effectively to parental failures along these
lines and urge comprehensive sex education programs in schools.
Analogous arguments are presented concerning the school's role in
health education, religious education, moral training, and the like.
Should the schools do what parents fail to do or do ineffectively?

Family incomes vary widely. Should schools provide free services
to students who cannot afford to pay while charging others for the
same provisions? Should the school serve as a social agency when
economic opportunities are limited for some learners?

What are your beliefs about these and similar issues? (Information
on the foregoing questions occurs throughout this book, especially
in Parts II and III.)

**18   Who Shall Control Education in General and
      the Curriculum in Particular?**

Some recent publications include the belief that the American Federation of Teachers and the National Education Association through
their local units have taken control of schools away from local school
boards, administrators, accrediting associations, and other groups.
Legally, schools are creatures of the states; local school boards develop
their policies. However, differences often exist between what the law
says and what actually happens — whether the case in point be school
programs or some other aspect of society.

Who should control the curriculum of a given secondary school?
Shall the local board of education determine how many years of
English are required for graduation? Shall lay advisory committees, the
local business community, organized labor, or other groups determine
what is to be taught?

Many years ago, some extremists among the progressive education
movement were believed to have made the point that students them-

selves should determine what the curriculum should be in schools. Although that belief never gained much recognition, the question is still appropriate.

Who should control the curriculum?

19 What Criteria Shall Be Used in Evaluating the Excellence of a Given School?

The evaluative criteria typically used by accrediting associations and state education departments are being questioned. So are the values of such factors as the number of merit scholarship winners in a school, performance on standardized achievement tests, the quality of the school building, and the public relations program.

Is it possible and important to measure growth in individual responsibility for learning and the quality of what students do while engaged in independent study? Or is it sufficient to use data from the usual standardized achievement tests? Having defined school goals in terms of changes in student behavior, can a school discover whether these changes actually have occurred? Or is possession of knowledge a sufficient test of educational outcomes? Do qualitative judgments have a place in evaluation, along with the collection of quantitative data and the professional interpretation of the data? What criteria deserve highest priorities? What is a workable scheme? (See Chapters 32 and 33.)

Again, what do you believe?

20 How Shall Increased Funds Be Spent to Improve Educational Quality?

Educators' professional organizations frequently argue that increased funds should be spent for higher salaries for teachers and for smaller classes. However, some persons contend that those factors alone do not produce better educational quality, so increased expenditures are also needed for technical devices, clerical services, and instruction assistants to aid teaching and learning. These people also ask for more free time for teachers so that they may keep up to date, confer more with their professional colleagues, and perform other professional tasks. Generally speaking, schools spend much more money on buildings and less on tools than do industrial organizations.

Should financial input be related more scientifically to educational output? (Chapters 27, 28, and 30 will explore this question in more detail.) Does curriculum improvement require different criteria than schools use now in spending the funds they receive?

Who is responsible for increased accountability in the use of school funds, materials, spaces, and the time of learners and teachers? How is the content of curriculum related to accountability? Who will determine the performance criteria that show the productivity of the institution?

What do you think? Do you have ideas about what expenditures school officials might reduce in order to have more funds for the research and development of new ideas? Are industrial development ideas appropriate for schools?

FACTORS THAT AFFECT THE CURRICULUM

Answering the foregoing questions reveals a number of factors that enter into a definition of the curriculum: content, methods, and structure. We use the term *structure* in a broad sense to include organization, configuration, facilities, resources, time, and numbers — the educational setting for teaching and learning.

The answers also point out the human dimensions in curriculum. The characteristics and needs of individual students are basic considerations. Equally important are the needs and characteristics of each teacher, especially the manner in which individual competences are utilized. The school principal is a key also in each school as far as the curriculum is concerned.

Political, social, economic, and other cultural forces outside the school also influence the curriculum. Various supervisors and administrators and a host of other persons are doing research, producing materials, issuing pronouncements, raising funds, and taking political action. Vigorous statements by prestigious individuals and groups influence what teachers do. Research focuses on particular learning theories and teaching methods creating special styles in teaching and learning. Foundations, governments, corporations, and organizations provide funds to foster particular curricular ideas and special programs for the education of teachers and students. These influences and others are explored in some detail in chapters 2 and 3.

A TIME OF INNOVATION

Recent surveys by the National Association of Secondary School Principals reveal numerous exemplary programs in the use of television, video tape, data processing, telephone amplification, dial-access systems, minority studies, drug studies, use of learning packages, differentiated staffing, flexible scheduling, team teaching, independent study, use of teacher-counselors, changed grading systems, and other innovations. Today's secondary schools are especially innovative in challenging many traditional beliefs about curriculum content, methods, and structure.

Are these curricular innovations merely fads that teachers and principals follow in order to be up-to-date? Consider what often happens when a course outline is revised, or the schedule is changed, or a learning resources center is added to the curriculum. The revision may exhilarate the teachers and students, but an evaluation after the change has operated for a while shows limited or no pupil gains. Curriculum restructuring requires coordinated, innovative approaches. Attempting to alter any one aspect of the curriculum — content, for instance — without varying teaching and learning methods and structure in a carefully conceived *instructional system* limits the effectiveness of the changes. All factors must change together if the maximum potential benefits are to be realized.

DEFINING CURRICULUM

The conventional way to define curriculum is to refer to the variety of instructional activities planned and provided for pupils by the local school or school system. The definition is all right; it simply lacks vigor. Curriculum is a vital, moving, complex interaction of people and things in a freewheeling setting. It includes questions to debate, forces to rationalize, goals to illuminate, programs to activate, and outcomes to evaluate. These topics are what this book is all about. Part I initiates the process.

Chapter 1 aims to help you clarify your own present opinions. Chapter 2 lists the authors' basic beliefs about teaching and learning. You must accept, reject, or modify these beliefs — and possibly add some others — as background for your work. Chapter 3 helps you to understand the current pressures for curriculum change.

Part II of this book helps you to understand the curriculum issues and major developments in eleven secondary school subject areas. Career education, common learnings, mini-courses, special projects, extraclass activities, and adult education are discussed in Part III. Part IV deals with the educational setting, and Part V suggests ways to organize for change, the need for different teaching roles, and how to plan and conduct experimental studies and demonstrations. Some pitfalls to be avoided are identified. The final section, Part VI, discusses ways to evaluate present individual achievements and program developments with a look ahead to the future.

By the time you finish this book, you will have a sound, coordinated basis for secondary school curriculum improvement in your school. This broad operational plan is more likely to produce significant gains in learning for each student than would a narrow, segmented approach to change. As part of the improvement program, you will take important steps to professionalize the teaching staff and to recognize their individual differences. You will understand that secondary school curriculum improvement requires more than revising content. All aspects are interrelated.

TOPICS FOR STUDY AND DISCUSSION

1. From the twenty issues listed in this chapter, select the one that interests you the most. Read as much material on this issue as time permits, then prepare a case on one side or the other to present to your colleagues.
2. What other educational issues affecting curriculum planning and development seem important to you? List at least one and indicate the arguments on either side.
3. Who should decide issues of curriculum development? What are the roles of teachers, school administrators, parents, and the public? What is the role of the curriculum expert? Which goals are local, state, or national concerns?

SELECTED REFERENCES

Cawelti, Gordon. "Issues in Competency Based Education," *Educational Leadership* (Nov. 77), pp. 86–91.
 The need for clearer goals and sharper focus on general education is offset by confusions between capability and competence, difficulties in setting minima and maxima, and a tendency to omit the fine arts and physical education.
Cunningham, Luvern I., "Educational Leadership: The Curious Blend," *Educational Leadership* (February 1976), pp. 323–326.
 Today's issues are more complex than ever before as the goals of schooling are less clear and the conflicts about them more pronounced. The resolution demands improved leadership.
Curtis, Thomas E., and Bedwell, Wilma M. *Curriculum and Instruction for Emerging Adolescents.* Reading, Mass.: Addison-Wesley Publishing Company, 1977, pp. 81–129.
 Unit II gives a historical survey of educational purposes, cultural determinants, and behavioral science theories and provides a basis for middle school education for emerging adolescents.
Foshay, Arthur W. *Curriculum for the 70's: An Agenda for Invention.* Washington, D. C.: National Education Association Center for the Study of Instruction, 1971.

Foshay emphasizes student participation in curriculum plans, the subject disciplines as general education, and humaneness in education.

Goodlad, John I. *Facing the Future — Issues in Education and Schooling.* New York: McGraw-Hill Book Company, 1977.

Sixteen papers deal with such topics as curriculum development, program development, team teaching, and nongrading. Although some discussions focus on elementary schools, all are relevant for the secondary level.

Gross, Ronald, and Osterman, Paul, eds. *High School.* New York: Simon and Schuster, 1971, pp. 108–121.

The Montgomery County, Maryland, Student Alliance, a group of high school students, criticizes the schools for creating fear, dishonesty, destroying eagerness to learn, and a number of other shortcomings. They have twenty-four suggestions ranging from the evaluation system through the curriculum, to the need for students on the school board.

Hechinger, Fred M., and Hechinger, Grace. *Growing Up in America.* New York: McGraw-Hill Book Company, 1975, pp. 90–158.

In Chapter 5, the Hechingers make an interesting historical statement about the influences on educational issues by politicians, educators, and others, including Thomas Jefferson, Horace Mann, Boss Tweed in New York, St. Louis Superintendent William J. Harris, President Nicholas Murray Butler of Columbia University and President Charles W. Elliot of Harvard University, John Dewey, and some people in the present era.

Hunkins, Francis P. *Perspectives on Curriculum Development, 1976* Yearbook. Washington, D. C., Association of Supervision and Curriculum Development, 1976, pp. 83–129.

This is a interesting historical view of how the curriculum has evolved in this country — not a comprehensive treatment but rather a provocative look at some highlights that relate to many of today's issues.

Popper, Samuel H. *The American Middle School.* Waltham, Mass.: Blaisdell Publishing Company, 1967, pp. 187–225.

Popper analyzes the differences between theory and practice in junior high schools and suggests a technique useful in resolving curriculum issues and planning improvements.

Saylor, J. Galen, and Alexander, William M. *The High School: Today and Tomorrow.* New York: Holt, Rinehart and Winston, 1974.

The authors highlight issues facing secondary schools and suggest possible solutions.

Silberman, Charles E. *Crisis in the Classroom.* New York: Random House, 1970.

See especially Chapters 4, "Education for Docility," and 8, ". . . Reforming the High School," pp. 113–157 and 323–369. The first reference criticizes what elementary and secondary schools do to pupils; the second suggests some solutions — both documented from school situations.

Tanner, Daniel, and Tanner, Laurel. *Curriculum Development.* New York: The Macmillan Company, 1975, pp. 100–144.

The authors' discussion in Chapter 3 can help you understand how issues affecting the curriculum develop, are sometimes resolved, and often continue to challenge persons and groups.

Trump, J. Lloyd. *A School For Everyone*. Reston, Va.: National Association of Secondary School Principals, 1977, pp. 3–27.

> Part 1, "Rationale for Improvement," raises questions about who shall speak for education and why different designs are necessary, and suggests some bases for decision making.

Van Til, William. *Issues in Secondary Education Today*, and Beck, Robert H. *A History of Issues in Secondary Education*. Seventy-fifth Yearbook of the National Society for the Study of Education, Part 2. Chicago: University of Chicago Press, 1976, pp. 1–64.

> The society's Yearbook Committee identified nine crucial issues related to youth, society, content, and methods. Van Til and Beck explain some implications of these issues for today's schools and provide the historical bases for them.

2

Some Viewpoints
to Consider

Now that you have examined some of your beliefs about the curriculum, you need to know the special biases of the authors, because this book represents a selective rather than an encyclopedic treatment of the secondary school curriculum. As you read this chapter, make notes to indicate your present agreement, disagreement, or uncertainty relative to opinions expressed here so that you may discuss the ideas with others.

We do not believe that the only way to improve the curriculum is to abandon the secondary school for some alternative enterprise. Nor do we believe that changing the name of a school or the grades it includes or who controls it will insure the kinds of curriculum improvements that we urge in this volume.

We know that it is difficult and time-consuming to improve the curriculum. One of us has worked with a group of schools in a longitudinal effort to follow a model of curriculum improvement for a period of years. Some schools found it possible to reach most aspects of the model, while others were unable to do so for a variety of reasons, as indicated in a publication mentioned in the bibliography at the end of this chapter.

We believe in the comprehensive type of secondary school with a balanced curriculum designed to serve the widely varied interests and talents of *all* the children in the United States. We believe that similar goals should guide curriculum developments in other countries.

Conversely, we reject such ideas as the following: some curricular areas are more important than others; some methods of teaching and learning may be used constantly to the exclusion of others; some young people are more important than others; and youths in one part of the country are more important than youths in other parts.

We assume that a basic purpose of education is to develop further the curiosity and creativity found in all small children. We accept the challenge to help each person discover interests and develop talents as effectively as possible. Of course, we recognize that people exist in a variety of social groups, so we must emphasize effective communications and relationships among individuals and groups for the maximum benefit of both. We believe that the school, as an educational institution, must not isolate itself from the families that produce the pupils or from the society in which the school exists.

Educational programs need to reflect better understandings regarding the place of the school in society. What students do in school needs to relate more closely to what they may learn at home and in the community, recognizing vast variations in all three locales. Moreover, schools need to understand that the communities and homes have been expanded unbelievably through television and other mass media. The school curriculum must utilize these outside forces constructively.

We believe that nowhere in the world have so many children and youth been educated so well as in the United States. We also believe that this superiority lies in the constant search for better ways of teaching and learning. We foresee even more rapid changes in curriculum content, methodology, and the educational setting. We think that schools need to make better use of the professional talents of teachers and principals, the potential capacities of learners, the purchasing power of school moneys, the resources of communities, and the findings of educational research.

This book represents our efforts to implement better the recommendations of many individuals and groups that have issued statements designed to change the curriculum during this century. Since you have studied many of these statements in your courses on the history of secondary education, we do not repeat them here. However, you may wish to review the proposals in the references as indicated.

The references include the *Seven Cardinal Principles of Education* listed in 1918 by the NEA Commission of Secondary Education;[1] the ten functions of secondary education as summarized in 1937 by what was then the Department of Secondary School Principals of the NEA;[2] *Planning for American Youth*,[3] published in 1945 by the National Association of Secondary School Principals, based on the NEA's Educational Policies Commission's comprehensive statement, *Education for ALL American Youth*,[4] and the 1963 and 1971 statements of the NEA Project on Instruction.[5]

Those landmark statements emphasized the need for changed curriculum programs, broader in scope, that would include all aspects of human needs and developments. The goal was to help the greatly increased numbers of youths with more diversified environments cope better with the problems they faced. These developments today are more rapid and complex than ever before.

SOME RECENT POINTS OF VIEW

The 1970s have produced a number of statements relative to needs and developments in secondary school curriculum improvement. A few highlights from three of these statements provide further challenges for students and practitioners who seek improvement.

1. A task force established by the Charles F. Kettering Foundation provided a number of recommendations in 1973.[6] Significant educational change can be accomplished only through the cooperative efforts of educators, students, and citizens. Educators need to take the initiative in stimulating citizen involvement. Collective-bargaining arrangements need approval by local boards of education only after a series of public hearings are held to allow maximum citizen improvement.

[1] NEA Commission on the Reorganization of Secondary Education, *Cardinal Principles of Secondary Education*, U. S. Bureau of Education Bulletin 1918, no. 35 (Washington, D. C.: Government Printing Office, 1918).

[2] "Functions of Secondary Education," *Bulletin of the Department of Secondary School Principals* (January 1937).

[3] *Planning for American Youth* (Washington, D. C.: The National Association of Secondary School Principals, 1945).

[4] *Education for ALL American Youth* (Washington, D. C.: Educational Policies Commission, National Education Association, 1944).

[5] *Schools for the 60's*, Project on Instruction, National Education Association (New York: McGraw-Hill Book Company, 1963).

[6] B. Frank Brown, Ch., National Commission on the Reform of Secondary Education *The Reform of Secondary Education: A Report to the Public and the Profession* (New York: McGraw Hill, 1973).

Individual student rights are balanced with individual student responsibilities to the school and society. Schools need to identify, post, and widely disseminate the responsibilities that students are expected to accept, based on the involvement of citizens, students, teachers, and administrators. An interdisciplinary approach to curriculum should place particular emphasis on the areas of English and social studies, with special focus on student responsibilities. Alternative programs for older students, developed cooperatively by high school and community college personnel, are essential.

Work-study programs give all high school–age students the opportunity to develop marketable skills prior to graduation. Individual class schedules in high school provide time during the school day for students to leave the building and perform youth services in their communities.

School districts planning alternative programs must develop evaluation plans that include written comprehensive examinations, demonstrations of minimum competencies, completion of objectives, and fulfillment of school-student contractual agreements.

2. The National Association of Secondary School Principals (NASSP) developed a statement in 1975, *Secondary Schools in a Changing Society — This We Believe.*[7]

Schools need to assume leadership to attain public agreement about the purposes of secondary education in order to provide common ground for school action. Secondary schools need to coordinate community use and family service agencies so that student referrals will be timely, appropriate, and articulated with the school environment.

The secondary school curriculum should be redesigned and placed in a more comprehensive setting to provide opportunities for service and work, serious contact with adult institutions, and experiences that span age and ethnicity. Multicultural understandings are interwoven with a number of subject areas throughout the curriculum, including English, social science, science, and the fine and practical arts. Career awareness and career preparation are goals that are appropriate in most subject areas. Secondary schools need to identify and organize the learning resources of the community as well as those of the campus. In the spirit of offering extended educational opportunities for youths, college courses should be provided on the high school campus.

The NASSP acknowledged the pervasive impact of the media and the marketplace on the educational networks of youth. These "other curricula" require an ability to analyze and criticize and a framework

[7] Scott D. Thomson, Ch., The Task Force on Secondary Schools in a Changing Society *This We Believe* (Reston, Va.: The National Association of Secondary School Principals, 1975).

of personal values with which to read the various configurations.

The NASSP believes that, on balance, the reforms of recent years have made valuable contributions to secondary education and thus should be continued. A new flexibility and attention to individualization has entered the secondary schools.

Free public education includes all education programs organized and sponsored by the school both on campus and in the community. It encompasses all learning opportunities and options for youths that lead them constructively toward legal adulthood, now age eighteen. The student may "stop out" of school but does not drop out of education. The student may phase in and out of full-time classwork according to his or her overall program, but learning continues under school sponsorship.

3. The recent publication *A School For Everyone*,[8] developed by one of the authors of this book on the basis of a six-year Model Schools Project, describes a design for a secondary school described as "based on both old and new ideas." The following outline characterizes some of the recommendations in that book. The secondary school should:

a. Make sure that every student is known totally, educationally speaking, by a teacher adviser who monitors the student's progress throughout the time her or she is in contact by the school, helping to diagnose needs, plan programs, make and change schedules, evaluate results, and plan accordingly for the future. (These procedures go far beyond the typical homeroom or the programming done by school counselors or assistant principals.)

b. Recognize individual differences among teachers by helping each one discover and exploit personal interests and skills constructively with the aid of nonprofessional clerical, instructional, and general assistants.

c. Develop a supervisory-management team that separates responsibilities for working with teachers to improve the educational program from performing such routine matters as keeping the building clean, operating buses properly, keeping public relations in order, purchasing supplies and equipment, doing the many other important tasks that have to be done but not by principals and assistant principals.

d. Provide curriculum relevance by drastically reducing the required content in all the subject fields so students have more

---

[8] J. Lloyd Trump, *A School For Everyone* (Reston, Va.: National Association of Secondary School Principals, 1977).

time to devote to their own selected special fields as related to their own special interests and careers.

e. Develop better utilization and coordination among the three locales for learning: schools, homes, and communities.

f. Evaluate and report pupil progress to emphasize individual achievements in the required areas and special projects as well as give information on norm-based measures that enables a student to know the areas in which he or she does best or may need remedial work.

g. Develop systematic programs for motivating students, teachers, and supervisory-managers through presentations, discussions, materials, reward systems, options in environments, continuous progress opportunities, cooperative planning, conditions for study and work, and personnel policies.

h. Improve interaction skills and human relations by means of systematic programs at all levels.

i. Provide students in their school time with a variety of activities, locales, and materials in relation to all levels of interests and ability. These activities may be done alone or with differing numbers of other students in a variety of locales and with appropriate learning materials. The emphasis is on alternatives according to student needs.

j. Utilize time, numbers, spaces, supplies, and equipment in relation to educational goals rather than to conform to conventional policies applied uniformly to all schools.

k. Recognize that the building — an old one remodeled or a new one — must not dictate the educational program but rather serve it. The beauty of the building is in form and function. The size reflects the idea that learning occurs also in homes and the community.

l. Utilize different and more comprehensive methods for judging the school programs in place of conventional uniform program evaluation techniques.

All the foregoing goals have significance for secondary school curriculum improvement. They are described in more detail in this book with suggestions for implementation (see Chapters 19 through 33).

ESTABLISHING PRIORITIES FOR CURRICULUM IMPROVEMENT

As you read this book and think about curriculum improvement, you will need to select your directions carefully. Obviously, you cannot do everything at once even though you are likely to discover soon that one change affects other curricular aspects. You will need to decide what matters most.

We devote the rest of this chapter to some priorities we believe deserve early consideration. The order of the subsequent topics is not significant. We repeat, you need to set your own order of priorities. Some of the topics represent educational clichés; almost everyone writes and talks about them. The questions are: Will you do something about them? And which ones will you tackle first?

Refining Curriculum Content

A major overhaul is needed in the curriculum content of all subject fields. The task includes identifying the differences between *basic materials* and those that are in the realm of *creativity* and *special interests,* for today's conventional schools often require much content that pupils neither want nor need. Inclusion of unnecessary material causes many students to lose interest — they may rebel or become underachievers. Even worse, they may lack the time and energy to follow their special interests and to develop their unique talents.

A three-way division may help teachers in a local school solve the problem of required vis-à-vis elective content. First, as suggested earlier, the required content in all areas of human knowledge is what everyone in the society needs to know to live adequately. A second level is what a given student needs to know and do in order to enjoy hobbies that arise from special interests that the school has stimulated through the required content and the motivational presentations that will be described in Chapter 21. The third level aims to provide content for students who wish to discover options in careers.

In history, for example, teachers need to provide answers to these questions: What content is essential for everyone in order to help make effective decisions? What content is needed for learners who become interested in a hobby of special interests in some aspects of history? What content is necessary for the learner who plans to become a professional historian, to make a living by using or developing some aspects of history? The same questions are relevant for all areas. Even though a local school uses a state or city curriculum, the teacher needs to make the three-way separation available to students.

Required learnings. To determine basic, or fundamental, education, teachers and curriculum experts must identify the facts, concepts, skills, and appreciations that are *essential* in our society for anyone who is educable. Beyond that minimum, the schools should also identify the content that is *desirable* for most people and *enriching* for the specially talented. It is possible that national groups will identify this curriculum content for all persons in the United States. Then other groups can add materials needed by persons in a given state. Local teachers will complete the content by adding topics regarded as essential for the local community and region. The foundational content must be arranged logically and sequentially so that the students progress continuously from the time they enter the school program until they leave to go to work or to continue in a higher institution.

The required work should be held to a minimum. The evaluative question is, What progress has been made toward identifying essential content? For example, what facts about the history of the United States are *essential* for the "good American"? What mathematics does the typical person — not the engineer or scientist — need? Is memorizing the names and dates of the popes essential for proper religious behavior?

Typically, students should have to devote only one-half of their school time to basic learning. The rest of the time should be used to pursue special interests, no matter how transitory, with the professional aid of an appropriate teacher. Unfortunately, most of today's curriculum-planning and curriculum-development projects add to the student's burden of required learnings rather than reducing the quantity through refinement.

Creativity and depth education.   The teacher should provide extra information and make assignments that will motivate students to go beyond the fundamental or required content in creative ways or in greater depth. Such a program would eliminate the outmoded "required-and-elective" system, which often limits the breadth of experience for students in the upper years by keeping them away from fine and practical arts or from specialized work in mathematics or literature. The average student may complete the essential content by the age of fourteen (earlier or later, recognizing individual differences) so that basic education beyond that occupies only 10 to 20 percent of school time. (Some time is required to keep up-to-date, refresh memory, or correct wrong information learned earlier). The rest of the time is devoted to creativity and depth studies in the world of work or advanced studies leading to the university.

The teacher should use content that has been developed nationally and regionally, only accepting or criticizing what the experts have done. The time and effort saved may be spent more profitably on planning how to relate local content to the essential national and regional materials.

Motivation

The quality of a student's learning is related directly to the effectiveness of motivation. Young people, like all of us, are motivated by contacts with stimulating personalities or exciting ideas. Students want to write poetry when they are in contact with a great poet or a teacher who loves poetry and knows how to stimulate other people's interest.

Motivation depends on the nature of the assignments and the diversity of learning experiences. It also is stimulated by placing students in situations where each can work at her or his own pace. Conversely, motivation is destroyed when the able student must sit in class until less able learners catch up or are removed for remedial work. It is impaired also when a student is in a class beyond personal capacity and consequently is frustrated by comparisons with other students who are much more able and interested at the moment than he or she is.

Evaluation, of course, directly influences student motivation. How the teacher reacts to an individual's independent study efforts is crucial. Young people who are constantly compared with others in an unfavorable manner soon lose interest.

Much of the material in Part IV of this book bears on improved motivation. We believe the importance of motivation calls for basic changes in the curriculum setting. Many practices in today's schools destroy interest and produce the considerable number of reluctant learners and disinterested students who occupy such a noticeable place in the secondary classrooms of this country. On the other hand, we are not enchanted by motivation that results from a fear of failing crucial examinations such as those given in many European schools or the College Board Examinations of the United States.

Problem Solving

Although it may be unrealistic to assume that a school's curriculum can be organized entirely around problems for students to solve, the excellence of instruction and learning will be influenced by the degree to which students can pick areas of the curriculum to analyze, divide those areas into meaningful parts, attack each aspect intellectually and systematically by collecting appropriate information and interpreting effectively what they discover, and then arrive at defensible solutions. Students do not have to discover everything for themselves, but the process of discovery and analysis is to be encouraged and learned to the fullest extent possible.

The assignments that teachers provide for students should stimulate the higher mental processes. Some memorization, of course, is essential to learning, but the memorization should enable students to engage in higher mental activities rather than merely passing the next examination or participating in a discussion during the next ten minutes.

Value Development

Values are learned best by practice, but they also develop as students encounter vicarious experiences in listening, viewing, and reading. The instructional program should help them relate appropriate knowledge from various fields. Habits of extensive reading, writing, and oral communication, and values that call for creative efforts, are developed systematically by the school curriculum, not by accident.

The school program speaks louder than the goals expressed in a curriculum guide. A curriculum that requires the fine arts only through grade 8 says very loudly to the students that the fine arts are unimportant in the lives of citizens. (No wonder so many homes are poorly decorated and our cities have so much ugliness in them.) A school curriculum that says to students, "This year you must care about science [or United States history] and then you can forget about it for two years [or completely]," is not developing the idea that a person should *always* keep eyes and ears open for new developments or interesting ideas in all areas of human knowledge.

Individual Student Goals

Each person should strive for the following educational goals: the skills of study, the desire to study, and the state of keeping constantly up-to-date in all areas of human knowledge while seeking new truths and better ways of doing things. A curriculum designed to further these goals differs in many respects from what exists in many of today's schools, where a subject is required at a given stage in a student's development, a grade is given and credit is extended largely on the basis of local examinations, and then the subject may be forgotten. The evaluation of progress should emphasize the educational goals listed above. To realize these goals, each student must spend relatively more time in independent study — sometimes individual and sometimes in small groups — and comparatively less time in standard-sized classes doing much the same things as the others in the class.

Individualization of instruction that aims to develop maximum potential requires the emphasis in evaluation described in Chapters 32 and 33. The school then compares the individual mainly with past accomplishments rather than with others in the class.

Individual programing requires flexible scheduling so that based on a professional decision of teachers and counselors, a student at any given time may spend greatly increased amounts of time working in a science laboratory, an art room, or the gymnasium, or engaging in some civic, aesthetic, or work experience outside the school. Responsibility for learning is developed only as people have opportunities to make their own choices. Although the school should reserve the right of final decisions about a student's program, the aim should be to give each one as much responsibility as possible.

The diverse goals of individual students may be served also by introducing many more electives into the school's program in the form of mini-courses. Such courses may be of a standard length or may vary with individual interests and talents. Some schools may offer fifty, one hundred, or even more such courses on an elective basis for from one week to six weeks. For example, a school known to one of us has nothing but mini-courses for the final six weeks of the school year. The exception to that rule is that students who have not finished regular subjects must spend that six weeks on the completion of those subjects rather than on the mini-course program. Chapter 31 includes examples of such programs.

Other schools are creating "mini-schools" within an existing building in order to provide more alternatives. One mini-school has continuous-progress arrangements to permit each student to progress at his or her own selected pace along with other features of individualized programs. Another mini-school serves as a headquarters for students, all of whom are scheduled into various community places for their learning. Still another is for students who are unable to advance in conventional programs and require the special type of help that remedial curricula and methods typically provide. Other mini-schools emphasize one aspect of the curriculum, for example, fine arts or science. This approach contrasts with the arrangements that some other school systems have provided in what are called alternative schools. Obviously, there are some advantages to providing such programs on a single campus rather than forcing students to change to a completely different locale. Also, a school thus may provide conventional programs for students and parents who prefer those arrangements.

Teacher Goals

The basic goal of every teacher, insofar as students are concerned, is to become dispensable as rapidly and as completely as possible. That purpose requires that the teacher place more responsibility on learners. It colors assignments and activities in ways that are described throughout this volume. The teacher's success is measured in terms of what the pupils do when the teacher is not present — what they do in the resource centers or at home at night, on Saturday, or during the summer months.

A second basic goal of teachers is to become more professional. This goal requires that they go far beyond their efforts to obtain higher salaries and more elaborate teaching certificates with increased hours in their subject areas or in the professional field of education. Teachers need to discover what they must do themselves and what can be done by less costly clerks and instruction assistants. They have to understand what they must teach personally and what students can learn largely by themselves through the use of such devices as programmed learning (teaching machines and teaching books), television, recordings, and films.

Professional teachers also spend considerable time keeping up-to-date, conferring with their professional colleagues, improving their preparation for teaching, improving evaluation of student progress, and meeting with individual students at their request. No professional teacher should be scheduled with groups of students for more than twelve or fifteen hours per week, so that each will have time for such professional activities.

A third teacher goal is for each to do what he or she is most competent and most interested in doing. Today's schools largely ignore individual differences among teachers through such procedures as the self-contained or self-sufficient classroom, in which one teacher is expected to perform all services for students in a given subject field or grade level. The principle of individuality is also violated by uniform salaries, standard class loads, uniform retirement, and a host of other standard personnel policies. Teachers need to meet regularly with other teachers to plan what each may do best and to give each the privilege of doing it.

School Climate

The relationships that develop among students, teachers, supervisors, and administrators are extremely important for each group. The increased power of teacher organizations has provided teachers with higher salaries and improvements in working conditions, developments that were sorely needed for many years. In some cases, however, the results are undesirable relationships that affect the school climate adversely.

When teachers seek more power, they sometimes oppose school

supervisors and administrators whose assigned responsibility is to improve teaching and learning in the schools. Teachers and students have conflicts when teacher organizations limit teacher contributions to extraclass activities outside the usual school day.

Other developments outside the schools can also affect school climate adversely. Teachers and administrators are blamed for the decreasing achievement of students on certain standardized, norm-based tests. Parents and other taxpayers blame the schools for the increased use of drugs, racial violence, changes in behavioral mores, dress, and the like. Criticism that does not look at the changing world outside the schools is both shortsighted and incomplete. Students, aware of these criticisms, sometimes react unwisely against both teachers and the school.

Constructive efforts to improve school climate involve reassessment of positive needs and the relationships among all the people involved. Also needed are local studies of factors in society that affect schooling. Motivation for curriculum improvement can result from such efforts. Constructive action can solve problems and improve the climate; destructive approaches produce frustrations. Later chapters provide specific ways to improve curriculum content, methods, and evaluation.

Point of View

Those who would improve the curriculum must constantly and honestly examine what they believe. We have stated our concerns so that readers may know the points of view that illuminate and influence the concepts presented throughout the rest of this book.

We are critical of many practices that exist in today's schools. We believe they reflect inconsistencies between stated purposes and procedures used to accomplish the goals. Those who study curriculum development and try to change schools translate beliefs into positive action. What results from their work will be different from and better than the program that exists today.

TOPICS FOR STUDY AND DISCUSSION

1. Discuss the changes in secondary education curriculum goals that appear in statements issued during the past half-century. What others would you add?
2. What curricular goals deserve highest priority today?

3. Consider a subject area, perhaps the one you teach. At two given ages
— for example twelve and seventeen — what content is essential for
all or most pupils?
4. Take some typical topic or unit in a subject you teach; list some hobbies
or careers that would be open to pupils who learned more than the
essentials required of everyone.
5. What motivational factors other than those listed in this chapter should
curriculum planners consider?
6. React to the beliefs about curriculum submitted by the authors. Are
there any you would reject or others you would add?

SELECTED REFERENCES

The Adolescent, Other Citizens, and Their High Schools. The Report of Task
Force '74. New York: McGraw-Hill Book Company, 1975.
  The Institute for Development of Educational Activities, Inc., of the
Charles F. Kettering Foundation provides further recommendations to
those in the 1972 National Commission on the Reform of Secondary Education. The report covers many issues about community involvement,
control of schools, student responsibilities, and alternative programs.
Bailey, Stephen K.; Macy, Francis U.; and Vickers, Donn F. *Alternative Paths
to the High School Diploma.* Reston, Va.: National Association of Secondary
School Principals, 1973.
  Chapter 1 describes a regional learning service in central New York,
where learning consultants help dropouts identify goals and prepare for
regional, state, and national examinations. Chapter 2 describes the need
for and recommends external high school diplomas for dropouts of various types. The emphases are on varied locales and methods of learning.
Beane, James A. "Curriculum Trends and Practices in High Schools," *Educational Leadership* (November 1975), pp. 129–133.
  Survey data from 232 high schools indicates relatively few changes in
curriculum and requirements for graduation. Most of them "remain subject to the traditional criticisms made by progressive educators."
Brown, B. Frank, Ch. *The Reform of Secondary Education.* New York:
McGraw-Hill Book Company, 1973.
  See especially Part IV, "Alternatives to Secondary Education." The
discussion on nonformal sources of secondary education, including television and alternative programs and schools, provides recommendations
for nonconventional approaches to schooling. Also, Part VI, "Issues and
Dissent," highlights differences of opinion among members of the National commission on the Reform of Secondary Education, established by
the Charles F. Kettering Foundation.
The Curriculum: Retrospect and Prospect. Seventeenth Yearbook of the National Society for the Study of Education, Part 1. Chicago: University of
Chicago Press, 1971.
  Fifteen authors cover curriculum development from the 1920s to the
present and look into the future.

Curtis, Thomas E., and Bidwell, Wilma W. *Curriculum and Instruction for Emerging Adolescents.* Reading, Mass.: Addison-Wesley Publishing Company, 1977, pp. 133–141.

Accepting the premise that personalizing education is basic in the middle school, in Chapter 8 the authors present a variety of requirements for required and elective curricula. Integration of disciplines, correlation of experiences, balance, and planned sequences are essential ingredients.

Della-Dora, Delma. "Democracy and Education: Who Owns the Curriculum?" *Educational Leadership,* vol. 34, no. 1, pp. 51–59.

Who owns the curriculum? The author answers, "We all do."

Eurich, Alvin C., ed. *High School 1980.* New York: Pitman Publishing Corporation, 1970.

Twenty-five authorities state what they believe will happen in the change process, in the curriculum areas, in the utilization of persons and resources, and in evaluation.

Feyereisen, Kathryn V., et al. *Supervision and Curriculum Renewal: A Systems Approach.* New York: Appleton-Century-Crofts, 1970, pp. 130–152.

The authors urge the process of systems analysis for designing curricula, ranging from objectives to content to methods to media to evaluation with more precise decision-making processes than schools conventionally use.

Frymier, Jack Remmel, et al., *A School for Tomorrow.* Berkeley, Calif.: McCutchan Publishing Corporation, 1973, pp. 3–36.

Read Chapter 1 for Frymier's summary of what needs to be done to improve schools.

Gibbons, Maurice. *The New Secondary Education.* Bloomington, Ind.: Phi Delta Kappa, 1976, pp. 91–133.

The goals of schooling need to go far beyond the limit of the junior and senior high school years. The methods include teaching students to develop and implement their own programs as teachers help them organize suitable experiences. The "present-practice-test" methods of instruction are inadequate.

Gorman, Burton W. *Secondary Education: The High School America Needs.* New York: Random House, 1971.

This book makes proposals for improving all aspects of secondary schools, including "The High School of 1990."

Havighurst, Robert J., and Dreyer, Philip H., eds., *Youth.* Seventy-fourth Yearbook of the National Society for the Study of Education, Part 1. Chicago: University of Chicago Press, 1975.

Elizabeth Douvan, in "Sex Differences in the Opportunities, Demands, and Developments of Youth" (pp. 27–45), and Helen S. Austin, in "Young Women and Their Roles" (pp. 419–434), highlight the rapidly changing roles of females in our society and provide specific recommendations for required changes in school curricula due to those developments.

Osen, D. S. K. *Student Perception: Selected Innovations in Secondary Education.* Ann Arbor, Mich.: University Microfilms, 1970.

The author's doctoral dissertation reports on the reactions of a sample of students and graduates of three California high schools to the ideas of

J. Lloyd Trump as found in a considerable number of publications. The author also predicts the future impact of "The Trump Plan" in this study done at the University of Southern California under the direction of Professor William Georgiades. Includes bibliography.

Passow, A. Harry. *American Secondary Education — The Conant Influence.* Reston, Va.: National Association of Secondary School Principals, 1977.

James Bryant Conant's recommendations, repeated in the appendix, were developed for both junior and senior high schools. Included are two that had lasting impacts: counselors, and individualized programs for students. Most of the twenty-one for senior high and fourteen for junior high received some attention. Possibly most important was Conant's commitment to the education of *all* youth.

Scribner, Harvey, and Stevens, Leonard. *Make Your Schools Work.* New York: Simon and Schuster, 1975, pp. 21–99.

Part II discusses breaking the lock-step of entrance and promotion, the nine-month school year, the one-teacher limitation, learning outside school, youth teaching youth, using spaces other than present school buildings, systematic reexamination of all programs, local identification of needs, breaking the diploma bind, and funding the further education of dropouts.

Trump, J. Lloyd. *A School For Everyone.* Reston, Va.: National Association of Secondary School Principals, 1977.

In Chapters 3–20, the author consolidates his ideas for improving schools, including suggestions on how to start and how to judge the results.

Van Haden, Herbert I., and King, Jean Marie. *Innovations in Education: Their Pros and Cons.* Worthington, Ohio: Charles A. Jones Publishing Company, 1971.

Van Haden and King outline significant components, advantages, difficulties and some assessments, leaders, and locations in innovations under the following categories: individualized learning, accountability, curriculum expansion and improvement, reorganization, and personnel utilization and improvement. The content relates also to Parts IV, V, and VI of this volume.

Vaughn, Jacqueline B. "The Expanding Role of Teachers in Negotiating Curriculum," *Educational Leadership* (October 1976), pp. 21–23.

Classroom teachers are urged to assure their participation in the process of change.

3

Influences on the Curriculum

American society constantly undergoes cultural and social change. Entrenched traditions continue to be challenged. Present changes bring a new emphasis on personal choice and the worth of cultural diversity. More than any other institutions, public schools reflect the common bonds and transcendent values of society. The task of the public schools is to encompass basic values and reflect social, economic, and cultural change.

The secondary school curriculum continues to need redesigning in order to reflect pragmatic, worthy procedures and accommodate innovative, desirable changes. Opportunities for experiences in the world of work as well as contact with adult institutions are becoming part of the academic curriculum. If a definition of the secondary school curriculum includes what teachers teach and how they teach, then the forces that affect the curriculum may be summarized as follows:

1. a changing concept of student needs, rights, and responsibilities
2. changing parental demands for explanations of what the school is doing and what it ought to be doing

3. court interpretations of the law as it affects students
4. legislation in the various states dictating what students shall be taught and how they shall be taught
5. national movements reflecting philosophic approaches to content and instructional procedures
6. the militancy of teacher organizations demanding economic and professional benefits with the willingness to strike to obtain them
7. movements, such as accountability and "back to the basics," that are calling for more precise methods of evaluating classroom results

A number of societal pressures are being applied to schools. For instance, there is a struggle for control of the curriculum; ethnic minorities, teachers, administrators, parents, and students are demanding a greater say. School boards no longer rule with an iron hand. Competent, concerned teachers are asking to be consulted in the selection of textbooks, tests, and other resources. Parents resent teachers' behavior when they leave the classroom for the picket line. Conscientious students are disturbed by the loss of learning experiences resulting from protracted teacher strikes.

SOCIETAL PRESSURES

Societal pressures on the school curriculum are associated directly or indirectly with the scientific and technological developments of the age and the resulting automation of many human activities. This has come with great rapidity; uncertainty and confusion accompany it. The agricultural revolution and the industrial revolution each took centuries for full manifestation, but the scientific and technological revolution matured almost within a decade.

The social order surrounding the schools is casting its reverberating problems — mobile populations, unemployment, poverty, delinquency, and changing home conditions — into the laps of curriculum planners. Many of the ills of modern society are attributed to the collapse of stable home life. The decline of a strong kinship system in an urban society has left the family rootless, mobile, and small. The directed activity of government agencies and planning commissions has replaced family-centered living. Social action, once face-to-face and personal, has now become indirect and bureaucratic. The results are congestion, disorganization, and delinquency. While these conditions are not prevalent throughout the country, they are found in large segments of urban populations and must be recognized as affecting many school programs.

In this country any extensive mobility of population is certain to create racial and ethnic problems. The mass exodus of blacks from the South to urban centers in the North and the invasion of suburbia by various ethnic groups have created social problems of great magnitude. Combined with all this, of course, was the Supreme Court's decision to integrate the public schools. Educational planners must resist pressure from those who believe that racial and ethnic understanding can be effected by instructional processes; they must develop organizational practices that provide equal status of membership in groups.

Supreme Court decisions have done much to clarify religious issues in the schools. Bible readings and prayers have been invalidated, but religious holiday celebrations, released time, and transportation of parochial pupils remain administrative problems that involve conflict and often constitute curriculum pressure.

One of the most stultifying factors in curriculum development is the infliction of regulations by state legislative and regulatory bodies. These are the avenues by which special interest groups such as patriotic, civic, or labor organizations can influence the instructional materials of the classroom. Some states require by law that communism be studied; others require certain units of history. In one state, the harmful effects of alcohol are supposed to be taught in five different subject-matter areas, and the principal of the school is subject to a fine for failure to do so. Although that law is not enforced, it is typical of how pressures through legislative enactments can clutter up curriculum objectives.

STATE AND FEDERAL GOVERNMENT

Probably the greatest factor in the change from a purely locally conceived curriculum is the stepped-up activity of state and national governments in the field of education. Even the most ardent critic of federal aid to education will have to admit that such aid is now an accomplished fact, the federal government has elected to channel a large part of its efforts through state departments of education. The debate may go on over federal aid and resulting federal control, but it is purely an academic question. Participants in federal aid know that purse strings have built-in control factors. Financial responsibility is necessary; otherwise irresponsible spending, wanton waste, and even graft may result.

The role of the U. S. Office of Education in the development of new curricula is very much in evidence. Previously, its activity had been primarily consultative, but with the passage of the National Defense Education Act of 1958, it began to disburse funds and its influence in curriculum making was established. The national government's interest in research phases of education has a certain amount of respectable antiquity. A historical survey of such interest would include the creation of the Smithsonian Institution in 1877, the passage of the Morrill Act for land grant colleges in 1862, the creation of the National Academy of Science in 1863, and the creation of the U. S. Office of Education in 1867. Historical precedents for federal aid in the vocational education field include the Smith-Hughes Act of 1917, the George-Dean Act of 1936, the George-Barden Act of 1946, and the Vocational Education Act of 1963.

The entrance of the national government into curriculum making on a broad base came under Title III of the National Defense Education Act, which provided financial assistance for strengthening science, mathematics, and modern foreign languages. Subsequently, this activity was broadened to include English and social studies. Financial assistance has been used in a variety of ways to improve instruction in these fields. The general pattern includes an examination of existing curricula, design and development of new curricula, testing and refinement of curricula in practical situations, and the production and distribution of new curricular materials.

The most sweeping of all federal aid to education came with the Elementary and Secondary Education Act of 1965. Financial assistance from this act has far-reaching effects on curriculum making. It provided for the allocation of large sums of money to various states for programs of instruction and instructional materials. Emphasis was placed on new programs and innovative procedures for teaching. This was truly federally aided curriculum construction. Although distribution of the funds was under the supervision of the various state departments of education, to label the act itself anything less than a form of governmental pressure would be misleading.

One of the most direct influences on curriculum planning has been the requirement for sex equality resulting from Title IX in the regulations of the Department of Health, Education, and Welfare (HEW) as ordered by legislative enactments of 1972. Content and instructional areas of health education, physical education, and extraclass activities have been redesigned. Regardless of what the curriculum content or expenses involved in participation may be, opportunities for both sexes must be equal.

A summary of recent federal legislation affecting school curriculum includes:

1. type of training afforded teachers through the Educational Professions Development Act, the Teachers Corps, and special vocational education grants

2. completion of federal desegregation efforts in many southern and border states through efforts of HEW, the Department of Justice, and federal courts

3. enactment of more than a half-dozen significant sex equality bills affecting education and employment

4. expenditure of more than $30 million to develop advanced measures of educational assessment to identify what is learned in schools

5. extensive federal investment in public television programs that require curriculum ingenuity as to content and production

6. major activity in support of the arts and humanities, including sponsorship of "artists in schools" programs in hundreds of local communities

7. state educational agencies receiving between one-third and two-thirds of their revenue from the federal government; this is especially true in vocational-technical education

8. grant awards: $750,000 to eighty-one recipients for innovative programs in art education

While a federal takeover is not inevitable, there is a strong case for local school officials keeping a guarded eye on all curriculum planning. Historically, education has been a state function in the United States, but most of the control and planning of instructional programs has been left to local school authorities. In recent years, however, more and more state-dictated regulations have affected subject-matter content, materials selection including textbooks, and instructional methods as controlled by teacher-training programs.

Space here will permit a brief description of two state programs that illustrate the ever-increasing influence of state agencies on the public school curriculum. A plan to achieve a comprehensive, systematic reform of California's intermediate and secondary schools has been instituted.[1] According to the chief state school officer, the plan is based on the recognition that fundamental changes are required to motivate a mounting number of "turned-off" students and to reverse sliding student achievement levels. The old mass-production approach, which fails for too many young people, will be replaced with a new system that recognizes individual differences and responds to them. The program, called *personalized education,* includes the following highlights:

1. Each student must be allowed to progress in school as quickly or slowly as necessary to gain the skills required by the adult society.

[1] George W. Neill, "The Reform of Intermediate and Secondary Education in California," *Phi Delta Kappan* (February 1976), p. 371.

2. A new learning environment must be created that offers optional times, places, approaches, and groupings for learning activities.
3. Emphasis in the school curriculum must be on skills, competencies, and personal capabilities demanded by a complex and changing society.
4. Credit and noncredit "furloughs" must be available to permit students to leave and reenter the school system.
5. Demonstrated competence in an area of study rather than "seat time" in class must be required as the basis for awarding credit to students.
6. A continuous program of "planned experiences" must be provided to place all students in contact with people whose racial, ethnic, socioeconomic, or cultural backgrounds are different from their own.
7. Students, parents, staff, and others must be involved in the decision-making process at the school level.

In 1974, the State Board of Education of Michigan appointed a Task Force to Study Secondary Education in the state. The objectives for the task force were the following:[2]

1. to examine the thirty-two recommendations of the National Commission on the Reform of Secondary Education and advise the State Board of Education on their individual merits and possible implementation
2. to review the present Department of Education progress in regard to secondary goals, secondary school expectations, and student needs assessment at the tenth- and twelfth-grade levels; and to advise the State Board of Education on the progress in regard to the implementation of these programs, including vocational education and career education
3. to study various state and national reports on the reform of secondary education or new reports from task force members and advise the board on the merits of any such proposals that may have implications for statewide consideration in Michigan

The Michigan Task Force report included the following significant curriculum recommendations for the secondary schools:

1. that the content of the traditional high school curriculum be revised to reflect the goals and objectives of the local school community
2. that every high school establish an affirmative action commit-

[2] Judy L. Bauer, "Reform of Secondary Education in Michigan," *Journal of the Michigan Association of Secondary School Principals* (Winter 1976), p. 58.

tee composed of students, former students, faculty, and community representatives

3. that curricula be realigned to provide students with a range of experiences and activities broad enough to permit them to take full advantage of career opportunities in their communities

4. that a wide variety of paths leading to completion of requirements for graduation from high school be made available to all students

5. that tests be routinely administered quarterly or monthly to help adolescents obtain credit for work done outside the classroom

6. that class rank and grade-point average be discontinued as qualifications for college entrance

7. that secondary school personnel work with private and government agencies toward the provision of a job for each high school graduate who chooses not to continue beyond high school education

8. that financial support be provided by the state legislature for area skills centers

9. that work-study programs be developed

10. that allowance be made for variable time schedules, including day and night classes, longer and shorter class periods, and year-round school programs;

11. that student evaluation be ongoing and individualized

12. that responsibility and decision making for matters that affect the learning situation be shared among students, staff, and parents

13. that open schools, schools without walls, street academies, and skill centers be considered viable alternative delivery systems for secondary education

In the two programs just described, there is no doubt that state influence is very strong in curriculum-making decisions.

THE ACCOUNTABILITY SYNDROME

The accountability syndrome is certain to influence curriculum decisions for some time to come. Causes for emphasis on accountability may be traced to the ever-increasing demand for educational dollars. The federal government has poured billions of dollars into the educational mix, and negotiated teachers' contracts continue to call for ever-increasing financial obligations on local school boards. As demands increase and inflated dollars shrink, educational constituencies become more concerned over value received. Congressional representatives, taxpayers, school board members, and school patrons all ask the same question: what are we getting for our money?

Educational leaders have been ready to assure the public that increased support for education means better schools. Teacher organizations have promised better educational results from better pay. The public is becoming increasingly concerned that educational results do not match educational promises. Either better educational programs have not been forthcoming, or educational leaders have not been able to identify results satisfactorily.

Manifestations of the accountability syndrome may be found in such movements as national assessment, performance contracts, differentiated staffing, and so-called taxpayer revolts. Those who originally opposed national assessment on the basis that results would provide for an unwholesome comparison of various school systems are now demanding national assessment data to prove their schools better than those of their neighbors. Bills are being introduced into state legislatures to make provisions for state assessments, and soon local assessment will be in vogue.

One of the problems that continues to plague educational planners is the lack of reliable evaluative criteria. School boards act as policy-making bodies, professional administrators do the implementing, and the general public passes judgment on the effectiveness of the product. No agency, however, has responsibility for encompassing an assessment function in any meaningful way. School patrons may vote down a bond issue, but no one really knows what the negative vote means. Seldom do the people have ways of communicating their concerns in such a manner as to insure improvement in the school curriculum.[3]

Theoretically, education has a conceptual flaw. There is no aspect of the system that regularly generates effective data, nor is there anything in the concept that requires the system to pay any attention to the feedback if it should appear. The secondary school curriculum is particularly vulnerable to this phenomenon. In a period when critics are demanding proof of results and educational leaders have no effective way of showing results, the discovery of effective evaluative criteria must be a high priority on the curriculum planner's agenda. Perhaps with the development of sophisticated systems analysis and computerized data, pertinent assessment may become a reality.

DECLINING TEST SCORES

Declining test scores have received widespread attention from the press, educators, and the public in general. On the secondary school

[3] M. T. Hinkemeyer, "Curriculum Theory and Public School Problems," *The Clearing House* (May 1976), pp. 398–400.

level, most of the information comes from reports of two national testing groups, namely, the American College Testing Program (ACT) and the College Entrance Examination Board (CEEB). Both these testing groups have attributed the causes of declining test scores to the increasing number of students taking the test, many of whom are less qualified.

For some critics of U. S. secondary schools, declining test scores represent a confirmation of their worst fears about schools; that is, the schools are failing in their primary task of educating students. Many educators, on the other hand, take a defensive position by blaming social factors, including parents, television, and the lack of a purpose among youths. It is important to note that real assessment of the cause of declining test scores lacks any real data that show a collection period of at least ten years. The only safe assumptions to make are either that the content of tests is changing or that the pool of students taking the tests is changing. Any other assumptions in the matter are complex and must be reflected in curriculum planning.

There may be some clues for curriculum designers in a survey made of selected secondary school principals, but these are only opinions and lack supporting data. The principals gave the following reasons for declining test scores:[4]

1. difficulty in maintaining standards of discipline in today's schools
2. breakdown of the family unit, leading to less parental control
3. less-effective teaching of skill subjects (reading, writing, mathematics) coupled with teacher reluctance to assign homework and demand compliance
4. extensive use of mass media with a resultant adverse impact on reading and other basics
5. decline in teaching of factual material due to an attempt to make school more humanistic
6. inadequate preparation for and management of innovative programs such as the open classroom
7. lack of appreciation for the value of education; many high school students view education as irrelevant to their goals and getting ahead in today's world
8. decrease in enrollment in the more difficult high school courses; students who are more involved in humanistic pursuits that are not measured by back-to-the-basics examinations
9. introduction of electives, such as mini-courses, of a nonquality nature; in many cases, relevancy has replaced goals and standards

[4] Donald J. Nelson, "What's Behind the Test Score Decline," National Association of Secondary School Principals *Bulletin* (May 1976), pp. 78–79.

10. lack of proper supervision of the instructional program by administrative personnel due to the vast amount of time spent on noninstructional problems, such as crime and discipline
11. lack of clearly defined objectives for the various levels of the total school system, which makes accountability meaningless
12. less structure and control over the educational process by the school as a result of court decisions relating to student rights
13. increase in school holding power and consequent encouragement of students of lower ability to take the admissions tests
14. more able students "turned off" by the competitive nature of admissions testing
15. restrictions imposed on administrative leadership as the result of teacher contracts

The whole area of standardized testing is in turmoil. Some critics are questioning the validity of standardized tests, while others are pointing to extensive abuse in the use and interpretation of test scores. The National Education Association and the American Federation of Teachers are on record as favoring either abolition or complete revision of the tests. The crux of the situation probably lies in the fact that instead of being defensive, both supporters and opponents should pool their respective competences to improve design, construction, administration, and interpretation of standardized tests. In the meantime, purposeful curriculum changes may be in limbo.

NATIONAL STUDIES, COMMISSIONS, AND REPORTS

Secondary school educators responsible for the revision and improvement of the secondary school curriculum must scrutinize the many publications that come from studies and reports of organizations and commissions concerned with the progress of education. Two of the reports directly concerned with secondary education are reviewed here, but secondary school curriculum makers should feel the responsibility for complete coverage of all related publications in the field of education.

Mention was made in Chapter 2 that the National Association of Secondary School Principals has published a statement on secondary education prepared by a task force entitled *Secondary Schools in a Changing Society — This We Believe*. Pertinent in the discussion here, this report urges consideration of the following conclusions about the role of secondary schools:

1. Although the schools can focus on transcendent values that remain firm in any society, they must also manage dimensions of change that require skill and patience.

2. Schools can be effective when goals are clear. A mobile, plural-
    istic society places temporary and divergent demands on its
    educational institutions. Herein lies the core of the problem
    faced by contemporary secondary schools.
3. The focus in secondary schools over the past generation on
    better buildings, on modern curricula, and on a higher-quality
    teaching staff, failed to recognize a larger world that was grad-
    ually forcing youth into holding ponds surrounded by abstract,
    passive, synthetic experiences.
4. The basic responsibility of the secondary schools within the
    total context is to instruct. This does not mean, however, that
    learning should be confined to the classroom. Superior instruc-
    tion can occur within a variety of settings, both on and off the
    school campus.

In their yearbook on secondary education, the National Society for
the Study of Education points to nine issues that must be considered in
curriculum decisions for the secondary schools:

1. how to foster to the fullest the development of the individual's
    potentialities and experiences as a self-actualizing person.
2. how to help youths develop and apply humane values in order
    to achieve the democratic dream
3. how best to equip youth with vision, knowledge, and compe-
    tences needed to cope with social realities
4. how to utilize the relevant experiences of humankind in the
    education of contemporary youths
5. how to incorporate the modern school setting with the total
    environmental experiences of youths
6. how subject-matter content can take into account social reali-
    ties, human values, needs of individual learners, and bodies of
    knowledge from disciplinary and interdisciplinary studies
7. how more effective methods of school organization can be
    created
8. how teaching strategies can be mobilized to make better use of
    instructional resources and learning experiences of youths
9. how all the elements in the educational enterprise can be used
    more effectively in administering, supervising, and evaluating
    the secondary school program.

Criticism from both right- and left-wings of philosophic thinkers is
pertinent to secondary education. Much of the left-wingers' writings
advocate the abolition of formal education, while the right-wingers call
for extensive revision or the return to established policies such as
back-to-the-basics.

The National Commission on Reform of Secondary Education proposes that formal education not be required beyond the age of fourteen. This would make most secondary education voluntary. The Carnegie Study, *Crisis in the Classroom,* says students are in an intellectually sterile and aesthetically barren atmosphere. In order to make progress, the pragmatic curriculum worker will probably need to take an eclectic approach in his or her philosophic decision making in relating to the criticism.

CONFLICTING FORCES

Education is marked by conflicting forces that would direct what the schools ought to be teaching and the way students ought to be taught. This is hardly a new phenomenon. It can be traced through much of the history of education.

For secondary school curriculum makers, one immediate conflict is associated with those who would espouse a more humanistic approach to educating youths and those who proclaim the need for a back-to-the-basics movement. There are many other conflicts in education, however, so too much attention should not be focused on this one. Advocates of back-to-the-basics blame all the problems of education on a curriculum marked by openness that offers alternatives to meet youthful needs.[5] They point to declining test scores, student unrest, teacher militancy, and scores of poorly prepared, unemployable youths as evidence of a need to return to fundamentals.

What back-to-the-basics means is not always clear. To some, it means emphasis on the reading, writing, and arithmetic in the elementary schools. To others, it means more formal organization of school programs with emphasis on rigidity of discipline. To still others, it means greater emphasis on morals and things related to "the good life." Whatever it means, curriculum planners in secondary school education must realize that it involves many thoughtful, disturbed citizens. It behooves secondary educators either to take steps to effect a more basic program or to prove to parents that present programs do not neglect basics and that the humanistic approach does offer valuable alternatives to youths.

The humanistic movement may be associated with much of the recent progress made in the secondary school curriculum. More attention is given to the individual student's needs, fears, and desires, and one-to-one relationships are emphasized. The open school offers an organizational pattern for the development of individualized instruc-

[5] Ben Brodinsky, "Back to the Basics: The Movement and Its Meaning," *Phi Delta Kappan* (March 1977), pp. 522–527.

tion and a series of alternatives for youths. These alternatives relate to organization for classroom instruction, curriculum pattern, and student relationships. Here are some examples:

Modular schedules	Career Education
Student self-scheduling	Alternate twelfth-year program
Differentiated staffing	Adjusted graduation requirements
Curriculum clusters	Year-round school programs
Ungraded classes	New approaches to student
Mini-courses	attendance
Subject-matter laboratories	New emphasis on student rights
Adjustable classroom space	Measurement by performance
Large-and small-group instruction	objectives
Optional time for independent	Measurement by competence
study	objectives
Team teaching	

Advocates of humanizing processes in the schools are not in conflict with the back to the basics forces. They contend that the teaching of basic skills is inherent in every individualized instructional plan. The preceding alternatives are only part of the search for better ways to reach the individual student. Conflict comes when back-to-the-basics proponents claim that such alternatives lead to a neglect of teaching basic skills.

If progress is to be made in building imaginative, innovative secondary school curricula, certainly critics must be satisfied that basic skills are not neglected and that alternative programs are adding to the individual development of students in a positive way.

The most puzzling question in this context is how much schools really have changed.[6] The atmosphere may be different and the schools may seem different, but has the institutional character changed? Are the purposes and functions any different? In other words, how much impact have all the proposed changes made? Could it be that more than ninety percent of all the secondary schools in the nation are much the same as they have been in the last two or three decades? Answers to such questions are not easy to find.

THE PRESSURE FOR CLAIRVOYANCE

In every period of curriculum study and development, those responsible for the process are tormented by the uncertainty of their ability

[6] Leonard B. Stevens, "The Paradox of School Reform," *Phi Delta Kappan* (February 1976), p. 371.

to evaluate future needs. The philosophic seers of education haunt the practical-minded curriculum builder with demands of proof that what the pupils are learning today will be applicable in their world of tomorrow. This might be labeled the pressure for clairvoyance.

At present, this pressure for prediction involves the two searching questions that follow. The first question is certainly not new, and the second is rooted in the necessity for balance in curriculum matters.

Are Scientific and Technological Values Being Stressed at the Expense of Social and Moral Values?

The question of relative values is always present in planning the school curriculum. It is posed in many different forms — Are the values realistic? Are they consistent? Are they applicable? Are they in balance? Thoughtful critics of today's curriculum ask whether the student, engulfed in the mastery of the ever-increasing scientific and technological knowledge, has the opportunity to develop discriminating judgment of social and moral values. This is a question of balanced emphasis. In a larger sense it raises the question of whether people will be able to live in the automated technological world they are building.

Today's curriculum emphasizes the development of problem-solving ability for scientific and technical pursuits. Individual competition is stressed in myriad ways through competition for scholarships, academic groupings, and prizes for the intellectual elite. Too little attention is given to balancing these experiences with activities that enable youths to think in terms of social solutions and moral obligations. Scientific and technical pursuits are unquestionably necessary, but they are not enough in a world troubled with social inequalities. The unsolved problems of today and tomorrow are related to social behavior.

Adult leaders are forced to make decisions concerning the welfare of humankind in a world of thermonuclear capabilities, expanding global populations, rapid technological evolution, and unprecedented leisure. This calls for ability and experience quite different from the scientific thinking that created such conditions. It calls for discriminating powers in areas of social values where the search for answers is both frustrating and confusing.

Are the Students' Experiences Within the School Consistent with the Experiences They Face Outside the School?

Educators training youths for the future must establish some form of reference for beliefs and expectations. What is at stake is the standard of values of humankind. A regrettable mistake in the past has been to assume that school life, neatly compartmentalized into Carnegie units of subject matter and supplemented with the "socializing" effect of extraclass activities, inherently provides discriminating powers for social decision making. This assumption ignores both the violent clashes among peoples, classes, and races outside the school and young people's awareness of these clashes. Educators who foster such bland curriculum experience fail to understand youth's intensive search for a cause. The whole panorama of youth in "protest" ought to make clear to educational leaders how hungry young people are for opportunities to participate in serious decision making in the realm of social problems.

The schools are charged with the task of preparing youths for "life," and, paradoxically, young people find little in educational experiences that is either applicable or germane. They are part of a world of work, war, race tension, sex exploitation, economic affluence, economic distress, and organized protests against the social order. These are not bookish things and are not related to any basic set of facts. They raise questions in the minds of students for which the classroom provides only limited answers. The question might be asked: When will the curriculum contain honest courses on sex, anthropology, history, psychology, and religion? When will international affairs, race prejudice, poverty, and egocentric amusement activities be given equal importance with the scientific and technical areas of problem solving?

The choice confronting modern educators is not necessarily a choice between humanism and liberal arts on one hand and science and technology on the other. It is more a problem of the balance of relative values. It is senseless to debate the importance of one against the other. They are both supplementary and complementary. The plain fact is that both the social and scientific transition will make a chaotic world unless better communication is established between the proponents of human values and the new mechanistic forces.

A survey of emerging social problems reveals a whole new concept of work and the jobs involved, materialistic efficiency resulting in forced leisure, and millions of human beings — formerly nameless, silent, and oppressed — entering the mainstream of civilization and demanding the fruits of an abundant life. These social problems are complex and solutions are difficult. They call for the highest type of curriculum soothsaying. They point to young people's need for experiences that enable them to be aware of their social environment and to be flexible and imaginative in dealing with it. The past is only a prologue, not a pattern, and yesterday's dying echo must not determine tomorrow's theme.

TOPICS FOR STUDY AND DISCUSSION

1. Identify pro and con factors concerning whether the schools should prepare youth to change society or merely to make satisfactory adjustment to societal conditions.
2. What is the role of the school in the great moral issues of society?
3. The opponents of federal aid to education have contended consistently that federal control of education is a certain concomitant of federal aid. Find evidence in present federal aid programs that justify this fear.
4. What would be the merits of a national curriculum for education?
5. Analyze the school's responsibility for the maintenance of balance between the pressures of a technological age and the maladjustment it may cause in the social order.
6. What dangers are inherent in statutory regulations of subject matter to be contained in public school curricula? What authority should be vested with this power?
7. What will be the total effect of the accountability syndrome on the public school curriculum?
8. There is general agreement that effective evaluation of the educational product is necessary. Why has so little progress been made in this direction?
9. One theory advanced for declining test scores is that young people are weary of taking tests and no longer apply themselves. Evaluate this position.
10. Identify the main dilemma in the proposals of back-to-the-basics advocates.
11. Summarize proposals of the present group of national studies and commissions on education as they affect the secondary school curriculum.

SELECTED REFERENCES

Alexander, William M., and Sayler, J. Galen. *The High School: Today and Tomorrow.* New York: Holt, Rinehart and Winston, 1971.
  Through the efforts of two well-known authorities in secondary school curricula, all facets of modern high schools are analyzed. The book contains an overview of future secondary schools and points to the principal who must be an innovator of new curricula, techniques, organizations, and administrative practices.
Bailey, William J. *Managing Self-Renewal in Secondary Education.* Englewood Cliffs, N. J.: Educational Technology Publications, 1975.
  Bailey proposes to bring about effective change through a systematic management of behavior. Helpful suggestions and sample forms are provided for organizing and planning change. There may be some lack of fresh ideas and an overabundance of practices already tried. This is illustrated by the space devoted to the merit of large- and small-group discussions.

Bernard, Harold W., and Huckins, Wesley C. *Humanism in the Classroom.* Boston: Allyn and Bacon, 1975.

Based on first-hand observation of innovative schools across the nation, this valuable book offers authoritative help for evaluating and effectively utilizing current educational innovations. It covers such timely topics as behavior modification, accountability, team teaching, programmed learning, open education, organizing for change, and much more. Also, it contains a helpful glossary and dozens of enlightening cartoons, illustrations, charts, and graphs.

Havighurst, Robert J., and Dreyer, Philip H., eds. *Youth.* Seventy-fourth Yearbook of the National Society for the Study of Education. Chicago: University of Chicago Press, 1975.

The National Society for the Study of Education publishes two yearbooks each year devoted to a particular topic and composed of essays by the most knowledgeable people in the field. This 1975 edition, which is devoted to essays on development of those between the ages of fifteen and twenty-four, is one of the most useful that the NSSE has published and one that should be a valuable source book for secondary school principals and curriculum planners.

Roberts, Arthur D. *Educational Innovation: Alternatives in Curriculum and Instruction.* Boston: Allyn and Bacon, 1975.

Emphasizing theory into practice, many of the chapters in this book include concrete, practical suggestions for emphasizing ideas. Teachers who want to improve their instructional techniques, curriculum coordinators who are hoping to develop stronger curricula in a system, and principals and superintendents who want the best possible programs for their schools will find recommendations on many of the latest innovative programs and ideas.

Rubin, Louis. *The Future of Education.* Boston: Allyn and Bacon, 1975.

Nine leading experts assess the problems faced as an educator each day. Viewpoints are expressed, arguments presented, and helpful suggestions made to aid in teaching today and planning for tomorrow. Included are understanding social change, implications of imminent social change, environments for learning, and research needed for tomorrow's schools.

Schaffarzick, Jon, and Hampson, David H. *Strategies for Curriculum Development.* Berkeley, Calif.: McCutchan Publishing Corporation, 1975.

This publication represents the experiences and views of people who have directed or assumed major roles in large-scale curriculum-development projects. Specific topics covered include perspectives on curriculum development, specific approaches to curriculum development, focus on instructional materials, evaluation of the Kettering Project, and comparative studies of curriculium-development procedures.

Thompson, John Thomas. *Policymaking in American Public Education: A Framework for Analysis.* Englewood Cliffs, N. J.: Prentice Hall, 1975.

Principal objectives in policy-making theory are put forth in a conceptual framework for public education. Visual models are used to delineate the relationships among various subsystems at all levels of the public education structure. An Eastonian model is applied to show how policy is formed.

Van Til, William. *Curriculum: Quest for Relevance.* Boston: Houghton Mifflin, 1971.

This volume points to the fact that the struggle among forces in American society for curriculum change grows sharper. Roadblocks in the quest for relevance are identified as follows: present curriculum patterns fail to illuminate social realities, meet individual needs, or develop humane values; the integration of knowledge in subject matter areas is lacking; and no socially oriented proposals for humanizing education gather momentum.

Wilson, Craig L. *The Open Access Curriculum.* Boston: Allyn and Bacon, 1971.

Student needs are the focus of this treatise concerning the curriculum. Open access deals with the availability of educational opportunities for all students. Greater emphasis is put on the philosophical principles of curriculum development than on how to develop curricula. Material is especially pertinent to problems for students in urban areas.

II
Issues and Action in the Subject Areas

4

Business and Distributive Education

A study of the business education programs in secondary schools over the nation reveal many interesting changes, which reflect evolving social, economic, and technological conditions. The daily needs of people are in a state of flux due to changing social and economic conditions. Thus, employers have new attitudes and expectations concerning employment requirements. Technology is changing the business office in the same degree it is changing everyone's daily life.

Despite these conditions, the basic twofold objective in business education remains the same: to provide the student with the fundamentals of business and economic education, and to furnish the skills necessary for occupational success. An interesting commentary on business education is that it has always provided vocational training, yet not until the passage of the Vocational Education Acts of 1963 and 1968 was it afforded recognition in the vocational education field and provided financial support accordingly. Business education is one of the few disciplines that has consistently provided students not only with consumer and economic knowledge and skills, but also with marketable knowledge and skills.

The physical placement of the business education department and its curriculum associations is debatable. The question is whether it shall continue as a separate entity or be moved into and associated with the other areas of vocational education. Many business education leaders appear willing to concede the logic of the subject's direct association with vocational education. While on the surface this matter may not appear to be vitally important, a final decision will strongly affect the shaping of philosophic curriculum concepts.[1]

The extent of offerings in business education programs will vary depending on the school's size, type, and philosophy. Many schools offer what might be termed a minimum program. Other schools include a wide variety of innovative subject-matter material that keeps pace with technological developments. A minimum program ought to include a bookkeeeping-accounting area, a distributive area, a stenographic-secretarial area, a data-processing area, a general clerical area, and a general business area.

The general business area appeals to students not interested in preparing for a specific business occupation but who desire a broad overview of business and want to become acquainted with the development of consumer and economic knowledge. Writing letters and reports, preparing income tax returns, buying insurance, arranging credit, and using banking services are only a few of the inescapable business aspects of daily living. Responding to these common needs, business departments are opening their basic courses to all students.

Students pursuing the regular business sequence that traditionally involves shorthand, bookkeeping, and typing are obtaining economic background and developing marketable skills necessary to obtain jobs within the business world. Thus a student who elects to study in the bookkeeping-accounting area is preparing for a job as an accounts clerk, bookkeeper, junior accountant, or accounts payable–receivable clerk. With experience and further training, the scope widens to the occupations of accountant, cost accountant, and auditor.

Students preparing themselves for occupations should have access to all subject matter that prepares them for a specific job. For example, students preparing for stenographic and secretarial occupations need shorthand, machine transcription, business English, typewriting, and secretarial practice, but they also should have experiences in general business, business law, and accounting. Students preparing for computer and accounting occupations need their regular courses supple-

[1] Dean R. Maklory, "Business Education," National Association of Secondary School Principals *Bulletin* (January 1975), pp. 95–100.

mented by general business, business law, consumer economics, and business management. One of the values of business education is that it prepares the student to be not only a producer but also a consumer in modern society.

Secondary schools making an effort to keep their business education program abreast with technological developments may encounter new titles assigned to subject offerings, for example, micrographics, reprographics, word processing, data processing, and simulations.

Micrographics is a title applied to the storing of records in microforms. Because the use of microfilm and microfiche is becoming so prevalent in business, office workers need to understand how to establish retention schedules, how to purge files of unnecessary information, how to prepare records for microfilming, and how to use various retrieval systems.

Reprographics deals with the proliferation of new types of reproduction equipment. Office workers must decide which type of available equipment is best suited for each reprographic job. They must know how to paste up copy for duplication to avoid retyping, which cost factors are related to specific jobs, and how to keep duplicating costs under control.

The development of automated, self-correcting, programmable typewriters has provided the impetus for establishing word-processing centers. These machines increase office workers' capacity for transcribing letters, memoranda, reports, and other documents. Schools are setting up word-processing laboratories for integrating advanced typing, machine transcription, and automated typing.[2]

The need for office workers to be familiar with data processing has caused subject matter in this field to be introduced as a separate course or integrated with accounting. Since data-processing equipment is expensive and soon becomes outdated, many business education curriculum directors are hesitant to go beyond programs that involve little or no hardware. When more complicated equipment is needed, program directors are turning to hands-on experiences through cooperative work placement of students in business houses where equipment is available.[3] Other methods involve the teaching of concepts of storing, manipulating, and retrieving data through terminals connected with computers located elsewhere.

A growing number of business educators are giving their students realistic experiences by teaching them by means of simulations. These

---

[2] Terry M. Frame, "Word Processing is No Myth," *American Vocational Journal* (December 1975), pp. 23–25.

[3] Norman F. Kallaus, "Simulating an Effective Information System," *Business Education Forum* (May 1975), pp. 23–24.

simulations are of two types. One is a flow-of-work situation, where work is processed through a simulated organization much as it would be in a real-life situation. The other is a position simulation, where students assume particular career roles such as clerk typist, secretary, or administrative assistant. They are given a variety of office tasks, such as processing incoming mail.[4] Students not only get hands-on experience in a variety of jobs, but also come to see the office from a variety of perspectives — supervisory as well as subordinate — and they learn how to transfer basic skills to a variety of jobs.

REVISIONS IN SHORTHAND

Shorthand courses emphasizing theory in a long, drawn-out procedure are being questioned. There is a tendency to place ever-increasing emphasis on the ability to produce useful transcript. This, of course, means giving more attention to the practical application of shorthand. The simplification of shorthand has been in progress for some time; major systems of shorthand are being revised in this direction.

Shorthand systems may be classified as alphabetic, symbol, and machine. Each of these systems provides varied degrees of competence. There are ranges of accomplishment that students will achieve within the three systems, alphabetic shorthand generally providing the lower limits and machine shorthand the higher limits. In certain cases one limit will be desirable, while in other cases a rate somewhat in between is more appropriate.

Although alphabetic and machine shorthand systems have been gaining in use, symbol systems are taught in most secondary schools. The needs of students taking shorthand, research findings related to the system, and the time to be devoted to the teaching of the system are important factors in selecting a system of shorthand.[5]

Advocates of alphabetic shorthand stress the fact that students do not need to learn new symbols, as they are already familiar with the longhand alphabet. Consequently, principles involved are fewer and require a shorter time to master. The optimum uses of alphabetic shorthand are probably for personal note taking and for transcribing short dictated items.

The symbol systems of shorthand lend themselves more appropriately to use within business offices for taking dictation directly from an

[4] Nancy Wolff, "The Real Side of Simulation," *Business Education Forum* (January 1975), p. 8.

[5] Dean Clayton, "Essential Elements of Shorthand Instruction," *Business Education Forum* (December 1974), pp. 12–13.

employer. Students enrolled in symbol shorthand classes are generally preparing for a predetermined position.

Machine shorthand also lends itself to secretarial positions. Students going into court or conference reporting will select machine shorthand. In the future, computer transcription of machine shorthand will be used widely.

As new and revised systems of shorthand are introduced, curriculum planners will need to evaluate each system carefully, keeping students' needs in mind. The essential elements of instruction — student, teacher, and system — cannot be separated. Once these three are harmonized for best results, shorthand should no longer be the business education course with the highest dropout record.

Accelerated shorthand programs should be taken by capable students who need a program condensed into one year for use in postschool education. Many of these students are college bound and will use their shorthand for note taking at lectures and seminars. Part of them will earn needed financial assistance doing secretarial work for campus personnel where a high degree of business efficiency is not necessary.

Personal-use shorthand, frequently called notehand, emphasizes special techniques for converting expressed ideas into capsule statements. It translates original meaning rather than original words, emphasizing the ability to get the gist of remarks rather than taking them verbatim. This is a one-semester course and should enroll both boys and girls.

There will be a continued need for a two-year vocational shorthand program, but it must be adjusted to meet changing conditions. Such a program no longer attracts the brightest students, who are usually in the accelerated or the personal-use courses. Therefore, recognition must be given to the need for more student help in spelling, punctuation, and proofreading. There is an advantage, however, to such homogeneous grouping: it results in a narrower spread of learning activities and calls for more intensive, direct teaching.

Those planning the shorthand phase of the business education curriculum must concern themselves with the proper selection of students, adequate theory presentation, proper motivation for maximizing skill-building efforts, provisions for individual rates of learning, and full utilization of the various media for facilitating learning. Skill building and the fusion of shorthand, typewriting, and English usage ability must receive continual stress.

An innovation in the teaching of shorthand and transcription in many secondary schools in the introduction of machine shorthand. While mechanized shorthand may be confined to large urban and suburban schools for some time to come, there is ample reason for business education planners to investigate the feasibility of such processes in all secondary schools. The shorthand machine is fairly inexpensive, light, and compact, but it does require additional space in a business education department and a separate system of instruction. However, business offices must install and use shorthand machines in order to give any validity to shorthand machine instruction in the schools. It is not known how rapidly this will happen.

BOOKKEEPING: A QUESTION OF SURVIVAL

Serious questions are being raised about bookkeeping. There is need for reshaping objectives and reorienting areas of emphasis, for much of the present teaching perpetuates obsolete business forms and business activities. Extensive streamlining is necessary to acquaint students with modern business situations. The accounting operations of so many business corporations are tailored especially for their particular activities that only a minimum of training is essential for positions with these corporations. Most of the training is obtained on the job or at a special school provided by the particular business. A certain measure of rethinking on the semantics of bookkeeping is also in order. Many of the everyday English words used in bookkeeping in a technical sense do not retain their usual meaning. Thus simplification and reduced obscurity are needed.

Whether bookkeeping remains in the business education curriculum is a moot question. Strong defenders of the subject would have all business education students take an elementary bookkeeping course. They point to its basic values for vocational pursuits in the business world, citing the need for a basic understanding of combination journals, handling cash, use of business papers as source information, depreciation and bad debts, and the like. They also point out that bookkeeping is a good preparation for advanced study in accounting, since it provides an understanding of record maintenance and develops the ability to organize quantitative data.[6]

These proponents of the basic values of bookkeeping further enhance the subject's position in the business education curriculum by listing the factors good teachers can emphasize to relate bookkeeping to economic literacy. These include (1) private enterprise in a market-oriented economy, (2) calculation of the role of profits in a capitalistic economy, (3) productive costs — fixed, variable, average, and marginal — and (4) general business activities such as withholding taxes, controlled inflation, and marketing stocks and bonds.

[6] Cleo P. Casady, "The Value of High School Bookkeeping Courses," *Business Education Forum* (October 1974), pp. 19–21.

Boosters of bookkeeping also point to the personal use value of the subject. They contend that bookkeeping helps meet general education objectives by teaching future citizens to keep records, plan family budgets, prepare tax returns, reconcile bank statements, and understand financial statements.

Good processes in the teaching of bookkeeping emphasize individualized learning. The use of "practice sets" has many of the characteristics of modern simulation procedures. Curriculum planners for all business education programs have excellent opportunities for providing individualized instruction through the use of pacing, differentiated assignments, independent study, programmed materials, small-group instruction, simulation experiences, and gaming device activities.

NEW APPROACH IN TYPING

In the teaching of typing, the time-honored procedure of having students develop speeds measured in so many words per minute with minimum errors is being looked at askance. Business educators advocate that a student's typing ability be measured in terms of ability to do functional production work. Speed and accuracy remain relatively important, but the multiple uses of variations of the typewriter call for additional skills.

In addition to necessary skills in typing, students should attain facilities for greater practical services. Basic reading, spelling, punctuation, and proofreading should be concomitant learnings. Time for perfecting these fundamentals may be attained by reducing the time spent on practicing such infrequently used typing needs as legal documents, bills of lading, and quantities of invoices, statements, and receipts. Emphasis should not be on training students for initial positions, but rather on preparation of executive secretaries. For such preparation, a student needs a thorough understanding of the basic skills of communication.

Typewriting was the first subject in the business education field to be suggested as being valuable for personal use. Curriculum planners now generally accept the dual role of typing instruction for vocational pursuits and personal use. The more enthusiastic advocates of typing instruction suggest that one year of the subject be required of all students. They would retain the second year for those planning vocations requiring additional typing ability.

New directions in typing instruction point to intrinsic values that can be built into good teaching of the subject. Studies of elementary school children reveal that typing has a favorable effect on general academic achievement, improves word skills and English mechanics, and stimulates certain types of creativity. So why can't secondary school typing achieve the same ends if they are stressed as objectives? Creativity takes the form of self-expression in typing accomplishments. Instead of teaching six rigid business forms, the instructor teaches only one, and the student is encouraged to concentrate on the organization of thought, the division of paragraphs, and the proper grammatical structure. Much of this kind of typing is done from direct dictation or rough drafts.

Accomplished typists are frequently asked to type from the rough draft of a letter. This requires acute concentration and discrimination. Students must learn to make necessary corrections without changing the meaning. In such activities, they are required to think as they type. This raises the typist from the level of a mechanical reactor to that of an intelligent participant. The process requires experience in what might be called "think-and-type" situations.

Any change of objectives or emphasis does not lessen the need for stressing skills. Since typing is basically a skill subject, it will continue to require from one-third to one-half of a student's instruction time to insure both competence and confidence. New approaches to teaching the subject will make typing classes more stimulating and afford students greater breadth of learning.[7]

In some places these new approaches result in innovative occupational programs such as flexible laboratory instructional programs for students who cannot schedule regular typing classes. This individualized instructional program is designed primarily for non–business education students who desire to acquire employable skills in clerical office occupations so that they may obtain immediate part-time employment or full-time employment upon graduation.

Special typewriting programs are being developed for civil service typewriting, medical typewriting, and legal typewriting. Each of these courses has as a major focus the development of language arts skills required of office workers related to the particular profession. The range of possibilities for specialized typewriting courses is limited only by the school's human and physical resources.

DISTRIBUTIVE EDUCATION

Distributive education is in the family of vocational education subjects that are supported by federal aid to education. It came into being with the George–Dean Act of 1936 and was greatly strengthened by the George–Barden Act of 1946. It also shares in the greatly increased support furnished by the Vocational Education Act of 1963.

[7] L. J. West, "Implication of Research for Teaching Typewriting," *Delta Pi Epsilon Research Bulletin,* no. 4 (1974), p. 1.

Distributive education is vocational because it involves supervised training on the job. The typical program organizes learning in the classroom for part of the day and in regular distributive merchandising jobs for the remainder of the day. Salaries are provided students for their merchandising work. Federal moneys are furnished to supplement the salary of the distributive education coordinator (the teacher in charge of a distributive education program) and furnish certain other fringe benefits for the program.

The coordinator's duties go beyond classroom teaching to student counseling, job placement, and program public relations. Distributive education classroom work includes receiving, selling, merchandising, sales promotion, and control. The related classroom program usually involves required general education classes such as English and social studies and commercial subjects such as salesmanship and commercial law. Frequently, typing and bookkeeping are background requirements.

The on-the-job training is designated as the cooperative phase of distributive education. On-the-job activities provide students with practical experience and enhance their respect for what they learn in school. They become familiar with job opportunities, job requirements, salary scales, business procedures, and the exacting requirements of the business world. In many cases the money they earn enables them to stay in school. Dropouts are very few. Another benefit is that a secondary school that sponsors a distributive education program establishes better relations with businesses. The distributive education coordinator becomes familiar with the needs of the business community, and she or he is in a position to interpret educational problems to business leaders.

Although distributive education is a comparatively new subject in the secondary school curriculum, leaders are constantly seeking new ways to organize classes, new methods of instruction, and new ways to utilize staff resources to develop more effective programs. This is in keeping with an age of continual change.

Distributive education curriculum leaders recognize that an improved and widely expanded distributive education program can make a definite contribution to the solution of many social, economic, and educational problems of a community. Programs of distributive education are associated with problems of dropouts, teenage unemployment, and changing patterns of the distribution of commercial products.

New Teaching Methods

Distributive education coordinators are experimenting with team teaching and programmed instruction methods. Where programs involve more than one teaching coordinator, the team idea is feasible. Even when there is only one coordinator, faculty members from related fields — such as English and social studies — can be enlisted.

The enlistment of cooperation with other teachers in the school is a good practice. It helps overcome the isolation that characterizes many vocational education programs. Vocational students like to feel they are part of the total school program. In situations where the distributive education teacher teams with part of the academic faculty, students have the opportunity to relate to a variety of learning situations. These same experiences may be obtained through programmed instruction, although experimentation to date offers no conclusive evidence.[8]

One of the most successful teaching methods associated with distributive education programs is the use of a sales laboratory. Here the distributive education coordinator can demonstrate the tenets of modern merchandising, such as self-service and centralized check-out, in a learning-by-doing fashion. Instruction is more realistic in this environment, and students obtain vocational competence with greater ease. A well-organized sales laboratory enables students to make direct application of classroom theories under directly supervised instruction. The equipment and facilities in a sales laboratory may include cash registers, showcases, display stands, display windows, marking machines, wrapping counters, gummed tape machines, and other merchandising paraphernalia.

TRENDS IN BUSINESS EDUCATION

Changes in the business education curriculum reflect a reduction in the rigidity and specifity that marked the field for a long time. Business education classes formerly were open only to students seeking training for a specific vocation and who exhibited the necessary skills for competence in a chosen field. Relaxation of those objectives and the opening of classes to students with a wide variety of needs marks current business education programs.[9] Today many schools permit students to select from the entire business curriculum those courses they believe will provide them with the knowledge and skills they wish to acquire. A sequence of courses is required only of those who designate a specific vocational objective.

Business educators recognize that some knowledge, skills, and attitudes are best acquired in a business setting. This has led to the

[8] James G. Bennett, "The Need to Evaluate Distributive Education Instructional Materials," *Business Education Forum* (May 1975), pp. 22–23.

[9] E. Crooks, "Business and Office Education Revisited," *American Vocational Journal* (March 1977), pp. 44–45.

development of extensive cooperative work experience. During the senior year, students are placed in a part-time position and supervised by both teacher and employer. They normally are paid for their work, and the educational experience becomes an integral part òf their school program. Cooperative work experience, along with simulated business activities within the classroom, give a practical aspect to students' education.

The use of mini-courses is invading the business education field also. Many of the mini-courses are service oriented, so they appeal to both business and nonbusiness students. Drawn from subject matter that was formerly unit material within semester or yearly courses, the mini-courses are designed to give students wider choices and more opportunities for exploration. Examples of mini-courses are money management, insurance, contracts, records and accounts, advertising, and investments.

It is inevitable that career education would have its effect on the business education curriculum. Instructional materials are placing more stress on occupational requirements for entering and succeeding in job situations. Business education departments are providing try-out experiences for middle and junior high school students. The exploration of business careers is a popular topic in guidance materials and, strangely enough, a field that has long been associated with job placement objectives is now being given due recognition in the all-encompassing career education concept.[10] Certainly career education is a familiar topic to the business educator.

Individualized instruction is more prevalent in business education classes today. In such areas as accounting, much of the work has always been somewhat individualized, but the development of modular scheduling and other schedule adjustments have been accompanied by competence-based instruction, learning activity packets, and teaching-learning units.[11] The business education curriculum is marked by greater flexibility than ever before.

A somewhat belated trend comes from the recognition that learning to spend is as important as learning to earn. More attention is being given to the development of economic and consumer awareness and competence. Consumer and economic knowledge, attitudes, and skills are developed in such courses as general business, business law, and consumer economics. Units on income tax and financial reports provide students with the opportunity to acquire economic and consumer

[10] Robert A. Ristau, "Career Education in Basic Business," *Business Education Forum* (April 1975), pp. 5–6.

[11] Ronald D. Hahn, "Similarities Between Traditional and Individualized Instruction for Beginning Shorthand," *Business Education Forum* (January 1975), pp. 11–12.

competence. Too often in the past, business education teachers have focused their interest and attention on the teaching of shorthand, typewriting, and accounting at the expense of economic and consumer concepts and abilities that students need.[12]

One of the best statements concerning what direction the curriculum in business education should take may be found in a statement by the Policies Commission for Business and Economic Education,[13] These trends are in keeping with the better curricula being developed by business education curriculum personnel:

1. Every secondary school should provide opportunities for students to prepare for careers in business.
2. The time devoted to preparation for business occupations should depend on the student's abilities, interests, and personal qualities.
3. The sequence of learning experiences should be planned so that the student will achieve his or her highest occupational competence upon completion of the program.
4. On-the-job experience through cooperative education should be an integral part of the student's program.
5. Opportunities must be provided for secondary students to develop an understanding of how the business system operates.
6. Requirements relating to the development of personal and social economic competence should be reciprocally recognized by the respective departments of the school.

TOPICS FOR STUDY AND DISCUSSION

1. Develop criteria for the placement of data processing within the business education curriculum.
2. What changes would occur in business education courses if they were performance-based?
3. How can situations regarding declining enrollments in shorthand classes be remedied?
4. Are the goals of business education and career education compatible?
5. One authority writing in the area of distributive education makes the statement that jobs available to students in the field of marketing are not related to the subject matter being taught. He would have distributive education courses integrated with other related disciplines in the curriculum. Develop a counterargument.

[12] Larry L. Luing, "Expanding the Role of Business Education," *Business Education Forum* (February 1978), pp. 3–7.

[13] Policies Commission for Business and Economic Education, "This We Believe About Business Education in the Secondary Schools."

6. Discuss the merits of on-the-job experiences with simulated experiences for business education seniors.
7. Bookkeeping courses in the secondary school curriculum are now being labeled accounting courses. What is the significance of the change?
8. Word processing has been a part of business education courses for a long time. Why has it been given a new birth with the invasion of technology?

SELECTED REFERENCES

Abbott, Helen Lawson. *Human Relations Skills of Beginning Office Workers in Occupational Adjustment.* Atlanta: Georgia State University, Ph.D. Dissertation, 1973.
 Abbott develops a list of critical requirements in human relations behavior that contribute to the successful occupational adjustment of beginning office workers in three roles: relationships with supervisors, other employees, and individuals outside the firm.
Beryle, Milton K. *Your Career in the World of Work.* Indianapolis: Howard W. Sams & Co., 1975.
 Beryle presents significant information on proper work attitudes, managing money, banking, insurance, social security, wage and tax statements, and consumer responsibilities. He gives job summaries and lists career opportunities. This is a comprehensive guide for business education teachers in guiding graduates into business occupations.
Coleman, Marion G., and Henson, Oleen M. *Effective Secretarial Education,* 12th Yearbook. Reston, Va.: National Business Education Association, 1974.
 The authors describe and evaluate new ideas and techniques in secretarial education. They explore methodology in shorthand and typewriting instruction, and they cite research of significance to the business education teacher.
Maxwell, Gerald W., and Winnett, William L. *Relevance in the Education of Today's Business Student,* 11th Yearbook. Reston, Va.: National Business Education Association, 1973.
 This book is a dialogue between business educators and those segments of society most concerned with business education. It contains interviews with students, parents, entry-level employees, teachers, and curriculum directors, as well as community business leaders.
Policies Commission for Business and Economic Education. "This We Believe About Business Education in the Secondary Schools."
Ristau, R. A., and Lambrecht, J. J. "Business Education Keeps Pace." *American Vocational Journal* (September 1974), pp. 40–42.
 This is a good summary of classroom teaching developments in business education. The authors make several predictions for developments in the future and show relationship between career education and business education.

5

English Language Arts

The English language is a living thing and thus is in a state of constant flux, but the teaching of English has changed relatively little over the past several decades. Probably the most significant changes over this period have been the "activity" or "experience-centered" programs popular in the thirties and forties and the communication theory of semantics popular in the early fifties.

The most important development of the seventies, the elective program, is reaction to the traditional English curriculum; ironically, it features student-centered experiences, which were also stressed in the earlier periods. The elective programs range all the way from a limited program in the senior year to programs for the entire secondary school English curriculum. Already English curriculum workers refer to a conflict between the elective program and the traditional program.

The traditional English program is based on the division of English into written composition, language study, and literature. Units of subjects are allocated to the various grade levels according to the logical development of content. Usually grammar and composition are studied in the freshman and sophomore years, American literature in the junior year, and English literature in the senior year.

In a modernization of this program a sequential step arrangement is developed and the psychological rather than the logical is stressed. Each grade level includes material about the structure of the English language, writing effective prose, and reading literary forms, with subject matter developed sequentially according to the students' learning levels.

THE ELECTIVE PROGRAM

The elective program in the English curriculum developed out of the necessity to rescue students from boredom and disinterest arising from the myriad of experiences available through other forms of communication, especially the public media. Teachers who find it increasingly difficult to sustain interest in long, frequently repetitive experiences with the written and oral form of the language are turning to the development of the mini-course, the elective course, and similar formats of in-depth organization in a wide variety of subjects for briefer periods.[1]

A definition of an English elective curriculum is not complicated. It simply means that all or part of the courses in the English curriculum are organized around a theme, unit, or topic. These courses are presented in time sequences according to needs of students and the subject matter involved. They may continue for a week, a month, three months, six months, nine months, and sometimes a semester. The main features of an elective program are that none of the courses is required and that wide varieties are presented for selection. Many programs do require that students must have a certain minimum of experiences in specified areas of the English program.

Another of the most important features of the English elective program is the opportunity offered students to select the program they want to study at any particular time. Frequently, the choice of instructors accompanies the election of the course. Since students are able to choose the classes they want, it is more likely that they will have sustained learning experiences. In the traditional program, for as much as a year they are locked in courses that suit neither their interest nor their ability. Many elective courses are planned personally by the teacher. This leads to enthusiastic and interesting teaching and a classroom atmosphere that is much more conducive to learning.

Another significant factor in an elective program is the number of

[1] Theodore Hipple, *Teaching English in the Secondary Schools* (New York: The Macmillan Company, 1973), pp. 43–45.

student-centered methods and activities. Small-group discussions and the independent pursuit of information are both part of the flexibility of an independently planned course where time and content are controlled by the teacher or the curriculum planning group. Most elective courses contain numerous activities that lead to total student involvement.[2] For example, in a survey of one course in an elective English curriculum, students reported that they had participated in more creative, student-centered activity than in any other course in their entire school curriculum. In writing assignments, students frequently prepare more than they are assigned, and participation on a volunteer basis leads to wide writing experiences, including innovative composition, poetry writing, and written critiques of classmates' contributions.

The following objectives for elective English programs are the most frequent:

1. To better meet the needs, ability, and interests of students in regard to language arts skills.
2. To give students the freedom and opportunity to make mature choices.
3. To improve the attitude of both students and teachers toward language arts programs.
4. To broaden the experiences of students in language arts programs by the use of a wide variety of subject matter.
5. To provide the opportunity and stimulus for improved instruction in language arts skills through better planning, methods, and instructional materials.

The following pages contain an example of a large Midwestern high school's elective English program for grades 10 through 12. This program was selected as an example because it recognizes both the abilities and the interests of the students. Ability is evaluated through phasing. While there is nothing new about phasing, it is still a standard model for matching the difficulty of materials to students' abilities.

CENTRAL HIGH SCHOOL   *Phase Elective Semester Courses*

General Description: Students at Central High School may choose from a listing of thirty-five semester elective English courses during grades 10 through 12. These include a range of courses from basic composition to rhetoric, logic, art of the film, film workshop, English usage, the American dream, literature of the South, satire, and Shakespeare. All courses are phased according to level of difficulty,

---

[2] Edmund Farrell, *Deciding the Future: A Forecast of Responsibilities of Secondary Teachers of English, 1970–2000* (Urbana, Ill.: National Council of Teachers of English, 1971).

with most of the courses phased 1–2 or 3–4–5. Some courses are recommended for one year only, others for the entire three years.

The main objective in the program is to provide students with the opportunity to have a variety of choices in their English program. Each of the courses has built-in learning experiences in basic language skills, including work in composition. Each student is required to have a theme folder showing his or her writing skills.

The process of electing an English program requires students to change courses as well as instructors at the end of each semester. It also requires that students give serious consideration to the choices they make. The departmental schedule for twenty-nine English teachers is determined by the courses that students elect.

The elective courses have no grade-level requirement, but some do have grade-level recommendations. They are phased according to level of difficulty. Phasing is a way of describing courses by assigning them a range of numbers from 1 to 5 to indicate degrees of difficulty:

Phase 1 — Courses are designed for students who have problems with writing and speaking and need help with basic skills.

Phase 2 — Courses are for students who do not have problems with basic skills but need to improve and refine them.

Phase 3 — Courses are for those who have mastered the basic skills and are ready to use these skills to gain new experiences.

Phase 4 — Courses are for students who have demonstrated ability with reading, writing, and speaking skills and who want special experiences in these areas.

Phase 5 — Courses are for students who are seeking a challenging academic experience in the use of basic skills.

Basic Composition (recommended for sophomores, juniors and seniors)   (Phase 1–2)

This course is designed for students wishing to improve their writing skills. It focuses on the basic process of finding material and structuring it for presentation to the reader. Assignments are given to help improve sentence structure, word usage, organization, and spelling. This course concentrates on effective writing and well-developed paragraphs.

Advanced Composition (recommended for juniors and seniors) (Phase 3–4–5)

Students work on a wide range of essays and topics. They have experiences in organizing and developing ideas through a variety of methods. They learn to recognize how word choice, sentence structure, and imagery affect the communication of ideas.

Rhetoric and Logic (recommended for juniors and seniors)   (Phase 3–4–5)

**CENTRAL HIGH SCHOOL ENGLISH DEPARTMENT
COURSE OFFERINGS**

Course Title	Phase Level	Open To:	Fr.	So.	Jr.	Sr.
Basic Composition	1–2			x	x	x
Advanced Composition	3–4–5				x	x
Rhetoric and Logic	3–4–5				x	x
Writing for Readers	3–4–5				x	x
Writers' Workshop	4–5					x
Communication Studies	3–4–5			x	x	
Creative Speaking	2–3–4–5			x	x	x
English Usage	2–3–4			x	x	x
Industrial English	1–2–3–4–5			x	x	x
Language and People	3–4–5				x	x
Reading Improvement	1–2			x	x	
Reading and Research	3–4–5			x	x	
Individualized Reading	1–2–3–4–5					x
Print and Flick	1–2			x	x	x
Art of the Film	3–4–5				x	x
Film Workshop	1–2–3–4–5				x	x
Newspaper Reporting	3–4–5			x	x	
Editing for Publications	3–4–5			x	x	x
Newspaper Production			x	x	x	x
Yearbook Production			x	x	x	x
People in Conflict	1–2			x	x	
Contemporary Literature	1–2–3				x	x
American Dream	2–3–4			x	x	x
American Studies	3–4–5				x	
Language of Poetry	3–4–5			x	x	x
Literature of the South	3–4–5			x	x	x
Mythology	3–4–5			x	x	x
Nonfiction	2–3–4			x	x	x
Science Fiction	3–4–5			x	x	
Major American Writers	3–4–5			x	x	
Major British Writers	3–4–5				x	x
People, God, and the State	3–4–5				x	x
Satire and Humor	3–4–5					x
Shakespeare	3–4–5				x	x
Humans/Animals/Nature	1–2			x	x	x
Supernatural and						
Detective Story	1–2			x	x	x
Magazine Reading	1–2				x	x

The students study clear thinking as a preliminary to clear speaking and writing. They examine propaganda techniques and a variety of logical fallacies.

Writing for Readers (recommended for juniors and seniors (Phase 3–4–5)

This is a course for students who enjoy writing, who want to enhance their skills in creative writing, and who enjoy thinking, talking, and writing about people, places, and things in fiction, nonfiction, poetry, and plays. From their own experiences, the students write approximately one creative paper per week.

Writer's Workshop (recommended for seniors who have completed Writing for Readers)   (Phase 4–5)

The workshop is open to students who have demonstrated in Writing for Readers an ability to write independently and productively. Students continue to enhance their skills in writing readable prose or poetry. The class produces a creative writing magazine.

Communication Studies (recommended for sophomores and juniors) (Phase 3–4–5)

This course is designed to help students express themselves more effectively in a variety of communicative situations. It investigates the communication process and traces humanity's historical quest for more efficient methods of imparting knowledge and discoveries. Special emphasis is given to the importance of language in the communication process, with exercises designed to help students improve language skills in writing and speaking.

Creative Speaking (recommended for sophomores, juniors, and seniors)   (Phase 2–3–4–5)

This course emphasizes problems that a student must solve in order to communicate clearly and effectively when *speaking* to other people. Individualized training and practical experience in all phases of speech preparation and delivery are included. Each student learns to speak with clarity and conviction; to select and limit speech subjects that are clear, interesting, and significant; to arrive at rational judgments; and to support her or his own thoughts with relevant material from authoritative research sources.

English Usage (recommended for sophomores, juniors, and seniors) (Phase 2–3–4)

This course utilizes both traditional and modern grammar to present accepted principles of English usage. The course is designed for students who recognize deficiencies in their language and who desire a systematic study of grammar and usage to improve their English. Practical application includes the writing of multiparagraph essays that emphasize the kind of clear, correct usage expected in many academic, social, and vocational areas.

Industrial English (open to sophomores, juniors, and seniors) (Phase 1–2–3–4–5)

This course is designed to help the student who is also enrolled in industrial education courses. Emphasis is given to reading and writing skills that relate to improved performance and understanding of vocational concepts: reading directions, handwriting, spelling, syllabication, and technical vocabulary.

Language and People (recommended for juniors and seniors) (Phase 3–4–5)

This contemporary course is designed to investigate linguistically the structure, development, and growth of language and its function in society. Oral and written research projects provide opportunities to discover the conditioning role of language as a symbolic shaper of human behavior. Language in its cultural context helps the student to understand and master characteristics of current language and to become familiar with situations in which language humanizes.

Reading Improvement (recommended for sophomores and juniors) (Phase 1–2)

Reading improvement is a course designed to help the student read with less difficulty and more enjoyment. Attention is given to vocabulary skills, methods of studying assignments, improving listening, and increasing reading speed and comprehension. This course is designed for students who read below their present grade level and wish to improve reading skills.

Reading and Research (recommended for sophomores and juniors) (phase 3–4–5)

This course emphasizes the development of advanced reading skills needed by college-bound students. Exercises in vocabulary improvement, verbal analogies, reading comprehension, and reading speed help prepare the student for college entrance examinations. By preparing a major term paper, the student can read extensively in areas of interest, become familiar with libraries, and develop writing skills required for future research papers.

Individualized Reading (recommended for seniors)   (Phase 1–2–3–4–5)

This course is for the responsible student who likes to read and who is capable of carrying out individual reading programs that will involve written papers of various kinds and lengths. Readings will be determined by conferences with the teacher. The written work must show the extent and direction of student readings and will be a major means of evaluating student reading.

Print and Flick (recommended for sophomores, juniors, and seniors) (Phase 1–2)

The purpose of this course is to involve the student in the critical reading of literature and the critical viewing of films in order to be able to evaluate the final and total communication of both. During the first quarter, the student responds to film techniques and the film's plastic elements, which, when combined, produce meaningful communication. In the second quarter, the student draws relationships between the two forms of communication.

The Art of the Film (recommended for juniors and seniors) (Phase 3–4–5)

Students view many short films, often several times. Emphasis is on technique and theme. Students also watch feature-length movies both on television and at the theater. Reviews are written and reports made.

Film Workshop (recommended for juniors and seniors; prerequisite: Print/Flick or Art of the Film plus approval of the instructor) (Phase 1–2–3–4–5)

Students in this course are provided with the opportunity of working with and making many kinds of films. Some film-making activities include pixillation, animation, documentary, experimental, and narrative films. Students script, shoot, and edit their own films.

Newspaper Reporting (recommended for sophomores and juniors) (Phase 3–4–5)

Students study methods of reporting as a basis for clarity and precision in writing. Students conduct interviews to gather information and to learn what makes news and how news is gathered. They write a minimum of one news story per week and three major research projects. Students study such special skills as the lead paragraph, story types, copyreading, and headline writing.

Editing for Publications (recommended for sophomores, juniors, and seniors; prerequisite: Newspaper Reporting)   (Phase 3–4–5)

Students study skill areas needed for editing newspapers, books, and magazines. Areas studied include the structure and organization of publications staffs; layouts and design of publications; editorial and magazine writing; uses of photography and artwork; copy preparation, copyfitting, and printing instructions; and press law and libel. This course is recommended for students considering journalism as a career and those seeking editorial positions on the various school publications.

Newspaper Production (noncredit; open to all students by application)

This extracurricular staff meets daily for both semesters during the school day to produce the student newspaper. Positions are usually available for four to six freshmen, six to eight sophomores, eight to ten juniors, and ten to twelve seniors. Students interested in working on this staff must be appointed by the sponsor and the present staff.

Yearbook Production (noncredit; open to all students by application)
This extracurricular staff meets daily during the school day to produce the student yearbook. Students interested should have a B average and must be appointed by the sponsor. Students from all four class levels are encouraged to apply.

People in Conflict (recommended for sophomores and juniors) (Phase 1–2)
This course focuses on people-in-conflict situations — conflict with themselves, their environment, their society. Students study aspects of the human struggle to realize dreams and the forces — war, prejudice, family, peers — that oppose attainment of these goals. Materials for this course include *The Red Pony, My Shadow Ran Fast, Pudd'nhead Wilson,* and selected nonfiction.

Contemporary Literature (recommended for juniors and seniors) (Phase 1–2–3)
Mature students read selections by today's authors covering novels, drama, nonfiction, and science fiction. Group discussions, special projects, and theme assignments accompany the study of works such as *In Cold Blood, Flowers for Algernon, 15 American One-Act Plays,* and *Manchurian Candidate.* Each student is required to select two other books during the semester: one as a personal choice and one as a requirement.

The American Dream (recommended for sophomores, juniors, and seniors   (Phase 2–3–4)
America began as a wilderness and a dream. That dream has grown and changed, molded and developed by what is uniquely American. Students look at the origins of the dream and see how it exists today. They do this by discussing poetry, short stories, and longer works such as *The Great Gatsby* and *Death of a Salesman.*

American Studies (open only to juniors; offers credit in both English and U. S. History)   (Phase 3–4–5)
This course offers a combined study of American literature and American history as interrelated thematically and chronologically The literature segment includes selected short stories, novels, poems, and plays; the history segment includes various documents and reserve materials as well as the basic text. Students work with

two teachers, one from the English staff and one from the history staff, for back-to-back periods. This course, a two-semester sequence open only to juniors, gives two credits — one in U. S. History and one in English.

The Language of Poetry (recommended for sophomores, juniors, and seniors)   (Phase 3–4–5)

Poetry is the central focus of this course. The subject matter is as wide as Carl Sandburg suggests when he speaks of poetry as the "synthesis of hyacinths and biscuits." Not only is the subject matter varied but so is the form; poetry is read that ranges from sonnet to song lyrics. Discussion and written work give the student an opportunity to explore poetry.

Literature of the South (recommended for sophomores, juniors, and seniors)   (Phase 3–4–5)

The literature of the South provides a rich and fascinating field of study. Through the works of novelists, poets, dramatists, and journalists, students gain a better understanding of this fascinating part of the nation. In this course, students attempt, through reading and research, to identify some of the characteristic traits and ideals that have made the South a literary haven.

Mythology (recommended for sophomores, juniors, and seniors) (Phase 3–4–5)

Classical mythology is one of the principal sources for the allusions and symbolism in Western culture in general and literature and art in particular. In this course, students study some of the main works of classical mythology from which an abundance of allusion and symbolism originates. In addition to Homer's *Iliad* and *Odyssey*, students read some stories of pre-Homeric heroes. They also read some myths from non-Western cultures that illustrate universally recurrent mythological themes.

Nonfiction (recommended for sophomores and juniors)   (Phase 2–3–4)

Most reading done by adults falls into the category of nonfiction. In this course, students concentrate on a range of nonfiction, much of which is based on the lives of people past and present. Some of the reading material consists of short pieces on contemporary issues, including editorials and personal essays.

Science Fiction (recommended for sophomores and juniors) (Phase 3–4–5)

Science fiction is more than stories about robots and spaceships. Science fiction writers extend their views of the present to future extremes in order to illustrate the conditions of people in society. This course examines the present and the future as presented in writings such as *1984* (Orwell), *Brave New World* (Huxley), *Anthem* (Rand), *Fahrenheit 451* (Bradbury), a thematic anthology of short science fiction stories, and other works of the student's own choice.

Major American Writers (recommended for sophomores and juniors)　　(Phase 3–4–5)

Poe, Hawthorne, Melville, and Irving are four of the early American writers who helped establish the position of the American writer in world letters. Thoreau, Twain, and Crane forged new paths in American writing and thinking. Hemingway, Faulkner, and Arthur Miller have continued dealing with themes and structures begun by the early American authors. This condensed survey of American "greats" acquaints the students with their literary heritage and contemporary expression as well as offering opportunities to write about these literary works.

Major British Writers (recommended for juniors and seniors) (Phase 3–4–5)

This course is designed as a one-semester chronological survey of the finest that has been written in the language we speak. Starting with the Anglo-Saxon origins of our language, the student reads from the medieval period of Chaucer and the Elizabethan English of Shakespeare. Continued reading and writing deals with special emphasis on selected works of the seventeenth and eighteenth centuries, the Romantic and Victorian poets, as well as representative British prose, including novels.

People, God, and the State (recommended for juniors and seniors) (Phase 3–4–5)

The conflict between human loyalty to God and loyalty to the demands of political expediency is basically one of conscience and of morality. This course examines the nature of this conflict in terms of the political and moral choices that great men and women in high office must make. Such literary works as *Oedipus, Antigone, Julius Caesar, Murder in the Cathedral*, and *A Man for All Seasons* will serve as a basis for this study. Discussion and written work give the students an opportunity to examine their reactions to this conflict.

Satire and Humor (recommended for seniors)　　(Phase 3–4–5)

Students explore such questions as why humor and satire have increased in importance and popularity in the 1970s. They also learn to recognize the devices of satire and humor by studying the many different kinds — jokes, tall tales, autobiographical sketches — in a variety of forms — short stories, articles, novels, and cartoons. In addition, students write expository themes and experiment with their own humorous writing and projects.

Shakespeare (recommended for juniors and seniors)   (Phase 3–4–5)

For the modern student, Shakespeare offers perhaps more than any other author the whole spectrum of human experiences and emotions. The content of the course consists of several representative plays (including tragedies, comedies, and histories) as well as some lyric poetry. Students are encouraged to approach the plays from both a literary and a theatrical point of view. Projects and individual activities range from writing expository papers to developing research topics, to producing scenes or passages from the plays.

Humans/Animals/Nature (recommended for sophomores, juniors, and seniors   (Phase 1–2)

This course explores the relationship between animals and humans. Specifically, students read, discuss, and write about a variety of stories concerning animals. Materials will range from *Aesop's Fables* to contemporary paperbacks.

Supernatural and the Detective Story (recommended for sophomores, juniors, and seniors)   (Phase 1–2)

As long as people have questions about themselves, they will be interested in the mysterious and the unexplainable. Tales of the supernatural and detective stories form the subject for the reading in this course. The student reads a variety of works in prose, poetry, and drama form for pleasure as well as analysis. Classroom participation includes oral as well as written activities.

Magazine Reading (recommended for juniors and seniors)   (Phase 1–2)

Magazines deal with the real and vital concerns of complex society and provide exciting information that helps students cope with their world. In this course, the student investigates the common types of magazines: pictorial, digest, weekly news, sports, fashion, consumer, mystery, science fiction, special interest or hobby, home, and teen-age. Activities generated from their magazine reading include developing adult leisure reading tastes; supplying entertaining reading experiences; discussing interesting articles; increasing vocabulary; presenting a demonstration speech; and writing expository paragraphs and letters.

Media Studies (recommended for sophomores and juniors) (Phase 1–2)

Through a study of media, the student investigates how people use communication processes to understand and control their environment, themselves, other people, and machines. A study of the various media — magazines, movies, newspapers, paperbacks, radio, records, and television — result in oral reports and written essays.

The Bible as Literature (recommended for seniors)   (Phase 3–4–5)
Modern civilization is greatly indebted to the Bible, both the Old Testament and the New Testament. Students are able to document a vast amount of detail and allusion that relates to the literary heritage of our culture. In this course, the Bible is studied not only for its intrinsic and humanistic values but also for its influence on the great body of Western literature.

MINI-COURSES

The preceding Central High School elective English program is an example of a semester plan for all courses. The following pages contain examples of courses of varying length of time and content. They are selected from the elective English program of secondary schools all over the nation. Space permits only grade placement identification and objectives of each course.

THE LANGUAGE OF DRUGS

The Language of Drugs, part of the eighth-grade program, is an eight-week course that integrates all areas of English instruction within a topic that is of compelling interest to a junior high school student.

Objectives: The purpose of the course is to use the broad topic of The Language of Drugs as a vehicle to insure greater competence in English. The usual compartmentalization resulting from separate handling of spelling, grammar, literature, and composition is avoided, and students, carried along by their interest in the topic, participate in activities designed to enrich their knowledge of the subject and at the same time to strengthen the English skills appropriate to their grade level.

THE MYSTERY STORY

The Mystery Story is a nine-week elective mini-course recommended for grades 9–12.

Objectives: This course introduces the student to the genre of the mystery story, its patterns, and its terminology. It attempts to develop the student's ability to read for detail and understanding and to write creatively and critically. The cultural value of the mystery story is examined in both literature and film.

POETRY AND MUSIC

Poetry and Music is a one-semester elective for seniors in which they pay serious attention to the lyrics of contemporary rock poet-singers. They are asked to evaluate the personal, political, religious, and social messages and implications of the songs and lyrics. Once this effort is well underway, poetry from the English and American traditions is presented to encourage students to locate connections and related themes.

Objectives: (1) To bring to the surface the social, religious, political, and personal meanings of rock music today; (2) to compare and contrast with lyrics of the past; (3) to encourage students to evaluate their own positions.

POETRY: HUMAN NEEDS

Poetry: Human Needs is a six- to nine-week elective for high school students. The core of the course is contemporary poetry, but other media such as film, art, and music enrich the understanding of the poems. The course works best with average to advanced juniors but can be adapted for slower students.

Objectives: The goal of this elective is to help students understand and appreciate what it means to be a human being by approaching poetry from the viewpoint of human needs: the need for physical security, for safety, for love and belonging, for esteem, for self-actualization, for beauty. Emphasis is also given to techniques in reading poetry, but not at the expense of the content. Use of other media provides an experience in an interdisciplinary approach to study.

NONVERBAL AND VERBAL COMMUNICATION

Nonverbal and Verbal Communication is a nine-week course designed for students who wish to learn about the effects of body language and vocal intonation within the communication process, the powers and limitations of words, and the importance of feedback and listening to communication.

Objectives: Students will experience the impact of actions and symbols in interpersonal communications, assess the impact of vocal intonation, evaluate the powers and limitations of words, improve listening skills, practice giving effective feedback, and learn to adapt their use of the communication process to ever-changing situations in the world around them.

PEOPLE: TWENTIETH CENTURY

People: Twentieth Century is one unit in humanities, a year's elective program for interested seniors who experience the cultural past in relationship to the contemporary and express the results of their study in highly imaginative, individual, or group projects.

Objectives: The course attempts to introduce a variety of experiences that increase the students' sensitivity to art forms, and knowledge of the cultural past and present and to provide the opportunity to examine values in light of cultural heritage. The goal of this course is to develop the students' concept so that new ideas may be internalized and reflected in choices that help build lifestyles.

MYTH AND MODERN SOCIETY

Myth and Modern Society is a nine-week elective English course open to sophomores, juniors, and seniors in senior high.

Objectives: The course attempts to answer the questions, How has myth influenced our culture? What similarities are found in myths of various cultures? What myths prevail in our modern world?

HINDU RELIGIOUS LITERATURE

Hindu Religious Literature is a nine-week mini-course offered to eleventh- and twelfth-grade students, of all ability levels.

Objectives: Students are introduced to the major concepts and cultural traditions of Hinduism as shown in the sacred literature. Through readings, class discussion, and written assignments, students explore Hindu religious and philosophical speculation on the origin and meaning of life and the relationship between people and the divine.

HUMOR IN AMERICAN LITERATURE

Humor in American Literature is a one-semester, nongraded elective course for the average student, although many academic students take the course.

Objectives: To survey American literature as seen in its humor; to acquaint the students with the specific techniques used to create humor; to develop a broader sense of humor that will include all the genres; to see humor as a human quality that provides pleasure but also functions as a vehicle for serious comments on human nature.

EVALUATION IN ELECTIVE PROGRAMS

With the emergence of the elective program, the problems of grading become more complex. As has been suggested, in this program a student can enroll in an English course that lasts for six to nine weeks or an entire semester. In a year's time it is possible for a student to have four to six different teachers and as many groups of classmates. There may not be enough time in the elective course program for teachers to adjust testing procedures for individual abilities and for the student to find out what the teacher wants.[3]

Teachers in an elective curriculum are faced with using an old grading system in a new program. With the recent emphasis on behavioral objectives, the stultifying procedures involved in the traditional program are difficult to adjust to time and productivity. In other words, traditional testing is neither applicable nor adequate. Many innovative teachers are turning to pass/fail techniques, with the teacher specifying passing grade criteria and frequently with student participation in the establishment of the criteria. Students can understand better what they are learning from activities through a process of formal self-evaluation. When students sit in judgment of their own learning behavior, needed changes are apparent and more easily facilitated.[4]

ANALYSIS OF THE ELECTIVE COURSE PROGRAM

The critics of the elective course language arts program are sure to make comparisons with traditional programs. They contend that several questionable assumptions are related to benefits of elective programs. Advocates of elective course programs contend that these courses are arranged to meet student interests, needs, and abilities. Critics question why many courses reflect teacher, not student, interest, why so many courses parallel college and traditional high school offerings. Programs invariably are not based on a systematic analysis of student needs. The most traditional English program can lay claim to serving the needs of its students with the same confidence elective programs can. There is little evidence that teachers vary their instruction in accord with particular abilities of students nor that students do any better because they have chosen their own courses.

Advocates of elective programs point to the opportunity teachers are given to specialize. These advocates further point to the fragmentation of the English curriculum and the lack of integrated sequential teaching of skills in the traditional program. Any specialization that results in the compartmentalization of instruction in composition, reading, speech, and various types of literature is likely to be detrimental to the English program and the professional growth of individual teachers.

Curriculum workers constructing elective courses are enamored with

[3] Philip DiStefano, "Can Traditional Grading Survive the Elective Program?" *English Journal* (March 1975), pp. 56–58.

[4] James B. Van Hoven, "Reporting Pupil Progress," *Phi Delta Kappan* (February 1972), pp. 365–367.

the idea that the brevity of the course and frequent changes of teachers are leading factors in sustaining student interest.[5] Those adverse to this idea claim that courses are not long enough for students to explore in depth, which causes them to accept artificiality as a sound working concept.

The choice of courses in and of itself has a meaningful, positive effect on both affective and cognitive responses. Critical analysis shows this assumption to be true for affective responses. Students in a high school where the elective program is used had more positive attitudes than students in a neighboring school with a traditional program, but they did not achieve higher scores on writing samples and reading and writing tests. To be sure, the comparison was made with paired students. Curriculum workers adverse to the elective program are vehement in their denunciation of the idea that teachers in a traditional program will not share the responsibilities for student failure because they had no part in the formation of the program.

The critical viewpoints on the elective course program may be summarized as follows:

1. Elective programs do little to overcome the weaknesses of traditional programs.
2. There is the same lack of personalized teaching within individual courses.
3. There is too much repackaging of content from traditional courses.
4. Claims of innovative designs are exaggerated.
5. There are too many literature courses based on survey and genre, language courses dealing with narrow matters of usage and syntax, and composition courses reflecting naive notions about the composition process.

Despite the criticisms and cautions offered by many thoughtful and conscientious curriculum coordinators and English language arts teachers, elective programs represent a massive shattering of the structures that have shackled English curricula for years. They have created a new sense of satisfaction among teachers and have demonstrated that all students need not study the same material at the same time in the same way. Age and ability are not prime factors in what students shall study. They participate in the planning that incorporates their individual goals.

[5] R. Baird Shuman, *Creative Approaches to the Teaching of English: Secondary* (Itasco, Ill.: F. E. Peacock Publishers, 1974), p. 142.

CREATIVE WRITING AND COMPOSITION

There is something distinctive about labeling a course *creative writing;* it appeals to a student's sense of doing something new or original. Teachers who teach courses in composition, rhetoric, or exposition may be viewed as those assigned to the dull drudgery of daily repetition of the correct format of written thought.

Veteran teachers may question the distinction between creative writing and the routine assignments they make for theme writing. There are differences to be sure, but all writing is interpretive, selective, and styled. A knowledgeable teacher of a composition course would not fail to emphasize voice, tone, and metaphor. The same teacher teaching a course in creative writing would stress cause and effect, organization, and punctuation.

The intrusion of linguistics and the acceptance of dialect as a correct format have expanded the role of the English teacher. Framers of modern English are very conscious of this expanded role. Nevertheless, in the field of writing, the basic need for students to express themselves remains the same.[6]

Conscientious secondary school English teachers are haunted by the criticisms of lay "experts" and college English professors that secondary school classrooms do not prepare students adequately, particularly in the study of language and composition. Points of ineptness concerning secondary school students come mainly from two facets of English teaching, the study of the language and the teaching of written composition.

There is a deeply rooted belief bordering on mysticism that a mastery of grammar will inevitably lead to "correct" and "proper" English and that with this knowledge a student is guaranteed successful use of English. Hence written composition and creative writing are merely exercises demonstrating this accomplishment.

THE USE OF THEMATIC UNITS

A major concern of English teachers today is making English teaching as effective as possible while attending to students' interests and abilities. There is, too, a desire to reduce the segmentation of the English curriculum, i.e., to unify the subject matter. These aims deserve even greater consideration as English departments move from the tra-

---

[6] John H. Bushman and Sandra K. Jones, "Getting It All Together Thematically," *English Journal* (May 1975), pp. 54–60.

ditional curriculum structure to the English elective/mini-course design. The thematic unit fits very well into this reconstruction of the secondary school English curriculum.[7] It provides a structure in which the teacher can effectively unify the teaching of oral and written composition, literature, language, and media.

The thematic unit can be effectively taught in almost any secondary school. If the school has a traditional curriculum structure, the teacher simply divides the semester into six-week or nine-week segments and teaches thematically. If it is an English elective/mini-course curriculum, each thematic unit becomes a course within itself.

It is important that the teacher using the thematic approach realize that the linguistic or social theme is secondary to the teaching of language arts: in essence, the theme is the vehicle through which students come to write, read, and speak.

Whether the theme be *love* or *war* or *alienation* or *social welfare,* it is important that the students write from their own experiences, either real or vicarious. The emphasis of any writing program should be process rather than product. Students should be encouraged to view writing as an on-going process moving from an unsophisticated use of word phrases and sentences to a more mature, well-developed sense of writing.

Obviously, the study of literature plays a central role in the thematic unit. By design, the unit fosters student involvement by emphasizing the literary work itself. When the students investigate the work and its relationship to the theme, they are in fact identifying its relationship to themselves. Thus the major emphasis of the thematic unit lies in the personal response of each student to his or her own work. The unit is dominated by neither historical nor formal characteristics, for although these characteristics are important in the study of literature, they are not of primary importance. Students should not work to find how a particular literary piece fits into an overall historical survey nor should they try to determine the formal aspects of the work. Attention should be focused on the work itself — what the author has to say and how.

Curriculum directors and teachers should consider the thematic unit for inclusion in a language arts program because it works well in an elective course program and it gives both students and teachers another alternative for meeting students' needs while covering a wide variety of material. Yet it can be compacted and deepened according to the best judgment of all concerned.

---

[7] C. Brooks, "Comments on Thematic Arrangements of English Literature," *Journal of General Education* (Winter 1977), pp. 324–329.

LITERATURE AND THE LANGUAGE ARTS PROGRAM

In the English department of some secondary schools, there may be a dichotomy between the teachers of literature and teachers of composition. Some teachers express strong preference for teaching one or the other. Others argue about the values involved. Frequently, the college preparation of English teachers is heavily loaded with courses in literature. The elective course English program offers opportunities for teachers to teach courses in their areas of specialization.

The debate about the relative importance of literature and composition is senseless, for they are complementary and should have common objectives as well as integrated teaching procedures. Literature mirrors human life. It is through literary works that students gain knowledge about people. Literature is indispensable in the education of youth because it relates the interaction among all levels of culture and social status.

Literature reflects hopes, joys, desires, disappointments, and frustrations of people everywhere. It can play a unique role in fostering better human relationships among all people, especially if the subject matter realistically reflects the multicultural and multiethnic composition of society. Reading literature gives students access to great ideas and truths that have been reflected through generations in complex, symbolic ways.[8]

Literature is the opus of the artists, and artists break apart the card houses of false notions and easy answers perpetrated by people who think they have divinely inspired answers. On occasion literature may describe interpersonal conflicts, but it frequently expresses in the most powerful ways the human tendency to elect new goals, new hopes, and new anchors in life. In other words, literature confronts students with choices, and skillful teachers as well as knowledgeable curriculum coordinators will select and organize material that provides students with important preparation for experiences in democratic living.

From the viewpoint of curriculum development, it is desirable to search for new means of presentation and new organizational formats, and to perceive new trends. All this poses a problem because secondary school literature textbooks are organizational packages that are not conducive to the study of trends or patterns. The novel, the short story, poetry, and drama all pose distinctive subject-matter organization problems.

A survey of the teaching of literature shows variations in the way some innovative teachers search for methods to interest, even excite,

[8] Jesse Perry, "Toward a Multi-Cultural Curriculum," *English Journal* (April 1975), pp. 8–9.

students in various selections within the framework of traditional forms of literature. For example, one teacher claims the short story to be the most satisfying of all literary forms for students. He holds that the brevity of the short story makes it ideal for classroom discussion and permits students to deal in depth with a wide range of subjects. An outline for teaching the short story might include: (1) visualizing the setting; (2) seeing conflicts; (3) understanding decisions; (4) seeing value judgments and conflicts; (5) sensing tone and mood; (6) seeing character; (7) understanding character; (8) seeing "stock" characters; (9) understanding the plot; (10) seeing the sequence of events; (11) understanding the story line; and (12) understanding structure.[9]

Many secondary school students reject the study of poetry. Some think it is "sissified" and some "just do not like the stuff." It probably takes more artistry to teach poetry than to teach any other form of literature.

Students must be helped to view poetry as a condensed form of expression. They must be helped to realize how much of their own feelings and emotions poetry relates. Teachers of poetry should stress the channels of responses offered to students. For example, students should be encouraged to keep diaries of their own thoughts as they probe poetry for meaning and form of expresson.

Poetry offers an opportunity to help students see how complex their own thinking processes may be. They can learn how ideas can be juxtaposed, how to probe for different layers of meaning, and how many elements can focus on one idea. Students are shortchanged when they are urged to "appreciate" poetry. The understanding of poetry is the premium product.

A most important factor in the teaching of the novel is preparing students to read a long work. The teacher should prepare a series of interesting activities so that students are receptive. As the novel is read, a continuation of relevant activities will facilitate reading and deepen insights for sustained interest. The climax in the study of the novel is vested in the past reading activities. Students should be encouraged to reexamine their own values in relation to those of the author. In the final analysis, values are established in the interplay among author, teacher, and fellow students. The sharing of thoughts, ideas, and conclusions can make the study of the novel a valuable experience for the student. It may be noted here that the personal involvement of each student with the literary characters is much more important than the usual formal dissection of literary works and the memorized recognition of literary forms.

[9] Charles R. Duke, "Teaching the Short Story," *English Journal* (September 1974), pp. 62–64.

Finally, the drama brings students in contact with many literary immortals, such as Shakespeare. Modern psychological concepts should prevail in teaching the drama. Plays should not be dissected into acts or scenes in any sequential order. The whole play should be read so the student receives the impact of the author's main ideas. The drama is an action type of writing, so the flow of action should be the keynote in helping students understand the mood of a play. Students can learn to appreciate the drama even more if they became involved in writing or presenting plays.

CONTROVERSY OVER THE TEACHING OF GRAMMAR

Some scholars are sharply opposed to a blind faith in unvariable forms of teaching grammar. Curriculum planners should evaluate traditional grammar as it is taught in the schools in order to assess the value of changes offered by advocates of a new grammar. The traditional study of grammar dealt with parsing sentences and memorizing rules to identify parts of speech and to correct false syntax. In parsing sentences, students were asked to identify the part of speech of each word and then relate it to applicable categories. It was necessary for students to memorize rules of grammar so that they could prove the correctness of word choice when the occasion demanded or, more accurately, when the teacher demanded. The rules were supposed to insure that the student would not use incorrect syntax.

An early modification of traditional grammar was to place emphasis on parts of sentences as well as parts of speech. Thus attention now is given to subjects, predicates, objects, and modifiers, each of which is encompassed by grammatical rules. Emphasis is placed on sentence structure and sentence analysis.

Advocates of structural linguistics espoused a revolutionary approach to the teaching of grammar. Probably the most important force in the new movement was Noam Chomsky's *Syntactic Structures*.[10] The central theme of structuralism relates to language as a system in which each separate part is related to all other parts. A system of language is discovered by selecting a part and establishing its relationship to all other parts.

Structuralism has peculiarities of its own. The structuralists insist that speech is the real language. According to them, meaning should not be considered until phonology, morphology, and syntax have been disposed of, which means in practice that meaning is given little attention, or that it is dealt with indirectly. In spite of certain limitations,

[10] Noam Chomsky, *Syntactic Structures* (Hague, Netherlands: Mouton, 1957).

structuralism is attractive because it offers insight into the nature of linguistic systems, into the way language is put together.

Modern linguists advocate a structural approach to grammar teaching, by which usage determines correctness of form. They view usage as distinct from grammatical structure. They see spoken language as the primary source of grammatical data for written language. If a great many people use a certain structure in oral communication, it becomes acceptable usage. These scholars suggest that language be viewed as a psychological, historical, and sociological phenomenon rather than a corrupt descendant of a more perfect parent.

The structural linguistic approach to the teaching of grammar offers exciting vistas for teachers who are discouraged with the futility of teaching grammar in the traditional manner. Opposing forces, of course, say that although usage is a powerful factor in linguistic change, it is not an adequate criterion in itself accepting or rejecting such change. These forces hold that for the sake of logical consistency, certain rules must be maintained, and that any change creates more problems than it solves.

It is apparent that the threshold of a counterrevolution in the teaching of grammar has been reached.[11] The term *new grammar* is appearing with increasing frequency. Perhaps greater accuracy would dictate the identity of several new grammars. An outmoded and incorrect grammar is being replaced by new grammars that actually describe the structure of English as a unique language.[12] The linguist refers to the step beyond structural grammar as generative transformational grammar. It deals with complex structures and identifies rules governing transformations that users of a language have habitually followed without consciously recognizing them as rules.

A generative grammar is a set of rules that describe the structure of every normal sentence in a language, and these rules dictate automatically which sentences are normal. Structural grammar is occupied with the question of *how* one knows the structure of a given sentence. What are the signals, word order, function words, endings, and so forth that convey grammatical meaning and indicate structure? On the other hand, in generative grammar there is no such concern. Instead of worrying over how the structure of a language is determined, generative grammarians will state as explicitly as possible what the structure is. To do this, they use quasi-algebraic formulas instead of everyday language in stating rules; they contend that everyday language is

---

[11] Dwight L. Burton and John S. Simmons, *Teaching English in Today's High School* (New York: Holt, Rinehart and Winston, 1970), pp. 28–54.

[12] Doris V. Gunderson, "Research in the Teaching of English," *English Journal* (September 1971), pp. 792–796.

often ambiguous. Quasi-mathematical statements force the grammarian to be explicit. It should be pointed out that the use of such abstract symbolism is often confusing and distressing to many English teachers. It is probably necessary to trust the generative grammarian as to the necessity of such procedures.

While it is not too difficult to describe generative grammar, transformational grammar presents quite a different problem. A grammar can be generative without being transformational, and, at least theoretically, the reverse is true. The problem in describing transformational grammar is that it can be a great many things, some of them quite different from the others.

Generative transformational grammar has much to offer, but it is still very much in the formative stage. Basic and far reaching changes are constantly being made. Those who pioneer in introducing transformational grammar into their English classes today must be prepared to find it obsolete tomorrow. Even now, disturbing rumbles can be heard from those proclaiming the merits of stratificational grammar.

New linguistic theories and new revolutions in grammar are likely to keep turning up for some time to come. Curriculum makers in the field of English cannot sit back and hope that the whole thing will go away. The new grammars promise to describe the workings of the English language accurately, and they have a direct application in teaching students how to write English sentences. Perhaps a breakthrough is imminent in the teaching of the most difficult of all skills — teaching students to write well.

General acceptance and implementation of the newer approaches to the teaching of grammar will be related closely to the training of knowledgeable teachers. It will be necessary in many instances to reeducate teachers in the actual linguistic structure of the language.

CENSORSHIP

When censorship is rampant in a nation frightened by uncontrollable social problems, the English classroom is certain to be a prime target. The English classroom provides a setting for the expression of both noble and ignoble human behavior. The traditionalist who believes censorship a duty looks first at human experiences that are either moral or immoral.

Immorality is likely to be equated with sexuality and implicitly related to obscenity. Textbooks and all reading materials used by English teachers are scrutinized for obscenities and labeled immoral and thus unfit for student consumption. While the cornerstone of U. S. democracy as promulgated by the public school system is the ability to make choices, these critics — claiming their objective to be the salvation of democracy — would deny secondary school students experiences in making choices between the moral and the immoral.

Curriculum builders need to remember that obscenity is narrowly construed when it is limited to sexuality. The abuse of power, racism, sexism, and brutality can also be considered obscene.

Censorship, once begun, is hard to contain. It can soon spread to include any idea or attitude the censors find objectionable. At best, it can do little to protect morals. True morality is based on choice; therefore making it impossible for students to choose not to read a book makes it impossible to be moral. Censorship does not generate virtue, only fear.[13]

Most teachers, administrators, and curriculum coordinators are quite willing to engage in self-assessment and self-evaluation and are willing to be held accountable for the quality of instructon and the moralistic values therein contained, provided the evaluative criteria are broadly based and not hampered by unrealistic restrictions. Unfortunately, in many situations the forms of appraisal are anything but broadly based. Teachers are finding their efforts hampered by censorship of print and nonprint media, the release of data from standardized tests by state and national agencies, the indignant but vague demand for a return to the "basics" and an accountabilty system created and imposed by people outside the educational profession.

TOPICS FOR STUDY AND DISCUSSION

1. Critics of the elective English program fear that many students will miss reading the classics. How serious is this problem?
2. Carefully assess the program of Central High School. What additions or deletions should be made?
3. Are mini-courses a fad or a realistic answer to needed motivation for students in language arts classes? List advantages and disadvantages.
4. Develop a position paper on the pros and cons of the elective English program critics.
5. What are the advantages of teaching the language arts through the use of thematic units?
6. Is the ability for creative writing a "gift," or can it be developed in any student of average intelligence? Document your answers.
7. If you were a consultant to a language arts program, what advice would you offer for improving the teaching of literature?
8. Evaluate the effects of modern linguistics programs on the purposes and objectives of teaching grammar in the secondary schools.

[13] Sandi Brinkman, "The Public Education System: Future or Funeral?" *English Journal* (September 1974), pp. 42–44.

9. Why is the teaching of writing skills considered the most difficult of the language arts objectives?

SELECTED REFERENCES

Applebee, Arthur N. *Tradition and Reform in the Teaching of English.* Urbana, Ill.: National Council of Teachers of English, 1974.
  This perceptive account of the forces that have shaped English as a subject of study evaluates the shifts of emphasis in the philosophy of education as reflected in the teaching of English. It points to the continuing tension between two views of English: as a body of knowledge and as a means of gaining new perspectives on life.
Bergman, Floyd L. *The English Teacher's Activities Handbook.* Boston: Allyn and Bacon, 1975.
  This handbook of over 1000 activities for use to encourage creativity among students can be used by an experienced or beginning teacher. It is virtually an encyclopedia of classroom ideas for innovative English lessons in the language arts and instructional communication.
Doll, Ronald C. *Curriculum Improvement: Decision Making and Process.* Boston: Allyn and Bacon, 1974.
  Doll offers an in-depth treatment of systems, open education, and humanistic approaches; includes new evaluation procedures developed over recent years; and deals with accountability and current efforts to determine the competence of teachers.
Duke, Charles R. *Creative Dramatics and English Teaching.* Urbana, Ill.: National Council of the Teachers of English, 1974.
  Emphasis is on the fact that dramatics form an excellent pathway for finding solutions to many of the problems in the teaching of English. Teachers are urged to make extensive use of the creative ability of secondary school students. Playwriting is presented as a motivational activity and a problem-solving technique.
Dunning, Stephen. *Teaching Literature to Adolescents.* Glenview, Ill.: Scott, Foresman and Company, 1974.
  This book was designed to integrate theory and practice in the teaching of literature. Attention is given to helping teachers bridge the gap between the classics and much of the works of modern authors. It is a good treatise for curriculum planners since it presents lists of appropriate works suitable for students of varying degrees of motivation and intellectual abilities.
Hass, Glen, et. al. *Curriculum Planning: A New Approach.* Boston: Allyn and Bacon, 1974.
  This foundations book in curriculum has been highly praised for its flexibility in modular, independent study, and traditional classes. The case study format helps develop case studies about a real school to apply skills learned. Prerequisites, rationales, objectives, preassessments, and postassessments presented at the beginning of each section of readings

are designed for helpful self-examination. Additional learning activities include suggested projects, additional readings, films, and related material.

Judy, Stephen N. *Explorations in the Teaching of Secondary English.* New York: Dodd, Mead & Company, 1974.

This source book for the experimental teacher encourages the teacher to discover methods through experimentation. It is designed to assist the teacher who searches for his or her own effective model. Aims and issues are explored, as well as problems and perplexities. Each of the major language forms is discussed.

Lee, Helen C. *A Humanistic Approach to Teaching Secondary School English.* Columbus, Ohio: Charles E. Merrill Books, 1973.

This is another book, common to the field of English today, that encourages teachers to discover their own best way of teaching English. This book describes numerous examples of personalized learning while steering clear of prescriptions for how to teach. A particularly strong section of the book deals with speaking and usage. It stresses the social realities of language usage.

Lefevre, Carl A. *Linguistics, English, and the Language Arts.* Boston: Allyn and Bacon, 1970.

The author emphasizes his own personal brand of linguistics. He presents a structural bias of transformational grammar and includes listings of teaching suggestions for aiding beginning teachers. He advocates the theory that secondary teachers stress intellectual inquiry and not try to make their students "junior linguists."

Martin, Charles B., and Rulon, Curt M. *The English Language: Yesterday and Today.* Boston: Allyn and Bacon, 1973.

The authors present an excellent in-depth study of the varying dialects of American English and the classroom implementation of the premise that dialects are legitimate, grammatically sound forms of our language. Another outstanding feature is the inclusion of the most up-to-date research in the area of transformational grammar. Many illustrative examples and problems are included. Other languages are often used for contrasting analysis with English in order to exercise the student's understanding of the main concepts of language study.

Parker, Robert P., and Daly, Maxine. *Teaching English in the Secondary Schools.* New York: The Free Press, 1973.

Many books aimed at helping English teachers are as traditional in content as they are in style, but the authors of this book make a concerted effort to depart from the traditional. It is suitable for the novice as well as the experienced instructor. It leads to a reexaminaion of teaching methodologies and content.

Shepherd, David. *Comprehensive High School Reading Methods.* New York: Charles E. Merrill Company, 1973.

The material is concentrated on the reading problems of the secondary school. Techniques are analyzed for integrating the solution of reading problems throughout the entire public school span. The author takes the viewpoint that reading must be taught as a component of all secondary school subject matter.

Shuman, R. Baird. *Creative Approaches to the Teaching of English: Secondary*. Itasca, Ill.: F. E. Peacock Publishers, 1974.

This is a collection of essays about various aspects of the teaching of English with English methods or approaches as part of the focus. The book is divided into six main sections: literature; drama; grammar; writing; spelling and punctuation; and vocabulary. Each chapter is written by a specialist in English education.

The Teaching of English. Seventy-sixth Yearbook of the National Society for the Study of Education. Chicago: University of Chicago Press, 1977.

As the Yearbook Committee looks at the teaching of English in the mid-1970s, it appears clear that English education is in a period of transition. This yearbook presents a comprehensive review of the state of English teaching today. Part of the topics presented include: changing content in the English curriculum, evaluating growth in English, the future direction of English teaching, values in the English classroom, and language and the nature of learning.

6

Fine Arts

Teachers of the fine arts in the nation's schools are being challenged by a variety of circumstances — the move toward accountability, the interest in management by objectives, the tightening of the budget, the trend toward interdisciplinary studies, and the strong emphasis on the basics. Fine arts curriculum planners are seeking ways to move from the narrow role of preparing a small number of talented students for performance and exhibition to a broader role that uses interdisciplinary approaches to stimulate all students and involve them in learning both about and through the arts.[1]

The emphasis that curriculum makers put on the fine arts is one of the real tests of their faith in a comprehensive school program. The so-called fundamental subjects are always assured of a secure place in the learning experience of the student, but the arts are usually considered of secondary importance, and their fate fluctuates according to

[1] Gene C. Wenner, "Arts in the Mainstream of Education," *Music Educators Journal* (April 1976), pp. 28–36.

societal whims or economic pressures. Considering the fine arts mere entertainment and ignoring their meaningful values that ennoble and elevate will only foster mediocrity in an age searching for excellence.

Instead of producing merely specialists who can fit into technological slots, the schools must produce generalists who can improve the art of living. The truly comprehensive curriculum emphasizes all types of learning activities. All students need experiences in understanding music and the various art forms. These experiences should be extensive enough to include something for those who create, those who perform, and those who consume. Students need to learn how to exercise social responsibility in making personal and group decisions about the arts. School programs should reflect a balanced image of social and artistic values.

One of the basic tenets of a good education is the development of discriminating taste. The school should help students be as critical of a singer without a voice, or an art form without imagination, as they would be of a public official without integrity. In many respects, the fine arts help prepare youths to take part in making civic decisions that will not be stereotyped or prejudiced. People are responsible for the quality of art in their homes and the aesthetic choices they advocate in their communities. The arts are involved in decisions about civic planning, housing, and urban renewal. If the aesthetic and cultural levels of society are to be raised, the educational insights youths gain from the fine arts program of the schools will be the cause.

The increased leisure time of an affluent society gives the schools cause for placing greater stress on learning experiences that contribute to the purposeful, intelligent, and satisfying use of that leisure time. Growing patronage at art exhibits, the ballet, symphony concerts, and other aesthetic and cultural activities indicates that interest does exist. Youths need educational experiences with music and art forms as preparation for even greater understanding and enjoyment of such profitable leisure-time ventures.

ART

Art, one of the most sophisticated forms of visual experience, is the visual language of all people. It is an integrating process of sensing, thinking, feeling, and expressing. To understand art, one must understand one's fellow beings and the many forms of visual expression people employ. The development of such understanding is not an easy process; it is frequently deep and complicated. The infinite subtleties employed in visual expressions require artistic sensitivity for interpretation. This educational learning activity should have a place in the secondary schools.

National Interest

It is hardly necessary to stress the importance of art in the life of a nation. It is paradoxical, however, to compare the lofty position art occupies in the cultural affairs of this nation and the indifference it receives in the nation's schools. An increased emphasis on art in public life may be noted. Galleries are crowded and new ones are being built. Great works of art are topics of conversation. A sympathetic government offers financial encouragement to art projects, and large mail-order houses are adding original paintings to their lists of merchandise. In the commercial world, advertising, product design, packaging, and television programming are constantly seeking new artistic and colorful ways of increasing product appeal. Communities of all sizes are engaged in serious planning for improved artistic appearance and creative architectural design.

This may not be exactly a renaissance of art, but a favorable climate for a flowering of the arts certainly exists. However, a survey of the programs of the nation's public schools does not reflect a fervent activity in the field. Research data indicate that the students either do not have the opportunity or are not availing themselves of the opportunity to pursue art courses. This is especially true of the secondary schools: slightly more than 50 percent of them offer art courses, and around 15 percent of the students are enrolled. Only a limited number of the small schools attempt to teach art.

Secondary art education has been less well supported than other areas in the curriculum, and yet a slow but general growth has been evident over the last quarter-century. Art now has a secure place in the secondary curriculum after many years of scattered and uncertain status. In recent years, regulations have appeared in state after state to insure that these gains will be maintained. Some states require a minimum period of art study in secondary schools — usually in grade 7 or 8. More often, the decision regarding required or elective status for art has been left to local school districts. Among all trends in secondary art, this gradual increase has been the most encouraging.

Secondary art has benefited from the great popular surge of interest in the arts, although the boom in art museum construction, the nationwide appearance of state and local art councils, and the spiraling consumption of arts and crafts materials have not reflected the interaction between school and community that one might have expected. Perhaps the conservativeness of academic traditions in education is too strong for art to be allowed to find its own level of prosperity. Alternatively, the situation still reflects those traditional American values where education is viewed as predominantly utilitarian and vocational.

The kinds of art that are taught in secondary schools and the way in which art is taught seem to suggest that as schools employ more art teachers, the subject matter of art becomes more specialized. Although strong statements appear in the literature regarding the need to teach art history and art criticism, subject matter continues to follow divisions based on studio work — often to the neglect of the more intellectual studies. Where two art teachers are employed, most likely one of them will focus on the fine arts and the other on the crafts. With the addition of more art teachers to a staff, the subject-matter preferences of the teachers themselves are most likely to color the curricular offerings.

Subject areas that have grown markedly in popularity in recent years include jewelry, ceramics, photography, printmaking, sculpture, and drawing. The basic design or generalized Art I courses are disappearing in favor of the specificity desired by both students and teachers. Different viewpoints are expressed regarding the appropriateness of this pattern, but it does exist, especially in large senior high schools.[2]

Middle and Junior High School Art

Art educators encounter a great deal of difficulty in being optimistic about conditions in the middle school and the junior high school. The middle years are usually the last opportunity that all students have for contact with art in a programmatic way. An awareness of this induces art teachers to "cram," trying to present a comprehensive program to as many students as possible. This inclination is helped by the fact that the time allocated for contact with a given student rarely, in the best instances, equals more than a period or two a week. Added to the usual constraints of inadequate facilities, limited resources, large classes, and programmatic isolation are the expectations of administrators, students, and parents, who assume that the art program will produce art.

Students, parents, and administrators are demanding an accountability from a program area that has enjoyed a rather ambivalent attitude toward evaluation. Art teachers, in addition, are expected to contribute

---

[2] Guy Hubbard, "Trends in Secondary School Art, Emphasis: Senior High," *Art Education* (February 1976), pp. 12–13.

in a direct, meaningful way to resolving social issues such as the integration of minorities, assisting students with special needs, environmental concerns, and value sets. To compound the confusion, volume is often equated with quality. Consequently, the success of the art program at this level is easily reduced in terms of the amount and diversity of work produced.

A profound shift in societal attitudes is the cause of considerable stress in the junior high/middle school population. Art educators are confronted with students who increasingly question authority, reject absolutes, and challenge rules. They are quick to judge and are not reticent in their judgments. Consequently, art programs that maintain pragmatic, dictative practices or insist on an attentiveness to arbitrary and/or ill-defined experiences are trouble-bound.

Social pressures, institutional constraints, and teacher-training conflicts all come to center on the question of the appropriateness of content for the junior high/middle schools. What should be taught and how is perhaps the most controversial concern for art programs at this level. The value of traditional exercises in drawing, painting, sculpture, graphics, and crafts is being challenged by art educators. Social orientations are demanding that art education be relevant to the masses as the general curricular emphasis is promoting subject-matter integration.

One of the most pervasive movements in junior high/middle school art programming has been the emphasis on subject matter and instructional integration. These interdisciplinary programming efforts are based on the premise that fundamental relationships exist among all the arts and between the arts and other areas of education. These relationships commonly recognize the need for access to specific information, the need for basic and specialized skills development, and emphasis on creative activity.

Aesthetic education has emerged during the past decade as an alternative for art education. The distinction between the two is significant. Art education has, in reality, focused on teaching art to students, with the artist being the primary model in curriculum building. Aesthetic educational methodology places an emphasis on teaching the student through multiple arts experiences, striving to maintain a balance between cognitive and affective learning. This approach translates the artists' modes of activity into a structure for learning, sometimes called the arts process.

Counter to the preceding interdisciplinary trends are the efforts to enhance art as a viable end in itself. Art programs in many junior high/middle schools are providing experiences in jewelry, film making, photography, and environmental art as well as basing instructional activities on temporary art forms such as pop, op, and minimal art. Added to these efforts has been the introduction of visiting artists into the schools so that students might have a "live" model to observe and emulate.

The choice of art at the middle school level appears to be to re-evaluate the nature of art when viewed as an end in itself, to integrate art into aesthetic education contexts, or to extend art into all education. Whatever the decision, the art teacher will certainly share in determining the course of the program.[3]

Administrative Problems

Very few administrators would deny the value of art as a school subject. They would generally agree to its inclusion in the curriculum of the elementary school but, as has been suggested before, there is a marked lack of support in the secondary schools. Secondary school administrators contend that their curriculum is overcrowded with more basic requirements. They also point to their inability to secure qualified teachers.

However, the inclusion of subjects in the secondary school curriculum is determined partly by the significance attached to the subject.[4] There is no research to prove that one subject is more important than another for all students. Once it is decided that art is a valuable area of instruction, its status in the secondary school curriculum will be improved. The next problem will be scheduling. Numerous schedling patterns are feasible. No doubt some type of flexible scheduling will make it possible to enlarge the scope of curriculum offerings that are necessary to take care of the ever-increasing experiences needed by secondary school youth. How much art should be required, how many times per week art classes should meet, how long the class period should be, and what the size and composition of art classes should be are problems to be settled by local curriculum planners. Some phases of art instruction can be handled well in large groups, while other types will need individual attention. Certainly, every secondary school will want to encourage the very talented students to do creative work in depth. They can do so in individual studio cubicles.

Solving the problem of an adequate teaching corps is a formidable task. Consideration of the quality, experience, expertise, special abilities, and limitations of art personnel is necessary if good results are to be secured. This is a situation where training and qualifications

[3] David W. Baker, "Trends in Secondary School Art, Emphasis: Middle and Junior High School," *Art Education* (February 1976), pp. 10–11.

[4] M. D. Day, "Effects of Instruction on High School Students' Art Preferences and Judgments," *Studies in Art Education* (Winter 1976), pp. 25–39.

do not always insure adequate teaching. And conversely, art classes cannot be assigned to any inept member of the staff who happens to have a vacant period. One answer to the teacher problem will come through encouraging more young people with artistic ability to enter teaching education. Until such a time as an adequate supply of teachers is available, several things can be done to alleviate the shortage. Larger classes can be used for basic instruction. Certain aspects of art instruction, mainly those involving individual direction, lend possibility to the use of staff members with limited training but a reasonable amount of artistic ability. It is not unreasonable here to suggest the incorporation of talented laypeople; they could be used effectively in extraclass art activities.

Visiting Artists

The National Endowment for the Humanities and the National Endowment for the Arts, geared toward postsecondary education and aimed at integrating the arts more deeply into the curriculum as an essential ingredient of literacy, undertook the educational objective of making the performing arts more available to students outside the schools and of supporting artists to work for varying amounts of time with students and teachers at the secondary and elementary levels. Such a liaison led to an Artists-in-Schools and Artists-in-Residence Program in a valiant effort to redirect priorities in art education. Federal aid has declined since 1970, but support has been given to Artists-in-Schools Programs by school systems and state departments of education who have taken over administration and funding.

Looking back over this period, one ought to have witnessed some experimental programs that died due to premature evaluation (CAREL), some that were modified through adoption by local agencies (ARTS IMPACT), and others that are newly emerging on a national scale. Along with these few named developments and other alternative approaches, there is intermittent discussion voicing conceptual ambiguities and contesting methodologies in efforts to rationalize a proper basis for the inclusion of the preceding activities.

The Artists-in-Schools Program is an interesting development. An artist of some reputation is invited to spend a year in the school as a teacher, adviser, and critic. Professional educators have been quick to criticize the program because even though the artists are not certified teachers, they are paid out of local school funds.

Some art teachers have accepted the program as an inspirational and skillful supplement to their own work. Others are critical because they believe the artist in residence lacks the experience to have the proper perception of students and the unique goals of the school. Although it is probably impossible to evaluate such a program properly until more data are collected, many schools report an excellent experience with visiting artists. They bring to the student an image that exemplifies the success and enjoyment of their profession even though only relatively few secondary school art students will become professional artists. Yet the association brings a better appreciation of what the professional does.[5]

Necessary Skills in the Art Classroom

Frustration comes in the classroom when students become dissatisfied with their shortcomings. Teachers may accept this as a signal to change projects rather than as an opportunity to help students develop sufficient skills to enjoy the thrill of accomplishment. A learning program in art is certain to present a number of problems of technique and design. If students are not sufficiently skillful in mastering these problems, they are likely to lose interest in a project.

The art teacher should strive at every experience level to develop sufficient skills in students to solve immediate problems. For example, drawing ability can be a major hurdle between conception and completion of a creative idea. Drawing is a skill that can be learned. This does not mean that copybook methods need to be employed or that students must draw photographically, but it does allow for imitative experiences under the skilled guidance of the teacher. These imitative activities can be drawn from the works of the masters and the skills of the teacher. Students need to draw well enough to express what they want to say. The ability to see and the ability to express reactions to the visual world are closely aligned. Each reinforces the other; each motivates the other. As ideas become more complex, the need for expression motivates the development of greater skills. As skills develop, the urge to originate new situations leads to still greater creativity.

The experience of creating pleasing objects and arranging them in satisfying visual situations is a practical aspect of art. Students must understand art as a visual means of communication through drawing, painting, sculpture, and the creation of personal symbols. This means that skills need to be developed through experiences with a variety of graphic and structural media.

Some art authorities are suggesting that students be encouraged to delve more deeply into a single experience and carry it through with a single process for greater development of skill and understanding.

[5] Marvin J. Spomer and Richard L. Brink, "Debate: A. I. S.," *Art Education* (April 1976), pp. 28–29.

Some schools are experimenting with individual project ideas whereby students have the opportunity to be creative with material that is important to them. The student uses such an approach, not for the sake of being different, but as a tool for learning and as a basis for creativity.

It is questionable whether a good teacher would constantly change materials and activities in order to hold the interest of the student. To do so is to push the entertainment or novelty value of art. Students like to improve in what they are doing rather than constantly dashing through new experiences. Creativity achieved through depth study and with adequate skill brings personal satisfaction. Art has a built-in motivation: it is fun to do when it is done well.

Creativity

In all programs of education, emphasis is on the creative approach and the experimental attitude. In fact, the concept of creativity has permeated the educational world so deeply that it is now in danger of becoming a cliché. Basically, all art teachers more or less view their job as one of fostering creativity. The problem is to agree on what creativity means.

Judging what is or is not creative essentially depends on the degree of difference that may be noted between any two given objects. This means that every art object occupies its own unique position in space and is thus separated from all other objects. It exhibits visible, physical differences from any form made before. The creative student produces art objects unlike those produced by others.

In its purest sense, the creative act is based on standards of visual differences. It cannot be classified as either good or bad, beautiful or ugly, and it is inconsequential whether it is functional or nonfunctional. Whether creativity can be taught is worth pondering. Generally, all students possess some ability to perform creatively, but the teacher's role in helping students express themselves creatively is unsettled. In the broadest sense, the teacher would merely act as a critic who corrects the student's work according to standards of visual difference.

Advocates of the purest forms of creativity contend that the methods of teaching must be personal, expressive, and as creative as the expected aesthetic product itself. They hold that the student must be freed from prototype learning where the obvious thing to do is to copy the works and styles of the masters. They believe the creative teacher does not produce in the student the image of the teacher. When aesthetic ends are predetermined and developed creatively, the growth of essential skills is concomitant. This does not allow for the usual method of developing skills by checking errors against the ideal model.

Modifications in approaches to creativity. One of the pivotal points in discussing creativity in art concerns the cause of student discouragement, which usually occurs when students feel that they can no longer successfully pursue the task at hand. Those who disapprove of imitation or copy work claim that students find themselves in this position when they are unable to produce the objects they have been urged to copy, and this leads to discouragement, causing them to cease trying altogether. Counterclaims of those who believe in the necessity of imitation for the development of basic skills point to the possibility of the same result if students grasp creative ideas that are beyond their skill to produce. Hence it appears that the counterclaims of one group nullify the claims of the other, giving cause for indecision on the part of curriculum planner.

The psychologist might ask why people assume that imitation and creativity are mutually exclusive. Such an attitude does not hold with an intelligent diagnosis of imitative behavior. It suggests that imitation does not tolerate variations, elaborations, refinements, or simplifications. It denies that the student who imitates has the ability to develop more personal images with the help of a good teacher. Actually, there must be some imitation in all creative activity. According to the gestalt hypothesis, students bring to the learning situation their own learning environment, a collection of at least partially imitative experiences.

The extent to which creative people have imitated others is difficult to determine. It is questionable to say that pure originality allows for no outside influence. This would mean that students do not influence each other and that a teacher's influence must be negated. Such instructional theories bewilder practical educators. They have accepted the idea that students should have creative experiences and that art is a suitable vehicle for these experiences, but their practical sense causes them to question the omissions of the development of basic skills and techniques for such experiences.

Art and Special Education

Art has much to contribute to the special education field, both at the academically talented level and at the mentally handicapped level. There is no doubt that the really gifted artistic people come from the higher intelligence levels of the social order. The artistic future of the country is crucially dependent on the identification and encouragement of potential artistic leadership. The future painters, designers, artisans, and architects will provide the resources for the aesthetically enlightened consumer. Many students among the academically talented have artistic talent, but they frequently lack enough exposure and educational encouragement to discover their potential.

In some instances, the talented student's inability to enroll in art is a scheduling problem. In other instances, it results from a pseudo-erudite attitude that art is not exactly scholarly, or that it is not a likely college preparation subject. More flexibility in scheduling will help solve the first problem; the problem of attitude is something else. School administrators who really believe in the comprehensive school are going to consider art a basic subject and afford it an important place in the educational program.

A strong case can be made for the need for art in the educational program of the academically talented. These students should have experiences with visual and sensual images; otherwise, they fail to develop the ability to make adequate aesthetic and perceptual judgments and discriminations, since so much of their work deals with the factual, the analytical, and verbal abstractions. Since these students have few opportunities for innovative creative behavior, they need the freedom provided by art.

Attention must also be given to those in special education, who represent the opposite of the superior ability group. While about 15 to 18 percent of the school population are considered academically talented, about 6 percent are mentally handicapped. This group is not inartistic, but it does need a more sympathetic approach. These students require a careful selection of art activities that convey a sense of permanence and solidity. Tentative conclusions from limited research indicate that a program of studies for the mentally handicapped must be qualitatively different in methods, activities, and tools.

Drawing and painting are meaningful to retarded students in the early grades, but as they mature they adjust better to work with crafts in such materials as copper, leather, and clay.

Present and Future Trends

It is simple to say that art affects everybody, that a civilization without art is impoverished, and that the person who depends on others for providing vicarious artistic experiences is barren indeed; but to demonstrate the value of art in the school, such courses must have a prominent position in the curriculum, and getting administrators to include them is not easy.

Curriculum planners must stress the fact that art provides students with experiences that are satisfying and directly useful to them in their daily lives. Through art, students develop their critical faculties and discover constructive avenues for emotional expression that enable them to contribute artistically to the creation of a more satisfying environment.

Future citizens must learn to create wholesome, satisfying experiences beyond those necessary for making a living. Since they live in a world of colors, forms, lines, textures, space, and motion, they need to develop the ability to explore things creatively through their senses. All students have a relative amount of talent in creative expression, so they should have an opportunity to work on their own ideas, concerns, and imaginative projections.

It is difficult to identify curriculum issues in art education. They are somewhat philosophical and thus do not lend themselves to categorical treatment. Art educators tend to group themselves into what might be labeled progressives and conservatives. The approaches of these two groups parallel division of thought in many other sections of education.

The progressive art educators are in the residual stream of progressive education. Theirs is the psychological and sociological approach associated with freedom of expression. The most fervent abhor any form of copying and would deemphasize drawing. They would have the teacher act as a keeper of material and a guide for students who venture into experiences of self-expression. The teacher would enter the classroom without plans of any kind, taking cues from the students' interests and desires. Of course, just as practices were modified following the heyday of progressive education, so have modifications been affected in art education today. The progressive group has continued to emphasize creativity.

The conservatives also aim at creativity, but they identify and develop it differently. They would emphasize the development of skills and techniques, holding that drawing ability is basic to a student's growth in art. They would stress visual accuracy and perspective, contending that basic art education is learning to draw cubes, cylinders, and human figures. Extreme conservatives would have each art lesson be a drawing lesson. They contend that to copy well is a virtue, not a sin, and that nonverbal perceptual and expressional skills are essential to understanding. In summary, the conservative approach to creativity points to the necessity of having skills and techniques commensurate with desired creative expression.

It is fortunate that the extreme view of neither the progressive nor the conservative group dominates curriculum planning in art education at the present time. The best programs reflect a conciliatory attitude toward the desirability of student proficiency in both skills and creative expression. It is true, however, that the approach to creativity continues to be a point of debate.

Every indication is that art programs will continue to be exploratory.

They will involve a wide variety of broad units of experience based on the role and function of art in all human ideas. This concept is based on the thesis that humanity is revealed in part through its visual artistic expression and that these revelations are unique in particular art forms. It suggests that a major function of art education is to teach students to incorporate themselves in art expressions and identifies a difference between *doing art work* and *being deeply involved in it.*

More stress will be put on the development of *understanding* of art and the art method. In the past, too much emphasis has been put on art *appreciation.* Students have been encouraged to appreciate art for art's sake, or because it is the cultural thing to do. Little thought has been given to the idea that real appreciation can come only through understanding; that is, art can be liked or disliked by the students according to their reactions to what the art form really means and not simply because a teacher has said it is good art and ought to be appreciated.

Less emphasis will be placed on the learning of technical processes as an end in themselves or in the building of specialized, sequential skills for college studio training. A student's art experiences will be evaluated more in terms of the effect these experiences have on total behavior. The art product will be only one continuum in the art process. There will be an orientation of art experiences toward personal enjoyment of all social living, including home and family relationships.

There is no doubt that art curricula are going to reflect more diversity in purpose from both the artistic and practical standpoints. Differentiation of programs both for the gifted and the mentally retarded is indicated. Exploration will be continued in the use of art as a therapy for the mentally retarded and the physically handicapped. There will be more concentration on the "service" aspects of art programs in school and community life. The practical function of artistic knowledge for use in community beautification appeals to the average citizen who is asked to support art programs in the school.

A discernible trend in curriculum experimentation may be seen in the movement to use art history as a point of departure for student experiences. This involves a reduction of time spent in the manipulation of art media and an increase in time devoted to surveying outstanding works of art with attention to understanding how they were created. This may indicate a pendulum swing from overemphasis on direct experiences.

Art is a highly individualized enterprise. It is the rightful inheritance of every school youth, and it is entitled to a secure position in the school curriculum. With the present emphasis on individual learning, art is especially worthwhile, since it offers extensive opportunities for the realization of this important educational objective. The highly personal quality of response to visual design, inherent in individual experience in art expression, helps youths develop their own aesthetic standards and values. In time, these become the standards and values of the nation and its people.

In secondary school curricula, advanced placement programs are giving new status to art. Advanced placement in art history has created new courses in museums, and the openness of the studio art course has impelled many teachers to rethink both the methodology and the content of their work. More students than ever are taking additional course work — particularly life drawing — in local museums and art schools. The continued growth of university and art school enrollment attests to the success of senior high teachers in developing the special capabilities of the talented while fulfilling the need for art as a vital dimension of general education.

MUSIC

Position of Music

Among the fine arts, music probably enjoys the most stable position in the curriculum. Music educators are winning the struggle for general acceptance of music as part of the regular curriculum offerings. The transistor tube has brought everyone the possibility of music every waking hour.

Not too much space is needed here to identify the value of music in the educational experience of youth. Music has the facility for widening the cultural horizons of a nation. It is part of the culture of all peoples, from the primitive to the highly sophisticated. The history of America can be traced through the folk music of its people; Brahms, Beethoven, and Bach are symbols of old world culture.

Music provides an insight into what is beautiful, artistic, and intellectual. It has companionship with art, poetry, and drama. As students are exposed to better music, they learn to understand it and their musical tastes are raised. As consumers of music through all the popular media, they desire better quality and gradually their cultural taste improves.

By exposing students to meaningful tonal and rhythm patterns, the music program of a school gives students an increased sensitivity to music that can make all their future musical experiences more enjoyable. The music curriculum should not be designed to make musicians out of all students, but rather to help them be musical to the extent that their experiences will be more enjoyable and worthwhile. Music offers unlimited opportunities for gifted and interested students, whether they specialize in it or not.

A music program offers definite vocational possibilities, even though it may not stress them. It is estimated that about 11 percent of the adult population earn all or part of their living through some association with music. The school program can ether be basic or supplementary to the training of future wage earners in the field. A well-rounded music curriculum will take care of the many and varied abilities and interests of the total school population.

Music educators have two major curriculum objectives: give music status in the curriculum as a recognized discipline, and to make music available to all students.

Music as a Discipline

There is convincing evidence that music is worthy of recognition as a valuable subject in the curriculum. The basic contribution it makes to daily living pleasures and the promise it holds for purposeful use of leisure time in a technological society could be sufficient reasons for making it part of the general education of youth, but music educators claim that music is inherently comparable to the accepted disciplines even without these supporting relationships.

It would be regrettable if schools in a space age society were to neglect music, which is so much a vital part of the humanities. Music has form and design, cause and effect. It is a means of communication as important and eloquent as the written word — perhaps even more so — and it is intelligible to all people if they have experience in its interpretation. It serves both the mind and the spirit. Music illustrates literature and history; it brings civilization to life.

Music draws its sources from great novels, sonnets, and biblical tests. The librettos of opera illustrate the ties between music and literature. Although it has been said many times, the fact remains that music is truly a universal language. It is structured around linguistic symbols that convey impressions, express ideas, communicate thought, and create moods.

Music compares very favorably as a discipline with the highly respectable fields of mathematics and science. To understand music thoroughly requires a rigorous mathematical intelligence. It involves thinking in terms of precision, exactness, and quantitative as well as qualitative analyses. Music has a theory and value system that involves ratios, numerals, fractions, measurements, and arithmetic symbolization. In its most sophisticated areas — such as composition, harmony, and counterpoint — music requires the same high level of abstract thinking as does mathematics.

Any dichotomy between music and science is related to purpose and use rather than basic values. Both encompass systems of knowledge and both are capable of dissemination of this knowledge. The tenets of science are order, balance, symmetry, and proportion. These tenets are analogous to those of music, and both scientists and musicians are probing for the truth through experimentation, exploration, and logic.

General Music Program

A major objective of the advocates of music in the curriculum is to make musical experiences available to all students. Music educators claim that there is no such thing as a genuinely unmusical person and that even a monotone is not incurable. The kaleidoscopic nature of music offers experiences for every student through singing, playing, creating, or listening.

Heretofore, the music program in the secondary school has consisted of choral groups and instrumental groups. The students involved were selected for their interest or ability in performance. This necessarily limited the opportunity for musical experiences. To overcome this limitation, general music education programs have been introduced into the secondary schools.

General music education programs are designed for all students who want to enjoy the benefits to be derived from all forms of musical study.[6] Those with no previous background or those with a lack of interest in music are encouraged to enter the program. They are provided with exploratory experiences in singing, listening, and playing. Desirable musical skills are matured and new ones discovered.

More success with general music courses has been enjoyed in vocal than in instrumental music. Too often the instrumental teachers support the idea in theory, but in practice they are happy to have any student join the vocal classes as long as those with high intelligence, excellent motor coordination, healthy lungs, and money to buy an instrument are assigned to them. Singing should be a basic activity in the general music program, but this does not mean that instruments should be neglected. Instrumental work should also be included — even the study of banjo, guitar, piano, and organ.

Regardless of the organizational pattern of the general music education program, certain fundamental objectives need to be met. Basically, students should be provided with opportunities for exploring and

[6] June Thomsen Getter, "Music is Part of the Humanities," *Educational Horizons* (Fall 1974), pp. 38–40.

understanding music as a cultural force in society, individual talents should be discovered and developed, and discrimination that leads to understanding and appreciation of worthwhile music should be stressed. General musical experiences should include a study of the theory of mechanics of music. And, probably more important, every student should have the opportunity to participate in some form of music for pure personal pleasure.

Administrative Problems

Curriculum designers should direct their attention to several problems that music programs have. Mostly administrative or philosophic in nature, such problems affect the ultimate outcome of the program. One of the problems is associated with a common attitude of music teachers, who are too frequently performance oriented. Their programs are centered around marching bands and public appearances of choral groups. While school officials may stress the public relations value of these things and parents may get satisfaction from the public performances of their sons and daughters, the real values of music lie in the opportunities given students to experience a variety of musical activities in depth.

The full fruition of a musical program is frequently hampered by scheduling problems, allotment of academic credit, and correlation with other school activities. Imaginative programs of flexible scheduling can do much to alleviate the scheduling problem. Students should not be denied an opportunity to have music as part of their schedule because they have other important subjects to pursue. If music is accepted as an academic discipline, allotment of academic credit becomes an academic matter. A ridiculous procedure is to substitute marching in the band for physical education credit or to allow less credit for music because it is not one of the "solids." Because music has much to offer, both supplementary and complementary to other subjects and activities, the correlation of music with other school activities can be exceptionally fruitful to the total school program. This correlation is a desirable administrative accomplishment.

Another problem is that many music teachers complain that their classes are overloaded with undesirable students. They claim that vocal music classes are frequently dumping grounds for such students. If music commands the proper respect in the school and the general objective is to have every student share in the music program, there should be no undesirable students in any music class. The solution to all these problems hinges on better curriculum planning and mutual

respect and cooperation between music teachers and their administrative superiors.

Music Education Issues

The major issue in music education today is the selection of content or
subject matter to be presented to students and how this content or
subject matter is to be used. Much of the controversy centers around
the questions of whether the music will be confined to the so-called
classics and whether it will be presented in its original form. Some
music educators are vehement in their defense of unadulterated classical music. They hold that the only way students will be able to judge
the barrage of musical stimuli they hear daily is to develop aesthetic
judgment and discriminating taste through introduction to a wide
repertory of the world's foremost music and then to pursue depth study
of as much of it as time permits. These music educators warn against
the questionable procedure of predigesting music for students or adul-
terating it by removing all difficulties and complexities, which they
see as "mutilating" and "homogenizing" musical art.
     Music educators who desire a wide variety of musical experiences
for youth hold that the avowed purpose of music education should be
not only to transmit the great musical heritage of the past, but also to
lend direction in shaping the future. They have no quarrel with challenging the student's ability to reach the various levels inherent in
music, but they think that some music must be altered and other music
deleted in order to fit the student's level of ability. They contend that
an important task of music education is to bring the student and music
into congenial and beneficial association.
     The liberal group believes that students deserve opportunities to
grasp the impact and value of the widest variety of musical art. This
includes contemporary serious music as well as so-called popular
music. Contemporary music may be distasteful to those who will not
admit that changes are occurring in music. New aesthetic values are
involved, and accepting these values means accepting unmusical
sounds that may be labeled noise, and there is always conservative
resistance to innovation. But future musical history will recognize the
landmark contributions of many of the contemporary composers.
     The liberal viewpoint does not deny the value of acquainting
students with Bach and Wagner; it merely holds that students' knowledge of the classics should be supplemented by association with perish-
able popular music and the tuneful music of Broadway shows so that
they will have a wider field of experience. Classical rigidity excludes

too much desirable music from youth. Boredom, sometimes associated with stereotyped music, may account for some of the extremes in musical fads that young people pursue outside the school music program.

There is some contention over what attitudes students should develop toward music. This is identified with the difference between "liking" and "interest" and between "entertainment" and "pleasure." The sensible position would appear to be held by those who say that the immediate *liking* of a piece of music is not a valid criterion for including it in a music program. Many fine pieces of music require repeated hearings and close attention before students like them. It is unlikely that all students will ever like all music. What is important is that they find it *interesting* enough to explore and discover musical meaning. Doing so leads to the development of musical insight.

Specific Outcomes

As has been suggested before, basic observations about humanity place music at the core of human experience. Demonstrated in all societies — undeveloped or socially and culturally advanced — is the phenomenon that human beings have a capability and need for forms of emotional expression that transcend the limits of physical and verbal description.[7]

Most music educators agree that all persons with normal sensory endowments have the capability to use music at some meaningful and expressive level. These capabilities range from the self-initiated, self-taught folk level to highly developed technical and artistic levels. Societies and subsocieties are pluralistic in their musical tastes and preferences. School populations are mostly pluralistic and multicultural; thus to involve unselected and diverse student populations in musical experiences, schools must offer varied and diverse music programs.

Charles H. Benner, past president of the Music Educators National Conference,[8] suggests the following minimum specific outcomes for public school musical experiences:

1. skill in listening to music; ability to use one's voice confidently in speech and song; ability to express oneself instrumentally on some one of the folk, social, keyboard or ensemble instruments; ability to respond to musical notaton

[7] Charles H. Benner, "Music Experiences in School Settings," National Association of Secondary School Principals *Bulletin* (October 1975), pp. 1–4.

[8] Ibid. p. 9.

2. awareness of structure and design in music; recognition of the relationship between social and political development and art forms; awareness of the place of music in contemporary society
3. an attitude that values music as a means of self-expression — that looks to music as a source of renewal of mind and body, as an experience that extends the dimensions of life and living

Benner further suggests that to meet the musical needs and interests of all secondary school students, including those who do not participate in select performing ensembles as well as those who do, the secondary school music program should feature the following:

1. Opportunities should be available for participation in musical activities, the object of which is satisfying experience in informal and social uses of music rather than formal public performance.
2. Small ensembles (combos, quartets, miscellaneous groupings, and so on) should provide an opportunity not only for the advancement of individual musicianship, but also for experiences in a type of activity that can be continued pleasurably and profitably in adult life.
3. Stringed instrument instruction and orchestral ensembles should be included in the high school music programs. Historically, musical literature for the orchestra is extensive and the sounds and timbres of the instrumentation are varied. The adaptability of the orchestra in combining with vocal and choral groups, drama, and dance places the orchestra in a position of having versatility and a high-level musical and aesthetic function.
4. School instrumentalists should have opportunities to play more than one instrument. Musical experience in learning to play one instrument enables them to play other instruments.
5. School instrumentalists, as "school musicians" and in order to become "music-participating adults," should have opportunities to participate in vocal experiences (and students in vocal organizations should have opportunities to participate in instrumental activities).
6. Musical activities should provide experiences that relate the musical and dramatic arts—music, theater, and dance.
7. Opportunities should exist for experience in creating, composing, organizing, and arranging musical forms and sounds.
8. The music literature of the secondary school music program should provide an acquaintance with representative music of the past, with contemporary forms of folk, social, and commercial music and emerging forms of musical expression.

9. Finally, experience in music should be made available to special students—challenging experiences for the gifted and talented and appropriate experiences for students with neurological, physical, or learning disabilities.

What Is a Good Music Program?

Curriculum directors and music instructors continue to strive for the best music programs possible. In achieving this objective, difficulty arises in establishing a formula for determining program effectiveness. Objectives can be established and philosophy formulated, but many times they contain high-sounding phrases and nothing spelled out in sufficient specifics to be practical. Eunice B. Meske, professor of music at the University of Wisconsin, has formulated a series of statements that are suitable for evaluation procedures. [9] Her statements are paraphrased here:

1. Clearly stated long-range goals for the music program have been developed cooperatively by music teachers, other school faculty, and community personnel.
2. Music teachers have worked together to translate these long-range goals into specific objectives.
3. Music teachers have devised a total program which provides opportunities for every student to work toward these objectives.
4. Every student participates in some type of music class at least one semester during his secondary school career.
5. The music curricular offerings include classes that make it possible for students to explore a wide variety of performance, listening and creative activities.
6. Within each class the music teacher identifies specific musical skills and understandings to be gained, and develops semester and yearly objectives for their acquisition.
7. Within each class the music teacher has developed ways of evaluating individual progress toward the attainment of these musical objectives; grades are not determined solely by "attitude" and "attendance" but by acquisition of content.
8. Content and objectives of courses where students re-enroll (large ensembles) are designed so that students do not simply repeat activities with different music. A student is required to

[9] Eunice B. Meske, "My School Has a Good Music Program — I Think!" National Association of Secondary School Principals *Bulletin* (October 1975), pp. 7–12.

complete different objectives each semester so that he or she continues to extend musical skills and broaden musical understanding.

9. The teacher avoids the pitfall of choosing for study only music he or she likes; the teacher introduces literature of many periods and cultures, including (but not exclusively) our own, in every music class.

10. No student is excluded from participation in a performing group because of lack of knowledge or skill; students may begin their music study of an instrument or voice. Teachers recognize that the purpose of music classes is to help students learn — not simply to allow them to use musical skills they gained in private study.

11. No student is excluded from participation in a performing group because of finances. Such hidden requirements as purchase of a specified quality instrument, private study, outfits that match, or funds to make trips to Europe (which often result in a music program reserved for the "upper class") are avoided.

12. Offerings in performance skills include small ensemble classes. These activities are not offered as an extension of the large ensemble program but as a valid alternative without participation in large ensemble required as a prerequisite.

13. Students have frequent contact with practicing professional musicians, through school concerts and recitals, visits by professionals to classes, and field trips by students to concerts, recording studios, television stations, record shops, and the like.

14. Students are introduced to career possibilities in music not only in its performance, but in the many supportive fields such as music merchandising, recording engineering, music library science, music criticism, instrumental repair, and piano tuning. Provisions for learning skills for these occupations are made when feasible.

15. Music classes grant academic credit on a par with other classes requiring similar time and effort of the student.

16. The school schedule offers music classes throughout the day, rather than only at hours that force students to choose between music and physical education, music and early dismissal, or music and participation in a work-study program.

17. The equipment for music includes adequate equipment for multiple listening stations, electronic devices for recording and creating music, a music laboratory equipped for individual study and including items such as an electronic or guitar lab, an extensive library of music of all types and books about

music, and space for individual and small-group activities, as well as the equipment needed for large-ensemble activities.

18. Public performances are presented as the outgrowth of musical study rather than as the purpose for organizing a performing group. Performing groups are seen as music classes where music is studied, rather than rehearsed in imitation of a professional organization.

19. The principal keeps lines of communication open between administrators and music teachers, making it possible for each to keep the other informed of interests and concerns.

20. The principal, other administrators, and teachers avoid the pitfall of evaluating the music program against stereotyped views of "what a program should be," based on one's own school experiences (bad or good).

21. The principal recognizes the contribution of a music program to the total curriculum and evaluates its success using criteria similar to those used for any subject in the humanities. The principal avoids evaluations based solely on the number of first-place awards brought home from spring competition.

22. The principal does not evaluate the music program purely in terms of the instructor's popularity, the department's value as a public relations arm of the school, the ability of the Parents Club to raise money for trips, or the size of the band on the football field (in comparison with the rival school down the highway).

23. Teachers see their first responsibility as "selling music," rather than "selling themselves," thus avoiding the personality cult that can easily become rampant in a school where the primary focus is on the reputation of a performing group made up of a small minority of the student body.

24. The students are enthusiastic about music and school music activities, demonstrating their enthusiasm by enrolling in elective classes of many kinds, supporting performances presented by schoolmates, continuing their musical involvement after school days are over.

The Tanglewood Declaration

The Tanglewood Declaration is already a landmark in music education. This declaration was formed at a symposium held at Tanglewood, Massachusetts, summer home of the Boston Symphony Orchestra, during the summer of 1967. The Tanglewood Symposium was composed of philosophers, scientists, labor leaders, philanthropists, social scientists, theologians, industrialists, and government officials. The field of music was represented by music educators and professional musicians. The symposium addressed itself to "Music in American Society." The major accomplishment of the Tanglewood Symposium was the *Tanglewood Declaration,* which is well on its way to becoming a benchmark in American music education. It is a starting point for curriculum planning in the secondary music field. The text of the Tanglewood Declaration follows:

> We believe that education must have as major goals the art of living, the building of personal identity, and nurturing creativity. Since the study of music can contribute much to these ends, *we now call for music to be placed in the core of the school curriculum.*
>
> The arts afford a continuity with the aesthetic tradition in man's history. Music and other fine arts, largely nonverbal in nature, reach close to the social, psychological, and physiological roots of man in his search for identity and self-realization.
>
> Educators must accept the responsibility for developing opportunities which meet man's individual needs and the needs of a society plagued by the consequences of changing values, alienation, hostility between generations, racial and international tensions, and the challenges of a new leisure.

Music educators at the Tanglewood Symposium agreed on the following points for curriculum implementation of the Tanglewood Declaration:

1. Music serves best when its integrity as an art is maintained.
2. Music of all periods, styles, forms and cultures belong in the curriculum. The musical repertory should be expanded to involve music of our time in its rich variety, including currently popular teen-age music and avant-garde music, American folk music, and the music of other cultures.
3. Schools and colleges should provide adequate time for music in programs ranging from preschool through adult or continuing education.
4. Instruction in the arts should be a general and important part of education in the senior high school.
5. Developments in educational technology, educational television, programmed instruction, and computer-assisted instruction should be applied to music study and research.
6. Greater emphasis should be placed on helping the individual student to fulfill his or her needs, goals, and potentials.
7. The music education profession must contribute its skills, pro-

ficiencies, and insights toward assisting in the solution of urgent social problems as in the "inner city" or other areas with culturally deprived individuals.

8. Programs of teacher education must be expanded and improved to provide music teachers who are specially equipped to teach high school courses in the history and literature of music, courses in the humanities and related arts, as well as teachers equipped to work with the very young, with adults, with the disadvantaged, and with the emotionally disturbed.

Future Trends

The ultimate purpose of a music program will be served when students come into meaningful contact with the vistas of musical heritage and have experiences that carry them beyond their present expectations. A student is musically educated when he or she can make aesthetic quality a matter of choice rather than chance.

To this end, music programs will emphasize objectives that develop significant musical competence, musical understanding, and a knowledge of the whole range of music literature. Essential aims of a music program will continue to be emphasized. These give students a measure of musical independence — the ability to sing, to play an instrument, and to read music.

New courses are being introduced in listening and in the understanding of musical literature. Listening courses are geared to challenge the emotions, stimulate the imagination, and engage the mind. Stress is laid on the student's ability to discriminate quality in performance and composition and the ability to perceive elements of form within the abstract.[10]

Specialized courses in both music history and theory are being made available for gifted and interested students. Music theory courses provide students with opportunities to improvise music and to write rounds and canons. They may not learn to write masterpieces, but they will be making discoveries that underlie mature musical achievement. Part of this is learning to isolate rhythm from melody and harmony.

Curriculum guidelines in music are being directed toward having students arrive at a level of musical and intellectual comprehension that is challenging. Programs feature a variety of styles and periods, media and performance, and musical forms. Significant proficiency in

[10] B. Reimer, "Patterns for the Future," *Music Educators Journal* (December 1976), pp. 22–29.

performances is being stressed. The curriculum organizational pattern will vary from school to school, but the best programs will be the ones that include musical experiences for all students according to their interests and abilities.

It may be noted that extensive space here has been devoted to this field. It is out of the conviction that the fine arts are going to loom large in the future lives of the citizenry. It has been suggested that a balanced program of instruction is a desirable curriculum goal. Proper emphasis on the fine arts will make this a realistic goal.

The pleas of music educators for recognition of music as a discipline should not go unheeded by curriculum planners. Their job is to balance the amount of study and performance in the arts with the peripheral and materialistic experiences of other areas of the curriculum. It is time that any unwarranted faddish aura be dispelled from the whole field of the fine arts.

TOPICS FOR STUDY AND DISCUSSION

1. Assess the role of art in the secondary schools in relation to its carry-over value into meaningful employment.
2. It is stated that a basic tenet of art is the development of discriminating taste. Is this true or is the development of such ability a total educational objective?
3. What needs to be done to upgrade the role of art education in the secondary school area?
4. Develop a basis for discussion about the dichotomy between the necessity for mastery of drawing skills and the development of creativity.
5. Is music really a discipline or is it merely status claim on the part of music educators?
6. How can one account for the rapid development of general music programs in the secondary school curriculum?
7. Prepare a brief for or against the so-called watering down of the classics in music in order to make them more palatable for youthful consumption.
8. What is a meaningful relationship between man's social and political developments and the art forms?
9. Prepare a model evaluation form for a good secondary music program based on Eunice B. Meske's proposed criteria.
10. Trace the common elements in the various forms of purpose and objectives presented in this chapter.

SELECTED REFERENCES

Arnheim, Rudolf. *Art and Visual Perception*. Berkeley and Los Angeles: University of California Press, 1974.

As the title suggests, this book is based on psychology and firmly grounded in gestalt theory. Throughout the explication of the various elements of visual experience, the concepts of simplicity, structure, similarity, and the interplay of psychic forces are important factors for comprehending the nature of phenomena and in determining how artistic or aesthetic responses are affected. The principle of simplicity is woven into each aspect of what can be taken in or apprehended as an integrated configuration.

Baker, Rachel. *All About Art.* New Haven, Conn.: Fine Arts Publication, 1971.
The content of this book is based on a tested art curriculum. It teaches elements of design and the principles of art. It is divided into sixteen chapters — the language of art, line, shape, texture, value, color, space, mass, repetition, contrast, pattern, composition, painting, sculpture, architecture, and graphic arts.

Glenn, Neal E.; McBride, William B.; and Wilson, George H. *Secondary School Music.* Englewood Cliffs, N. J.: Prentice-Hall, 1973.
The authors discuss the need for a program of music in the secondary schools to be worked out both theoretically and practically. The theoretical gives continuity, stability, and direction to the teaching of music. The practical makes theory explicit and applicable to particular cases. The material in this book proceeds from the assumption that everything has relationship when developing an adequate music teaching program for the modern secondary school.

Hardiman, George W., and Zernich, Theodore, eds. *Curriculum Considerations for Visual Arts Education.* Champaign, Ill.: Stipes Publishing Company, 1974.
The authors identify and justify the unique and contextual features that visual arts contribute to the framework of general education. They also explicate critical issues related to the process of curriculum development and evaluation in the visual arts. The content of the book is based on an analysis of articles on art in a series of reputable magazines.

Hobbs, Jack A. *Art in Context.* New York: Harcourt Brace Jovanovich, 1975.
This book is a refreshing change from the standard historical presentation of visual art. As the title suggests, the understanding of a work of art can be significantly increased if it is examined within the cultural framework of its time. An introduction is given to the perceptual basis and visual elements of experiencing art. There is also a discussion of reciprocal relationships between the artist and society, which result in change and stimulate new artistic developments.

Klotman, Robert. *Teacher Education in Music.* Washington, D. C.: Music Educators National Conference, 1972.
This is a report of a commission that was assigned the task of developing a set of recommendations for strengthening teacher education preparation and music education in its many ramifications. It identifies the need for well-prepared music educators who will function in various instructional modes and roles. It makes clear the problems of the music educator in dealing with students from widely disparate socioeconomic backgrounds.

Landon, Joseph W. *Leadership for Learning in Music Education.* Costa Mesa, Calif.: Educational Media Press, 1975.

This book is aimed at all levels of music education. The central theme is that a music program is as good as the persons who influence it most, that is, students, teachers, music educators, and administrators. Students will have the most influence on their own learning when they have capable teachers who know and care enough about music to do something about it. The discussion of schools of philosophy relating to music would be valuable to any music educator.

Marple, Hugo D. *Backgrounds and Approaches to Junior High Music*. Dubuque, Ia.: Wm. C. Brown Company Publishers, 1975.

Suggestions are made for bridging the gap between elementary school music and the junior high school. Three established methods of teaching music to adolescents are discussed. Included is a historical background of the junior high school and role of music involved. A large amount of space is devoted to the development of general music, with ensembles and special classes stemming from them. There is a penetrating discussion on the problems of junior high school music programs, centering on the lack of consensus over what the content of courses should be.

Ocvirk, O. G., et. al. *Art Fundamentals: Theory and Practice*. Dubuque, Ia.: Wm. C. Brown Company Publishers, 1975.

This book offers a wealth of visual and written material as well as sound instructional guidance for the student of visual art. Without denying the subjective dimensions of artistic creation and appreciation, the authors argue persuasively for the importance of developing one's capacity for appreciation and one's expressive capabilities. The text provides some educational means toward these goals. Numerous studio problems that lend themselves to critical evaluation are presented, along with supplementary theoretical and historical material.

Sunderman, Lloyd Frederick. *New Dimensions in Music Education*. Metachen, N. J.: The Scarecrow Press, 1972.

Music education for youth in the inner-city, urban, and suburban schools is discussed in detail. Included are secondary school curriculum materials from many sections of the country. Sunderman points to the need for administrators and curriculum planners to be concerned with the wholly new musical era of the 1970s. This is a good book for all who are preparing to teach music.

Tellstrom, A. Theodore. *Music in American Education*. New York: Holt, Rinehart and Winston, 1971.

The general plan of this book is to assign the first chapter of each section to the evolution and establishment of a major educational movement. The author then demonstrates how the principles involved are transposed into action in the area of music education. He makes suggestions about how the structure of future educational policies will more likely reflect the conditions and environment of the times.

7

Foreign Languages: Modern and Classical

Declining enrollments in modern foreign language classes, at both the college and the secondary school level, have been a source of concern among teachers, curriculum directors, and administrators. It has resulted in a flurry of reevaluation of teaching objectives and methods.

In the case of the secondary schools, the study of foreign languages has been urged on students for reasons that either no longer exist or were false in the first place. The primary reason given to academically inclined students for the study of foreign languages was that it was a college entrance requirement. While there still may be a few prestigious colleges or universities that include foreign language as an entrance requirement, the number is decreasing rapidly. No longer is it logical to advise students that they cannot get into college without a foreign language. A second reason usually given to students for taking a foreign language was that it would prove valuable to them when traveling in foreign countries. Since an affluent society has made it possible for young people to travel extensively over the world, they have learned that English is practically a universal language and that feeble attempts to use a foreign language are ineffective.

The foreign language curriculum and its methods of instruction are an example of how practice can get out of touch with reality. While foreign language teachers and counselors were engaged in the practice of eliminating students on the basis of college preparation, they were arbitrarily screening out the experiences for other students who might have been attracted to languages. Secondary school students are alert to their teachers' use of false concepts, which include studying a foreign language for its necessity in national defense, tourism, international banking, and possible employment in a foreign country.

THE ADVENT OF THE AUDIO-LINGUAL APPROACH

Curriculum planners will remember that the study of foreign languages was given increased impetus with its inclusion in the National Defense Education Act of 1958. This act selected mathematics, science, guidance, and foreign languages as subjects to be favored with vast sums of federal money for improvement of programs in the nation's public schools. Since new emphasis was given to the study of modern foreign languages, it was logical that new approaches to teaching and learning would emerge.

A recognition of the merits of the audio-lingual system resulted from experiences of the military in teaching foreign languages. The armed forces established language-training schools at which students were given intensive training in a language for several months through speaking and listening to the language, analyzing its structure, and participating in a limited amount of reading and writing. Linguistic scientists analyzed the soundness of the audio-lingual method. They pointed to language as a living, vital, and ever-changing force involving people and their cultures. They claimed that a static concept of language made up of isolated sounds, words, and grammatical rules failed to teach a language as it really is. They emphasized the need for a phonetic analysis of characteristic foreign sounds as pronounced by a native, to be followed by training in recognizing these sounds as influenced by their position in words and sentences.[1]

Two major objectives emerged in the promotion of the audio-lingual approach. The first advocated that listening comprehension and speaking should become more important than reading and writing in the study of a second language. The other objective suggested the mastery

[1] Theodore B. Kalivoda, "Communication in the Foreign Language Classroom," *Hispania* (May 1976), pp. 294–301.

and retention of a complexity of skills. It can readily be seen that the realization of both these objectives required consistent study over longer periods. It involved teaching a language rather than teaching *about* a language. Enthusiastic advocates of the audio-lingual approach pointed to a future time in American secondary education when all high school graduates would be bilingual.

Many foreign language educators still believe that the audio-lingual approach is probably the best way to teach languages if the objective is practical communication. These authorities contend that in the final analysis, this approach will also do a better job in teaching the writing and reading of a language.

The audio-lingual approach to modern language teaching is not startlingly new, nor is it a radical departure from the traditional fundamentals of good language teaching. It is more a rearrangement and a shifting of emphasis. After the initial orientation lessons, taught in English, the modern foreign language becomes the language of the classroom. Students are encouraged to think in the foreign language, not to translate it word for word into English. For example, on seeing or hearing the Spanish *manzana* a student decodes it into the English *apple,* thinking in Spanish of a fruit to eat or to shine and give to the teacher. The language being studied is considered adequate for communication in its own right, without recourse to English or any other language. Formal translation from English to the particular foreign language is avoided during the first two years of study. No student is asked to read what he or she does not aurally understand.[2] Grammar is acquired initially by imitation and repetition in natural situations, not by formal analysis. A study of formal grammar and the reading of the language are delayed until the advanced stages of study. The contention is that the ability to comprehend the written word is more thoroughly developed if adequate time is spent on learning to hear and speak the language. When these primary skills become automatic in informal discussion, reading and writing begin to play an important role in language behavior.

WHEN SHOULD FOREIGN LANGUAGE STUDY BEGIN?

During the renaissance period in modern foreign language teaching following the impetus given by federal funds in the National Defense Education Act, many problems associated with the audio-lingual approach appeared. Lengthy debate ensued over when foreign language

---

[2] Jeri Hanly, "Bridging the Gap in the High School Class," *The French Review* (March 1976), pp. 476–482.

study should begin and how long the sequence should be. Foreign language educators and curriculum experts in the field advocated the elementary, middle, and junior high school as the initial beginning, declaring the traditional two-year sequence of the senior high school almost worthless. Some authorities contended that the third grade was about the right time to begin foreign language study. One writer in the field cited the following quote from a language specialist:

> Childhood is the ideal period for acquiring a native or near-native pronunciation. Medical evidence, experimentation, and objective observation have proven conclusively that children learn foreign languages more quickly and more accurately (at least as far as pronunciation is concerned) than adolescents or adults because of the flexibility of their speech organs and their lack of inhibitions that are typical of older children. To children, a new way of expressing themselves, particularly if it is associated with a normal class activity, presents no problem.[3]

Other authorities set the seventh or eighth grade as the best time to begin a language sequence. The Curriculum Committee of the National Association of Secondary School Principals recommends the introduction of a modern language no later than the ninth grade, preferably in the seventh or eighth grade. It recommends a minimum of four years of sequential study — as long as such is profitable — through the tenth or eleventh grade, even though third- and fourth-year classes may be small and individual study and practice may be necessary. It is contended that patterns of speech and communication skills established in the first foreign language greatly reduce the difficulty of progress in a second. The four-year sequence gives the student time to study a second foreign language if he or she desires.

Other authorities believe that the first grade or even the preschool years are the time to introduce foreign language study. Very few modern language authorities would disagree with the early introduction of language teaching, but they are very apprehensive about certain practical aspects of such early introduction since the students may lack seriousness of purpose. The school may use it to impress patrons and have no plans for continuity or evaluation. Such procedures could dull the students' curiosity and interest in languages and cause them to avoid language study in later years. A lapse in the study of a language is a serious deterrent to progress. A final factor that causes language authorities to

[3] Frank M. Grittner, "Foreign Languages and the Changing Curriculum," National Association of Secondary School Principals *Bulletin* (October 1974), pp. 71–78.

question the early introduction of modern language study is the lack of capable language teachers in the elementary grades.[4]

The United States Office of Education sponsored an experimental program called Foreign Language in the Elementary School (FLES). As a stimulator, the program enjoyed reasonable success. Elementary school enrollments in foreign language jumped from 200,000 in 1955 to 2 million in 1965. There is little evidence that any substantial number of programs have been instituted below the first grade. Most of the programs start at the third or fourth grade, but the recent trend has been to move them to the seventh or eighth grade because of practical problems of financing, staffing, and articulation.[5]

Many testimonials tell of successful foreign language programs in the elementary schools, but evidence is less than conclusive of the unequivocal acceptance of foreign language as an integral part of the elementary curriculum as advocated by proponents of FLES. Many students in the FLES program change to another language when they enter secondary school, which defeats the basic purpose of a six- to eight-year sequence.

An interesting development in the placement of foreign language study in the school curriculum is the continuation of the exploratory concept for the middle school and the junior high school. Some advocates of this concept no longer contend that it should be evaluated for its continuity purposes but rather for the opportunity it offers younger students to explore the world of languages. As an example, the purpose of the exploratory program is stated in this manner:

1. It is to provide, for all students, a foreign language learning experience that is worthwhile for its own sake.
2. It is to provide the main basis for enabling each student to judge whether he or she wishes to pursue further study of a foreign language.
3. The program is self-sufficient; that is, there is no attempt whatever to make it fit sequentially with subsequent foreign language instruction in the senior high school.
4. The emphasis is on breadth; that is, the program offers a bona fide sampling of many aspects of foreign language learning.
5. The program is nonselective; that is, its purpose is to provide a language learning experience for all students. Therefore, such

[4] Douglas Morgenstern, "Eight Activities for the Conversation Class," *The Modern Language Journal* (January–February 1976), pp. 35–38.

[5] Charles R. Hancock, et al., "A Study of FLES and Non-FLES Pupils' Attitudes Toward the Study of French," *The French Review* (April 1976), pp. 717–722.

things as IQ, grade-point average, vocational aspirations, and other alleged predictors of success are considered irrelevant.

6. The class has a "low-pressure" atmosphere. While each unit of work is covered thoroughly, there is no compulsion to cover a specified amount of material within an allotted period.

7. Homework is minimal in such a program although some students may choose to participate in certain out-of-class project activities or may wish to do outside reading in areas of interest.

PRESENT TRENDS IN MODERN FOREIGN LANGUAGE TEACHING

As a result of a dearth of evidence testifying to the success of audio-lingual methods of teaching modern languages, the trend is toward a more eclectic approach. There is a broadening interpretation of the guidelines that set parameters for audio-lingual teaching. Increasing latitude is given to the introduction of reading and writing skills. Researchers warn of the dangers of excessive reliance on pattern drills that can lead to boredom and fatigue.[6] They also warn of excessive reliance on students' ability to discover for themselves principles that underlie patterns of language. It is suggested that grammatical instruction be interspersed to prevent the mere parroting of set phrases.

The curriculum of the comprehensive school continues to contain an adequate amount of modern foreign language teaching. Curriculum leaders recognize the importance of another language for the well-educated student.

Emphasis is given to the general education values of foreign languages. Stress is put on intercultural linguistic values rather than on the so-called training of the mind. Although utilitarian values are important, they are not in themselves a major reason for having a complete language program. The real objective is the understanding of other cultures that leads to the understanding of their people.

An important advantage of the study of a modern foreign language is that the student can associate the language with actual living conditions of the people using the language. For example, much is to be gained by a student who studies French in a French school and lives in a French home. Many schools work out exchange programs with other countries whereby students live abroad for a year. Exchange students coming to this country serve the dual purpose of improving their study of English and contributing to the language classes in the

[6] Maria P. Alter, "A Modern Case for Foreign Languages," *The Modern Language Journal* (April 1976), pp. 155–160.

schools where they are based. These programs have far more merit than the limited junkets sponsored by modern foreign language tour groups. Frequently, the tour communication procedures are mundane and do not contribute to the development of language skills.

The value of the language laboratory is problematic. It certainly is not fulfilling the great advantages claimed for it by those who sold elaborate rooms of hardware to the secondary schools in the early days of the audio-lingual approach. Enterprising teachers probably will continue to use language laboratories to give students examples of correct communication skills. In other schools much of the equipment is silent and collecting dust. Teachers in schools where affluence is not prevalent have learned to substitute the tape recorder for proposed language laboratories. It is probably one of the most important instruments in supplementing communication skills in modern foreign language programs.

A NEW PREMISE GAINS SUPPORT

The lack of research in the foreign language field and enrollment uncertainties have raised questions concerning some time-honored concepts. Foreign language educators have consistently advocated a multi-year sequence of courses, each course dependent on the preceding one, designed for the above-average student. Now both parts of this premise are being questioned, especially the allegedly necessary sequential nature of language study.[7] Thus foreign language curriculum designers are considering mini-courses as an alternative to the third and fourth year of study. The assumption is made by foreign language educators that anyone who has studied a foreign language for two years should then be free to choose additional foreign language courses from a variety of mini-course options. The preferred time to offer these mini-courses is after the completion of the second year. Several considerations support this recommendation. In the first and second years, students gain a basic vocabulary, a command of basic grammatical structures, and familiarity with some simple cultural concepts, and they have had opportunity to apply what they have learned to listening, speaking, reading, and writing. This should provide a dependable preparation for the pursuit of different avenues in the foreign languages.

At the end of the second year, the greatest degree of dropout occurs; only about one-third of second-year students enroll in the third year. Many discontinue their study of foreign language at this point because

7 W. T. Gordon, "Free Expression or Re-expression," *The French Review* (October 1976), pp. 79–82.

they think they have satisfied college entrance requirements, but others drop out because in most cases the third year is heavily literature oriented, which is not to their liking. Diversification is much needed at this juncture, and mini-courses offer a means of providing it.

Most academic fields now offer elective courses on a semester or even shorter basis. As long as these short-course opportunities are not available in the languages, numbers of students will decide to develop their programs by combining a number of semester courses and thereby rule out another year-long foreign language course.

In many small high schools and some larger ones, too, insufficient enrollments result in dropping the third- and fourth-year courses or in combining the two. A group of mini-courses means a more attractive curriculum for those two years than a combination of the usual upper-level courses, and they can mean the existence of opportunities for advanced study where none existed before.

Although the importance of relating mini-course topics to the interests of students and the backgrounds of teachers is stressed, a listing of topics that have been developed in a number of schools may be helpful to faculties just starting out to establish such courses and to curriculum directors and other staff members who may be involved in the venture. Most of the possibilities, which are listed here under three headings, are applicable to all secondary school foreign languages. Specific content and length of course are left to the discretion and imagination of each teacher or foreign language department.

GROUP I: LANGUAGE

General Listening — Comprehension Skills
Listening to Radio Broadcasts
Corrective Phonetics
Everyday Conversation
Vocabulary Building
Playing Games Using a Foreign Language
Grammar Review
Reading for Fun
Reading Mysteries
Reading Technical Materials
Writing and Presenting Skits
Personal and Business Correspondence
Composition
Journalism
Business Language
Shorthand in a Foreign Language
Reading Newspapers and Magazines

GROUP II: LITERATURE

Course on a specific author
Introduction to Literature
Overview of any one century
Course on one specific work
Overview of any one country or culture
Adolescent Literature
Overview of any one genre

GROUP III: CULTURE

Art	Education
Music	Industry
Famous People	Trip Planning/Traveling
Geography	Gestures (Kinesics)
History	Latin Americans in the U.S.
Current Events	Latin American Revolutionaries
Sports	Transportation
Fashions	Recreation and Leisure
Food	Living Accommodations
Great Monuments	Urban Life
Political Systems	Rural Life
Media	French Canada
Role of Women	French West Indies
Family Life	Teenage Life

Sorting mini-courses into categories such as these can be helpful in examining a mini-course program for its scope; only rarely, however, will a given course fit neatly and completely into the language, literature, or culture category.

VARIETY IN PROGRAMS

Modern foreign language programs in the secondary schools are in a state of flux. The lack of overwhelming success of the audio-lingual approach, the turn to alternative programs following the second year of study, and the different types of secondary schools involved make it difficult for modern foreign language teachers and curriculum directors to design successful programs. The following examples are said to be successful in their respective schools:

DREHER HIGH SCHOOL, COLUMBIA, SOUTH CAROLINA
The program consists of four years of French, German, Spanish, and Latin and two years of Russian. Foreign language courses are divided into semesters so that students who are incapable or unwilling to continue may take another subject after a half-year rather than after an entire year. During the first three semesters, emphasis is placed on the oral skills, and written skills are introduced. So that students may profit to the maximum from their foreign language experience, a resource center and a laboratory are available in addition to the classrooms — each supervised by an aide. In the resource

center are foreign language books from classics to comics, reference books, audio-visuals such as slides, filmstrips, tapes, cassettes, posters, and records. The language teachers have developed materials whereby students may work at their own speed. The classroom is used to present and develop lessons. Students who grasp the lessons quickly are permitted to go to the resource center to work on units for enrichment.

The central purpose of the program is to permit the teacher to work with smaller groups of students, thus allowing more individual attention and not sacrificing the time of other students. Capable students who grasp the required material quickly are able to work on materials for enrichment.

XAVERIAN HIGH SCHOOL, BROOKLYN, NEW YORK

All incoming freshmen select a language that they will study three hours per day during the freshman year. They have the option of choosing French, Spanish, or Italian. In their freshman studies, they take a grammar course, a literature course, and an area studies course. In the beginning, all three teachers try to teach the rudiments of the language. Thereafter, speaking the language constantly, they are very quickly able to diverge into their three particular areas of specialty. Because of the larger number of students who take Spanish, saturation is continued in the sophomore and junior years, when students take world history and American history taught in Spanish. The objective is to achieve fluency in writing, reading, and speaking modern language.

ST. MARY'S ACADEMY, PORTLAND, OREGON

The second-, third-, and fourth-year French classes are set up so that the students may progress at their own rate. Basic minimum requirements for grammar, vocabulary, and speaking and writing skills are defined for each level. Credit is given upon the accomplishment of those requirements. The continuous-progress philosophy is based on the fact that each individual learns in his or her own way and at his or her own rate. Because the major material to be covered is in learning packets, each student or group of students may move from one packet to another at his or her own speed. There are approximately eighteen packets each for second- and third-year French, designed to take the average student approximately two weeks to complete. The fourth-year packets, of which there are about twelve, are a little longer. Tests must be passed with a grade of 80% or higher. The packets include both group and individual work; each includes activities for reading, speaking, listening, and writing. It is believed that facility in a language involves an integration of basic listening, speaking, reading, and writing skills. Plugged into these are pronunciation and vocabulary skills as well as an awareness of the grammar and the culture underlying the language. Different students master these skills at different rates and by different means, so an opportunity is provided for these students to progress in French at the rate and by the means most compatible with their own learning styles.

PROSPECT HIGH SCHOOL, MT. PROSPECT, ILLINOIS

The regular Russian program offers experience with conversation, grammar, literature, reading, and writing. The program of individualized instruction offers one-third of the program (vocabulary development and declensions) on an individual basis. The materials provide for various rates of progress, and evaluation is based on progress only; there is never comparison between students. Two class periods per week are provided for drill, study, and testing. This should result in an increase of vocabulary retention and a capacity for using Russian declensions. The materials are in a state of constant change, for they reflect the ability and level of the students enrolled. The main purpose is to improve general knowledge in vocabulary and declensions, thus giving students greater success in the course, yielding higher grades, and retaining enrollment at the advanced level of study.

LIVE OAK HIGH SCHOOL, MORGAN HILL, CALIFORNIA

The German program at Live Oak High School is totally individualized and includes more than forty courses at five levels of language instruction. For each course, there is a series of learning activity packets, which provide specific performance objectives, step-by-step guides for the study of texts and tapes, worksheets, oral drills, checklists, and guides for testing procedures. Each course is divided into a number of units, ranging from two to ten. Each unit consists of sixteen assignments, and each of these must be completed at the 90-percent mastery level. Credit is given on the basis of the number of units mastered, not on the time spent.

CLASSICAL LANGUAGES

The future of classical language teaching in the secondary schools is problematic. As far as enrollment is concerned, Latin is more than holding its own, but Greek is practically nonexistent. Little or nothing is being written about Greek, and only a few schools offer Greek. Surprisingly, the teaching of Latin is not losing ground. The flow of students into Latin classes has been steady all during the increased emphasis on the modern foreign languages.

Increasing use of either of the classical languages is going to depend on the number of teachers available to handle the teaching assignments adequately. Most of the present teachers are nearing retirement age, and the supply of beginning teachers is small. Prospective Latin students should begin the study of Latin in the secondary school with a minimum of three years' work. If this study is started in the seventh or eighth grade and then dropped until the college years, a problem of continuity arises. As already mentioned, very few students will continue the study of a language after a period of disuse.

The history of the teaching of Latin presents an interesting paradox. Although Latin ceased to be used as a vernacular language by A.D. 800, it was still taught as a spoken language in the sixteenth and seventeenth centuries because it formed a universal means of communication. The practice of teaching it as a spoken language was followed in the early American schools. Thus it may be seen that the teaching of the language was started in this country by the oral-aural method. As the country developed and French became the language of diplomacy, it became more difficult to perpetuate the teaching of Latin as a spoken language. Hence the transformation from the oral-aural method to the grammar-translation method. This change did not bother the Puritan philosophy of devotion to the training of the intellect. Rather, it enhanced it. It also decided the method of teaching other languages from that point until modern times.

Teaching Methods

Today, teaching methods in Latin are in stages of experimentation and revision, especially at the college level, and the experimentation probably will be reflected in the future training of Latin teachers. Changes in teaching methods are being approached in different ways. Most of the revised programs stress the reading of the language; a few emphasize the development of oral ability.

Extensive experimentation on the oral-aural method of teaching Latin has been done by Waldo E. Sweet of the University of Michigan and Father Most of Loras College, who have combined the direct method with a scientific linguistic method. Their premise is that learning a language is the same as learning a set of habits in any other activity. This involves extensive drill and repetition of language patterns.

It is doubtful, however, that the oral-aural procedure will ever be used as extensively in Latin as in the modern foreign languages, since Latin is not a means of modern communication. It is likely that the reading of the language will continue to be stressed more and more, with a marked curtailment of grammar-translation.

Who Should Study Latin?

Because of the tradition that has developed around the study of classical languages, and because of the character and operation of the elective system, students studying classical language do not represent the broad spectrum of student ability. Students who enroll in Latin are likely to come from the upper third of the ability range. Those who are enthusiastic about the teaching of the subject accept this as a desirable situation. They would encourage students with proven linguistic ability to enroll in a three-year minimum program somewhere between grades 7 and 12. This could either precede or follow the study of a modern foreign language or perhaps run concurrently with it. None of the advocates of Latin consider it a general education subject suitable for all students. What, then, will be the future of Latin? Interest and enthusiasm for the subject remain constant among the students and parents, but curriculum emphasis varies according to educational objectives. Where scholarly and cultural objectives are foremost, Latin is firmly entrenched. Where the practical and functional uses of a foreign language are the main objectives, Latin may become an early mortality.

The Future of Latin and Greek

There is no doubt that Latin and Greek will continue to be studied by classical scholars at the college level. The future of the teaching of the classical languages at the secondary school level is far more uncertain. As has been stated before, Greek has almost disappeared from the secondary school scene. But it is hazardous to predict the future of Latin with any certainty.

Those who predict an early demise of Latin claim that it is a dead language and that it is a waste of time to teach it except to satisfy the needs of a few classical scholars. These people mean, of course, that Latin is no longer a means of communication and therefore lacks any practical use in the marketplace.

The proponents of Latin deny that it is a dead language. These classical scholars and curriculum planners place much of their faith in the future of Latin on the continuing popularity of the subject as reflected in secondary school enrollment figures. It is the second most popular foreign language being taught in the public high schools of the nation. There are 1,167,000 boys and girls studying Latin in grades 7 to 12 and, in seventeen states, it has a higher enrollment than any other foreign language. The advocates of Latin contend that the reason students continue to enroll in the subject is because both they and their parents have a high regard for its value. They also claim it makes a direct contact with the classical past from which Western civilization sprang.[8] It gives direct access to the thoughts of people who lived during one of the most important periods in the history of humanity. They brush aside the argument that the study of history and literature can do the same thing in a much easier fashion. They hold that it is a fallacy to substitute the abstract for the concrete in cultural and humanistic areas when the concrete is essential.

Probably the strongest argument for the continued teaching of Latin comes from those who point to the contribution it has made to the modern foreign language field. It is the mother of five important languages of Europe and the Western Hemisphere. Over 30 percent of English words are Latin derivatives. There is also the contention that Latin is the only foreign language in which stress is still placed on grammar. Many of the critics of present-day education believe that American students need a sense of grammar and style, and they can get it more easily and concretely from the inflected language than they can from its modern counterparts. Hence the study of Latin makes a valuable contribution to the understanding of English as well as the modern foreign languages.

TOPICS FOR STUDY AND DISCUSSION

1. Cite justifications for calling the traditional two-year foreign language programs a waste of time.
2. To some people, the use of the word *hardware* is rather harsh when applied to a good modern foreign language laboratory. Why do the critics use such a word?
3. What factors are important in determining the starting grade level of foreign language teaching?
4. Weigh the educational values of foreign languages as being (a) disciplinary, (b) practical, and (c) cultural.
5. Evaluate the thesis that a language becomes the means of penetrating the culture of a given society in the broadest anthropological sense.

[8] R. McKeon, "Latin Literature and Roman Culture in Modern Education," *Journal of General Education* (Winter 1977), pp. 296–302.

6. Probe the conclusion that many languages are interchangeable as far as disciplinary values are concerned.
7. What factors will determine whether Latin will continue in the secondary school curriculum?
8. Play the devil's advocate and develop the thesis that the audio-lingual approach to the teaching of foreign languages has been oversold.
9. Prepare a positive or negative argument on the similarity of a linguistic approach to the teaching of English and the teaching of a foreign language.
10. Probe the question of survival of modern foreign language in the public schools.

SELECTED REFERENCES

Allen, Edward David, and Valette, Rebecca M. *Modern Language Classroom Techniques*. New York: Harcourt Brace Jovanovich, 1972.
This handbook shows the teacher ways of implementing and supplementing existing materials. The emphasis is on teacher-made materials with treatment given to the general overview of the language class, specific techniques for teaching the language itself, development of language skills, and suggestions for teaching culture.
Ferguson, John. *Utopias of the Classical World*. Ithaca, N. Y.: Cornell University Press, 1975.
This book contains the kind of information that teachers of classics require in order to help students understand the relevance of ancient thought in their own lives. The book illuminates rather than duplicates other contemporary accounts of millennial pursuits. The subject matter brings a sense of relevance to a course involving ancient studies. It also enriches a wide variety of courses in social studies and philosophy according to periods under consideration.
Gaeng, Paul A. *Introduction to the Principles of Language*. New York: Harper & Row, 1971.
Gaeng attempts to outline for the beginner the major principles of the science of language in straightforward and concise terms. He presents the accomplishments and results that have been achieved in the field of linguistics over the past 150 years.
Jokobvits, Leon A., and Gordon, Barbara. *The Context of Foreign Language Teaching*. Rowley, Mass.: Newbury House Publishers, 1974.
The authors question the feasibility of functional bilingualism in the foreign language classroom. They suggest a new focus on the learner's creative and intellectual needs. They advocate a high foreign language aptitude, a genuine communicative need and an integrative orientation into the new language and culture. The authors reject the hypothesis that second-language learning is sequential and suggest a return to the natural and unstructured environment of first-language acquisition. As an alternative, they offer a transactional model that is sensitive to the context of language usage.

Parks, John H. "The Classics in the Curriculum." *Peabody Journal of Education* (May 1970), 331–339.

This article includes an evaluation of the traditional reasons given for maintaining the classics in the curriculum. It offers as a substitute a justification of the classics along the same lines as those usually given for modern foreign languages.

Rivers, Wilga M. *A Practical Guide to the Teaching of French.* New York: Oxford University Press, 1975.

This book is intended to provoke discussion, not to provide final answers. It will prove useful to the neophyte teacher as well as provide a source of ideas for the experienced classroom worker. The book focuses on materials and ways of presenting language lessons with an eye to the development of a critical sense and a creative involvement of the learning process between the teacher and the student. The amount of substantive information about language in general and French in particular is unusual for a book of this type. Particularly important is the sensible treatment of problems of translation.

Westcott, David. *A Teacher's Notebook: French.* Boston: National Association of Independent Schools, 1974.

The material found in the curriculum section is the same as may be found in public school guides. The sections on testing and materials to aid the teacher are valuable to any classroom teacher. A variety of textbooks is evaluated for use in audio-lingual or traditional teaching methods. The equipment list should be very helpful, as is the section devoted to teachers' aids, which includes a suggested basic library. All the material in this publication should be very useful to the beginning teacher as well as a good compendium of source material for the experienced teacher.

8

Home Economics

Many stories have developed around the theme of a lifelong search for an ideal or a precious object that is ultimately found on the searcher's own doorstep. In curriculum studies, this is the story of home economics. Curriculum makers look constantly for subject matter related directly to the lives of students — subject matter that has practical application and will lead ultimately to a vocational pursuit. Home economics involves learning activities that meet these requirements, yet it is a field that has been received with something less than enthusiasm by administrators, parents, and students. In many instances, it has been a subject forced on all junior high school students and relegated to elective status in the senior high school.

Parents often are not enthusiastic about home economics, although it is a subject that will be involved in the lives of all students who someday will be establishing their own homes. Some parents advise against students taking home economics, contending that mothers should teach their children the art of homemaking in their own homes. There has been a limited enrollment in home economics for many years. Recently, however, enrollment figures have shown a steady increase.

Home economics is an area of education that has as its major concern the total well-being of the family. Chaotic social conditions in many sections of the country have caused educational planners to reevaluate the responsibilities of the family. Home economics programs need to be restructured to accommodate mobile families with multiple parental obligations.

TITLE CHANGES AND DEVELOPMENT

A brief look at the history of home economics reveals changing attitudes and objectives. At one time, the field was known as *domestic science*, probably because the title sounded scientific. In those days, the two main subjects were cooking and sewing, with students enrolled for cooking one semester and sewing the next. The present title, *home economics*, became associated with the subject as increased emphasis was placed on economics as applied to the home and family.

Home economics gained stature in 1917 with the passage of the Smith-Hughes Act, which allocated federal money for the support and development of home economics as a vocational subject. The use of the term *vocational home economics* began at this time. This and later legislation was designed to emphasize the contribution of home economics education to the vocation of homemaking. This required the broadening of the field to include child care and guidance, family relationships, and home management. It also meant the inclusion of principles of other disciplines such as science, psychology, sociology, and economics.

A dualism existed in home economics curricula of the secondary schools in the early years. A school would offer either vocational or nonvocational home economics, depending on whether the school received federal funds for the support of the program. It was also marked by the certification of teachers to perform in either one type of program or the other. Federal legislation dealing with vocational home economics set up definite time schedules for teachers that enabled them to plan work with students in school that carried over into the activities of the home.[1] Vocational teachers were hired on a twelve-month basis with fringe benefits, including a paid vacation and travel allowance. This meant that students were also enrolled in twelve-month programs. Although they did not report for daily classes during the summer

---

[1] Bertha G. King, "Vocational Home Economics Education," *Journal of Home Economics* (March 1976), pp. 34–36.

months, they were expected to pursue extended experiences under the teacher's guidance and supervision.

Critical Views

Home economics has its usual share of critics who would change trends and limit developments. Some of these critics contend that as it is now conceived, home economics is not a field at all, or that at best it is entirely synthetic. They point to the fact that principles of science are involved in health and housekeeping practices, principles of psychology and sociology determine child care and family relationship, and principles of economics are basic to the whole structure of family finance. These critics propose to retain these learning principles in the setting of their own discipline and thus save valuable student time in already overcrowded curricula.

Other critical groups are alarmed by the invasion of home economics into the sacred tenets of the home. They hold that marriage, child rearing, and family intimacies are too complicated for secondary youths to comprehend. They would have the school confine itself to the teaching of the fundamentals. These alarmists are never too specific about what the fundamentals are.

Some critics of vocational home economics claim that there is too much federal dictation in the programs. However, most administrators of schools that have the vocational programs work on the assumption that federal directives can be instrumental in the development of good learning situations. Recent surveys show many nonvocational programs with offerings broadened to include the same comprehensive activities as the vocational classes. Heretofore these nonvocational programs have involved mostly cooking and sewing and even after revision many of them have inherent limitations.

Regardless of the critics, home economics is enjoying its best enrollment to date. Over 95 percent of all public secondary schools of the nation have classes in home economics. Close to 50 percent of all students take one or more courses in the field. There is little doubt that homemaking of some form or other will continue to be taught in the secondary schools.

HOMEMAKING IN A CHANGING SOCIAL ORDER

In recent years the term *homemaking* has been used more and more in connection with home economics. Although there are numerous vocations in the field of home economics, such as home economists for utility companies and several types of government positions, the chief vocational pursuit is homemaking. It furnishes a practical application of classroom teaching and requires no on-the-job training. Everybody agrees that it is important, and few can escape the ultimate need for its basic content. Homemaking in the modern social order is an inclusive process involving foods and nutrition, clothing selection and construction, child care and training, family relations and social graces, home furnishings and equipment, consumer education and money management, and the many problems related to family health.

Home economics, like most of the other subjects in the school curriculum, is bound to be affected by the changing social order in an automated, technological society. Those making curriculum decisions concerning home economics must be very conscious of the social forces that are shaping modern family living. If the subject is to be worth a prominent position in the curriculum of the comprehensive secondary school, it must earn this position through the vital contribution it makes in helping students face the complexity of modern living.

There is little value in comparing the modern home with the nostalgic image of a patriarchal father reading the Bible and conducting family prayers before an open fireplace. Those are scenes from another era. Home life today must be evaluated in terms of a changing social order, and the home must be assessed as a changing social institution. What is viewed by some as the collapse of the home and family life is nothing more than necessary adaptations of the institution for survival in a culture now predominantly urban and technological rather than rural and agrarian. The employment of both father and mother outside the home calls for mutual responsibility in homemaking, although women will necessarily continue to carry major responsibility for the operation of the household and for the spiritual, intellectual, and aesthetic tone of the home. Any retreat to the simple life is impossible. The job of the school is to teach people to live well in an urban culture in an imaginative and creative way.[2]

As has been stated before, challenges in curriculum development in home economics are greatly increased by the complexity of American life. An inflationary economy practically necessitates multiple wage earners in the lower- and middle-income families. A modern home in the $50,000 to $70,000 price range, soaring prices of all commodities, and increased economic tax burdens negate the possibility of economic survival with only one wage earner.

The homemaker–wage earner is a new image emerging in the home economics field. Curriculum adjustment within home economics pro-

2 Jennette K. Dittman, "Hidden Persuaders in the Home Economics Classroom," *Journal of Home Economics* (March 1976), pp. 24–26.

grams and development of interdisciplinary courses related to modern family problems are resulting necessities. According to statistics, the working mother category includes 53.9 percent of all women over the age of 18 who work out of the home. Half of American mothers bear their last child at the age of 30; hence more than half of their lives remain for gainful employment. Care of the children of working mothers is an acute problem. Surveys show that 13 million women with children are in the labor force. Divorced, separated, and abandoned mothers create the problem of one-parent families. Six million children, nearly one in ten, are living in one-parent homes. One out of every eight families is headed by a woman. These statistics do not refute the idea that home economics is a subject for both sexes, but they do show the need for extensive adjustment in the field.

There is no doubt that the secondary school home economics curriculum should include programs adjusted to the needs of prospective homemaker–wage earners. Content for such programs should emphasize human relationships applied to both family and job responsibilities. Principles of management — including decision making, goals, values, standards, and the nature and use of resources — should be included in content. Integrated subject matter should include budgeting and consumer education. Materials and activities from physical education that emphasize physical well-being through nutrition, recreation, and exercise should be included. Child care and child guidance has a special kind of identity in the program for the part-time mother. The dual role that both parents play today in homemaking and wage earning complicates and broadens the scope of home economics education.

Thus it may be seen that modern home and family life needs to be analyzed critically by home economics curriculum planners. The schools serve all social, economic, and cultural levels. If the teaching of homemaking is to be the responsibility of the secondary schools, and if this responsibility is to be met realistically, the homemaking curriculum needs all the characteristics common to other secondary school fields, such as ability grouping, problem solving, content adjustment, and sensitivity to a changing technological order. Of particular concern to the homemaking field are such social factors as the mobility of people, crowded living conditions in urban life, stress of rapid change in employment conditions, necessity for living in diversity, and the need for a common value structure.

HOMEMAKING AT DIFFERENT ECONOMIC LEVELS

It is difficult to identify the modern home, for it has different characteristics on different cultural and economic levels. There are really three homes to be considered. While certain common denominators may be found in each, many problems of family living are peculiar to each.

In the upper income brackets, both parents are likely to be college graduates leading active and busy lives. The father will be out of the home much of the time in business pursuits. The mother may not be a wage earner, but she will be busy with countless social and civic activities. Much of the education of the children, both in and out of the home, will be done by tutors or in private schools. There is little likelihood that these children will be enrolling in courses in home economics. Those with sufficient mental capacity will be college bound. However, the need for homemaking skills is as great in this group as in any other.[3]

Homemaking is complex. Exceptional skills and capacities are needed to carry out family living. There is need for an understanding of the dynamics of human behavior, a perception of personal and family relationships, and an appreciation of the obligations and responsibilities of parenthood. It may be assumed that children of well-to-do families receive such instruction in a liberal arts education. It is difficult to determine whether this is true or not. Excessive divorce rates in these families raise a question.

Home conditions are quite different in middle-income families, the so-called white-collar group. There is a devotion to family activities in this group. It is true that both parents are very active, with the mother holding down a full-time position in many instances, but parents tend to participate in more things with their children, such as little league baseball, scout work, and other forms of recreation and sports. These families are together more. But here again, the children are likely to be college bound and the parents do not look to the secondary schools for teaching the art of homemaking. Classes in home economics will be pursued on an occasional elective basis.

The lower-income families, frequently called the blue-collar group, probably contribute more children to the school system than either of the other groups, and more students will be enrolled in home economics classes from this group. This is true because fewer of these students are college oriented and many of them are facing early marriage and parenthood either by choice or by necessity. Among the lower-income families, the roles of the father and mother are quite contrasting. The father and mother tend to lead separate lives. Most of the responsibility for homemaking falls entirely on the mother. The father is out of the home much of the time. He does his eight-hour

[3] Jamie B. Yule, "Expanding Our Concept of Home Economics Education," *Journal of Home Economics* (May 1975), pp. 23–25.

stint in a factory or mine and then spends most of his other working hours in pursuits of personal satisfaction such as bowling or fraternal lodge attendance. In these homes, children are tolerated, often lacking in security and affection. The role of the wife is a lonely one. There is a great need for a common meeting ground for satisfactory family life.

FACTORS INFLUENCING THE HOME ECONOMICS CURRICULUM

Planning a home economics curriculum today is complicated by problems different from any previous societal order. Research in family activities reveals new sets of values, all cogent to subject-matter content in home economics classes. Education of family members has a higher priority than ever before. The value of an education has been accepted even among lower-income families. Planning for the education of the children is a major family problem. And beyond the education of the children is the continuing education of the parents. Adult education has a greater enrollment than any other educational enterprise, and this will increase as life expectancy increases. Fortunately, the field of home economics has been a pioneer in adult education. This is true particularly of vocational home economics.

Securing an education may tie in well with family ambitions. The desire of the average citizen to get ahead and have the best for her or his children calls for careful financial planning involving savings accounts, insurance policies, and sagacious investments. Also involved here is the need for security in the home. Most families are ambitious to own their own home, which requires good money management.

The automation of the home, along with efficient management, provides time for many leisure-time activities. These pursuits can add much to the togetherness and enjoyment of family life. Careful planning can provide possibilities for creative expression in art and music. Hobbies and sports can be valuable and rewarding leisure-time activities. This phase of family living is increasingly important for its contribution to both physical and mental health. Relief needs to be found from the pressures and frustrations of modern living. The incidences of cardiac cases and mental breakdowns point to this need.

The personal well-being of each family member is part of good family planning. This revolves around the necessities of food, clothing, and good health.[4] Well-balanced diets, good eating habits, proper personal grooming, and sensible care of the body are all ingredients of such

[4] Becky L. Jones, "Consumerism: An Opportunity, Not a Threat," *Journal of Home Economics* (January 1976), pp. 22–25.

planning. Two very personal facets of the home concern family ties and religion. Gregariousness is a natural human instinct that is inherent in good family relationships. Love and respect among family members give meaning to such relationships. Wholesome religious experiences can be additional factors. Planning for church attendance and family worship are part of the American heritage.

SUBJECT-MATTER ARRANGEMENT

The content and sequence of course work in home economics is of primary concern to curriculum planning. A survey of existing curricula reveals two common patterns. One pattern shows a series of separate courses in sequence of relationships and difficulty. Such courses cover such topics as foods, clothing, home management, health and home nursing, family relationships, child development, and consumer buying. The second pattern has yearly courses designated Homemaking I, II, III, and IV. Each year a series of topics is covered. Parts of these topics are repeated in succeeding years, but in increasing difficulty and application. The proponents of this plan contend that it provides for the establishment of interrelationships among the topics.

Two major problems are found in the home economics programs of many schools. The tendency is to require the subject in the junior high school for at least two of the three years. This tends to dull students' eagerness to enroll in senior high school classes, which are usually elective. Senior high school teachers are critical of the fact that too much advanced work has been attempted in the junior high school, with the result that students either lose their zest for the subject or complain of forced repetition. This problem is likely to be present when programs are set up on a yearly basis labeled Home Economics I, II, III, and IV. It takes careful planning to avoid boring repetition in such programs. One of the hardest things to do is to control the degree of difficulty.

PRESENT TRENDS IN THE FIELD

The best thinking among home economics curriculum leaders is consistent with curriculum development in other subjects. In meeting the needs of the wide variety of students found in a comprehensive school program, it is necessary to build curriculum content on basic concepts and generalizations. Results of extensive research and conference planning suggest five major divisions of content for home economics courses. These include the following:

1. human development and the famliy
2. home management and family economics
3. food and nutrition
4. housing
5. textiles and clothing

These five major content areas are not suggested in any sequence or order; they are only for purposes of identifying what constitutes the field. Arrangement, adjustment, and application of this content will differ from school to school. Learning should be established in problem-solving situations where the development of skills and the evaluation of experiences are major objectives. Independent study and clinical activities may be provided by study in depth of subjects such as consumer education. Special survey courses may be arranged for the college bound, for business education students, or for seniors who for some reason or other have never had the opportunity to take courses in the field. Special school projects may be part of the program. They would include child care centers, clothing repair centers, and centers for social graces.

A closer look at the textile and clothing unit will illustrate a suggested approach. The skills necessary for the design and construction of clothing continue to be basic and necessary, as is an understanding of the values and uses of textiles. The major emphasis, however, is put on an understanding of the uses of textiles and clothing as a means through which roles in life may be identified and expressed.

Through problem-solving situations, students become acquainted with the basic values and purposes of clothing in communicating personality and desired impressions. A person can reflect and express personal values through clothing. Certain consequences can result from clothing choices: impressions can be striking or subtle; values can be established or destroyed. The history of societies and civilization can be traced through clothing choices. Thus it may be seen that a knowledge of the uses of clothing can be of far greater impact than skill in design and construction. Fame and fortune may come to the limited few who design clothing and a certain satisfaction may be gained by those who construct their own clothing, but the responsibility for the intelligent wearing of clothing is the problem of all.

The sociological and psychological changes in students' characteristics that affect curricular changes relate to the so-called sexual revolution. The open warfare between the proponents and opponents of sex education courses in the schools has perplexing aspects for the experienced secondary school principal. In a previous era, sex education was neither emphasized nor identified. Biology, health education, social studies, and home economics classes included units of material related to reproduction, child care, health hazards, and social implications of promiscuity. If queried, most principals could identify their sex education program, but they would be surprised at the question being put in such form.

The sex education controversy has implications for home economics education. Whether the sex education program aspects related to home economics are part of an integrated program of the school or continue as part of the home economics curriculum will vary according to the mores of different communities. The fact remains, however, that sex is a basic integral part of family life and as such is in the province of responsibility of home economics education. The major task is in the restoration of the role of the family as the behavior-constraining and behavior-defining agency for youth. Readily available contraceptives, increasing physical mobility, and a consumer-oriented economy with its explicit approval of self-indulgence do not uncomplicate the problem. Possible solutions for the sex education problem, as well as for the many other problems in the home economics field, will be found by teachers who benefit from broader concepts of teacher education that emphasizes the use of empirical research and problem-solving techniques.

THE HOME ECONOMICS CURRICULUM OF THE FUTURE

The vocational aspects of home economics undoubtedly will continue to be stressed. It is a field that fuses theory and practice. Surveys of future job opportunities for young people reveal two general types of employment. One will be in positions associated with technology and will require well-developed technological skills. The other will be in positions of service to people. Here, too, skill and training will be necessary for those who want to be in the best competitive positions. Home economics can contribute to the vocational preparation of students for both technological and service jobs either directly or indirectly. In the case of very capable students preparing for jobs of a technological nature, the role of home economics may be limited to the homemaking responsibilities of these students. This touches on the question of whether intellectually gifted students should enroll in home economics classes.

In the past, enrollment in home economics has not been as high as it should be. Yet 95 percent of American women marry and have an average of three children each. This means that regardless of training and job position, students are almost sure to be homemakers. Therefore it is reasonable to assume that part of their preparatory education should contribute to this ultimate responsibility. Some authorities lament the waste of womanpower in the present technological order. These authorities would load the secondary school preparation of capable girls as well as boys with science, mathematics, and foreign languages. Psychologists maintain, however, that no school subject is markedly superior to another for "strengthening mental power," and the undeniable need for educating homemakers is merely avoided. The question that faces the planners of home economics curricula is one of designing home economics classes that will challenge capable students. Instruction needs to reach the rich potential these students have, both intellectually and artistically. This instruction should include concept development and critical thinking on a high level. It is the responsibility of the comprehensive secondary school to prepare students for the dual role of making valuable contributions both within and outside the home.[5]

The need for people in service occupations has developed rapidly with the urbanization of the population. People living within limited space and lacking opportunities to be self-sufficient need the services of many others. These service jobs have become more and more specialized, so that those who render the services must be trained. Whether the home economics curriculum should include vocational preparation for all service jobs is an open question that should be answered. Much of the content of home economics classes in the past has been applicable to the training for service jobs, but it has been homemaking oriented. A brief listing of some of the needed service jobs will illustrate this: child care services; clothing services and dry cleaning; institutional work — hospitals, motels, and hotels; housing and home furnishing — florists, gift shops, department stores; and specialized services such as shopping guides and companions to the elderly.

THE LAKE CLIFTON PROGRAM

Those who might doubt the important role a home economics program can play in a modern secondary school curriculum should take a look at the Lake Clifton High School program in Baltimore, Maryland. It is undoubtedly one of the largest in the nation, with an enrollment of 1500 students and 13 staff members. The program enjoys the luxury of having a waiting list of students.

Home economics at Lake Clifton is multidisciplinary, intricately interrelated, and structured with courses and prerequisites charted for emphasis on child development and family life, clothing and textiles,

[5] Evelyn Valentine, "An Award-Winning Home Economics Program in Action," *Journal of Home Economics* (September 1975), pp. 26–29.

comprehensive consumerism and homemaking, food and nutrition, and interior design. While students concentrating in one area are not scheduled into unwanted irrelevant classes, there is an adjusted amount of crossover, particularly for consumer and career education. About 90 percent of ninth-graders who choose an area of emphasis stay with it. Every effort is made to accommodate the needs of all students in the school. While the major areas of emphasis are sequential, any student enrolled in the school may elect to take a desired course.

Home economics students planning to go to college have access to college-entrance courses. Students planning to go to work are placed in work-study situations during the senior year, preferably in entry-level jobs leading to advancement and a stable financial future. Hospital kitchens, quick-food restaurants, shoe and clothing manufacturers, and other business establishments furnish the school's young people summer and part-time jobs.

Home economics curriculum planners interested in one of the most complete programs to be found anywhere should explore the Lake Clifton program in depth. The following outline of the class offerings will furnish a starting point:

    I.   Area: Child Development and Family Life Education
        Child Care and Development
        Child Development Lab I
        Child Development Lab II
        Child Development Lab III
        Child Development Seminar
        Family Life Education I
        Family Life Education II
        Family Health
   II.   Area: Clothing and Textiles
        Clothing I
        Clothing II
        Clothing for Young Men I
        Clothing for Young Men II
        Dressmaking
        Sewing with Knits
        Tailoring I
        Tailoring II
        Clothing Seminar I
        Clothing Seminar II
        Power Machines — Orientation to the World of Work
        Sewing for Others
        Needlecraft
  III.   Area: Comprehensive Home Economics (suggested courses recommended for *all* Lake Clifton Students)

       Preparation for the World of Work
       Family Health
       Personal Development and Human Relationships
       Introduction to Consumer Education, Home Management, and
          Family Economics
IV.   Area: Food and Nutrition
       Food and Nutrition I
       Food and Nutrition II
       Entertaining at Home
       Foods of the World
       Soul Food
       Foods for Children I
       Foods for Children II
       Food Service Program
          Introduction to Food Service
          Food Service Lab I
          Food Service Lab II
          Desserts and Breadmaking
V.   Area: Interior Decoration and Design
       Interior Decoration and Design
       Miscellaneous Decorative Furnishings
       Housing
       Basic Drafting
       Textiles and Home Furnishings
       Furniture Periods and Styles
VI.   Area: Fashion Merchandising
       Draping and Flat Pattern Design
       Fashion Advertising
       Fashion Merchandising
Number of Courses Offered — 42

OTHER PROGRAMS

A survey of other good programs across the nation reveals a broad concentration on consumerism, nutrition, and parent education. While programs may not be organized under those three headings, much of the interesting and stimulating content clusters around these areas of practical emphasis.

Offerings in the foods division include basic cooking, home entertaining, foreign foods and culture, and career-type food services. Interior design classes are given the assignment of decorating parts of a home within a specified budget. Basic drafting, consumerism, and furniture styles are studied. Students in family life classes are taught basic psychology for getting along with others and dealing with personal problems. Mock weddings and marriage crises are featured. Students in sewing seminars work at their own pace, having weekly conferences with instructors, both producing and designing garments.

A study of the following course content reveals interesting facets of innovative programs:

Food and nutrition. Quick foods — their worth, analyzing the quarter-pounder, alternatives to beef; scrutinizing health food stores; nutrition for athletes; gourmet approach to wild game; making jerky; foods good for the complexion; nutrition for aging people.

Family living. Children of divorce; alternative lifestyles; managing a career and a family; parent education; the childless marriage; nonsupport family management; facing retirement; food for working families; cultural heritage; sex stereotyping; women in the work force; alternatives to the Cinderella image.

Housing. The modular home; buying or renting; rising housing costs; mobile homes; flea markets; shopping in second-hand stores; saving energy; mortgage loans.

The preceding listings are not complete, but they do serve as illustrations of secondary school home economics programs that emphasize family living, the impact of consumer problems, and the ever-changing problems of adult life.

NEW EMPHASIS

Home economics educators continue to stress certain factors that they believe should be emphasized in a secondary school home economics program. There is every likelihood that these factors will continue to be stressed in the future.[6] The following summary identifies them:

1. Greater consideration is given to economic, social, and cultural conditions and needs of all persons, including such audiences as teen-age parents, older citizens, ethnic groups, the mentally handicapped, and people living in economically depressed areas.
2. Emphasis is on the preparation of individuals for professional leadership.

[6] H. T. Skitze, "Future of Secondary School Home Economics," *Journal of Home Economics* (March 1977), pp. 7–10.

3. Programs are designed to prepare males and females for combining the roles of homemaker and wage earner.
4. Consumer education, resources management, nutritional knowledge and food use, and parenthood education are included.
5. Ancillary services, activities, and other means of assuring quality in consumer and homemaking programs are provided.
6. Flexibility is the key to program development in home economics courses. Educational concepts and role adjustments are kept flexible in regard to changing societal needs.
7. The concept of life-long education is fostered. It springs from the fact that in an industrial society, living is not only a struggle for survival but also an enjoyment of the good things life affords.
8. A new direction that must be understood is that schooling is not necessarily synonymous with education. Recognition is given to the educational services provided by business and industry, churches, government, and other periphery agencies and organizations.
9. Home economics educators envision alternative designs for everyday living and critically evaluate and interpret the costs and benefits.
10. There is greater input into decisions made in the public realm that have impact on families.
11. There is creative adaptation to uncertainty and change that requires willingness to assume risks in directing change that affects family living.
12. The interdependence of resource availability and the development of human potential to affect resource distribution are recognized.

If the future home economics curriculum is to fulfill its role in a comprehensive school, there is no doubt that adjustments must be made.[7] Practically all students, including the intellectually gifted, will be future homemakers. If all girls and a substantial number of boys enroll, instruction must be adjusted to ability, as in any other subject. Many of the students who will pursue service jobs are already in home economics classes. New content and training in new skills will be necessary to prepare these students adequately. Home economics programs face a new urgency in helping youths adjust and make discriminating use of available resources, both human and physical. The students must learn to make sensible decisions in order to gain maximum

[7] L. C. Harriman, "Changing Roles: Implications for Home Economics," *Journal of Home Economics* (March 1977), pp. 11–13.

satisfaction and contribute significantly to the building of good homes and good communities.

TOPICS FOR STUDY AND DISCUSSION

1. What should be placed in an outline of learning experiences for both boys and girls in a family living course that would contribute to their readiness in establishing their own homes?
2. Weigh the values of home economics courses for general education, vocational education, personal development, and family life.
3. What common threads should permeate home economics, health education, sociology, economics, and business education? Should other areas be included?
4. Explore in depth the vocational home economics program sponsored by the national government as to its rigidity, its emphasis on motivation by contents, and its relations to modern family living needs.
5. Explore the theory that home economics should not be offered as a course in the secondary school curriculum — that it lacks subject-matter content and that the concepts involved ought to be developed in other more appropriate subjects.
6. How can the imbalance in home economics enrollment between the junior and senior high schools be justified?
7. Analyze the changing roles of men and women in a technological social order. What are the conclusions for curriculum planners in secondary school home economics?
8. If home economics curriculum planners are to come to grips with such vital problems as sex education, what should be the approach?

SELECTED REFERENCES

Bogert, L. Jean; Briggs, George M.; and Calloway, Doris H. *Nutrition and Physical Fitness.* Philadelphia: W. B. Saunders Company, 1973.
    The authors present basic facts about the principles of nutrition as well as progressive findings of nutritional research. Divided into three sections, the book discusses nutrients and their functions, food intake and utilization, and applied nutrition.
Concepts and Generalizations: Their Place in the Home Economics Curriculum. Washington, D. C.: American Home Economics Association, 1975.
    This publication demonstrates the responsiveness of today's home economics programs to the changing quality of human conditions and to changing values and patterns of contemporary living. It sets forth basic objectives for secondary school programs.
Cross, Aleene. *Home Economics Evaluation.* Columbus, Ohio: Charles E. Merrill Books, 1973.

The major focus of this book is evaluating student progress toward the accomplishment of those objectives selected for any given module, unit, or course of study. A theme that runs throughout the book is the involvement of students not only in evaluating their progress but also in determining objectives and in selecting methods of evaluation. A companion theme is the integral relationship of evaluation to the teaching-learning process. The intent of this book is to help home economics teachers to evaluate student achievement more effectively and to see evaluation as it relates to the teaching process.

Fleck, Henrietta. *Toward Better Teaching of Home Economics*. New York: The Macmillan Company, 1974.

This book reflects many changes in society. It reviews new ways to meet the increasing need for education in home and family living. There is a focus on the teacher and her or his competence in planning a program appropriate for students, the creation of an appealing and human environment for learning, and the effective use of many available resources. Consideration is also given to the dynamic use of teaching methods and materials, group processes, and evaluation procedures.

Hatcher, Hazel M., and Halchin, Lilla C. *The Teaching of Home Economics*. Boston: Houghton Mifflin Company, 1973.

Included is a treatment of important problems of teaching, such as the following: (1) developing relationships with others while growing as individuals, (2) being able to choose and use a variety of teaching techniques and resources, and (3) using, adopting, and developing home economics curricula. New terms that have come into use are adapted to home economics, for example, *humane teacher, lifestyles, self-actualization, empathy, accountability, people knowledge*, and *change agents*.

Kohlmann, Eleanore L. *Home Economics for Young Men: A Teaching Guide*. Iowa City: Iowa State University Press, 1975.

This is a resource guide for secondary school teachers who work with male students. It includes objectives, generalizations, and ideas for learning environments. It appears to reinforce stereotyped sex roles, but it should be helpful as a teacher resource since it was developed from the practical application of ideas that are advocated.

Lowenberg, Miriam E., et al. *Food and Man*. New York: John Wiley & Sons, 1974.

Lowenberg provides an up-to-date investigation into the interrelationships between modern consumerism and the production, processing, and marketing of food. It discusses the discovery of the functions of food in the human body, nutrition and the psychosocial basis of individual food habits, and how food has changed the course of history.

Nickell, Paulena, and Rice, Ann S. *Management in Family Living*. New York: John Wiley & Sons, 1976.

Here is a down-to-earth, humanistic book that deals with management as a path to a better way of life, a process for reaching goals and controlling outcomes of change. The goal-oriented, behavioral interpretation of management and decision making attempts to keep readers aware of today's focus on human resource development in today's family management. This book may be recommended for its readability, clarity of concepts, and documentation of research.

Oppenheim, Irene. *Management of the Modern Home*. New York: The Macmillan Company, 1976.

Home management is planned around the needs of today's families and individuals in the family. Oppenheim discusses such standard topics as values and goals in the management process, decision making, efficient use of time, household work management, the use of money, the family budget, and food buying for the individual and the family. She includes topics of current concern: the employment of women, the home and the environment, the low-income family, changing lifestyles, and the homemaker with a handicap.

Ruud, Josephine B., and Hall, Olive A. *Adult Education for Home and Family Life*. New York: John Wiley & Sons, 1974.

The authors provide an overview of the range of adult education programs for home and family living and tell how to develop suitable situations to meet the needs and interests of a variety of adult audiences. They point to the unique needs of adult students and analyze adult learning characteristics and motivations and their participatory patterns. They also list procedures and practices of programming for specific target audiences as well as ways to work with these audiences.

Whiton, Sherrill. *Interior Design and Decoration*. Philadelphia: J. B. Lippincott Company, 1974.

Whiton describes the dominant influences and characteristics of historical interiors, furniture, ornamental design, and architecture. New material includes interior design and architecture of today with emphasis on sociopsychological aspects of design.

9

Industrial Arts

Students who are free to select their exploratory experiences, both in and out of school, do so primarily in terms of work environment. Interest in the subject matter alone does not determine course selection. Students may select industrial arts because of the mechanical work environment, or the absence of the intellectual work environment, rather than merely an interest in construction or woodworking.[1]

As long as industrial arts courses are heavily oriented toward mechanical activity at the expense of equally legitimate opportunities for students to function and achieve in the other work environments, students with other than mechanical skills will not seek industrial arts experiences. Industrial arts teachers, regardless of their course content, must insure comprehensiveness in their teaching methods that will place students in a variety of work environments.

Industrial arts teachers must be especially alert to technological ad-

[1] Ralph Ressler, "Dumping Ground: Cause and Effect," Man/Society/Technology (December 1975), pp. 88–89.

vances in both industry and education. Two main characteristics of a modern industrial arts program should be the following: (1) major components of content should be derived from an analysis and synthesis of technological functions of industry, and (2) the laboratory approach to learning should provide a dynamic atmosphere that is characteristic of the world of work.[2] Curriculum planners in industrial arts have an obligation to keep up with technical advances in industry and translate them into the appropriate classroom-laboratory situation.

Studies of curriculum guides for industrial arts in the various states reveal a diversity of programs. In some states it is difficult to find published materials. In other states there is an abundance of material dealing with drawing, woodworking, metalworking, electricity, and radio. Far less attention is given to plastics, graphic arts, and power mechanics. Most of the curriculum guides concern themselves with the use of hand tools, the operation of machines, and related information concerning materials. It is difficult to find agreement on what should be taught. From a perusal of the available curriculum materials, it is reasonable to conclude that industrial arts in the hinterlands has not progressed very far from the concept of teaching basic hand tools and machine processes. Too often, the making of the "take-home project" is the ultimate objective. Most industrial arts curriculums need reorganization, both in their concepts and in their objectives.

CHANGING CONCEPTS

The term *industrial arts* is now being widely used by those connected with the field of industrial arts, and the industrial arts shop is the area designated as the laboratory for learning activities. The earliest term used in the field was *manual training*. Objectives were related to the development of skills in the use of hand tools, and woodworking was the major activity. Frequently, mechanical drawing was taught as a related subject. In some instances courses in woodworking and mechanical drawing were given in alternate semesters; in other cases the courses were given during the same semester on different days of the week. Enrollment in manual training was confined mostly to boys.

As increased technological knowledge brought new products and new industrial processes into everyday living, curriculum planners sought to incorporate this new information into the shop classes. There was a feeling that students needed a wider knowledge of materials and processes of industry. They also needed information about the use and maintenance of the many modern conveniences and labor-saving de-

[2] Albert J. Pautler, Jr., "Curricular Implications in a Technological World," *Man/Society/Technology* (May–June 1976), pp. 234–235.

vices coming into the home. To cover this wider scope of activity, the term *manual arts* came into use. Learning activities in the manual arts shop included the use of plastics, graphic arts, textiles, and bookbinding.[3]

The use of *manual arts* as a term to identify the field never gained wide usage, and it soon gave way to the current term, *industrial arts*. Programs of industrial arts have both technical and aesthetic aspects; many processes in the arts, such as ceramics, and different forms of crafts, such as weaving and leather working, are taught. The increased emphasis on a wide variety of activities in the industrial arts field soon identified it with the purposes of general education. Out of this grew the concept of the general shop.

Industrial arts has never emphasized vocational education. Confusion sometimes arises over this matter. The vocational overtones in industrial arts are secondary. Vocational education demands specialization and depth preparation that are not stressed in the industrial arts shop. The primary objective is to give students a wide range of preparatory experiences that will lead to later vocational choice or avocational pursuits. The theory behind the general shop is that students with wide experiences in industrial processes will adjust to the rapidly changing demands of a technological order. It presupposes that the job training of today may not be usable tomorrow. Vocational specialization too early may be wasted, but purposeful, planned experiences in a wide variety of industrial processes can result in intelligent vocational choices as opportunities occur. Even if no vocational choice results, avocational skills learned in general shop may result in personal satisfaction and worthwhile leisure activities.

Industrial arts experiences are for both boys and girls. Both are involved in the technological culture. It is doubtful whether any great number of girls will enroll in shop classes, but there is no reason to assume that they lack aptitude for it or that their needs are not as great as those of boys. Women are engaged in all phases of industrial life. They also share equal responsibilities in homemaking and recreational pursuits. Perhaps more experimentation is necessary for discovering the feasibility of a commonality of experiences including both industrial arts courses and home economics courses.

EARLY OBJECTIVES

One of the earliest lists of industrial arts objectives is *The Standards of Attainment of Industrial Arts Teaching*, published by the American

---

[3] Ronald M. Mangano, "Industrial Arts, Technology, and the Future," *Man/Society/Technology* (February 1976), pp. 141–142.

Vocational Association in 1934.[4] Objectives emphasized the manipulative skills in the use of hand tools and the execution of simple basic operations. The list remained essentially the same through revisions in 1948 and 1953, with the exception of added objectives for health and safety. It was a good listing at the time it was made, and it still contains many of the fundamentals of a good industrial arts program, but it does not adequately reflect the needs of the modern industrial order.

A study of industrial arts objectives recently compiled by leaders in the field shows a definite effort to meet the needs of youths in a complex society. These objectives include emphasis on problem solving, design, and experimentation as facets of a more wholesome approach to learning through intelligently organized experiences that help orient the student in the realm of industrial and technological subject matter. The proper emphasis given to the manipulative activities continues to be an issue, but more stress is being placed on the correlation of science and mathematics and the relationship of various industrial processes to lifelike situations.

The report of a U.S. Office of Education conference in 1960 includes four rather broad objectives. These objectives were the result of extensive surveying and summarizing of previously established objectives by recognized authorities in the field. They were meant to provide experience for the slow learner as well as the gifted and are worthy of careful analysis.

1. To develop in each student an insight and understanding of industry and its place in our culture.

There is no doubt that this objective is ordinarily the responsibility of courses in economics, sociology, and physical sciences, but industrial arts can show both the theoretical and the functional aspects of the occupational and productive activities of society. Industry is a dominant element of the modern social order. The school shares a heavy responsibility for helping each student understand this industrialization. Industrial arts can furnish basic training in skills, techniques, and information that will be of value for those who enter industry and the phases of business associated with industry. A desirable background also can be furnished for those who expect to go into advanced work in the various professional areas related to industry.

2. To discover and develop talent of students in the technical fields and applied sciences.

[4] American Vocational Association, Inc., Industrial Arts Division, *Standards of Attainment of Industrial Arts Teaching* (1934).

The fulfillment of this objective would bring a new type of student to the industrial arts shop. The stigma of being a dumping ground for disinterested students of questionable ability would rapidly disappear. Students would be guided into industrial arts courses as a result of their identification with scientific and technological pursuits. Future technicians, engineers, and production workers would gain basic experiences suitable to their aptitudes and needs.

The discovery aspect of this objective is worth careful analysis. The academically capable student is often cloistered in abstract subject-matter areas where the premium is on storing knowledge rather than applying it to practical situations. Part of these students graduate from secondary schools completely inept in the simplest of applications. Experience in industrial arts would not only aid in the discovery of technical abilities but would give confidence and satisfaction in the use of such abilities.

3. To develop technical problem-solving skills relative to materials and processes.

Problem solving continues to be a cardinal process for learning. There is a concentration of emphasis on problem solving in most of the subject-matter fields that are undergoing significant change in content and teaching techniques. When properly directed in industrial arts, this approach leads to creative thinking, the application of principles of science and mathematics, and technological know-how. The use of tools and materials divorced from problem solving may be glorified busy work, and this does not satisfy basic needs of students, whether they have much ability or little ability.

4. To develop in each student a measure of skill in the use of the common tools and machines.

This is one of the oldest objectives in the industrial arts field and it still is fundamentally sound. The skilled use of tools is essential in the many phases of industrial arts. This skill needs to be developed beyond the mere manipulative phases of the use of tools and machines. It leads to a necessary understanding of industrial processes and gives the student an opportunity to develop talents in technical fields. This ability is a means to an end in problem-solving ability.

MODERN OBJECTIVES

The basic objectives of industrial arts programs should be concerned with the contributions that can be made to general education. They must satisfy the ramifications of complex industrial experiences, as well as patterns of general civic and human relationships. Industrial arts experiences, if indeed they have progressed beyond the hand tool stage, need to be broadened beyond the materials and processes of modern industry to include unique patterns of human relations, such as those involved in the delicate balance between labor and management.

The November 1973 *Federal Register* contains a statement from the Vocational Education Amendments of 1968 concerning industrial arts: According to the amendments, industrial arts consists of those programs:

1. which pertain to the body of related subject matter, or related courses, organized about the technical, consumer, occupational, recreational, organizational, managerial, social, historical, and cultural aspects of industry and technology.
2. including learning experiences involving activities such as experimenting, designing, constructing, evaluating, and using tools, materials, and processes.
3. which provide opportunities for creativity, problem solving, and assisting individuals in the making of informed and meaningful occupational choices.

A comprehensive vocational education system must be capable of assisting all citizens to select, prepare for, and advance in occupations or careers of their choice. While industrial arts should not be charged with turning out the finished product, it should provide students with a broad understanding of the function and organization of major common elements in industry, develop a fundamental understanding of the principles of industrial sociology, industrial psychology, industrial economics, and industrial location, and give students an opportunity to identify important concepts about U.S. industry.

INDUSTRIAL ARTS IN THE COMPREHENSIVE SCHOOL

The role of industrial arts in the comprehensive school needs better delineation. For example, a basic concept of the comprehensive school is the proper balance of curriculum offerings to meet the needs of all students.[5] The connotation of balance appears to mean that students should have experience in subjects contributing to the educational,

[5] William K. McPherson, "Industrial Arts Education Identity Crisis," *Man/Society/Technology* (February 1976), pp. 138–140.

vocational, and citizenship aspects of their lives. It is sometimes referred to as a balance between the academic and the practical, or between the academic and the manipulative skills. Industrial arts represents a balancing subject in the curriculum as well as a subject that can exhibit balance within its own subject-matter area.

The industrial arts shop is unique as a facility for bringing together and synthesizing the various phases of a good educational program. Functional industrial arts should exploit this uniqueness and extend its benefits to all students. Things that make specific contributions to all youth should be emphasized. Industrial arts has the subject matter and activities to challenge the more able students. Attention should be given to the establishment of special, high-level classes that will attract students interested in science and engineering. Extensive experience in dealing with the less capable certainly ought to aid in charting sound programs for their needs. A minimum program for all abilities is a good objective.

The increasing complexity of our industrialized society and the increasing amount of mechanization encountered everywhere makes it essential that industrial arts experiences be regarded as basic and fundamental for all youth. There is definite evidence of need for reorganizing industrial arts objectives and content around modern industrial development and basic problems of industry, incorporating the accepted objectives of the comprehensive school.

There is no doubt that industrial arts as a part of general education can provide profitable and valuable experiences to all students in the public schools.[6] There are opportunities within its bounds to make positive contributions to the teaching of moral and civic responsibilities. It can also be an important adjunct to scientific research and experimentation.

There is a tendency to adjust industrial arts programs to provide more meaningful experiences for the college-bound student. This idea is commendable and has merit for those who plan to specialize in any form of engineering or highly developed industrial pursuit. However, the terminal student continues to deserve major emphasis in the industrial arts program.

The shop teacher would doubtless prefer to have students of average and above-average intelligence, and if vocational objectives are to be fulfilled in areas of industrial management and technological skills, this is a worthy preference. The ability to conceive from abstract ideas, to bring to life on the drawing board, and to execute a finished product from raw materials is the ultimate objective of every industrial arts

[6] Robert C. Andrews and Emanuel E. Ericson, *Teaching Industrial Education: Principles and Practices* (Peoria, Ill.: Charles A. Bennett Company, 1975), p. 247.

teacher. This does not mean that industrial arts cannot fulfill worthy objectives for students of lesser academic ability. Research studies continue to show that academic proficiency as expressed by IQ and other mental measurements has no correlation with the success of students in subjects that are primarily of the manipulative type.

In addition to providing students with knowledge for hobby pursuits and home mechanics efficiencies, industrial arts is in the pleasant position of being able to offer knowledge, skills, and techniques that can be used directly and immediately in gainful employment. It might be argued that this is vocational education and perhaps would include all vocational aspects, but no experience that becomes basic for life's work can be divorced from vocational experiences. The need for mechanical artists, mechanics, and technicians is ever present. Many skilled hands are needed between the drawing board and the launching pad.

It must be repeated, however, that industrial arts objectives are different from those of vocational education. The responsibility for preparing youths for job situations is the function of vocational education and should be identified as such. It is more important for students in industrial arts courses to learn of the complexities of American industrial culture and the resulting effects on the lives of people. The more technology and science expand, the more important it becomes for a person to understand industrial processes.

CURRICULUM TRENDS

There is a problem in bridging the gap between philosophy and theory in the new industrial arts programs. There are detractors as well as advocates of plans that feature technology as the basic content ingredient and the increased use of classroom activity procedures at the expense of laboratory experiences. There are those who contend that the tendency is to make programs with too many classroom activities and too few laboratory activities. The problem is to use industrial and technological processes as content and to keep relevant learning activities in the laboratory. If industrial arts is to be a vital subject in the curriculum, ways must be found to coordinate laboratory experiences with all phases of the program.

Those who advocate the increased use of classroom experiences in industrial arts programs point to the major responsibility the subject has for carrying out the aims of occupational education. These are classified as (1) development of technological and industrial awareness, (2) encouragement for exploration of individual aptitudes, capabilities, interests, and characteristics, and (3) development of skills and habits of hand and mind.

Technology Approach

Although industrial arts has been a part of the secondary school curriculum for a long time, industrial arts educators continue to defend its legitimacy and struggle with semantics of identity. They continue to make statements such as "Industrial arts *is* a school subject and is important in the general education pattern of all students." This same authority holds that industrial arts curriculum building concerns only content, that curriculum starts and ends with content. Outcomes are not part of curriculum but merely describe what values are to be achieved from the study of subject matter. Neither are methods a part of curriculum design; they only explain how subject matter is taught.

In contrast to the above, another industrial arts educator explains curriculum as the medium through which the aims, purposes, and objectives of education are implemented and realized.[7] He introduces the word *structure* (used interchangeably with the word *model*) as the vehicle for establishing various content levels to meet changing knowledge requirements.

Despite differences in approach, there is a growing agreement among industrial arts educators that the dominant objective of industrial arts should be to provide an understanding of American industry and an awareness of its changing technology. Programs using this as the basic objective are identified with a technology approach. In its simplest form, this approach redefines the old objective of "a degree of skill" as an understanding of the necessity for skillful use of tools rather than skill in the use of tools. In more complex form, technology as related to industrial arts is conceptualized as study of people as the creators of technology, incorporating the fundamental technical and cultural elements of the several areas of technology.

Paul DeVore proposes that an industrial arts curriculum based on the study of people and technology has the following characteristics:[8]

1. It provides a better base from which to implement the purposes and objectives of general education.

[7] Paul W. DeVore, "Structure and Content Foundation for Curriculum Development" (Washington, D. C.: The American Industrial Arts Association, November 1970), p. 1.

[8] Ibid., p. 2.

2. It is not limited or isolated by geographical boundaries, thereby evidencing the true nature of disciplined inquiry.
3. It is concerned with people as the creators of technology regardless of national origin.
4. It provides a meaningful relationship between technology and human culture. Historical, anthropological, social, and economic elements of the culture are important to the understanding of human technology, and a knowledge of human technology is vital to the understanding of any culture.
5. It identifies a knowledge area meeting the criterion of a discipline in the truest sense of the term.

DeVore structures the organization for content in a technology-oriented industrial arts curriculum around three technical areas:[9]

1. *Production* — providing goods and services of economic value for human needs and wants. Instruction would center around tools, materials, processes, machines, and organization and management of procedures related to fabrication, processing, and constructive technology.
2. *Communication* — providing information dissemination, storage, retrieval, and use. Subject matter would be related to information about sensing, encoding, transmitting, signaling, receiving, and decoding systems through the use of radiant energy and mechanical-chemical and electromechanical means.
3. *Transportation* — providing movement of people, materials, products, and services. Content would include information on propulsion, guidance, control, and structural and suspension systems for the solution of problems related to terrestrial, marine, atmospheric, and space environments.

If the proposals for a technology-based industrial arts curriculum are incorporated into the comprehensive secondary school program, industrial arts will undoubtedly take on a new image. Its position in general education will be solidified and its integration with other subjects will be axiomatic. It will necessitate the retraining of teachers and the opening of the industrial arts curriculum to the entire school.

Incorporation of Trades and Industry Courses

A present development in the industrial arts field is a movement to incorporate trade and industrial (T&I) education into the industrial arts

[9] Ibid., p. 12.

area. The matter is debated at professional meetings. Those who contend that the fields have separate identities suggest that industrial arts
is an educational program designed to provide opportunities for the
study of tools, materials, processes, products, and the roles of people
in the industrial enterprise, while trade and industrial education is a
special education designed to provide opportunities for the development of skills, knowledge, and attitudes that will lead to successful
entry and advancement within a trade or industrial occupation.[10] To
the untrained arbitrator in the matter, the preceding definition appears
to describe necessary elements of both fields.

Another authority attempts to refine the distinction between T&I and
industrial arts as follows: (1) education related to modern technology
versus education and training for a job in technology; (2) general information versus specific information; (3) exploration of multiple areas
versus specialization in one area; (4) a program based on creativity and
design versus a program based on function; (5) exercises and projects
versus production techniques; and (6) accent on appreciation and consumer utilization versus emphasis on construction and manufacturing.
From the distinction in the two fields emerges a clear-cut definition of
industrial arts. It is problematic whether industrial arts will be combined with T&I or whether they will operate as separate but compatible
fields; the possibilities furnish interesting speculation.

INDUSTRIAL PROCESSES IN THE SHOP

The length and breadth of a good industrial arts program depends on
the space and variety of industrial processes that can be accommo-
dated. Too frequently the industrial arts instructor is limited in knowledge and skill in teaching a number of industrial processes. Other parts
of this chapter mention many of the shop activities of a modern industrial arts program. The material that follows here is presented to
give a limited idea of new ideas being developed. Space does not allow examples in all areas.

Electricity and Electronics

Basic electricity has been one of the instructional areas of industrial
arts. Its content usually includes resistance, Ohm's law, schematic
reading, series and parallel circuits, inductance, capacitance, reactance,
and resonance. Much of this is related to home wiring.

---

[10] C. Thomas Dean, "The Industrial Education Concept: How Viable?" *American Vocational Journal* (February 1976), pp. 76–78.

In many industrial arts programs, the introduction to basic electronics is added to the program on electricity. This means the study of power supplies, amplifiers, and oscillator circuits, as well as heterodyning and the superheterodyne AM radio. Similarities and differences between vacuum tubes and solid state devices are also studied.

Electronics for advanced industrial arts students can be made interesting. The resistor cube appeals to the electronics student's sense of aesthetic form while covering basic principles taught in direct-current courses related to most electronic circuits.

Presented as a project, the resistor cube can give the student greater understanding and experience in circuit tracing, simplifying circuits with equivalent circuits, tracing electron flow from negative to positive, tracing current in a series circuit and parallel circuit, and addng voltage drops in a series circuit and a parallel circuit. It can also give a good review of the application of Kirchhoff's and Ohm's laws and give a good approach to the solution of an analytical problem.

A good problem is to give students a cube formed from twelve resistors, all with the same resistance value. The problem is to calculate the total resistance between designated points A and B. Variations can be made in the problem that can lead the students through a series of calculations that are somewhat difficult but nevertheless challenging.

Drafting

One of the usual projects of an advanced drafting class is the construction of plans for an imaginary house, a theoretical structure produced as a mental exercise. The lines drawn are usually "dead" lines, the walls do not line up, and modular concepts are imperfectly understood. Many students are unable to make the connection between a set of working drawings for a house and its function.

To depart from that process, the framework of the course can be redesigned. The term is divided into four nine-week quarters to permit the construction of a scale model of all framing and carpentry work. Home design, decoration, and financing are scheduled for the first nine weeks. Working drawings of plans, elevations, and details follow in the second nine weeks. The framing and carpentry drawings take up most of the third quarter, and construction of the model rounds out the term.

To enhance interest in the project, a general contractor may be chosen and field trips to actual construction sites may be made. One of the values of this redesigned course is that students become more realistic in their choices of building size, construction methods, styles, and materials. They are aware of cost factors in plumbing, heating, and electrical work. Realistically, the student model may be the design of a student's home some day.

Graphic Arts

If industrial arts is to be truly a complete program of industrial processes, it should include an adequate program in graphic arts. Many schools do include such a program.

A good project for graphic arts experiences for students is the making of a three-panel, two-color brochure. It calls for imagination, creativity, and mechanical aptitude to solve a variety of technical problems as students expand their skills in photo-offset lithography. The project motivates students because it is flexible in content and challenging in scope, emphasizing layout and design, cold type composition, copy preparation, camera work, stripping, platemaking, presswork, and finishing operations.

Skills a student may obtain from such a graphic arts project should include the ability to: draw a complete set of layouts including thumbnails, a rough, a comprehensive, and a working dummy; compose body and display type matter either mechanically or photographically; crop and scale artwork including continuous-tone copy; and strip one- and two-color flats in tight register.

The entire process is time consuming, but it causes the students to acquaint themselves with a host of graphic processes that are used in industrial work in this area of industrial arts. Work in this field has many job opportunities for the well-trained student.

Ceramics

Industrial arts curriculum designers who are interested in keeping their programs abreast of industrial processes should investigate the use of the Ram process as used in industry. This process will give ceramics classes hands-on experience with fast, modern manufacturing methods used to create a variety of products. Ram pressing forms a prepared charge of clay between two porous molds or permeable dies mounted in a press for molding by compression. The product is released by fluid pressure forced through the permeable dies.

The first step in the process is to check out suitable materials for die construction. Pipe casings for the steel shells may be used. It is important that they be durable enough to withstand the pressures of the compression process. The completed assembly usually consists of male and female die members. Shapes of the gypsum dies may be symmetrical or asymmetrical, as long as there is a positive draft. The upper half of the die assembly has registration pins for proper alignment with the lower half. Lugs are welded to the upper casing to secure a plate into which a T-bolt is placed, passing through the top of the press plate and holding the female member to the top of the press. The casing also has a speed connector for air tapped directly into the thick-walled shell.

The gypsum cement die may be reinforced with a metal rod or "spider." Some gypsum plasters for compression dies are expensive, but Ultraeal 30 is usually available, is not so expensive, and can be used for the permeable die. It has enough compressive strength for school laboratory experimentation.

A Foundry Project

Shell molding — a foundry method developed some time ago but until recently thought too expensive and too complicated for industrial arts — can be employed in any school metal shop at minimal cost, given a basic knowledge of foundry fundamentals. The process involves mounting a metal pattern to a plate and heating to 400–600°F. A silica sand combined with a thermosetting resin binder is then dumped onto the heated pattern and allowed to cure. The cured sand forms the shape of the pattern, and the hardened mold is separated from the pattern by means of ejector pins. The two mold halves are then clamped to make a complete mold cavity ready for pouring the molten metal.

Shell molding has several advantages over other casting methods. Tolerances can be more closely controlled, less draft is required, thin walls can be produced, metals can be poured at lower temperatures, sharp contours are possible, and smooth surfaces can be obtained.

Welding

Acquiring fundamental welding skills is an important objective of a good industrial arts program. A fallacy to avoid is the early transfer to a "live job." Many instructors believe that to maintain students' interest in welding, it is important to get the students involved in a practical project as soon as possible. As soon as a student can puddle a little, he or she is placed on project work that is to furnish most of the learning experiences.

Project work usually requires very simple welding and much grinding and painting, and it benefits someone else more than the student.

The welding involved in most projects brought into the shop can be done by any student with limited training.

To be of any use to the student, that kind of experience must be controlled. The task should be selected according to the needs of the class, and students assigned to it should need that particular experience. Well-planned and supervised live work can benefit a program, but busy work has no more place in welding than it does in the classroom. Projects that provide excellent motivation should be injected at intervals when needed, but this kind of practice does not insure proficiency for later job training and possible certification. The mastery of a variety of basic techniques is much more important.

Metallurgy

The study of the whole area of metals should be an important division of a modern industrial arts program. Powder metallurgy is an ancient process that can be made an interesting part of today's industrial arts laboratory work, and it is easily introduced using existing equipment. A demonstration unit fabricating a blind bushing can include a brief history of the process and an explanation of its essential steps.

Powdered metal parts are made by compressing metal particles into a precision die. The compacted metal is then ejected from the die and heated in a controlled atmosphere sintering furnace to bond the metal particles together.

Many kinds of metal powders have been developed, but copper-base and iron-base materials are the most commonly used. The compacting of the powder blend into an article of accurate size and shape is called briquetting. Compacting techniques include mechanical, hydraulic, and isostatic pressing. Pressures range from 15 to 50 tons per square inch.

Sintering is the operation in which the metal particles in the briquette are bonded under heat in a controlled atmosphere. Temperatures are determined by the blend and are usually 60 to 80 percent of the melting temperature of the lowest melting point of the constituent metal. The atmosphere prevents oxidation of the particles that could weaken or prevent the bond. Space here does not allow for a full description of the making of a bushing, but the well-informed industrial arts teacher can use powdered metals for the demonstration.

More Use of Research

One of the most encouraging aspects of curriculum development in the industrial arts field is the amount of research going on and the availability of results for industrial arts teachers. There has been a substantial increase in the number of studies using good research techniques. These studies are based on sound analytical endeavors to identify, classify, and organize content and experiences of industrial arts students.

As is true in so many fields in education, a discouraging thing about research in industrial arts is the lack of consistent findings, particularly those dealing with techniques and modes of teaching. Little experimental evidence indicates comparative superiority of any teaching method for any specific subject matter or any group of learners. The number of variables influencing teaching effectiveness is apparently so great that researchers have not been able to isolate and identify these variables precisely enough to permit an accurate description of "best" teaching methodology.

Regardless of outcomes, it is encouraging to find so much research and experimentation going on in the field. It is a harbinger of improved techniques for the future. At present, the questionable quality of many of the instructional strategies no doubt contributes to the lack of consistency in the findings of methodology studies. The experience of curriculum workers indicates that several revisions based on large-scale field tests are required to produce quality instructional materials and methods.[11]

THE FUTURE OF INDUSTRIAL ARTS

Industrial arts curriculum planners face a dilemma in deciding what direction programs should take. Several pertinent questions are involved. Will shop class teachers acquiesce to administrative pressures to make their special charge the less capable student who cannot make it in other areas of the curriculum? Will the shop idea be replaced by area program developments? Will industrial arts programs become theory-centered classes and primarily feeders to technical education?

Probably the best answers to the foregoing questions will be found in analyzing the stature industrial arts ought to maintain in a comprehensive school. Without doubt, the field has much to offer the slow learner and, especially, the handicapped.[12] This is a responsibility that industrial arts teachers ought to capitalize on rather than reject as a thankless task. Second, industrial arts is made to order for the contributions that can be made to a technological social order where in-

[11] Melvin J. Pedras, "A Syllabus for Industrial Arts Courses," *School Shop* (September 1975), pp. 35–36.

[12] W. E. Dugger, "Participation of Special Needs Students in Industrial Arts," *Man/Society/Technology* (March 1977), pp. 185–187.

creasing demands are for purposeful leisure-time pursuits. The great "do-it-yourself" mania that has swept over the nation has not come about by accident. These needs are genuine and they should be planned for in the education program of a comprehensive school. The industrial arts shop should be a laboratory for the development of purposeful industrial and leisure-time skills. Finally, industrial arts teachers must be cognizant of the impact technology is making on American industry. The body of science, techniques, and skills related to industrial development must be constantly reviewed for the purpose of making proper adjustment in industrial arts programs so as to attract and retain students of ability commensurate with the increasing difficulty of such programs.

There is a strong possibility that industrial arts theorists will outdistance practical thinkers in the rush to bring sophistication to the field. It may appear to the practical-minded industrial arts teacher that his or her shop is to become a citadel for physical science and mathematics rather than a place where students use skilled hands to shape industrial products, as formerly conceived. And indeed, this may be true. There are those who see the industrial arts program of the future rich in applied science. Principles of physical science will be evident in a large percentage of problem-solving, project-making activities of the future shop.

Those who would bring greater sophistication to industrial arts see students involved in making telescopes and studying astronomy, learning the lapidary art from geological investigations, and engaging in a wide study of electronics involving the building and understanding of radio equipment, high-fidelity sound, and even satellite tracking. Such programs would forego the regular auto mechanics course and teach the broad field of power, its resources, its conversion and use. The industrial arts shop would be an extension of the science laboratory. Students would see meaning in scientific principles by associating phenomena with familiar products and daily operations.

Industrial arts can make a valuable contribution to the secondary comprehensive school program. The opportunity is present for the development of an industrial arts program that will be vital in the lives of secondary school youths. Courage and vision on the part of industrial arts leaders can open many new vistas in the field.

TOPICS FOR STUDY AND DISCUSSION

1. What authenticity is there to the statement that industrial arts may have the unhappy distinction of being the most misunderstood subject in the secondary school curriculum?

2. What are the points of delineation between industrial arts and vocational education?
3. Surveys show a tendency to stress industrial arts more in the junior high school than in the senior high school. What objectives would determine this?
4 Industrial arts teachers are usually conscious of the "dumping-ground" stigma attached to their field. What assessment of responsibility may be made in this matter?
5. Contrast the development of industrial arts in different sizes of school districts according to community needs.
6. What logic is there in the proposal that industrial arts has aesthetic as well as technical value?
7. Identify the commonalty of experiences for students enrolled in courses of industrial arts and home economics.
8. Prepare a report for a local school board that would justify or reject industrial arts as a required subject in the secondary school curriculum.
9. Where should emphasis be placed in curriculum planning for a good industrial arts program for modern needs — on the unit shop or the general shop?
10. What answers should be given to those who ask why a good industrial arts program should have precedence over a specialized vocational education program in a comprehensive secondary school?
11. The requirements of engineering schools sometimes suggest mechanical drawing as a desirable subject for college preparation. Should provisions be made to separate this subject from the regular industrial arts program?
12. Refute the charge that increasing industrial and technological content in the industrial arts curriculum tends to limit laboratory experiences.
13. Critics of DeVore say his proposals are too theoretical and not likely to be implemented in the industrial arts field. Do you agree or disagree? Why?

SELECTED REFERENCES

Components of Teacher Education. Twentieth Yearbook, American Council of Industrial Arts Education. Bloomington, Ill.: McKnight & McKnight Publishing Company, 1971.
> This is a good compilation of material on industrial arts content with each chapter written by a different authority. Materials covered include technological dimensions of content, theoretical bases of content, scope and sequence of content, and elements of instructional methods.

DeVore, Paul W. *Structure and Content Foundations for Curriculum Development.* Washington, D. C.: American Industrial Arts Association, 1967.
> This is a valuable pamphlet on the relationship of the industrial arts field to technology. The function of industrial arts as a part of formal education is reviewed. DeVore proposes that the body of knowledge called technology contains the content reservoir from which industrial arts curriculum content can be derived.

Drake, George R. *The Complete Handbook of Power Tools.* Reston, Va.: Reston Publishing Company, 1974.

Each chapter is devoted to a different tool. It gives descriptions, major parts, cutting elements, controls, and adjustments. Hints for attaining professional results and the kinks of each tool are discussed. In addition to tool needs, workshop setups, and floor plans, electricity, lighting, and care of tools are presented. Charts are provided for English–metric conversions; choosing the correct drill, nail, and screw size; determining the proper wood joint; and illustrations of how to purchase the right size and amount of lumber.

Holland, John L. *Making Vocational Choices: A Theory of Careers.* Englewood Cliffs, N. J.: Prentice-Hall, 1973.

This is a career selection book for the identity of an appropriate work environment. The book should be an aid for early secondary youth to develop a self-image on which to base career-related decisions. Holland discusses several environments that affect career decision making, including mechanical, as characterized by aggressive behavior showing an interest in motor coordination; investigative, which operates by thinking rather than acting; social, which points to the need for attention getting; enterprising, which is marked by a manifestation of verbal skills, and artistic, which requires strong self-expression through artistic activities.

Industrial Arts in the Technologies. Morgantown: West Virginia University Publications, 1970.

This is a brief report of five predoctoral and five postdoctoral students who spent an academic year in building a model for industrial arts education. The result is a detailed rationale and structure of a model program for the education of teacher-scholars in technology. It forms the basis for a new type of industrial arts curriculum for secondary schools.

Johnson, Harold V. *Manufacturing Processes, Metals and Plastics.* Peoria, Ill.: Charles A. Bennett Company, 1973.

Johnson covers all metal processes thoroughly. He also covers materials structure, machines, planning, operation, production sequences, and relationships of all divisions in production. The book contains an excellent unit on programming and tape preparation in numerical controls and presents an in-depth treatment of foundry and a section on special casting processes. A special feature is the directions for performing commercially accepted tests on a wide variety of common materials.

Roberts, Roy W. *Vocational and Practical Arts Education.* New York: Harper & Row, 1971.

This book contains a historical development of the field and sets forth guiding principles for curriculum decisions. An attempt is made to put in proper perspective the relationship between vocational and industrial arts education. The use of the words *practical arts* in the book title will bother many industrial arts educators.

Sacks, Raymond. *Welding: Principles and Practices.* Peoria, Ill.: Charles A. Bennett Company, 1975.

Sacks develops well the theory and practice of arc welding, and he also covers gas and semiautomatic welding. Photographs and drawings supplement the materials, and good questions are presented for consideration.

Wagner, Willis H. *Modern Industry*. Chicago: American Technical Society, 1975.

The author provides up-to-date information about the organizational structure, equipment, materials, and processes used in manufacturing and construction industries. Simplified explanations range from the operation of an atomic energy plant, to the control of machines with magnetic or punched tapes, to the computerized typesetting process. This book has value for the planning of an industrial arts program for both teachers and curriculum planners.

10
Mathematics

Mathematics, inexhaustible as an area of discovery and creativity, satisfies both emotional and creative urges as well as scientific and utilitarian needs. Not only does mathematics have its useful aspects, but it also has philosophic, aesthetic, psychological, and historical aspects.

New uses of mathematics are being discovered constantly in the fields of physics, chemistry, and engineering, and even more astonishing uses are being found in other fields. The biologist is applying mathematical theory to the study of inheritance, industry is using mathematics in scheduling production and distribution, the social scientist is using ideas from modern statistics, and the psychologist is using the mathematics of game theory. The planners of the mathematics curriculum in the secondary schools must move rapidly to keep pace with the needs and development of these new applications.

The new uses of mathematics require a greater understanding of the structure of mathematical systems and less manipulation of formula and equation. There is more emphasis on the construction of mathematical models and symbolic representation of ideas and relationships.

Most computation previously done by humans is now done by machines. Both the changed emphasis and the increased use of mathematics cause the subject to be more and more a part of the total cultural pattern.

New programs, developed for both the elementary and secondary schools, are designed to attract more youths into the study of mathematics and to give a more realistic preparation to those who pursue the subject. A number of experiments have demonstrated the feasibility and advantages of teaching new topics in secondary school courses. New ideas, language, and symbolism help to give a better understanding of mathematics. Obsolete material is being replaced with more significant subject matter.

THE BEGINNING OF THE NEW MATHEMATICS PERIOD

During the period when important changes were first being made in the mathematics curriculum, quite a controversy raged over the use of the word *new*. While the difference of opinion was largely semantic, certain authorities took issue with the idea of calling the various reorganizations of subject matter new mathematics. To avoid this relatively unimportant argument, other authorities decided to use the term *modern mathematics*.

For purposes of clarification, it should be noted that the mathematics in the programs being introduced was not new; that is, it was not recently discovered. What was new was the emphasis given to topics that were not previously treated. This did not mean a rejection of much traditional subject matter, but rather an extensive reorganization of curricular material.

Probably the most important characteristic of the new mathematics was not in the content but in the spirit in which mathematics was approached. To emphasize the underlying unity and coherence of the subject and the interrelationships among the basic concepts, the new programs included such unifying elements as the concept of sets, the structure of the number system, coordinate geometry, inequalities and equalities, and appropriate mathematical language.

The new programs eliminated subject matter that had little relevance to modern needs. Elaborate and special cases of factoring, obscure geometry theorems, and logarithmic solutions of all the special cases of triangles by trigonometry were gone. Algebra was no longer presented as a collection of isolated techniques and formal mechanical procedures for solving verbal problems. Instead, the unified basic structure of algebra was used in developing algebraic skills. Such a point of view gave students more opportunities to explore and discover mathematical concepts on their own and to learn what constitutes mathematics and how a mathematician thinks.

DEVELOPMENT OF MATHEMATICS PROGRAMS DURING THE 1960S

Probably the best known and most widely used of the modern mathematics programs is that of the School Mathematics Study Group (SMSG), which was formed at a conference of mathematicians sponsored by the American Mathematical Society and financed by the National Science Foundation. In this program, students continued to manipulate numbers, but the prime objective was to develop an awareness of the basic properties of numbers. SMSG developed units of material for grades 4 through 12, testing the material in each unit extensively before publishing it as a textbook. Each unit presented topics and problems for mathematical analysis, repeating the topics in sequence for deeper treatment and continuous review. These concepts and their relationships form the structure of mathematics; therefore the program makers assumed that they were central to all mathematics.

SMSG courses dealt with relatively conventional topics rather than introducing new topics, but the organization and method of presentation had undergone definite change. The familiarity of experienced teachers with many of the topics was the basis for adopting the SMSG materials, since the teachers could use the SMSG units with relative ease following the directions provided in the teaching manuals.

In grades 7 and 8 the SMSG material covered elements of the total secondary sequence: abstract concepts, the role of definition, development of precise vocabulary and thought, experimentation, and mathematical truth. Although the course for grade 10 was predominantly plane geometry, it included some material on solid geometry, an introduction to analytic geometry, and a review of algebra. Grade 11 included trigonometry, vectors, logarithms, mathematical induction, and complex numbers. The grade 12 material had two divisions. One was a study of elementary functions such as polynomial, exponential, logarithmic, and trigonometric operations. It included an introduction of geometrically meaningful methods of handling areas, tangents, and maximum-minimum problems that gave students an intuitive background for calculus. The second division was an introduction to matrix algebra, including problems involving systems of linear equations and geometry. Careful attention was given to algebraic structure.

From this review of the secondary school area of SMSG mathematics, it may be seen that the old compartmentalization of subject matter has been dissolved by problem-solving techniques that require the use of the interrelated facets of the whole field of mathematics. These techniques placed a utilitarian value on mathematics.

The movement in mathematics that was most concerned with curriculum reform started with the formation of the University of Illinois Committee on School Mathematics (UICSM) in 1951. The committee grew out of a desire of the colleges of education, engineering, and liberal arts to improve their freshman mathematics courses, but soon the committee's interest and emphasis shifted to high school mathematics.

The UICSM program (often called the Beberman Program in honor of its director, Dr. Max Beberman) presented mathematics as a consistent, unified subject. Students were led to discover principles for themselves and to develop manipulative skills necessary for problem solving. It was an active process, with the student doing mathematics rather than being told about mathematics. The secondary school program, for grades 9 through 12, consisted of eleven units organized around the following topics: (1) the arithmetic of real numbers; (2) pronumerals, generalizations, and algebraic manipulations; (3) equations and inequations, applications; (4) ordered pairs and graphs; (5) relations and functions; (6) geometry; (7) mathematical induction; (8) sequences; (9) exponential and logarithmic functions; (10) circular functions and trigonometry; and (11) polynomial functions and complex numbers. Units 1 through 4 were intended for grade 9, units 5 and 6 for grade 10, units 7 and 8 for grade 11, and units 9 through 11 for grade 12.

In theory, the UICSM program was designed for all students. In practice, it is likely that the first two years were basic and the final two years were for advanced students. Some teachers thought the whole program was for only the more capable students. This opinion could have resulted from the inexperience of the teachers in the use of the material or from the faulty background of the students.

The University of Maryland mathematics project dealt exclusively with grades 7 and 8. Its objectives were development of precision in using the language of mathematics, appreciation of the structure of number systems, facility in the use of inductive and deductive methods of reasoning, and acquisition of an understanding of metric and nonmetric geometry. A strong thread of algebraic concepts ran through the program.

In grade 7, the Maryland program included such topics as properties of natural numbers, systems of numeration, symbols, factors and primes, mathematical systems, points, lines, curves, and planes. Attention was also given to proofs and equations in the system of real numbers. The grade 8 topics included the system of rational numbers, the system of real numbers, and the system of integers under addition. Logic and number sentences, equations, fractional number phrases, plane figures, and scientific notations for arithmetic numbers were covered. The Maryland program covered part of the material formerly presented in grades 9 and 10, and some question was raised about whether it was within the learning ability of all students in grades 7 and 8.

Several other modern programs for the teaching of mathematics have been developed within the last decade. Each is meritorious in its own right within identifiable objectives. These programs include the Greater Cleveland Mathematics Program, the Syracuse University–Webster College Madison Program, the Suppes Experimental Project, and the Ball State Experimental Program. Important contributions were also included in the *Report of the Commission on Mathematics* by the College Entrance Examination Board.

CURRICULAR IMPACT OF MODERN MATHEMATICS

Educators responsible for curriculum development in mathematics may be uncertain whether modern mathematics is catching on or whether those who adopted one of the several new programs have made the right move. It would be helpful for those in doubt to review a progress report made by the Commission on Mathematics.[1]

Since the major reforms in mathematics may be traced in part to the influence of the Commission on Mathematics of the College Board, it is of major significance to find what impact the commission's recommendations have had on the mathematical content of the curriculum of the secondary schools.

The commission recommended the following nine-point program:

1. strong preparation, both in concepts and in skills, for college mathematics at the level of calculus and analytic geometry
2. understanding of the nature and role of deductive reasoning — in algebra as well as in geometry
3. appreciation of mathematical structure ("patterns") — for example, properties of natural, rational, real, and complex numbers
4. judicious use of unifying ideas — sets, variables, functions, and relations
5. treatment of inequalities along with equations
6. incorporation with plane geometry of some coordinate geometry, and essentials of solid geometry and space perception
7. introduction in grade 11 of fundamental trigonometry — centered on coordinates, vectors, and complex numbers

---

[1] S. Irene Williams, "A Progress Report on the Implementation of the Commission on Mathematics," *The Mathematics Teacher* (October 1970), pp. 461–468.

8. emphasis in grade 12 on elementary functions (polynomial, exponential, circular)
9. recommendation of additional alternative units for grade 12: either introductory probability with statistical applications, or an introduction to modern algebra

The progress report made by the commission, based on a survey conducted by the College Entrance Examination Board, reveals how well the nine-point proposal is being implemented. Data were obtained by means of questionnaires sent to 2718 seniors who participated in College Board examinations. The general format of the questionnaire was relative to what the students had studied in secondary school mathematics.

The study indicates positive evidence of the commission's recommendations being incorporated into secondary school mathematics curricula. The following examples are pertinent:

1. Structure and properties of the number system had been studied by 85 percent of the students — more than three-fourths — prior to the junior year.
2. Approximately 90 percent of the students had studied inequalities along with equations.
3. Almost half the students reported their geometry course as including some coordinate geometry, one-third reported some solid geometry, and one-fifth reported both solid and coordinate geometry.
4. Indirect proof had been studied by 80 percent of the students, and propositional logic by about 65 percent.
5. Approximately 95 percent reported encounter with trigonometric functions prior to the twelfth year.
6. While only 35 percent of the students had studied complex numbers and 55 percent had studied the solution of triangles by logarithms, approximately 75 percent had studied complex number systems.
7. The data show an acceptance of sets as a unifying idea in mathematics. There is a general increase in acceptance after grade 7.
8. More than half the students had encountered the terms domain and range of a function, period of a function, and amplitude and frequency of a function.
9. Measures of central tendency and interpretation of data had been studied by about 40 percent of the students, and measures of dispersion by about 20 percent.

10. Seventeen percent of the students had enrolled in advanced placement courses in mathematics.

The data from the survey indicate that innovations by the Commission on Mathematics and other curriculum-reform groups have begun to appear in the programs of secondary school students and that recommended topics are being integrated into mathematics programs rather than attached superficially.

CONTROVERSY CONCERNING GEOMETRY

Curriculum reform will continue to center around the nine expectations of the Commission on Mathematics. But a puzzling issue remains unsettled: what to do with geometry. Authorities strongly disagree about content, length of time to be studied, and integrating relationships with other mathematical subject matter. It appears that the early introduction of geometric concepts on an intuitive level will be continued, the usual synthetic geometry will be changed to incorporate increasingly certain characteristics of coordinate geometry, and strong leanings toward the treatment of geometric transformations will emerge.

Great strides have been made in the development of the mathematical curriculum for elementary and secondary school students. Since the new mathematics was introduced, programs for arithmetic and algebra have been developed with a certain amount of universal acceptance. Such has not been the case with geometry however.[2]

Educators agree that the objective in the teaching of algebra is the development of properties for the fields of rational, real, and complex numbers. It is easy to grasp the notion of a field. But they cannot even agree on what the subject of geometry is about. To some, geometry is the study of geometric figures, while others think it is identified with a method of proof. Many authorities contend that geometry is the study of the invariants of transformation groups. Much of the controversy in secondary mathematics centers around whether transformation geometry is the answer. A modified "yes" appears to be emerging.

The many different classifications of geometries — Euclidean, affine, non-Euclidean, projective, algebraic, and differential — further complicate mathematics curriculum decisions. Each of these geometries may be studied in two, three, four, or any number of dimensions. In

[2] Richard H. Gast, "The High School Geometry Controversy: Is Transformation Geometry the Answer?" *The Mathematics Teacher* (January 1971), pp. 37–40.

fact, the problem is so complicated that agreement is almost nonexistent among mathematics curriculum planners.

Presumably, curriculum designers must decide on objectives for the formation and content of geometry. In one approach, a composite of authorities may be used. For a long time, mathematics teachers have been aware of the inadequacies of geometry courses based on abbreviated versions of Euclid's *Elements*. The following changes in course composition have been tried in this and other countries:[3]

1. the use of modified versions of the axioms
2. the simultaneous development of plane and solid geometry
3. the early introduction of metric ideas such as length of segments, angle measure, and area of plane figures
4. reliance on the properties of the real-number system
5. the introduction of coordinate geometry
6. the use of vector methods
7. the use of those transformations of the plane, called isometrics, that leave the distances between points unchanged
8. the inclusion of some non-Euclidean geometry
9. the development of Euclidean space as a vector space with an inner product
10. the development of the Euclidean plane as a coordinatized affine plane, with the real-number system used as the set of coordinates on a line and with a perpendicularity relation introduced in the plane

Two of the new mathematics programs developed in the United States are based on part of the preceding listing. The School Mathematics Study Group used the first five in varying proportions in two of their courses, Geometry and Geometry with Coordinates. The University of Illinois Committee for School Mathematics emphasized the ninth item.

Another approach to the format and content of geometry courses in the secondary school mathematics program would be to follow objectives as formulated by a recognized authority. Allendoerfer offers both objectives and approaches for the teaching of geometry. His objectives include the following:

1. an understanding of the basic facts about geometric figures in the plane and geometric solids in space

---

[3] Gail Spitler and Marian Weinstein, "Congruence Extended: A Setting for Activity in Geometry," *The Mathematics Teacher* (January 1976), pp. 18–21.

2. an understanding of the basic facts about geometric transformations, such as reflections, rotations, and translations
3. an appreciation of the deductive method
4. an introduction to imaginative thinking
5. an integration of geometric ideas with other parts of mathematics

Allendoerfer offers a selection of one of three approaches. First, the synthetic approach, which is the method used by Euclid and is familiar to all mathematics teachers. Second, the analytic approach, which solves geometric problems by means of algebra through the use of coordinate systems. And third, the vector approach, in which vectors are used to develop theory through the use of standard vector algebra.

The controversy over geometry is academic, but the decision about how to incorporate the subject into a mathematics program of a secondary school is real. Authorities in mathematics, both as individuals and in groups, have much to offer in the way of objectives and approaches, but the final decision must be made on the understanding of the nature of geometry and the conception of goals that individual teachers are trying to reach.

COMPUTER-ASSISTED INSTRUCTION

Many technological devices have promised hope for the improvement of instruction in the schools. Among these are educational films, television, language laboratories, programmed instruction, and teaching machines. For one reason or another, none of those devices has lived up to its early promise.

With the development of the electronic computer, a new technology raises hopes for improved procedures in education. Computer-assisted instruction (CAI) promises to provide some of the quantum jumps that have been hoped for in the past. Computer-assisted instruction has the flexibility and capacity for individualizing learning processes necessary for adaptive education. Sophisticated computer-assisted instruction has been developed in mathematics. The same thing is true for science, music, social studies, and English. Materials in other fields are under construction.

The three fundamental characteristics of computer applications to mathematics instruction as well as to other subject matter areas are: (1) the ability of a prestored program in a computer system to evaluate a student's responses and provide information regarding the correctness of these responses; (2) the active responding by the student; and (3) the opportunity to individualize instruction not only at the level of achievement, but in reference to the student's specific interests and abilities. These three characteristics involve individual pacing, logical presentation, small-step development, and immediate reinforcement.[4]

Computer-assisted instruction has had an impact on instructional methods. There is increasing concern for developing techniques that extend theories of learning to the actual learning situation. In view of the fact that a computer facility makes possible an environment for careful control of complex variables purported to contribute to effective and efficient learning, it behooves curriculum planners in mathematics to investigate the effects of feedback variables, types of review, and levels of achievement on growth of understanding for immediate and delayed retention.

A computer mathematics course focuses on a narrow but extremely important use of the computer: problem solving and problem investigation. Computer-assisted problem solving has great potential in aiding mathematics instruction.[5] Topics most usually taught are branching concepts, use of the quadratic formula, flow chart applications, use of interaction computer language, solving systems of equations, interaction techniques, nesting procedures, prime number problems, construction of tables and arrays, debugging techniques, approximating roots of equations, and organization of a computer system.

The impact of the electronic computer on the curriculum of the student cannot be overestimated. Elementary concepts of numerical analysis are mathematically based. Students need to be acquainted with the capabilities, limitations, and idiosyncrasies of computers.

ADJUSTMENTS IN PROGRAMS

The successful use of mathematics depends on knowing more than a vast body of inarticulated facts; unifying structures are requisite to practical problem solving. The school mathematics educators of the 1960s experimented with sets, numeration systems, axiomatic systems, mappings, and transformations, but not all these structures proved important in the development of mathematics as a body of knowledge.

In present-day mathematics programs, such topics as sets and numeration systems are being deemphasized and in some cases entirely omitted. A clear sense of structure and relationships continues to be essential. When unifying structures such as functions, transformations,

[4] Richard Johnsonbaugh, "Applications of Calculators and Computers to Limits," *The Mathematics Teacher* (January 1976), pp. 61–64.

[5] Aaron L. Buchman and Frank S. Hawthorne, "The Content of High School Computer Mathematics Courses," *School Science and Mathematics* (October 1975), pp. 543–549.

and systems are introduced into the mathematics curriculum, they must be made integral, operating elements in the program. Structures must be seen as summarizing and simplifying elements in mathematics.

The significance of mathematics for the vast majority of students lies in its usefulness in problem solving and other applications. Links between the world of mathematics and the world of reality are an increasing part of modern mathematics programs. Emphasis is on the unity of mathematics and the common procedures of mathematical thought. Distinctions between arithmetic, algebra, and geometry are disappearing. Ordering, indexing, counting, and measuring are treated together as major noncalculating uses of numbers. Variables are used in expressing functional relationships and in stating axioms and properties. Vectors are used to connect the concepts of algebra and geometry.

ACTION IN THE FIELD

Since mathematics is considered a basic subject, it continues to be a target for any back-to-the-basics movement in education. Similar to the charge that students cannot read is the charge that students cannot compute. Blame is placed on new mathematics programs that do not emphasize drill and practice. No rationale is presented that would determine the relative importance of computation within the set of all mathematics skills that a student ought to command.[6]

Some educators contend that the development of inexpensive pocket calculators will change both the kinds of computational skills that are taught and the ways in which they are taught. The electronic calculator is regarded as a supplementary tool that affords an alternative and an easier method of computation. A student may use a calculator to find numerical results to a problem without improving his or her theoretical grasp of the problem. There is, however, another point of view. A student who looks at how the calculator interacts with the problem may gain insight into the problem's theoretical aspects. It is problematic whether calculators will supplement or diminish the need for computational skills. It is reasonable to assume, however, that teachers will experiment with pocket calculators, focusing on their use as a basic tool in successful problem solving.[7]

[6] R. Taylor, "What to Do About Basic Skills in Mathematics," *Today's Education* (March 1977), pp. 32–33.

[7] H. O. Pollak, "Hand-held Calculators and Potential Redesign of the School Mathematics Curriculum," *Mathematics Teacher* (April 1977), pp. 293–296.

Four projects are under way that offer alternatives for updating mathematics programs. The first, under the sponsorship of the School Mathematics Study Group (SSM), is a course designed to include only mathematics concepts that are desirable for all students to know. In SSM, the traditional grade placement of topics is ignored; topics from arithmetic, algebra, and geometry are intermingled and arranged in a sequence that provides help in the development of a topic from several mathematics fields. Solution sets of algebraic equations are described and interpreted geometrically, while algebra is used to help describe points in coordinate geometry. The concept of function is introduced early and serves as a unifying influence in the discussion of many different types of mathematical content.

The School Mathematics Study Group has a special edition of the material for low achievers. The program introduces the same general content areas as the first two years of the basic version that was developed for average and above-average mathematics students. However, the material has been rewritten to have greater appeal to junior high school students whose elementary school mathematics achievement was very low. The reading level has been reduced, as has been the amount of reading to be done, and students are provided with addition and multiplication tables and flow charts for computational algorithms. This program reduces the computational demands on the students, freeing them to give more attention to mathematical concepts and relationships.

A third program that is ready for classroom use comes from the University of Illinois Committee on School Mathematics. It has been field tested and is designed to present elementary algebra, geometry, and probability from the standpoint of application. The emphasis is on the way abstract mathematical systems are applied to specific contexts and real-life situations.

Linear functions are introduced in the Illinois program as time-position relations of moving objects. Quadratic functions are used to describe gravitational motion. Systems of two or three variables arise from problem situations that involve cost functions. These variables can include uniform planar motion and systems of weights on an ordinary balance beam.

A fourth alternative mathematics program is offered by the Secondary School Mathematics Curriculum Study group at Columbia University. This program eliminates the usual separation of mathematics into several different branches and focuses on fundamental concepts and structures that underlie all branches. This is a new attempt to incorporate such thinking into secondary school mathematics courses, at least for capable students.

Unification is brought about by building the curriculum around fundamental concepts such as set, relation, mapping, operation, and basic structures such as group, ring, field, and vector space. This unified organization, along with the elimination of a number of traditional topics no longer considered useful, permits the inclusion of such modern applications as statistics, probability, computer-oriented problems, and linear programming.

The foregoing programs are not all-inclusive, but they do represent types of developmental efforts in secondary school mathematics. They further show that progress in modern mathematics programs continues along lines of synthesis, eclecticism, and measurable choice. Programs are being modified to meet the changing needs of students. Curriculum planners in mathematics will need to explore further the work being done in the Boston University Mathematics Program, the University of Oregon Studies, and the Unified Science–Mathematics Project at the Massachusetts Institute of Technology.

MATHEMATICS IN THE COMPREHENSIVE SCHOOL

It is evident that mathematics plays an important role in the development of a comprehensive school curriculum. The subject matter is constantly growing not only in advanced mathematics but also in the elementary phases of the subject. Mathematics is being called on today to meet a wide variety of needs that could not possibly have been anticipated a few years ago.

One of the main factors pointing to the significance of mathematics in a comprehensive school program is the changing emphasis in the field. It is moving away from human computation to an understanding and construction of the symbolic representation of factors that relate to scientific or social situations. As has been previously suggested, new mathematical ideas, language, and symbolism are being introduced to give a better understanding of the subject, thus widening the range of student abilities to comprehend and enjoy the subject.[8]

The cooperative effort of college mathematics professors and elementary and secondary classroom teachers in developing new programs of mathematics will lead to better articulation between secondary school and college mathematics programs. Practical applications of mathematical material, and better integration of mathematical subject matter with the total curriculum, will give greater continuity

[8] Richard E. Cowan and Robert C. Clary, "Identifying and Teaching Essential Mathematical Skills," *The Mathematics Teacher* (February 1978), pp. 130–133.

to the total school program and involve more pupils in mathematics than ever before.

One of the problems surrounding the introduction of modern mathematics programs into the curriculum is the determination of what level of student ability is best suited for such programs. Some educators contend that most of the programs favor the superior and college-bound student. Only experience and valid research will show if this contention is true. A good program in any subject-matter area in a comprehensive school will provide for the talented as well as the slow learners.

Accelerated programs leading to advanced placement should be part of the mathematical offerings of a comprehensive school. In many cases this acceleration allows the student to be exposed to a full year of calculus while still in high school. A competent secondary mathematics teacher will enrich classes for superior students with simplified or intuitive-level topics that are sure to be studied in college-level mathematics.

Unfortunately, some average and slow learners have developed a distaste and fear of mathematics that may be carried throughout their lives. Teachers must convince students that mathematics is worth learning, that there is a purpose in the mathematics program. In mathematics, learning is cumulative, and the slow learners will fall hopelessly behind if the program is not adjusted to them. Slow learners go through substantially the same mental processes as their more fortunate peers, but they have a different rate of perception. A well-adjusted program of mathematics in a comprehensive school provides for all rates of learning.

TOPICS FOR STUDY AND DISCUSSION

1. Evaluate the use of calculators by mathematics students for computational purposes.
2. Discuss the dichotomy between those who stress the identity of geometry and those who would integrate arithmetic, algebra, and geometry.
3. How does the back-to-the-basics movement in education correlate with the progressive concepts in modern mathematics?
4. Evaluate the impact of computer-assisted instruction on mathematics as compared with other subjects.
5. The introduction of pocket calculators into the classroom is the source of extensive debate. What is the answer?
6. What other alternative mathematics programs are available beyond those offered herein?
7. As a term assignment, construct a complete program of mathematics for a senior high school of grades 9–12.

SELECTED REFERENCES

Bassler, Otto C., and Kolb, John R. *Learning to Teach Secondary School Mathematics.* Scranton, Penna.: Intext Educational Publishers, 1971.
This book includes a large collection of specific exercises that either simulate aspects of the teaching process or identify recurring problems of content. Part I pertains to general pedagogical issues that must be considered to become an effective teacher of mathematics. Part II deals with specific subjects or mathematics at a particular grade level and the problems that are peculiar to these levels of mathematics teaching.

Butler, Charles H.; Wren, F. Lynwood; and Banks, J. Houston. *The Teaching of Secondary Mathematics.* New York: McGraw-Hill Book Company, 1970.
This book concerns the evolving program of secondary mathematics encompassing modern curriculum problems and means to effective learning and teaching of mathematics. Separate sections are devoted to teaching junior and senior high school students as well as specialized chapters on teaching algebra, geometry, trigonometry, and calculus.

Greenberg, Marvin Jay. *Euclidean and Non-Euclidean Geometries.* San Francisco: W. H. Freeman and Company, 1974.
Greenberg explores the postulates of both geometries in depth and discusses the historical development and philosophical implications of both. The major emphasis deals with the comparison between Euclidean and hyperbolic geometry.

Johnson, Donovan A., and Rising, Gerald R. *Guidelines for Teaching Mathematics.* Belmont, Calif.: Wadsworth Publishing Company, 1972.
The authors consider the foundations for mathematics instruction: the current status of the mathematics curriculum, some psychological-philosophical bases, and the goals and objectives of mathematics instruction. Specific sections pertain to highly pragmatic problems of day-to-day classroom teaching and detailed instructional activities related to specific aspects of the mathematics program. Part IV is devoted to ways to provide for individual learning differences.

Shaw, Robert A. "The Pendulum Swings Back in Junior High/Middle School Mathematics." National Association of Secondary School Principals *Bulletin* (October 1974), pp. 90–95.
Shaw contends that junior high school mathematics programs are in a state of flux. He takes a look at goals, behavior objectives, and learner-centered approaches, and questions the continuation of fragmentation in junior high school mathematics. There is a good discussion about the importance of evaluation.

Tankard, George G., Jr. *Curriculum Improvement: An Administrator's Guide.* West Nyack, N. Y.: Parker Publishing Company, 1974.
This easy-to-follow guide for helping determine what needs improving discusses current approaches and furnishes curriculum guides for finalizing programs. It defines the role of the administrator and provides a framework for evaluating his or her plans.

Triola, Mario F. *Mathematics and the Modern World.* Menlo Park, Calif.: Cummings Publishing Company, 1973.

Extensive artwork illustrates the relationship of mathematics to the modern world, and historical sections within each chapter portray the development of specific mathematical disciplines in the broader perspective of the times and social conditions in which they grew. The text concentrates on modern mathematics because almost all the branches of mathematics have undergone their most significant growth during or after the Renaissance.

Trueblood, Cecil R., and Jansson, Lars C. "Mathematics Curriculum Projects: Analysis and Comparison." National Association of Secondary School Principals *Bulletin* (November 1974), pp. 88–96.

The authors present a scheme for the analysis and comparison of mathematics programs being considered for adoption in school systems. They offer a model for accurate, comprehensive, integrated descriptions of programs under consideration. This book will be helpful for curriculum planners desiring to make adjustments in programs already being used.

11

Physical Education, Health, and Safety Education

Curriculum planners in the field of physical education are joining other subject matter specialists in proclaiming a new era; hence the birth of a new physical education program. Advocates of the new program admit that the idea has not yet swept the field but they do report encouraging gains.

A careful survey of what is included in the new physical education program and what objectives are espoused causes one to wonder what is new about it. This is the same evaluation given to supposedly "new" approaches to other subjects. Similarly, as in other subjects, the new physical education is a rearrangement of objectives to be emphasized and a new arrangement of teaching strategies to be used.[1]

The new physical education involves lifetime sports rather than the usual team sports. Movement education is stressed in the elementary school, and the individualization of instruction with the inculcation of

[1] George Leonard, "Physical Education for Life," *Today's Education* (October 1975), pp. 75–76.

strong self-concepts at every grade level is advocated. In the secondary school program, there is a deemphasis of dress regulations and uniforms and everything else that gets in the way of instruction and play. At levels below the secondary school, students learn ball handling. Since every student handles a ball and every student moves, no one sits around waiting a turn and no one loses.

Planners of new physical education programs are taking note of changes in adult physical activities as exemplified by the growing army of joggers, hikers, swimmers, and cyclists who are becoming increasingly knowledgeable about the benefits and long-term satisfaction of cardiovascular conditioning. They advocate a retreat from sedentary television activities to the tennis courts, lakes, streams, fields, and trails. Noted also is the creation of new games for the whole family such as yogi tag, frisbee, infinity volleyball, the mating game, and circle football. In these games, everyone is on the varsity and everyone plays. Further noted is the increase in dance, martial arts, and yoga, where body, mind, and spirit are in harmony.

ATTENTION TO MOTOR LEARNING

The latest area of emphasis in physical education centers around motor learning. A survey of programs for preparing teachers of physical education reveals such courses as Motor Learning, Psychological Basis of Activity, Psychology of Human Behavior, and Human Motor Performance. Despite the apparent simplicity of the term, there appears to be quite a diversity of opinion about how motor learning applies to physical education. An all-encompassing view is that all physical education is motor learning. One singular viewpoint stresses experimental aspects — to analyze and apply research findings to the learning of motor skills. Then there are those who discuss human movement from a conceptual viewpoint and talk about such elements as time, force, and space. Others are concerned with the physical activity from an integrated point of view and stress neurological and perceptual mechanisms.

Motor learning is the unique concern of physical education because it involves movement, and movement is the essence of physical education. Motor learning is the purposive integration of movements into effective patterns of action. By definition, it is the learning that may be observed and evaluated in terms of relatively permanent changes in motor behavior.[2]

[2] Charles Corbin, et al., Concepts in Physical Education (Dubuque, Ia.: Wm. C. Brown Company Publishers, 1974), pp. 22–24.

If curriculum objectives in physical education are to be based on motor learning, it brings a new dimension to program planning for physical education in the secondary schools. Curriculum expertise will need to include background in the various branches of psychology, physiology, neurophysiology, and human development. Much of physical education instruction has involved how to do things, but advocates of motor learning are more interested in *what* to do It may be noted, however, that although motor learning is identified in the long list of physical education objectives presented later, it does not dominate the listing. It is problematic what the final influence of motor learning will be in the shaping of the secondary school physical education program, but there is no doubt that curriculum planners must recognize its importance and shape programs accordingly.

STATE-MANDATED PROGRAMS

Physical education continues to be plagued by state-mandated programs. These programs result from the apparent neglect and low priority that local programs give to the field. The worst features of the state-mandated programs are the standardization of content and procedures and the lack of recognition of local needs. New York State has one of the better recently completed programs; certain of its features could serve as a model for curriculum development in other states.

The New York State program took two years for development, and it involved hundreds of physical educators and curriculum directors throughout the state. The program requires each school district to develop and implement plans to provide physical education experiences for all students. These plans must be on file and available for inspection. Objectives listed are: (1) to provide knowledge and appreciation of physical education, and (2) to make each individual aware of the effect of physical activities on the body. Activities are to be adapted to meet the needs of students who are temporarily or permanently unable to benefit from participation in the regular program.

The New York State program calls for the continued evaluation of the instructional program and the assessment of individual student needs.[3] Cumulative records on each student must be maintained. In grades 7 through 12, all students must have the opportunity for daily physical education upon request, and all students must participate in the program a minimum of three periods per calendar week during one

[3] George H. Grover, "New York State's New Regulations Governing Physical Education," *Journal of Physical Education and Recreation* (September 1975), pp. 29–30.

semester and two periods the other semester. This means that there can be no five-period program in one semester and none in the other.

Other facets of the New York program require comparable time in extraclass activities for those who exhibit a modicum of skills in regular classes. Athletes are not automatically excused. They too must show a modicum of physical education skills. A physician must exempt the handicapped, designating particular activities in which the particular student cannot participate. Other incidentals include diploma credit for physical education, the recognition of comparable off-campus activities, and the regulation of class size to conform to appropriate instructional patterns. Girls and boys must have the same degree of opportunity and equal facilities.

INSTRUCTIONAL OBJECTIVES

Physical education teachers tend to value certain kinds of objectives. Some believe that psychomotor skills should be emphasized while others contend that the primary purpose of instruction is to promote interests, attitudes, and values of physical activity. Another group points to the development of cognitive skills as a priority. No doubt a synthesis of objectives is needed to develop a workable curriculum. Objectives are usually stated in either general or specific behavioral terms.[4]

Teaching strategies are planned according to desired objectives. Structured skill-and-drill learning is used when psychomotor objectives are stressed. When affective objectives are used, a series of lead-off games, group activities, and informal learning experiences are associated with instruction. And in the case of cognitive objectives, there is much less emphasis on activity itself.

The process of teaching physical education is incomplete without some type of evaluation of results. Cognitive and psychomotor activities are much easier to evaluate objectively than are certain aspects of the affective domain. Students' ability to select, identify, name, diagram, explain, and compare are easily evaluated cognitive behaviors. Psychomotor behavior such as ability to perform, to demonstrate, and to execute a physical task are also relatively easy to measure. Problems arise in evaluating the results of affective domain objectives due to their subjective nature. One of the major needs for curriculum adjustment in physical education is to find ways to keep teachers from using objectives and methods that center around the affective domain without any regard for evaluation.

[4]Jo Mancuso, "Quality Secondary School Physical Education," *Journal of Physical Education and Recreation* (January 1978), pp. 42–52.

LACK OF STRESS ON OBJECTIVES

Periods of alternate stress and laxity are not representative of all physical education programs, but, unfortunately, such lack of continuity is the basis for many problems associated with the development of good physical education programs. Both professional educators and lay citizens must determine, once and for all, how to fulfill the objectives of a good program. Although many states have requirements for all students to be enrolled in physical education classes, the dodges used by school administrative officials are disturbing. Frequently, marching in the band or blowing a horn is substituted, and the academically inclined student needing an extra subject to go to college is excused from physical education. The development of high-powered athletic programs for public entertainment gives the lay citizen a mistaken image of the physical prowess of the entire student body.

It is difficult to understand the inconsistencies among educators' ideas regarding physical education. Every set of educational objectives published in the last half-century has listed health and physical well-being in categories of major importance. The comprehensive high school stresses the general welfare of all students and emphasizes a well-balanced curriculum, including subjects that contribute to physical and mental happiness throughout life.

Nevertheless, the curriculum-planning aspects of physical education have suffered from a lack of agreement on purposes and objectives. Advocates of the subject have also tended to claim multiple outcomes that have not been attainable due to insufficient teaching time, inadequate facilities and equipment, and large enrollments. Objectives range from narrow concepts of body building to wide concepts of general physical fitness and recreational activities.

Some physical education authorities would go beyond present exigencies and attempt to anticipate societal and cultural changes, necessitating a program with a wide variety of physical and recreational skills. But there is no doubt that the physical fitness aspects of the program continue to be stressed. The sedentary occupations in a technological culture and the excessive use of automobiles make it necessary for people of all ages to be inculcated with the need for intensity and frequency of exercise. Even athletic coaches are learning that their teams cannot attain peak physical condition by mere practice of the sport. The practice session lacks something that is needed to build strength and endurance.

It is doubtful that sufficient time or continuity of program is available in present-day school physical education activities to insure the physical fitness of every student. However, the value of a physical education program is only partially related to the physical fitness that students attain during their school days; the ultimate value must be measured in relation to the desire they develop for, and the satisfaction they derive from, being physically fit the remainder of their lives.

The previous statement might lead to confusion about whether physical fitness assures physical well-being, especially if mental well-being is also implied. It would be unfortunate to make this assumption. There is no doubt that physical fitness is a contributing factor, but in the absence of conclusive evidence to the contrary, it might be assumed that the stimulation of physical activity, rather than the strength and endurance developed by muscle-building activity, promotes physical and mental well-being.

This distinction is important in the development of carry-over values. Youths need well-rounded programs of both rigorous exercises and games and milder forms of the same activities, but it is the carry-over potentialities of the milder activities that are more evident in the pursuits from which adults derive physical and mental well-being. The average golfer cannot equate the physical benefits of the game with the rigorous exercise received, but one can build a strong case for the stimulation one gets from the physical activity and the exhilarating mental lift from the repartee one enjoys with playing companions.

Students who engage in competitive sports need a greater degree of physical fitness than those who do not, but the direction of a physical education program should not be geared to the necessity of competitive athletics. The major emphasis should be on helping the total school population obtain the degree of physical fitness and the basic skills necessary for the enjoyment of a variety of physical activities. When the dean of a school of physical education of a major university was called to task by one of his associates for granting two semesters of credit for a course in golf, he explained that it often took two semesters for a student to attain enough skill in the game to really "be hooked."

It is axiomatic that physical fitness is a prerequisite for the enjoyment of any physical activity. It is equally axiomatic that a satisfactory degree of skill is necessary for the enjoyment of physical activities associated with games and other recreational pursuits. Some physical education authorities claim that instruction in skills and intensive physical fitness development tend to be mutually exclusive. This need not be true if curriculum planners provide for a rational balance between the two activities and gear the program to the individual needs of students.

GUIDELINES

Physical education has much to offer in finding solutions to problems of student unrest. Secondary students appear to be bewildered and confused in some respects but conscientious and thoughtful in others. Investigation of the teen-age culture is needed to discover what students need, feel, and care about. This intensifies the relationship between physical and mental needs. It suggests that physical education should stress knowledge and attitudes and that the program of students should be designed to meet societal needs. Guidelines established for these purposes by a committee assigned to write a position paper for the American Association of Health, Physical Education, and Recreation include the following:[5]

1. A setting in which experiences will help students enjoy physical activity, to feel good about themselves.
2. Opportunities for vigorous activities through which there may be alleviation of frustrations and tensions.
3. Many avenues for self-identification and for identification with sex and peer groups.
4. A variety of opportunities to develop self-confidence, individual initiative, and responsibility to self and society.
5. Experiences that recognize a diverse range of human talents and interests, facilitating the discovery of specialized abilities together with the acceptance of limitations.
6. An atmosphere that relates and integrates the individual with the total environment.
7. Special attention to differences in physical development and maturity of individual students.
8. An environment that supports the rules necessary for the concept of fair play and for the safety of the participants.
9. Opportunities for students with severe structural or functional handicaps to participate in special activities adapted to their individual needs.
10. Coeducational physical education experiences.
11. Attention to the use of books, periodicals, and audio-visual media as resource materials.
12. Knowledge and experience in activities that will encourage and assist the individual to maintain fitness throughout life.
13. Leadership opportunities for each student.

The position paper committee recommends to secondary school physical education curriculum makers a common core of learning experiences for program building that includes the following suggestions:[6]

---

[5] Francis M. Kidd et al., "Guidelines for Secondary School Physical Education," *Journal of Health, Physical Education, and Recreation* (April 1971), pp. 44–48.

[6] Ibid., pp. 44–48.

1. The instructional program has as its foundation a common core of learning experiences for all students. This core of experiences must be supplemented in ways that serve the divergent needs of all students — the gifted, the average, the slow learner, and the physically handicapped. It must be geared to the developmental needs of each student.
2. The program should provide for a reasonable balance in activities commonly grouped as team and individual sports, aquatics, gymnastics, self-testing activities, dance, and rhythms.
3. Sequential progression in the specific skills and movement patterns involved in the activities included in the preceding grouping is essential.
4. There should be opportunity for elective learning experiences within the required program.
5. The acquisition of knowledge and understandings related to the development and function of the human body, and to the mechanical principles of human movement, is necessary.
6. Learning experiences (physical activities) should be designed to foster creativity and self-direction and to encourage vigorous activity, which includes emphasis on safety procedures.
7. Physical fitness — agility, balance, endurance, flexibility, and strength — should be developed.
8. Experiences that reinforce the development of behaviors, attitudes, appreciations, and understandings required for effective human relationships are important.
9. Special opportunities should be offered for students who find it difficult and uncomfortable to adjust to the regular program because of physical, social, or emotional problems.
10. The program should present basic skills that can be employed in a comprehensive intramural, interscholastic, and recreational program for all girls and boys.

The influence of the advocates of motor learning is reflected in the position paper of the American Association of Health, Physical Education, and Recreation. Physical education is defined as being an integral part of the total education program that contributes to the development of the individual through the natural medium of physical activity, hence, human movement. Secondary physical education is described as a carefully planned sequence of learning experiences designed to fulfill the growth, development, and behavioral needs of each student by encouraging and assisting him or her to:[7]

[7] Ibid., pp. 44–48.

1. develop the skills of movement, the knowledge of how and why one moves, and the ways in which movement may be organized
2. learn to move skillfully and effectively through exercise, games, sports, dance, and aquatics
3. enrich understanding of the concepts of space, time, and force related to movement
4. express culturally approved patterns of personal behavior and interpersonal relationships in and through games, sports, and dance
5. condition the heart, lungs, muscles, and other organic systems of the body to meet daily and emergency demands
6. acquire an appreciation of and a respect for good physical condition (fitness), a functional posture, and a sense of personal well-being
7. develop an interest and a desire to participate in lifetime recreational sports

PRINCIPLES OF A GOOD PROGRAM

A survey of the best thinking in the field of physical education reveals a consensus about what constitutes a good program. The major emphasis in physical education should be on instruction. This means that the teacher should constantly be engaged in teaching knowledge, skills, and attitudes in regard to physical activities. As has been suggested, it is desirable for students to improve their physical bodies, and in order to do this it is necessary to engage in strenuous body-building exercises. This should not be, however, the end objective. It is most important that students acquire attitudes and desires that will cause them to use their knowledge and skills to build strong bodies throughout their lifetimes. One of the main health problems of busy people is the tendency to neglect keeping in good physical condition and then expect the body to respond to a sudden burst of physical exercise in the same manner that it did formerly. This kind of exercise does more harm than good. One of the best outcomes of a good physical education program would be the built-in desire to use physical exercise in a scheduled, consistent pattern.

Instruction in physical education should be arranged in units of four to six weeks' duration. Successful experiences in physical activities are just as important as successful experiences in mental activity. Students need good exposure to an activity in order to understand purposes and to acquire enough skill to insure successful experiences. Short, fragmented units often end before a student has a chance to determine any measure of success or evaluation. Units of reasonable length are even more important if the students are heterogeneously grouped. The variance in time required for the learning of physical skills by different students necessitates extended periods of activity. This does not preclude the introduction of a variety of approaches for the accomplishment of these skills.

Variety is a desirable factor in physical education activities. It is intolerable to repeat the same activities in an identical manner every year. Learning should be purposeful and challenging. The worst offenders among dull repetitious activities are those teaching sport skills such as touch football, basketball, and softball. These games are not too complex and often occupy far more time than learning or even enjoyment justifies. Students frequently choose to play familiar games, for they derive security and pleasure from participating skillfully. However, the same pleasurable satisfaction can be obtained if the students are introduced to a wider variety of the less frequently played games. This procedure will offer many more students the opportunity to develop skills peculiar to their abilities. There is no more reason for having the same cycle of physical education activities every year throughout a student's school career than there is for repeating American history every year.

Evaluation in physical education is necessary as a measuring device and as a motivating factor. Students are intensely interested in the development of their physical prowess, and teachers should be concerned with this development as a fulfillment of their objectives. Adequate tests are available for physical fitness and skills of all types. Cumulative records on all students should be part of the repertoire of every physical education teacher.

Evaluation need not be limited to the measurement of physical prowess. Regular classroom evaluation should be made of subject-matter concepts and moral and social values. Students will maintain higher respect for physical education as a discipline if sophisticated classroom procedures are pursued. Successful experience is as important to student progress in physical education as it is to student progress in other subjects. It cannot be assumed that inherited capacity is the sole ingredient in superior performance. Excellence is a product of motivation, ability, and desire. It is relative to the individual pupil. Moral values can be equated, and excellence in performance can be judged, on an individual basis.[8]

Since sports are closely interwoven with physical education programs, attention should be focused on sports with the greatest carry-over values. Individual and dual sports offer the greatest promise here,

[8] L. D. Lomen, "Upgrading the Physical Education Curriculum," *Journal of Physical Education and Recreation* (June 1975), pp. 29–30.

namely, swimming, bowling, golf, weight training, tennis, and badminton. Sufficient time and effort should be provided to develop reasonable skills in these sports. If students use one or more of these activities throughout their active lives, then physical education has contributed to their well-balanced development.

Greater attention needs to be given to curriculum materials and class schedules in physical education. Too often, little or no direction is given to planning classes. A well-developed course of study should be an integral part of every program. Administrators should group students for a reason, rather than using physical education class as a miscellaneous dumping ground. Class size should not exceed the maximum of classes in any other department of the school. Classes of 60 to 100 students are intolerable if proper physical education objectives are to be achieved. No students — including varsity athletes — should be excused from enrolling in physical education, nor should they be permitted to substitute other classes.

Although most states require adequate training for certification of physical education teachers, there is still the need for upgrading the professional characteristics of many teachers. Only those who are properly trained should be assigned classes in physical education, and physical education teachers should view their teaching assignment with the same respect that any good academic teacher displays. Some school administrators prefer that their athletic coaches teach something other than physical education. The theory here is that too much physical activity is involved in teacing physical education and coaching athletics for a teacher to do a good job doing both. Neither experience nor research furnish a conclusive answer to guide staff assignments in the field.

CHANGE OF DIRECTION NEEDED

Physical education must become a viable and important subject in the secondary school curriculum. For this to happen, curriculum workers must separate superficial problems that tend to camouflage basic deficiencies. It is of paramount importance for students to transfer skills and knowledge that are obtained in secondary school physical education classes to future lifestyles.[9]

The present position of physical education in the curriculum is based on three questionable assumptions. The first is that students must be required or forced to enroll in physical education classes. The second

[9] Larry M. Abertson, "Physical Education or Physical Indoctrination," *The Physical Educator* (May 1974), pp. 90–92.

is that they must be externally motivated by grades, awards, and points. And the third is that students must have decisions about physical education made for them. Any capable, free-thinking adult strongly resents such regulations in his or her life. Why should youths be expected to react differently?

These three assumptions indicate that students are expected to be lazy, unconcerned, and incapable of making decisions. Perhaps present curriculum objectives and procedures unknowingly suppress students' natural interest, concern, and motivation. The curriculum in physical education must include a means for developing within the individual the ability to be self-directing, to make independent decisions, and to assume responsibility for these decisions. It is not contended that this is an easy task, but nothing less will assure the adoption of the important tenets of a good physical education program in adult lifestyles.

Secondary school physical education programs need to be planned around certain basic assumptions concerning youth. Students are interested in their own physical education experiences and they are by nature self-motivated. Students will assume personal responsibility in the decision-making process, but they need help in developing a rationale. The curriculum framework needs to be designed to contribute to the development of self-directing, self-reliant, fully functioning individuals.

As has been stated before, physical education is still in many areas a relentless repetition, in grades 7 to 12, of football, basketball, softball, and track and field. More advanced programs invoke the use of up-to-date methods and techniques and combine the talents and facilities of the school and community in teaching lifetime sports and leisure activities in coeducation. It is no longer uncommon to observe secondary school physical education programs that include activities from angling and archery to skish and yoga. The trick is to break out of artificial barriers of prelined gymnasium floors and 100-yard fields.[10]

Good programs include new methodologies, coeducational classes, individualized instruction, contract teaching, use of learning packets, performance-based objectives, and many other new techniques.

In the field of lifetime sports, many of the following will be found:

angling	dance
archery	deck tennis
badminton	field hockey
bowling	golf
canoeing	gymnastics

[10] Dean A. Austin, "A Developmental Physical Education Program," *Journal of Physical Education and Recreation* (February 1978), pp. 36–38.

handball	sailing
ice skating	scuba diving
joggers' circuits	skiing
martial arts	spelunking
mountain or rock	swimming
climbing	tennis
racquetball	weight lifting
recreational sports	wrestling
roller skating	yoga

HEALTH EDUCATION

Physical education and its related activities of health education, recreation, and safety present a real challenge to curriculum planners who believe in a comprehensive school program. This field separates the honest believer from the lip-service advocate. Probably no area of education is so important to the complete well-being of children and youth as health education, yet there is no area that has suffered more from indifference, uncertainty, and spasmodic emphasis. Students need certain basic experiences that can be provided only through health education. It is the school's responsibility to furnish these experiences. They are an inherent part of a real comprehensive school program.[11]

Health educators are struggling for identity of program and independence of operation. In a curriculum sense, health education has been neglected and overshadowed by emphasis on physical education. In too many situations, health education classes are scheduled in association with physical education and taught by physical education teachers who may or may not be competent in the health education field. In the worst situations, health education classes depend on whether rainy days preclude physical education classes using the outdoors or whether the gymnasium is available for boys and girls on separate days. A case can be made for the development of an independent health education program taught by health education teachers.

Today many people enjoy a high level of health and a greater life span than ever before, but it is difficult to identify reasons for this in the health education programs of the public schools. It is more logical to assume that the development of new drugs, better public health programs, and improved medical care are primarily responsible. Despite the possibility of a higher level of health and a greater life span, society is plagued by health problems such as heart disease, obesity, lung

[11] W. L. Yarber, "Utilization of a Health Inventory for Curriculum Development and Evaluation," *Education* (Spring 1975), pp. 235–240.

cancer, mental illness, alcoholism, drug addiction, and venereal disease. A solution to these problems must come in part from better health programs in the public schools, and much of this responsibility is centered in the secondary schools.

The basic concept in health education is to help the students see the desirability of achieving and maintaining a reasonable level of health. This is an individual responsibility and must be considered worthwhile by the student. The problem is to cause the student to see good health as a functional matter in his or her present life rather than as a delayed benefit. Too frequently, health classes stress physiological aspects of the student's life rather than healthy living.

Health is a personal matter. Whatever is taught, therefore, must become a part of the experience of each learner, and subject matter must be established in the context of his or her life. Knowledge about the structure and physiology of the body is of little value unless it contributes to the solution of actual health problems.

Effective health education needs cooperation between the home, the school, and the community. Attitude and desire for healthy living must be inherent in the total environment of the student. To be effective, a good school health program must be complemented by reasonably good health activities in the home of the student and in the living activities of his or her associates.

Good health education objectives include the securing of information and the building of good attitudes. This means students need to understand how their bodies function and how to avoid injurious things. Equally important is the development of proper attitudes toward living that will insure good mental health. The carry-over values of the health program are exceedingly valuable; it is here that attitudes are of paramount importance.[12]

Among the important understandings the health program should develop are those dealing with the causes and consequences of disease and illness. This should be related to the necessity of securing competent medical aid. The whole area of quack remedies and patent medicine should be covered. The average citizen faces a continual barrage of chicanery from the pseudomedical experts. While some of the products offered as remedies have limited value, others are worthless, and some are exceedingly dangerous.

A good health education program inculcates temperance and balance in health activity. Young people have a particular need to establish a proper sense of balance between healthy zest for adventure and foolish exposure to unnecessary hazards. In later years this means using good sense in the proper distribution of physical exercise in games and other

[12] W. L. Johnson, *Functional Administration in Physical and Health Education* (Boston: Houghton Mifflin Company, 1977).

activities. The social, economic, and psychological consequences of alcoholic beverages, drugs, and tobacco are basic teaching concepts in the health program. And (probably of equal importance in a well-fed nation) temperance in eating and the resulting control of obesity must also be taught.

The responsibility of the health education program is not only to furnish information, but also to guide the student's thoughts and actions toward the development of a behavior pattern that will enhance his or her total well-being. All students are required to make health decisions. The adolescent years are of significant importance in the final shaping of personality, a basic adjunct to good mental health. The ability to get along with people and the adjustment to sex as a natural and essential part of human existence are factors in developing a wholesome personality. Sex education should be taught naturally as a normal part of youthful development. Students need factual information rather than half-truths and fantasies. A good health program should help students understand the role of sex as a basic factor in a normal, healthy life.[13]

SAFETY EDUCATION

In many areas of the curriculum, it is apparent that safety is integral. Besides physical education, these include athletics, vocational education, homemaking, and all shop and laboratory courses. But since safety is closely allied with physical activities, and since coaches and physical education teachers are often enlisted as driver education teachers, safety education has been associated with the physical education curriculum.

In the more sedentary aspects of the school curriculum, safety is stressed in two ways: (1) by creating a safe environment throughout the physical part of the school, and (2) by using safety subject-matter content in appropriate subject-matter areas. The one part of the curriculum where safety is of major importance is in driver education.

The inclusion of driver education instruction in the secondary school program is debatable. It runs the gamut from being a state requirement for all students to being considered an unwarranted fad. Two factors weigh heavily in favor of driver education as a part of the formal training of youth. The first is the recognition that almost every person who reaches the legal driving age will be driving a car. The second is that the consequences of poor driving are so disastrous to the individual, the community, and the nation that this aspect of safety education simply cannot be neglected.

[13] B. Shimmel, "Sexual Health Care in the Schools," *Journal of Research and Development in Education* (Fall 1976), pp. 56–64.

A good safety education program stresses prevention and control of hazards that lead to accidents. The student is provided with opportunities to practice safe and skillful behavior and is encouraged to prevent complacency and carelessness. There should be continuity of purpose and objectives in the association of physical education, health education, and safety education. Each involves the general well-being of the individual, each demands a degree of self-discipline, and each necessitates the cooperative effort of the home, the school, and the community. The challenge is to create programs that help students live healthy and safe lives.

TOPICS FOR STUDY AND DISCUSSION

1. What changes will occur in secondary school physical education classes when the new physical education program is totally accepted?
2. How can objectives for psychomotor-dominated programs be reconciled with stress on cognitive skills?
3. What is the role of a state department of education in promoting curriculum changes within a state?
4. Compare evaluation procedures in physical education with those in more cognitive subjects.
5. What factors should be built into a program of physical education that will give some certainty of carry-over into adult lifestyles?
6. Evaluate the struggle of health educators to dissociate themselves from physical educators.
7. Develop a brief for debate on the subject "physical education classes should be elective."
8. Analyze the problems involved with physical education teachers who want to move their classes more to individualized instruction.

SELECTED REFERENCES

Briggs, Megan M. *The Place of Movement in Physical Education.* Boston: Plays, Inc., 1975.
   Briggs gives concise guidance in the presentation, subsequent development, and progression of movement in physical education. Content focuses largely on the presentation of lessons developed from a chronological point of view. Those seeking greater insight into movement concepts will find this book valuable.
Cratty, Bryant J. *Teaching Motor Skills.* Englewood Cliffs, N. J.: Prentice-Hall, 1973.
   In this collection of guidelines for teaching motor skills, support is given to theoretical positions with documented research. The author provides a good summary of information heretofore scattered throughout other books.

Healey, John H., and Healey, William A. *Physical Education Teaching Problems for Analysis and Solution.* Springfield, Ill.: Charles C Thomas, 1975.
  The role of problem solving in physical education instruction is explored. Those interested in relating theory to practice and translating ideas into action will find this volume interesting. Problem solving as a technique in methodology is the authors' main contribution.
Read, Donald A., ed. *New Directions in Health Education.* New York: The Macmillan Company, 1971.
  A collection of articles by noted health education authorities, this book presents the reader with some of the vital concerns of health education and offers some stimulating food for thought. It helps gain a fix on some of the critical issues in our society today and indicates some possible directions in which the health educator can go to confront the issues that are being raised.
Read, Donald A., and Greene, Walter H. *Creative Teaching in Health.* New York: The Macmillan Company, 1975.
  Emphasis is on creativity as it relates to such things as gaining insights into the needs and interests of students, the self-that-relates-to-others, use of behavioral objectives, creative use of the teaching-learning environment, the development of teaching techniques, and the evaluation of instructional outcomes. Important features include the application of the taxonomies of both the cognitive and affective domains in the construction of objectives and the presentation of suggested concepts for use within the more critical areas of the health education curriculum.
Safrit, Margaret. *Evaluation in Physical* Education. Englewood Cliffs, N. J.: Prentice-Hall, 1973.
  A different approach to measurement in physical education, this book draws heavily on newer measurement concepts developed in education and psychology. It advocates teachers developing their own tests rather than relying on standardized tests. There is comprehensive discussion of preparing objectives, properly evaluating, and establishing validity and reliability.
Singer, Robert N., and Dick, Walter. *Teaching Physical Education: A Systems Approach.* Boston: Houghton Mifflin Company, 1974.
  Singer and Dick present a systematic program for teaching physical education using an approach that is logical, conceptual, and practical. The text emphasizes the correct pedagogical techniques of instructing physical education activities using the primary components in the systems approach to learning: assessment of students' interests, characteristics, and skills; inventorying available resources; establishing necessary conditions and materials; and setting up terminal objectives.
Walker, June, et al. *Modern Methods in Secondary School Physical Education.* Boston: Allyn and Bacon, 1973.
  The authors attempt to help secondary school teachers analyze the learning patterns of teenagers and select and use the methods and techniques that will be most effective in a given situation. They try to unite both knowledge and theory with current practices in physical education and offer many practical suggestions based on their actual teaching experiences.

12

Science

Curriculum authorities who urge more science for all students point to present-day societal needs. Progress in applied science and technology has changed how people live, how they make a living, what they believe, and how long they will live. Few types of employment in the United States have not been changed and do not require a higher level of literacy in science than ever before. The government is spending large sums of money for science and technology. The number and complexity of decisions involving understanding of products, processes, ethics of science, and the relationship of science to society are ever-increasing. It is reasonable to conclude that if the masses are going to be involved in making scientific decisions, the schools must help all students understand scientific processes.

Possibly more progress has been made in reshaping and modernizing the school curriculum in science than in any other field. Both content and teaching methods have undergone extensive modifications. Greater emphasis has been placed on the dynamic qualities of the scientific enterprise. What science is and how it operates are considered more important than the results of science.

EVOLUTION OF SECONDARY SCHOOL SCIENCE PROGRAMS

Most of the curriculum decisions in science involved the initiation and implementation of programs in chemistry, physics, biology, earth science, and physical science. These programs were the results of several years of careful study and experimentation involving college personnel who were experts in their disciplines, classroom teachers trained in subject matter and method, and hundreds of boys and girls. Extensive tryout and revision were necessary. Usual curriculum decisions, such as the precise boundaries of the educational unit to be studied and the areas of the subject matter to be considered, were determined. The programs ran from kindergarten through grade 12; the basic purpose was to provide better articulation between colleges and secondary schools. Teachers were upgraded and retrained at summer and year-round science institutes sponsored by the National Science Foundation.

There were three salient differences between the new science courses and the traditional ones: philosophy, methodology, and content. Both teacher and student roles changed: The student engaged in inquiry and the teacher became a director, or guide, in the scientific process. Students came to understand science through active participation; they were not expected to stand by and watch teachers run through demonstrations. Rather than being led by the hand through lectures and field trips, students were called on to spend more time in challenging laboratory situations where real problems of science were explored scientifically. Heavy emphasis was placed on reasoning. Mere memorization of the laws of nature was less important than understanding how these laws affect people's lives.

The content of the new science material underwent radical changes. Almost everything taught in science classes was replaced with more relevant information. This is understandable when one remembers that scientific knowledge has doubled every ten years since the beginning of this century. Seven new science programs were developed, including two in physics, two in chemistry, and three in biology. Also, new approaches to general science and earth science were instituted.

CHANGES IN SUBJECT MATTER

In 1956 a group of professional scientists, concerned about the kind of science taught in American high schools, met at the Massachusetts

Institute of Technology with educators and teachers to try to improve the teaching of secondary school physics. A result of the meeting was the establishment of the Physical Sciences Study Committee (PSSC), which took as its prime objective the production of a physics textbook and supplementary materials to accompany it. PSSC Physics thus became the first in a wave of "alphabet" courses to follow.

The PSSC course emphasized the basic structure of physics, the acquisition of new physical knowledge, and the necessity for understanding rather than memorizing basic physics concepts. In the laboratory, the student was directed to first-hand experience in discovering and verifying physical phenomena. The program contained fewer facts than the usual course in physics, but it stressed concepts to be understood and used.

Compartmentalization was resisted all through the course. The course was designed to stress the interconnections between physics and the other sciences, particularly chemistry and biology. PSSC Physics was for academically oriented students. It did not cater to the wide variety of ablities found in a comprehensive secondary school. This may be one of the reasons why enrollments in physics continued to decline despite the introduction of the PSSC materials.[1]

To reverse this trend and to enroll more of the total school population, a revised program was developed at Harvard University. The Harvard Project in Physics was the outgrowth of the work of several hundred physicists and teachers who formulated, developed, and field-tested materials suitable for a wide range of student abilities. It was designed for the average student and thought to be suitable for more than half the secondary school population. As is the case with most innovative programs, much of the success in the use of HPP depended on the teacher's flexibility. The responsibility for structuring the course and the purposeful use of different media were very important.

Both the programs in chemistry were developed by groups sponsored by the National Science Foundation. The courses were not competitive, but rather two roads to the same destination. Both advocated a research chemist's approach with meaningful experimentation rather than the use of recipe procedures in the laboratory. There were, however, some basic differences in content, student experiences, and pedagogy.

CBA chemistry (the Chemical Bond Approach) dealt with the question "what is a chemical change?" To find the answer, a series of chemical systems was studied in detail, considering changes in bonding, structure, and energy.

The course emphasized laboratory work with the idea that students

[1] Miles A. Nelson and Donald G. Dietrich, "Declining Physics Enrollments: An Exploration of Reasons," *School Science and Mathematics* (November 1975), pp. 606–614.

will develop an appreciation of chemistry if they perform a chemist's functions. The laboratory was designed to help students identify a problem, design an experiment, carry out the technical operations, and arrive at a conclusion based on their own data.

CHEMS chemistry (the Chemical Education Material Study), like the CBA, emphasized models and model systems. The course began with an introductory section designed to help the student gain some familiarity with scientific methods and models and with such concepts as uncertainty in measurement, phase changes, chemical reactons, energy, molecules, the mole, conservation of atoms, kinetic theory, the electrical nature of atoms and ions, and chemical periodicity.

Like the CBA, the CHEMS course relied heavily on experimentation in the laboratory. In contrast to CBA, however, CHEMS made the laboratory an integral part of the learning process. Principles were developed through the student's laboratory discoveries.

Three programs were constructed in biology, all developed by the Biological Sciences Curriculum Study (BSCS). These courses differed from traditional courses in that they placed greater emphasis on molecular and cellular biology, on community and world biome, and on the study of populations. They stressed investigation and principles and higher levels of organization.

Nine unifying concepts ran through the three versions of BSCS biology:

1. changes of living things through time-evolution
2. diversity of type and unity of pattern of living things
3. genetic continuity of life
4. biological roots of behavior
5. complementarity of organisms and environment
6. complementarity of structure and function
7. regulation and homeostasis — the maintenance of life in the face of change
8. science as inquiry
9. intellectual history of biological concepts

About 65 percent of the content of the three biology courses was identical. For purposes of clarity, the three versions were labeled yellow, green, and blue. These versions did not represent a simple revision of old thinking in high school biology. On the contrary, all three were completely new starts based on the most up-to-date thinking at the time. None of the three courses was written for advanced or slow students; all were to be taught with equal facility to the average tenth-grader. The difference between versions was essentially in the approach to biology.

Probably the best known science program developed for junior high schools was the Individualized Science Curriculum Study (ISCS), which was produced at Florida State University under a National Science Foundation grant. The overall rationale for the program may be summarized in four points. First, the fundamental assumption underlying the ISCS program was that science at the junior high school level should serve a general education function for all students. Second, the program assumed that both processes of scientific inquiry and concepts of science provide a good basis for the organization of instructional materials and should be introduced simultaneously. Third, the ISCS materials were designed to allow the rate of instruction and the scope and sequence of content to vary with the individual student's background, interest, and ability. Fourth, the ISCS approach was activity centered because the project developers were convinced that students in the middle grades profit more by handling objects.

Procedures similar to those used in BSCS biology programs were used by the Earth Science Curriculum Project (ESCP), sponsored by the American Geological Institute. The ESCP approach to teaching earth science departed from the usual pattern. The concept of "science as inquiry" was stressed throughout.

Students were introduced to the use of significant figures, the various types of error, and the use of graphs. Mathematics used in the ESCP materials was not complicated but was used as the language of science. Fact was carefully kept separate from theory. A new departure in the material was the introduction of the interface concept. The theme of cyclical phenomena was used extensively and included such cycles as the hydrologic cycle, the rock cycle, the sunspot cycle, and various climatic cycles.

THE CHANGING SCENE IN SCIENCE

Most science educators are willing to concede that the development of the so-called alphabet courses in science made a valuable contribution to the improvement of the teaching of science in the secondary schools. Many of the problems that these courses were designed to solve remain unsolved, however, and curriculum planners generally criticize these shortcomings.

A survey and summary of the inadequacies identified in the alphabet courses include the following:

1. They were written to conform to the ideas and needs of single science enthusiasts.
2. They ignore the interdisciplinary approaches called for today.

3. The teaching materials cannot be used by 70 percent of the students.
4. The courses often omit treatment of whole areas of modern science.
5. They make no attempt to capitalize for teaching purposes on the machines and devices that are such an important part of modern living for every youngster.
6. The courses ignore the needs of general students and future citizens.
7. The courses are encyclopedic in content with respect to what are called fundamental principles of modern science. Most students become lost or bored with a welter of details that have little or no bearing on their present problems of living. However important the topics may be to the professional researcher, they serve to alienate students from science.
8. The courses place the emphasis in presenting science to the beginning student on the end products of science — the so-called key principles and modern ideas of science.

Science educators are now contending that science education must develop in the students both an awareness of the difficulties facing society and the capability to contribute toward solutions. A curriculum attempting to accomplish these ends must be multidisciplinary and must concentrate on developing problem-solving capabilities. Science courses must cease to be associated with only the very intelligent students. Science should be a thread running through all education and thus be available to all students.

As has been suggested, most secondary science programs are designed for a minority of the students, and no longer is the artificial labeling of courses as biology, chemistry, or physics appropriate. If science teaching is to result in scientifically literate citizens, all students must be involved in science activities.

Any change is at least in part a reflection of the needs of society. The current move toward the fusing of disciplines, conceptual schemes, or instructional procedures is such a response.[2] For several years it has been recognized that instruction in disciplines for the sake of increasing content competence is insufficient. The national curricular movement of the 1960s, with its stated objectives to increase scientific personnel, is no longer a vital force in the curriculum movement. There is no longer the pressing national security need, whether real or manufactured, for more scientists and engineers. The pressure is ever in-

[2] Gerald H. Krockover, "Science Education for the Future," *School Science and Mathematics* (November 1975), pp. 639–644.

creasing to produce a public that is literate in the interactions of the science-technology-society complex. This is in spite of reactionary activities pressing for skill development, short-range limited objectives, and job orientation.

There is a variety of individual projects and group efforts in progress that attempt to modify curricula as a response to the changing societal needs. Not unexpectedly, each group has its favorite terms that need operational definitions. Rubrics such as interdisciplinary, unified, integrated, correlated, coordinated, and comprehensive problem solving are part of the picture.

STATUS OF UNIFIED SCIENCE EDUCATION

From time to time in this century, science curriculum reform for elementary and secondary schools has been a topic for discussion, and occasionally the discussions have reached an action stage. In retrospect, many of the resulting changes seem to be very mild to today's science teachers even though at the time teachers may have regarded the changes as radical departures from tradition. Thus around the turn of the century, when biology was formed by combining botany, zoology, physiology, and anatomy, teachers probably thought they were on the cutting edge of innovation, and possibly they were. But yesterday's cutting edge is often today's trap of tradition.

The forces that worked toward the formation of biology as a school subject are still operating. Scientific knowledge and the realm of science are expanding, and the need for articulating, editing, coordinating, and so on, is as great or greater now than it was then. Professional scientists still need to specialize in a fairly narrow field of scientific endeavor for many reasons. However, the science curriculum needed by specialists in training is not the same as that needed by everyone.

As with the formation of biology, there is a current trend toward combining previously separate science courses and introducing elements of previously untreated sciences. The present state of this trend seems to be within the current curriculum development area known as "unified science education," which is sometimes shortened to "unified science." The latter term is technically inaccurate since unified science education does not deny the value of a professional scientist's being prepared and working in one of the specialized sciences.

What the concept of unified science education does assert is that science education, at least through the secondary school, should serve a general or liberal education function in its broadest sense. This assertion also includes science education for individuals who will eventually embark on a scientific or science-related career. The goal of scientific literacy for all individuals is often cited in this respect and has been defined in more or less operational terms.

The concept of unified science education itself has continued to evolve since it was first applied to a secondary school science program. The label *unified science* may be applied generally to any curriculum-development effort in which two or more previously separate science subjects are combined. There is a great diversity in the well-developed unified science programs that exist in schools. This diversity is expressed in different grade spans, degrees of individualization, staffing structures, course titles, and combinations of previously separate sciences.[3]

However, there is an increasing tendency to apply the term *unified science* only to planned instructional programs in which the boundaries between the specialized sciences are dissolved in favor of the pervasive ideas and characteristics that transcend all the specialized sciences. In an ideal unified science program of this type, each unit of instruction would include subject matter drawn from an assortment of the specialized sciences, including the natural, behavioral, and social sciences. Organizing themes for these units would be one type or a mix of types from the following: a major concept, a process of science, a specific natural phenomenon, or a persistent problem.

It should be emphasized that an ideal unified science course is not a "general science" course because a general course is composed of a series of units, each of which is essentially a short course in one of the specialized sciences. Nevertheless, general science courses do represent one step toward the unified science ideal and are thus considered under the generic heading of unified science education.

Distinctions between unified science, integrated science, coordinated science, integrated studies, and interdisciplinary science should be made, and they should reflect the usual attempt in science to be reasonably precise in terminology.[4]

It should be noted that of the approximately 170 different unified science programs identified by the Center for Unified Science Education at grade levels K–14, none seems quite to achieve ultimate unity. Therefore the term *degree of unification* gets used in discussions revolving around unified science programs in general.

Most of the 170 unified science programs have been developed locally, an additional factor that distinguishes them from conventional

[3]Albert V. Baez, "Educational Goals for the Seventies," *Science Education News* (October 1973), pp. 1–2.

[4] David H. Ost, "Changing Curriculum Patterns in Science, Mathematics and Social Studies," *School Science and Mathematics* (January 1975), pp. 48–51.

science programs. The reasons given for local development usually involve several perceived unique characteristics of the local school situation such as student needs, school facilities, and science teaching staff.

Another characteristic of most unified science programs that sets them apart from conventional science programs is that they are planned and conducted over a period of more than one year. Conventional secondary school science courses last for one school year and are not very well articulated with other courses in the school.

The various reasons and needs for establishing unified science programs have been fulfilled generally as shown by the evaluative studies that have been done. Among these findings are the following:

1. Increasing numbers of senior high school students elect science.
2. Students report a heightened self-perceived interest in science.
3. Students who go to college show no adverse effects in college science grades nor experience unusual difficulties in gaining admission to selective colleges.
4. Proportions of students aspiring to science and science-related careers are increased.
5. Achievement of scientific literacy, as measured by several instruments, is enhanced.
6. Students perceive the relationships among the sciences and the relevance of science to other social concerns more fully.
7. Teachers feel that science teaching is more rewarding and they are motivated to greater involvement in the total science program.

Each of the findings represents a desirable change in most people's perceptions of the science education scene. Taken as a group, they represent what might be called the pragmatic rationale for unified science.

There are also philosophic and psychological rationales for unified science curriculum development, but space limitations prevent full development of these dimensions.

Science educators, in order to structure a useful educational program in science that is compatible with present time constraints and expanding scientific knowledge, and to foster a modern answer to "what knowledge is of most worth?," develop school programs that dissolve the boundaries among the specialized sciences.[5] There are many promising paths to better programs.

[5] Don I. Phillips, "Challenges for Science Education," *Science* (December 1973), pp. 1048–1049.

FUSE — THE CENTER FOR UNIFIED
SCIENCE EDUCATION

The Federation for Unified Science Education (FUSE) was established in 1966 as an association of teachers with a mutual interest in developing instructional programs in science in which the differences between the sciences are dissolved or at least minimized in favor of major ideas and concepts that permeate science in general. The purpose of FUSE was mainly to provide a system of mutual help in solving common problems.[6]

In 1972 the Center for Unified Science Education was established by a grant from the National Science Foundation to FUSE to be located at Ohio State University. The center's mission was to disseminate the concept of unified science education and to facilitate the development of high-quality unified science programs in local schools.

To continue the objectives of dissemination and facilitation, appropriate resources were established at the center. Among these resources were a program description file, student instructional materials, a specialized library, test files, and a module bank.

In addition to being a resource area, the center developed unified science programs through consultation and long-range cooperation with school groups. These programs involve center personnel and people with unified science experience within the geographical region of a particular school.

In the FUSE concept, many techniques are possible for applying and implementing the unified science concept. The one most strongly advocated is a modular unit approach, which assumes that the unit is the basic component of a unified science curriculum. The unit is defined as an organized center of learning that lasts for a specified time, usually about six weeks. The modular unit is developed in successive stages. It starts with material being organized around a learning activity and follows with students selecting alternative modules that are appropriate to the chosen subject matter.

The interesting feature of the modular unit is that it is designed and assembled by local teacher teams using as components modules that already exist in other instructional sources. These sources include, but are not limited to, books, laboratory manuals, and films. The usual guidelines listed for a unified science unit include the following:

1. Be organized around a theme that is either (a) a concept that permeates all sciences, (b) a process of science, (c) a natural phenomenon, or (d) a problem.

[6] Barbara Thomson, "FUSE and The Center for Unified Science Education," *School Science and Mathematics* (January 1975), pp. 109–114.

2. Incorporate learning activities from several of the specialized sciences, including one or more of the behavioral or social sciences.

3. Be based on a few objectives that are clearly stated in learner terms and consistent with overall program objectives.

4. Provide learning activities for four to eight weeks of school time.

5. Incorporate a variety of learning modes, many of which include concrete experiences.

6. Be essentially self-contained, yet be an integral part of the local science program. The unit should be interesting to and usable by learners at a specified grade level.

7. Include an end-of-unit test based on achievement of unit objectives and contain only a few items of a purely recall nature.

8. Use a format that will lend itself to continuing evaluation of the unit in time.

9. Contain opportunities for learners to make some choices of what and how they learn.

10. Use commonly available equipment and materials, require a minimum expenditure for special equipment and materials, be compatible with local constraints, and capitalize on existing resources.

11. Be prefaced by a rationale that is addressed to both learners and teachers and that describes reasons for the unit's importance, interest, and so on.

12. Include several opportunities for learners to self-check their progress toward achieving the goals.

13. Be accompanied by a brief description of the teacher's role in teaching the unit.

14. Identify the source of the learning activities used in building the unit. Activities adapted from or located in other sources should be clearly linked to the unit.

15. Include a list of materials and resources required in the unit and their source or location.

16. Be accompanied by an accurate estimate of the number of hours of effort required to assemble the unit.

THE PORTLAND PROJECT

Science curriculum change can be initiated by a variety of means. It may be the result of administrative dictate or grass-roots undertaking. The integrated science curriculum known as the Portland Project is an example of a grass-roots program. It developed from a somewhat modest beginning into a full-fledged three-year secondary science sequence that has proved a viable vehicle for science education in a wide range of school situations.[7]

Two high school teachers engaged in a reflective dialogue concerning their respective classes in CBA Chemistry and PSSC Physics. They were concerned over a number of issues, but primarily the needless redundancy that existed in the two courses — for example, in the study of electrostatics, the basic atomic model, and gas laws. They questioned why students should be subjected to a fragmented representation of physical sciences. The opportunity to sequence topics from the two disciplines into a logical order offered considerable potential.

These two enterprising teachers led the way in securing grants from the National Science Foundation for putting their ideas into action. A task force of thirty-five scientists, science educators, and secondary teachers devoted various quantities of time as writers, consultants, pilot teachers and evaluators during a two-year developmental period. The goal was to develop a pilot program of integrated physics and chemistry to determine the feasibility of the approach.

Evidently, a number of teachers outside the Portland area were looking for a better way to approach secondary physics and chemistry instruction. Soon the program was being copied in forty-four schools in over twenty states. One of the interesting results of the Portland program was that it led to the development of the idea that the entire three-year secondary science sequence could use the idea of logical content development. The same creative idea was extended to include biology.

The idea of logical content development allowed topics to be sequenced in such a way that maximum advantage could be made of what had gone before and what would be studied subsequently. Instructional efficiency was increased by an approach of this type, and the resultant time savings allowed the inclusion of such topics as biochemistry and radiation biology.

Diversification and flexibility mark the use of the Portland Project scheme. The first-year course has proved able to fill a dual role effectively. In many schools it serves simultaneously as both a final course for students who desire only a single year of science and as a preparation for students who wish to continue with the second and third years of the sequence. In some schools the Portland Project course is the only science offered, while in others it is offered in parallel with conventional sequences of biology-chemistry-physics. Some science teachers have partially or totally individualized the materials, while others

[7] D. Cox, "Portland Project: Integrated Physics–Chemistry Course," *School Science and Mathematics* (January 1975), pp. 87–92.

use somewhat more traditional classroom techniques. In some instances the various parts have been offered as nine-week mini-courses.

The following topic outline for the entire three-year course of study may be of help to teachers and curriculum directors who may want to use all or part of the Portland idea:

First Year
Part One: Perception and Quantification
           I. Sensing and Perceiving
          II. Measurement, Distribution, Organization, and Communication
Part Two: Heat, Energy, and Order
           I. Heat
          II. Temperature and Chaos
        III. Energy
        IV. Nuclear Energy and Radioactivity
          V. Trends in Nature
Part Three: Mice and Men
           I. Reproduction and Development
          II. Genetics
        III. Genetics and Change
        IV. Populations
          V. Ecology
Part Four: Environmental Balance
           I. Our Spaceship Earth
          II. Pollution
        III. Water Pollution
        IV. Air Pollution
          V. Where Do We Go From Here?
Second Year
Part One: Motion and Energy
           I. Motion
          II. Newton Explains Motion
        III. Multidimensional Motion
        IV. Conservation
          V. Energy-Work
        VI. Kinetic Theory of Gases
Part Two: Chemical Reactions
           I. The Mole as a Counting Unit
          II. Combinations of Gases
        III. A Useful Form of $P = kDT$
        IV. Chemical Equations
          V. Electrical Nature of Matter
        VI. Basic Particles

SCIENCE AND THE ENVIRONMENT

Science educators are conscious of the growing concern over the destruction of the environment resulting either directly or indirectly from scientific discoveries. As the scientist uncovers the basic principles of nature, technology applies these principles to developing new products and new techniques. Frequently, the process of manufacturing the new products and the resulting consumer use by great masses of people are destructive to the environment.

Technology and progress are often equated. Business equates growth with progress, and the depletion of natural resources is seen as the development of natural resources. Industrial processes can cause pollution in all its insidious forms. Degradation of the environment and extinction of species are justified as necessary in supplying human needs. Industrial leaders contend that technology will ultimately solve environmental problems in the same fashion they were created. Evidence is offered in the form of smog devices, desalination plants, floating cities, and high-yield food production.

Preparation for solving environmental problems resulting from the technological development of scientific discoveries must begin in the schools. This means accommodations within the curriculum centered around problems of how to utilize technological possibilities in such a way as not to instigate social-cultural upheaval.

The science teacher is likely to need help in dealing with the broad scope of environmental problems. The social science teacher can have responsibility for developing concepts of humanity's place in nature, and the English teacher can guide students into contemplations of their role in controlling their environment. This can be reflected in the study of utopian novels. Science educators can use many of the best teaching techniques of the present-day school in developing curriculum procedures for helping secondary youths understand the crucial environmental problems created by scientific discoveries and technological development. Team teaching and the planning of interdisciplinary materials can be suitable activities.

The following is an outline for a suggested interdisciplinary course with emphasis on problems related to the preservation of a beneficial environment:

    I.   Chemistry Involved
        A.   Historical Background: Early Theories and Experimental Work
        B.   Development of the Atom and Atomic Structure
        C.   Bonding in Molecules
        D.   Bonding of Carbon: Introduction to Organic Chemistry, Biopolymers
        E.   Introduction to Solution Chemistry
        F.   The Study of the Nucleus: Radioactivity
        G.   Effects of Radioisotopes
   II.   Environmental Control
        A.   Air Pollution: Chemical, Biological, and Physical Problems

B. Water Pollution: Chemical, Biological, and Physical
    Problems
C. Solid Waste Removal
D. Radiochemical Pollution
E. Biological, Chemical, and Physical Methods of Pollution
    Control
F. Long-range Effects of Environmental Alteration

III. Natural Resources
A. Current World Supply of Natural Resources: Renewable
    and Nonrenewable
B. Sources of Resources
C. Present and Projected Rate of Consumption
D. Waste of Natural Resources: Methods of Reusing
    Resources
E. New and Potential Techniques of Extracting Resources
F. The Replacement of Natural Materials by Synthetic
    Materials
G. Relationship of Natural Resources to National and World
    Problems

IV. Ecology
A. Necessary Biological Background Material
B. Selected Examples of Ecological Systems
C. Current Problems and Possible Solutions
D. Potential Future Problems

V. Quality of Life
A. Population: Its Relationship to Available and Future Food
    Supplies and Natural Resources
B. Advances in Medicine
C. Genetics: Its Present Status and Potential Future Impact

VI. The Outlook for the Future
A. Concepts Expressed Through Literature
B. Legal Aspects of Control
C. Physical Well-being
D. Contemplative Relationship Between Science and
    Technology

INQUIRY TEACHING

The widespread commitment to inquiry places importance on the
improvement of questioning techniques by teachers. The teacher-
directed question is a valuable tool in inquiry science teaching. Yet
studies investigating the kind of questions teachers ask in science con-

sistently show that approximately three-fourths require only recall of information. Other studies confirm this fact when they report a limited time lapse between the teacher's questions and the pupil's response. Much of the success of inquiry science teaching will come with the improvement of the direction of learning by teachers through skilled questioning techniques. Teaching by the inquiry process is not easy. The teacher must be a careful organizer, a provider of materials, a skillful questioner, and an expert guide.[8]

The following is a listing of suggestions for the development of inquiry teaching:

1. Lesson materials and activities must be of interest to students that lead them to think, to question, and to discuss meanings.
2. There must be provision for a variety of levels and paths of investigation to accommodate individual initiatives, directions, and abilities.
3. There must be an involvement of concepts that are fundamental in developing an understanding of the nature of science.
4. Students must develop the ability to collect information, analyze and interpret data, and formulate hypotheses that lead to a solution of a problem.
5. The teacher's main role in inquiry teaching is to serve as a fellow investigator; to introduce concepts after students have had direct experience with materials, events, or situations; and to provide additional materials that reinforce the meaning of concepts.[9]

MINI-COURSES IN SCIENCE

Science teachers have been experimenting with the use of mini-courses where integrated sciences programs have been developed. The following suggested mini-courses briefly illustrate how such courses can be developed in science:

DISEASES FROM CITY POLLUTION

A nine-week mini-course to introduce the poisons people eat and breathe. The New York Indian and the early settlers lived in a clean

[8] Yehudah Freudlich, "The Problem in Inquiry," *The Science Teacher* (February 1978), pp. 19–22.

[9] Ronald K. Atwood and J. Truman Stevens, "Relationships Among Question Level, Response Level and Lapse Time: Secondary Science," *School Science and Mathematics* (March 1976), pp. 249–254.

city. Over the years New York City has become an overcrowded, garbage-filled area of potential disease and death. Students explore pollution, its cause, and how it can be corrected through field work, laboratory investigations, and classroom study. Who is responsible for New York City pollution? Who is responsible for cleaning up the ctiy? Who are the potential victims of the city?

PHYSICS FOR SPORTS

A nine-week mini-course to show how to improve sports skills through an understanding of the principles of physics that are involved. Actual sports equipment as well as laboratory models are used to investigate proper techniques. Students video tape themselves as they perform sports activities and analyze the motions in an attempt to improve performance. Why do power hitters hold the bat at the end? Why do quarterbacks hold the ball along the lacing? Why has the pole vault jumped from fifteen feet to almost nineteen feet in a few short years?

THE INVERTEBRATE WORLD

A nine-week mini-course to study the place of competition in life. By use of the microscope, laboratory work, and class investigation, students learn about animals that have caused more death and destruction to people and their property than all the wars put together. Students study how people have learned to make these animals work for them, how people use their greatest competitors to their own advantage. Which animal is used to wash dishes? What animal helps grass grow? Which tiny animal in the water has a big brother who can paralyze a horse?

PSYCHOBIOLOGY

A nine-week mini-course that attempts to explore why humans behave the way they do. People are the product of millions of years of life experience that is constantly shaping and determining how they will act and react to life situations. What can we learn about the baboon tribes of Africa? How did the giant tree lemur of South America affect us? How is it possible for scientists in laboratories to experiment with white mice and to predict how people in big cities will behave?

MAMMALS OF THE WORLD

A nine-week mini-course that introduces many different kinds of animals not found in the United States. The course explores the jungles of Africa and South America, the plains of Australia, and the heights of the Himalayan Mountains. How are these animals different from the animals we are familiar with? How are they similar? Why are these animals found *only* in their homelands and not in other parts of the world?

GREAT EXPERIMENTS THAT CHANGED THE WORLD

A nine-week mini-course that allows students to learn of and duplicate many of the important discoveries that changed the course of the world. Processes trace the development of machines from the wheel to the laser, of energy from fire to nuclear energy, of engines from the steam engine to the wankel engine, of the cell from an empty box to DNA. Explanations are given as to why Benjamin Franklin did not get killed while experimenting with electricity and how Alexander Fleming's cold may lead to a cure for cancer. Further discovery shows how Enrico Fermi came within inches of blowing up the city of Chicago.

HUMAN GENETICS

A nine-week mini-course that explores the process by which humans pass along their characteristics from parent to child and from generation to generation. The course develops an understanding of why humans are different from other animals. How did sickle cell anemia become such a widespread genetic disease? If your father and mother have the same blood type, can yours be different? What famous court case was determined because of blood type? Will it be possible to "mass produce" people through genetic engineering? Could we have five Wilt Chamberlains on a basketball team?

SCIENTIFIC PHOTOGRAPHY

A nine-week mini-course that investigates the many facets of photography. Basic still, table-top, motion picture, and microphotography are some of the techniques explored. Students learn about lighting, the use of meters, and darkroom skills. A camera can be a valuable and fun tool with a hundred uses. Learn to use it well at parties, on field trips, in the home, and in the classroom. Learn why and how the camera works in order to use it better. It is said that one picture is worth a thousand words. A good picture is worth 10 thousand words.

HUMAN VALUES AS RELATED TO SCIENCE

The secondary school is the appropriate place to construct proper perspectives relating to human values in the scientific enterprise. The day the atomic bomb was dropped, it became clear that science has the potential to do great harm as well as great good to human life. The student in secondary school science courses must consciously examine the value structures of science and their relationship to society.

Science has the potential to effect enormous changes in society. Major industries based on organic chemistry, synthetic organic chemistry, and electricity were created in the wake of scientific discoveries. The atomic bomb was the most graphic demonstration that such mechanisms existed. Heretofore, it was tacitly believed that scientific discoveries improved the lot of human beings; hence differentiation in values was not necessary. With the atomic bomb came the realization that the tacit values of science were inadequate.

Part of the science curriculum must be the development of explicit guidelines to aid students in establishing a value system in scientific thinking.[10] In the beginning a new humility must replace the arrogance of contemporary science. No longer is the scientist free to pursue the so-called truth without certain limitations needed to protect the welfare of human society. This in no way suggests that the truth will not continue to be the foremost objective of science, but it does call attention to the need for soul-searching responsibility on the part of scientists in contemplating the effects of scientific discovery on human existence.

The masses of society must understand the potential that science has for both good and bad.[11] No longer is it feasible for the scientific enterprise to be clothed in a mystique. Scientific knowledge needs to be clothed in language that is clear to the layperson. Science, after all, is both a cognitive and a social activity. The potential of science needs to be interpreted in nonviolent, noncoercive, and nonmanipulative fashion. The values established by secondary school youths need to be harmonious with the purposes of nations to curb the development of destructive forces that will ultimately lead to the destruction of the human race.

An ultimate value in science is to interpret the harmony between science and the forces of nature. Scientific discoveries increase the knowledge of national forces, and they have the potential for controlling and dominating those forces.[12] For the most part this is good, but value systems are needed to probe the fundamental question of whether the pursuance of scientific knowledge benefits the quality of

[10] Everett Mendelsohn, "Values and Science," *The Science Teacher* (January 1976), pp. 21–23.

[11] J. L. Carter, "Scientific Knowledge — The Inquiry Process and the Political Decision," *American Biology Teacher* (January 1977), pp. 47–48.

[12] D. S. Halacy, *Earth, Water, Wind and Sun: Our Energy Alternatives* (New York: Harper & Row, 1977), p. 186.

human life. It is the task of the school to provide experiences that aid the youthful scientists in establishing their own value systems. These experiences must not inhibit the search for truth, but the search for truth must not result in the ultimate destruction of the opportunity for the quest.

TOPICS FOR STUDY AND DISCUSSION

1. In what ways do the new science programs differ in philosophy and content?
2. Analyze the difference between PSSC Physics and the Harvard Project in Physics.
3. Assess the value of the alphabet science courses to the field of secondary school science.
4. Evaluate the main purposes of unified science education courses.
5. Why are most of the unified science programs developed at the local or practical level of science instruction?
6. Develop a rationale for a modular unit approach to the teaching of secondary school science that is compatible with modern psychological learning concepts.
7. Prove or disprove the idea that a science program such as the Portland Project increases instructional efficiency.
8. What is the extent of the responsibility of the secondary school science teacher for helping youths to be prepared to solve environmental problems?
9. Using the mini-courses illustrated in this chapter, develop a series of mini-courses on a chosen topic or area in science.
10. Prepare a defense for the thesis that no longer can the implementation of scientific discoveries be left to the discretion of scientists.

SELECTED REFERENCES

Anderson, Hans O., and Koutnik, Paul G. *Toward More Effective Science Instruction in Secondary Education.* New York: The Macmillan Company, 1972.
    The authors suggest areas that teachers need to think about as they design and plan instruction. They promote the process of inquiry and discovery as advocated by the American Association for the Advancement of Science. There is stress on teaching in science — not about science. Objectives for science instruction are developed and methods for implementing and evaluating science instruction are stressed.
Collette, Alfred T. *Science Teaching in the Secondary Schools.* Boston: Allyn and Bacon, 1973.
    This comprehensive reference for secondary school science teachers and curriculum coordinators discusses the significance and use of behavioral

objectives and analyzes theories of learning. It contains a chapter on integrating environmental problems with modern science programs. Ideas and tips on unit planning are shown, as are suggestions for the use of audio-visual materials.

Disch, Robert. *The Ecological Conscience*. Englewood Cliffs, N. J.: Prentice-Hall, 1970.

Sixteen different contributors identify environmental problems that may determine survival. Much of the material can be used for determining course content in updating the science curriculum.

Fischer, Robert B. *Science, Man and Society*. Philadelphia: W. B. Saunders Company, 1971.

This is a good source book for philosophic discussions of scientific content in the curriculum. The author claims that most science courses are *in* science; he claims his material is *about* science. He further claims that an approach to science that does not emphasize both substance and relevance is incomplete and unbalanced.

Hurd, Paul DeHart. *New Directions in Secondary School Science*. Chicago: Rand McNally & Company, 1969.

This book contains an extensive discussion on learning and the discipline-centered curriculum. How concepts are formed and how they may be taught are examined in terms of both the nature of science and the conditions for learning. The author evaluates new alternative courses for each science subject taught in the secondary school curriculum and examines the trends in secondary school science.

Tisher, R. P.; Power, C. N.; and Endean, L. *Science Education*. New York: John Wiley & Sons, 1973.

This book introduces teachers and teacher trainees to a variety of issues in science teaching, involves them in making decisions about science education, and fosters professional growth. The issues include the role of science in contemporary society and the implications for science curricula, the nature of contemporary science curricula, developing scientific literature, the effect of various strategies of teaching on the individual pupil, and the role and impact of the school on the nature of science education.

Werner, Vivian. *Scientist Versus Society*. New York: Hawthorn Books, 1975.

Werner discusses the right of scientists to go beyond the boundaries of human knowledge to discover the truth. The thesis of the book is developed through the profiles of six controversial scientists. In a time when humanism is being stressed in science instruction, this book has some interesting information.

13

Social Studies

Social studies is an evolving, changing field, so curriculum planners must be flexible, tolerant, and receptive to changing emphasis. It is necessary to define social studies; otherwise, just about anything may be included under the title.

In defining social studies, it is necessary to delineate the relationship between social studies and the social disciplines. One definition might be that social studies includes the social disciplines simplified for younger learners. Social studies is not tied to any one social discipline; rather, it represents an interdisciplinary combination of all social disciplines.[1]

Modern education, in spite of the zeal of many reformers, is an unhappy and unproductive experience for many secondary school students and remains a basic cause of much of the ferment in the various

[1] R. E. Gross, "Status of the Social Studies: Facts and Impressions," *Social Education* (March 1977), pp. 194–200.

subjects. Since social studies is taught in all grades and since many students evidence a certain amount of discontent with the subject, there are certain to be suggested reforms in the field.

Society places a premium on constant reevaluation and rationalization. The seemingly endless quest for newness is characteristic and all-pervasive in American society. This quest for newness has invaded the subject-matter areas of education, hence the new math, the new science, and the new English. Social studies has not escaped the newness syndrome.

The so-called new social studies movement was conceived in the spirit of relevance. It was designed to provide students with an inter-disciplinary approach to problem solving in the social sciences. History books, for example, in the new social studies involve the whole sweep of human experience; concepts from economics, anthropology, political science, geography, and sociology play a significant part in the new social studies. Similarly, every textbook in each of the other social sciences should necessarily incorporate material formerly reserved for separate subject-matter areas.[2]

It seems obvious enough that traditional disciplinary distinctions serve to compartmentalize knowledge. It is encouraging to report that disciplinary rivalry in academia appears to be lessening as an intel-lectual exclusivism. It is discouraging, however, to find that much of the new social studies still remains theoretical. A detailed study of new social studies textbooks shows only a few that differ significantly from the old. As long as traditional thinking maintains meaningful distinc-tions among social sciences, it will be difficult to demonstrate an or-ganic relationship among them, and unless an interdisciplinary pro-gram is implemented wholeheartedly, full justice will not be given to the social sciences. An interdisciplinary program is overdue, and value clarification based on cognitive moral development is advocated in order to give full recognition to the fields involved.

Social studies curriculum planners will find a great deal of solace in a survey of the other subjects where the term *new* has been applied. Progress has been slow, for American education is steeped in tradition and change is unwelcome and often feared. There has been some progress in social studies: the subject is taught differently today, and many forward-looking teachers are using problem-solving methods involving general study in the social sciences. Whether specific sugges-tions of curriculum planners are actually implemented is not always of central importance. The frontiers of the modern social studies curricu-lum will continue to be extended, and imaginative teachers will make

[2] Allan O. Kownslar, "What Should Be Done to the Social Studies?" *Social Education* (February 1975), pp. 89–93.

social studies classes a challenge and a joy.[3] If students learn to conceptualize, teaching has been effective. The new social studies may be summarized as changing:

1. from content and "fact" learning to conceptualization, problem solving, and value-conflict resolution
2. from cognitive learning to affective learning
3. from a history-centered curriculum to a social studies–centered curriculum
4. from a chronological conception of history to a theme-oriented conception of history
5. from a memory-dominant learning style to a discovery-method learning style

CITIZENSHIP, RESPONSIBILITY, AND MORAL VALUES

Social studies has long been given the responsibility for teaching youths to be good citizens. Some social studies curriculum planners contend that this should not be the sole responsibility of the social studies teacher but rather that the responsibility should be shared with all teachers in the school. It is a mistake to assume that students learn good citizenship habits in a social studies class and automatically practice them in all other school and community activities. This "citizenship transmission theory" is based on the assumption that there is a set of important moral concepts that can be organized and taught as subject matter.

American schools have used two general methods for teaching moral values. One method stresses direct educational procedures, such as telling students that honesty is always the best policy. Its adherents argue that teaching students certain virtues, such as honesty and responsibility, promotes sound character development just as prescribed patriotic ritual insures good citizenship. Advocates of these explicit procedures want young people to internalize particular social, political, and moral imperatives.

The other method of moral education stresses indirect educational techniques. Through their daily activities, teachers act as adult models for their students by demonstrating expected norms of behavior such as cleanliness and neatness. Punctuality, obedience, and orderliness permeate the classroom environment. Carefully chosen curriculum materials contribute to incidental teaching of values. Students learn about patriotism by studying the biographies of famous American

[3] Jory Berkwits, "The 'New' Social Studies," *The Social Studies* (January 1973), pp. 17–19.

statesmen. Changing social values and changing teacher behavior tend to make these two methods ineffective, however. During the past decade, educators increasingly have stressed new approaches to moral education. Value concepts have become increasingly important.[4]

Value concepts are identified by such terms as *value clarification, value analysis, humanistic education,* and *student self-conceptualization.* Within the social studies, indoctrination is being replaced by theories of cognitive moral development. The focus is how people reason about moral issues. Psychologists are presenting research results that are evoking interest among social studies curriculum planners who wish to apply cognitive moral development to social studies classrooms. Developmental psychologists believe they have discovered that mental processes develop in invariant sequences through a series of stages. The process of maturing involves the development of a more rational system of reasoning about situations involving more conflicts. Cognitive moral development stresses constant examination of the reasoning behind reactions to moral conflicts. Thus individuals move sequentially through stages of moral development.[5]

Value clarification can play a vital role in conflict issues, such as posed by the ever-present dilemma of individual rights versus group rights. Value clarification is not the imposition of a value system, but rather an attempt to have students carefully reexamine, explain, and justify whatever they value or cherish. If value decisions deal with a clash of interests between the rights of the individual and those of society in general, the student's value decisions must involve the realization of possible or probable short-term results.

Whether these new attempts to help students arrive at better moral judgments in social studies classes are successful will largely depend on the skill of curriculum directors and teachers in adjusting experiences and materials for student use. It is apparent that the emphasis is on students making their own decisions on moral values rather than copying the teacher. When modern students detect contradictions in their elders, they label it hypocrisy. Their problem is to solve the contradictions and arrive at their own beliefs and practices.

FREEDOM TO TEACH

Fulfillment of social studies teachers' responsibility for helping young citizens assume their rightful roles in the democratic order lies more

[4] Michael Scriven, "Cognitive Moral Education," *Phi Delta Kappan* (June 1975), pp. 689–694.

[5] Ronald E. Galbraith and Thomas M. Jones, "Teaching Strategies for Moral Dilemmas," *Social Education* (January 1975), pp. 16–17.

in the way they teach social studies than in the type of courses offered. Democracy depends on people's right to study and discuss issues freely. Equally important, it depends on a citizenry that exercises its rights, keeps well informed, and makes decisions after divergent points of views have been thoroughly explored. The responsibility for democratic citizenship cannot be developed within a vacuum. It must come from a study of societal problems and active participation in the solution of such problems.

The question of teaching controversial issues is persistent. It is closely allied with the question of whether social studies teachers should teach by prescription and indoctrination. In one sense, no vital social problem should be left undiscussed. But in order to keep from destroying the long-term objectives delineated for good citizenship, teachers must observe certain ground rules. Teachers who can successfully avoid indoctrinating students with their viewpoints are likely to be insipid and uninspiring. Here again, ground rules apply — chiefly those of respect for opposing viewpoints.

Basic to a democratic society is the freedom of teachers to teach and of students to learn. This should be stressed since court decisions, unfortunately, have not consistently supported these rights throughout the nation. It will take many years of litigation to delineate precisely the areas of teaching and learning that are protected. The present lack of judicial clarity places a heavy burden of responsibility on secondary school teachers.

A teacher's freedom to teach involves both the right and the responsibility to use the highest intellectual standards in studying, investigating, presenting, interpreting, and discussing facts and ideas relevant to his or her field of professional competence.[6] As professionals, teachers must be free to examine controversial issues openly in the classroom. The right to do so is based on the democratic commitment to open inquiry and on the importance of decision-making in a free society with the expression of opposing informed views and the free examination of ideas. The teacher is professionally obligated to maintain a spirit of free inquiry, open-mindedness, and impartiality in the classroom.[7]

Many state legislatures, boards of education, and school administrators have shown disregard for the teacher's professional role in dealing with controversy in the classroom. If the freedom to teach is to be meaningful, teachers must participate in decisions regarding

[6] David T. Naylor, "Censorship in Our Schools," *Social Education* (February 1978), pp. 19–21.

[7] Mohammed A. Shami, et al., "Dimensions of Accountability," National Association of Secondary School Principals *Bulletin* (September 1974), pp. 1–12.

the organization, presentation, and evaluation of instruction and in determining the competence of other teachers and administrators. The same is true of the freedom to learn: commitment to it demands student involvement in curricular decisions, even in the evaluation of instruction.

In 1974 the National Council for the Social Studies issued a position statement on *Freedom to Teach;* it is still timely. Part of this statement follows:

> Although the central concerns in evaluating teachers should be the quality of their performance in the classrooms and their relationships with their students, teachers should be encouraged to participate in community affairs. Such participation is important in its own right as well as for the modeling of active citizenship for students. Such participation is, indeed, a part of the freedom to teach; and to encourage it, boards of education must make clear that judgments of professional competence will not be biased by the teachers' personal religious, political, social and/or economic beliefs. In light of their role as agents of a democratic society, teachers' expressions must stop short of advocating the use of violence to achieve social or political change, but the legitimacy of the use of violence must still be considered a legitimate topic for classroom discussion. Boards of education and professional organizations have an obligation to protect teachers from unjustified attacks based on classroom performance or community participation. Dispatching the obligation calls for the education of members of the community, including students, concerning the legitimate roles of teachers as professional educators and concerned citizens, as well as support, moral and financial, for teachers when such attacks occur.

ENVIRONMENTAL STUDY

Environmental problems are a major concern to young people. A realistic approach to the study of environmental problems may be one of the answers to student motivation.

The world faces an environmental crisis. Resources are being depleted at an alarming rate, the air is being polluted beyond human tolerance, chemical waste is destroying both land and sea life; in fact, the whole ecological imbalance of the earth is reaching a danger point in the survival of human beings.[8]

[8]Thomas R. Tanner, *Ecology, Environment, and Education* (Lincoln, Neb.: Professional Educators Publications, 1975), p. 280.

While the problems involved in the environmental crisis affect most disciplines, human social behavior of man is doubtlessly the center of the problem. Herein lies an unsurpassed opportunity and responsibility for social studies teachers to develop an overriding concern for dealing with environmental problems in order that individuals, private enterprise, and governments at all levels will unite in seeking solutions to such problems. There needs to be developed a national and worldwide dedication to this objective.

Through involvement processes, students must learn how to relate and deal with nature. The development of value judgments, attitudes, skills, and concepts for solutions to environmental problems are transferable to a host of other social problems. Effective learning about environmental needs, problems, and issues can develop essential knowledge for the type of citizen that appreciates the interrelatedness of all resources and recognizes alternatives and consequences in the decision-making process, resulting in a respect for the dignity, worth, and values of others. This is the type of citizen that has an awareness of the realities and probabilities of the tempo with which change and solutions can be achieved. Young people equipped with the fundamentals necessary to meet environmental problems can apply such skills in seeking solutions to problems and issues associated with human rights, social behavior and interaction, and international relations.[9]

There can be positive values in moving subject matter concerning the environmental crisis into the center of the social studies curriculum. Focus on environmental problems will necessitate moving out of the classroom atmosphere in dealing with physical and cultural realities as well as social and economic behavior. It will be necessary for learners to investigate the interests and concerns of the neighborhood, the state, the nation, and much of the world. Air pollution from local factories, the disappearance of the Atlantic salmon, the building of honky-tonk communities in the Maryland wetlands, and the flooding of the dolly sods in West Virginia — all are part of the environmental crisis.

For those who complain of the dullness and irrelevance of secondary school social studies classes, a frontal attack on problems of saving the environment may be a sinecure. Most environmental issues involve a blending of theory and pragmatism for solution, an assignment of personal and civic responsibility, a shading of idealism and materialism, a tempering of necessity and justice, and a viable relationship between freedom and survival. These issues — these social studies — are what life is all about.

Young people may not be correct in their assessment of the irrele-

[9] Stanley P. Wronski, "A Social Studies Manifesto," *Social Education* (March 1975), pp. 150–152.

vance of much of the secondary school curriculum, but there are sufficient grounds for concern in the social studies.

SOCIAL STUDIES PROJECTS

The backbone of the changes in the social studies curriculum is based on the 110 or more research projects related to various facets of the social studies curriculum sponsored by the United States Office of Education and other cooperating agencies. Many of the projects are now in textbook or some other course-of-study format.

A brief summary of the findings and recommendations of the finished projects follows:

1. Emphasis is on ideas and methodology from anthropology, sociology, political science, economics, and social psychology. History and geography are not deemphasized, but they no longer dominate the field.
2. There is a distinct flavor of an interdisciplinary, integrated approach to curriculum development. This is particularly true of much of the new history material. Most of the discipline-oriented projects incorporate ideas from other fields.
3. Most of the projects show concern for the structure of knowledge. Patterns of concepts and generalizations are identified. The building of knowledge structures is considered an essential part of instructional strategy.
4. Practically all the projects claim to use discovery or inquiry teaching strategies. Some formalize inquiry into patterns such as problem solving, the scientific method, inductive thinking, or deductive thinking. Others claim that discovery strategies alone are more interesting and more effective.
5. A concern for values is evident. Most of the projects attempt to teach students to identify and analyze values in context.
6. More social realism and areas of conflict are suggested for the social studies classroom. Problems related to violence, social class, sex, and personal-social conflict are advocated.
7. Cross-cultural studies are a common means for contrasting values, establishing models for complex cultures, and perceiving uniformity and variety in human behavior.
8. More emphasis is placed on the non-Western world. Studies of Africa and Asia are highlighted. The new social studies materials reflect extensive field testing. There is an abundance of materials for both teachers and students. Sources of raw data are identified and the use of multimedia instruction is emphasized.

HIGH SCHOOL GEOGRAPHY PROJECT

The High School Geography Project is probably the most ambitious of all the new social studies endeavors. It is one of the activities in Project Social Studies that is part of the new social studies. It consists of six well-developed units and is titled "Geography in an Urban Age." The various units are (1) Geography of the Cities, (2) Manufacturing and Agriculture, (3) Cultural Geography, (4) Political Geography, (5) Habitat and Resources, and (6) Japan.

The course materials contain little that resembles rote learning or the description of earth features for their own sake. Rather, they focus on geographic concepts and skills. There is concern for the attitudes that students develop toward their fellow humans and their common habitat. Descriptions of parts of the world are secondary. Region-by-region coverage of the earth has been replaced by a selective treatment of topics involving important ideas and methods of problem solving in geography.[10]

The course brings together geography as it is taught in the secondary classroom and the frontiers of current geographical research and professional thinking. The design, preparation, and shaping of course materials are influenced by a kind of approach that would improve secondary school geography. The materials try to teach the ways geographers look at the world, and some of the methods they use to answer questions regarding spatial interaction, cultural diffusion, environmental percepton, and research within the realm of spatial science.[11]

The full impact of new high school geography with its implications for teaching methods and curriculum development cannot yet be determined. It is reasonable to assume that where the course is incorporated into secondary school curricula with sincere dedication, chances are good that the problem of geographic ignorance will be greatly diminished.

HISTORY IN PERSPECTIVE

The role of history in the social studies field poses basic problems of perspective and balance in curriculum making. The zealous advocates of history would dissociate it entirely from the social studies field.

[10] Francis X. Trezza, "Social Studies in the Seventies — and Beyond," *The Social Studies* (August 1974), pp. 162–163.

[11] N. C. Bettis, "Geography Curriculum Project," *Journal of Geography* (February 1977), pp. 69–70.

These advocates admit that the two are interdependent since history provides data for most of the social studies and uses principles and concepts derived from each of the social science disciplines. They contend, however, that history is the foundation of the social studies rather than vice versa.

The value of history may become an academic question. Rather than dominating the social studies field, as certain of its advocates suggest, history may be submerged deeper within the total order. A survey reported in a leading journal of history reveals that confidence and interest in the subject are waning and that many curriculum planners are beginning to doubt its usefulness for the individual and society.[12] Critics of the report are quick to come to the defense of history, but they admit that the old system of teaching the chronology of historical events no longer meets student needs, and they accept the desirability of teaching historical concepts.

Students are becoming increasingly interested in the study of current events without reference to their historical perspective. If this trend continues, history will continue its decline in importance in the secondary school curriculum. Critics of the subject say it holds its status now largely through state legislative requirements, and some schools are circumventing these requirements wherever possible. Assuming the critics of history are right, it behooves those responsible for curriculum decisions to find ways to make history more acceptable to secondary school students.[13]

In the face of the proliferation of knowledge that has a dominant effect on history, classroom teachers and curriculum directors need to make some selective choices about what to include in classroom learning situations. Too frequently a chronological study never reaches the last quarter-century of American history, yet this is part of the past that is most relevant and meaningful to students who are not interested in sacred tenets of historical lore. Perhaps a different, more flexible guideline would hold student interest. The idea of a thematic unit offers flexibility because it is basically interpretive and can include a broad sweep of history as recurring events. For example, an obvious theme of the present era is the exploitation of resources: each session of Congress sets forth guidelines to control the exploitation, and many young people are crusaders for conservation and thus are making history in their daily lives.

Using a thematic approach to preserve history as a viable subject for

[12] Organization of American Historians, "Bicentennial Report-Survey," *Journal of American History* (September 1975), pp. 64–72.

[13] Stuart Paul Marcus, "Is History Irrelevant?" *Social Education* (February 1978), pp. 150–151.

secondary school students suggests that teachers build many units around interesting themes.[14] Another obvious theme is federalism, which covers a whole panorama of events from the struggle of colonial legislators with royal governors to the struggle of the president with Congress over myriad issues. The potential themes appear to be numerous. Cultural changes, the pursuit of individual civil rights, foreign involvement, and the redefinition of national goals are only a few. Then, too, each of the many periods of history offers a host of themes pertaining to related events within the particular era.

The thematic approach to the teaching of history provides a criterion for selecting specific topics from which a teacher can develop instructional sequences for unit length. Such an approach gives the individual teachers the opportunity to lead their students into a meaningful, in-depth study of a selection of significant historical issues and events. Those who would worry over the omission of important historical events must remember that the purpose of the thematic approach is to select content that has enough depth and relevance to be interesting to students. Secondary students probably have been through at least one cycle of history in their previous school experience.

Social studies curriculum specialists are faced with another problem in planning the content of history courses due to unprecedented pressures for new approaches to the teaching of ethnic studies The earliest and most vigorous calls for ethnic studies programs were demands for Afro-American history in the 1960s. Keenly aware of the extent to which history influences student attitudes, black leaders demanded that Afro-American history be reinterpreted to enhance the black image in order that black students might develop more positive concepts. They called for the incluson of more black leaders in textbooks and called for the banning of textbooks that might be considered racist.

Other alienated ethnic minorities are following the pattern set by Afro-Americans. Chicano leaders are calling for a new interpretation of the way the Southwest became a part of the country. They contend that the United States prodded Mexico into a war in 1846 and seized Mexican territory in the process; consequently, Mexican-Americans are a colonized people within their native land. Puerto Rican militants protest their colony status that resulted from the Spanish American War.

Although less militant than other groups, Asian Americans — such as Japanese Americans, Chinese Americans, and Filipino Americans — have also been dissatisfied with the way American history has been taught. These groups contend that their image as "model minorities"

[14] Jesse Liles, "United States History: The Thematic Approach," *The Social Studies* (June 1975), pp. 121–124.

has minimized and obscured serious psychological and discrimination problems they have endured.

The ethnic problem is further complicated by the entrance of white ethnic groups, such as Polish Americans, Italian Americans, and Irish Americans, into the controversy. The white ethnic groups' demands for reform have intensified problems of conflict. Many nonwhite ethnic minorities interpret the efforts of white ethnics to establish ethnic heritage programs as another form of racism designed to divert attention from the serious plight of oppressed and alienated minorities.

Common threads run through the complaints and expressions of ethnic groups. Most of them stress ways in which they were colonized people, victims of discrimination and white racism, and how they remain politically powerless.[15] It is their belief that a restructuring of the social studies with the right ethnic heritage programs would enhance their groups' self-perceptions and contribute to their economic, political, and psychological liberation. This creates a serious and difficult task for the curriculum planner. Certain guidelines are in order for meeting the problem:

1. Ethnic programs should not result from crisis and pressure. They should not be hastily constructed to silence demands. The nature of learning, the broad social and psychological needs of students, and the structure of knowledge can be damaged in such a process. Ethnic problems may also be compounded by misguided efforts.

2. Ethnic studies programs that focus on one ethnic group have merit and can serve useful purposes. These specialized ethnic heritage courses will remain necessary as long as ethnic minorities have unique intellectual, psychological, and political needs and are excluded from total participation in society.

3. In planning for the future, curriculum specialists need to look beyond specialized courses to the modification of the entire curriculum for the inclusion of ethnic content and experiences. The total curriculum should reflect the role of ethnicity in American life and give valid descriptions of ethnic cultures. All students need to develop a minimal level of ethnic literacy.

To develop ethnic literacy and to acquire a sophisticated understanding of ethnic cultures in the United States, students must be exposed to a curriculum that is broadly conceptualized and includes content from American ethnic cultures. History is a vehicle for such an accomplishment.

[15] James Banks, "Teaching Ethnic Studies: Key Issues and Concepts," *The Social Studies* (June 1975), pp. 107–112.

SOCIAL STUDIES IN ACTION

The program of social studies at selected American secondary schools illustrates transitory stages in social studies development. There are two major avenues in the programs that meet needs and interests of a school's diverse student population. Students in grades 10 through 12 have a choice of programs ranging from full-year courses, as required by state departments of education, to a wide field of electives. Electives are designed to meet the needs of academically able students and those who learn from field work in the community. Developmental programs in basic skills are arranged with feeder schools. By the time a student is a senior, he or she should be able to incorporate these skills and basic concepts into fruitful independent study projects and research papers.

A partial listing of course offerings follows:

ASIAN AND AFRICAN CULTURE STUDIES   *Full Year — 1 Unit of Credit*
This course surveys life in cultural regions: Sub-Sahara Africa, India, China, and Japan. Students are given a chance to select areas of study. Emphasis in the survey of cultural regions is placed on traditional cultures and the impact of "modernization" in these areas. History and geography are used to understand why the patterns of life have developed in each region.

SURVEY OF EUROPEAN CULTURE STUDIES   *Full Year — 1 Unit of Credit*
A full unit of social studies is required of all tenth-graders. Students have the option of taking the full-year survey of European Culture Studies or three-fourths of a year of European Culture Studies and a nine-week elective.

Basic units in the survey course consist of study beginning with the Middle Ages, Renaissance and Reformation periods, modern changes in politics, economic systems, and international relations.

Students electing the three-fourths-year Survey of European Culture Studies will leave out the unit dealing with international relations to make room for the elective. The elective quadrant and the three-fourth-year survey course must be taken the same period.

AMERICAN HISTORY (AMERICAN STUDIES)   *Full Year — 1 Unit of Credit*
A full unit of social studies is required of all eleventh-graders in American History or American Studies. The basic areas of study include units arranged topically rather than chronologically. Units of study that constitute the large part, if not all, of the years' work include: The American People — Immigration and Reaction to Im-

migrants, Civil Rights Movements, Population Study; Government and Politics — Constitutional Theory, Political Leadership, The Branches of Government, Federal and State Relationships; American Economic Life — Basic Economics, Labor Movement, Agriculture, Growth of "Big Business"; American Civilization in Historical Perspective — Education, Creativity, Mass Media, Ideological Battles, Social Control; The United States in World Affairs — The Nation-State, Foreign Policy, 20th-Century Commitments, and The Expanding Nations.

CULTURAL AND PHYSICAL ANTHROPOLOGY

1 Semester — ½ Unit of Credit

The purpose of this course is to trace the origins of the universe to the evolution of human beings, through the development of humanity both physically and culturally. Students improve their understanding of humans as they learn to analyze the behavior of their closest relatives, the monkeys and apes. An excursion is taken to the zoo. Knowledge of biology is used in a study of primitive life on an actual fossil expedition. The opportunity to study past and present primitive tribes is offered. In all cases, students learn and use the techniques of the cultural and physical anthropologist.

SOCIOLOGY, AN INTRODUCTION   *1 Semester — ½ Unit of Credit*

This course is for students who are curious about the workings of society and what happens to people in their relationships with others. Study involves the investigation and analysis of human group behavior. Current "happenings" as reported by mass media and student observations and studies are used together with textbook readings. The nature of the course demands emphasis on discussions and group work. Students devise independent study in the community, using scientific methods of surveys, observation-participation, and interviews. A three-day sociology camp is held to provide experience in planning and accepting responsibility in group participation.

WORLDLY PHILOSOPHERS   *1 Semester — ½ Unit of Credit*

This course emphasizes philosophical discussions regarding people and government. Main activities include reading, analyzing, and discussing some of the world's greatest philosophers. The varying opinions of people and their governments are compared. A sampling of philosophers to be studied include Plato, Locke, Machiavelli, Nietzsche.

AN ANALYSIS OF THE ATLANTIC REVOLUTIONS
1 Semester — ½ Unit of Credit

This seminar on political revolutionary concepts includes a comparison of revolution in England, the American Revolution, and the French Revolution. Study is based on why the revolts took place, who the leaders were, the goals of each revoluton, the methods employed to achieve the goals, and the effects on the individual countries.

ANCIENT HISTORY   *1 Semester — ½ Unit of Credit*

This course deals primarily with Greek and Roman civilization from 1000 B.C. to A.D. 500. Emphasis is placed on the rise and fall of the great civilizations of the past and their flourishes of culture. Readings of ancient historians and research projects using libraries and museums are included.

ASIAN STUDIES   *1 Semester — ½ Unit of Credit*

Discussion and analysis emphasizing Indian and Chinese cultures is the basis of the course content. This specialized curriculum includes studies and readings concerned with Hinduism, Buddhism, Taoism, and Confucianism and the application of these philosophies to present-day Indian, Chinese, and American societies.

COMPARATIVE WESTERN RELIGIONS   *1 Semester — ½ Unit of Credit*

This course surveys the religious and philosophical background of the West. The ideas of Judaism, Catholicism, and the various Protestant faiths, along with their origins, beliefs, and modern-day influences on Western society, are discussed. Students are encouraged to compare these ideas with the Eastern (Buddhist, Taoist, and Confucian) religions and to evaluate the place of these ideas in their Western lives.

COMMUNIST THEORY AND DEVELOPMENT
1 Semester — ½ Unit of Credit

This course deals with the actual development of Communism, the economic system, and its coming into existence and the theoretical beliefs applied through the seizure of power. The nineteenth century is examined as it relates to the twentieth-century world. The practices of Lenin, Stalin, and Mao are examined.

CONSTITUTIONAL LAW   *1 Semester — ½ Unit of Credit*

This course includes a detailed observation of civil rights as interpreted by the Supreme Court. It poses questions concerning the rights of a juvenile, free speech, freedom of the press, and the rights of due process. The course is intended for students who have an interest in the law, either privately or as a career.

INTERNATIONAL POLITICS   *1 Semester — ½ Unit of Credit*

This course describes the methodology by which nations deal with each other and the reasons behind such relations. Concepts such as national security, total war, bipolarity, nuclear war, and proliferation are covered. Readings come from various sources.

THE "SICKNESS" IN OUR SOCIETY: SOCIAL PROBLEMS
                                            1 Semester — ½ Unit of Credit

This course studies the conditions involving human relationships that many people consider undesirable. Students select specific areas for study and then delve into an understanding of the problem using primarily sociological analysis. The cause and consequences of the problem and how the problem relates to other areas of human relationships are considered. Possible areas for study include crime and juvenile delinquency, poverty, and divorce.

DEATH AND DYING   *1 Semester — ½ Unit of Credit*

The purpose of this course is to encourage a more open attitude toward death. Students explore the American attitudes toward death and dying. In addition, students are required to submit a research paper based on opinion polls, questionnaires, and trips to old-age homes, hospitals, and cemeteries.

CONTEMPORARY WORLD PROBLEMS   *1 Semester — ½ Unit of Credit*

Students are given the choice of different vital world areas and their relevant problems for study. These problems and their effects on American foreign policy, and ultimately world peace, are examined.

ETHNIC STUDIES   *1 Semester — ½ Unit of Credit*

Students undertake historical and cultural study of selected ethnic groups in the United States, e.g., Italians, Afro-Americans, and Japanese. The current problems of race relations and ethnic identity are also handled. Readings from various sources are required.

PARTICIPATION IN THE COMMUNITY   *1 Semester — 1½ Credits*

Students will get credit toward graduation for work experience outside school. Through actual experience of working or observation-participation in community agencies and institutions, students become acquainted with the workings of the world outside school. Individualized problems for study are selected under the direction of a supervising teacher. Prerequisite: a job experience, with or without pay, in the community.

TRANSITION TO THE WORK ROLE   *1 Semester — 1½ Credits*
Students get credit toward graduation through a part-time job. Through this work experience outside school, students study the economic role of citizens and the structure and functions of economic institutions. Under the direction of their supervising teacher, they make periodic visits to the places of employment and study selected problems such as unionization and labor-management relations.

SUMMARY OF SOCIAL STUDIES TRENDS

The treatment of the social studies in this chapter is not complete. The social studies field is complicated — compounded by a wide diversity of opinions among social studies curriculum planners. As has been stated, there are those who emphasize the dignity and independence of the various social disciplines, and there are those who have espoused for years the value of an interdisciplinary approach that would conceptualize content into a meaningful whole.

The trends identified briefly in the foregoing material may be summarized as follows:

1. the identity of a movement that might be characterized as the "new" social studies
2. an obvious change resulting in a lessening emphasis on history
3. the effect of the Social Studies Project, resulting in the appearance of a variety of well-researched and carefully structured curriculum materials, including Project Geography
4. the increased significance given to *values* in social studies programs that emphasize value clarification and value analysis
5. the need for freedom to teach social issues in their real context, which will result in a rational and structured study of public issues
6. an emphasis on a more intimate and action-oriented concern for environmental problems with local needs, concerns, and resources being identified
7. the need for changing instructional strategies in the classroom that will bring about better conceptualization of content through the use of thematic units

8. finally, the presentation of a model social studies program based on selected American secondary schools

TOPICS FOR STUDY AND DISCUSSION

1. Would a nationwide curriculum in social studies satisfy objectives for the perpetuation of democracy in this country? Defend your position.
2. Is there a dichotomy between curriculum emphasis on concept development and the stressing of factual and chronological order in social studies?
3. Evaluate the thesis that pupils are justly bored with much of the content of the social studies curriculum.
4. Analyze the position of patriotic zealots who contend that the teaching of American history insures the perpetuation of democracy in the United States.
5. How far will the introduction of Afro-American courses go toward solving ethnic culture problems?
6. Discuss the relationship between the cognitive approach to teaching moral development and the responsibility of the school for good citizenship.
7. Critically analyze the Lincoln High School social studies offerings and suggest additions and deletions.
8. Are optional schools viable or are they merely futile efforts to relieve the tedium of academic learning?
9. Identify the sources of censorship that may be harmful to good social studies teaching.
10. Develop a plan for a local school to give leadership in efforts to improve environmental conditions within a local community.

SELECTED REFERENCES

The Associaion of American Geographers and the American Sociological Association. *Experiences in Inquiry*. Boston: Allyn and Bacon, 1974.
All the material in the book is authoritatively based on the instructional materials developed by the Sociological Resources for the Social Studies Program and the High School Geography Project. This study of social studies instruction drew on scholars from around the nation and had the financial backing to test more ideas and techniques than any smaller study could ever afford. The result: the "cream of the crop" of ideas and techniques that have been tested and revised over and over again until only the best possible information remains.
Cartwright, William H., and Watson, Richard L., Jr. *The Reinterpretation of American History and Culture*. Washington, D. C.: National Council for Social Studies, 1973.

While this volume contains virtually nothing on methodology, it is rich in topical chapters on American history and contains a wealth of teaching information.

Clark, Leonard H. *Teaching Social Studies in Secondary Schools.* New York: The Macmillan Company, 1973.

This is a handbook of ideas, approaches, and techniques useful in motivating and reaching students in social studies classes. While heavy on methodology, it also contains instructional media and materials. The appendix is rich in suggested sources of useful teaching items.

Ehman, Lee, et. al. *Toward Effective Instruction in Secondary Social Studies.* Boston: Houghton Mifflin Company, 1974.

This book deals strictly with the instructional process. It offers ideas for social studies teachers to become outstanding not only in their knowledge of the subject but in ways to convey this knowledge to students so that they enjoy the learning process. Sections on competence-based instruction, premises for evaluating student performance, and assessing instruction are offered.

Smith, Vernon H. *Alternative Schools.* Lincoln, Neb.: Professional Educators Publications, 1975.

Smith describes the development of alternative schools, including open schools, schools without walls, learning centers, continuation schools, and multicultural schools. He evaluates and projects the future possibilities of alternative schools. This is a concise and clear treatment of an important issue in secondary school curriculum studies.

Spiegel, Henry William. *The Growth of Economic Thought.* Englewood Cliffs, N. J.: Prentice-Hall, 1971.

Spiegel discusses various periods of economic development by systematically questioning how to cope with the fundamental economic problem of scarcity. The treatment of the modern economic period is designed to be comprehensive and cosmopolitan. A great deal of attention is given to twentieth-century economics.

Stevens, Lester P. *Probing the Past: A Guide to the Study and Teaching of History.* Boston: Allyn and Bacon, 1974.

This book combines a thorough discussion of the nature of the discipline of history with suggestions on the teaching of history. Included are sections on the relation of history to the social sciences and the use of visual materials, primary sources, interpretation, and textbooks in the teaching of history, plus illustrative text questions designed to evaluate achievement in history.

Sistrunk, Walter, and Maxson, Robert C. *A Practical Approach to Secondary Social Studies.* Dubuque, Ia.: Wm. C. Brown Company Publishers, 1972.

This book contains substantive material on the social studies. It has a practical aspect in the many pages devoted to courses of study and teaching units. Conceptual frameworks to explicate basic assumptions are discussed in Chapter 1.

Wesley, Edgar B., and Wronski, Stanley P. *Teaching Social Studies in a World Society.* Lexington, Mass.: D. C. Heath and Company, 1973.

A good broad picture of social studies education. Specific methods and samples from various curriculum projects are provided.

Zodikoff, David. *Comprehensive Teaching Models in Social Studies Education*. Dubuque, Ia.: Kendall/Hunt Publishing Company, 1973.

The book contains four chapters giving an explanation of the uses of a model and how models can be related to the study of a community. The author points out the fact that a model is simply a concise picture of clear statements of what is to happen through instruction or learning.

14

Vocational and Technical Education

The growth of vocational education, especially in recent times, has been phenomenal. Enrollments in federally reimbursed programs have shot up from 4 million to about 14 million, and a forecast of 20 million is made for 1980.

Not only have the numbers of students and teachers increased dramatically in recent years, but the breadth and depth of programs have also grown to meet the educational needs of students interested in a wide variety of occupational areas. To house this rapid expansion, a multitude of new school plants and untold numbers of additions to existing facilities have been constructed. Most of them combine a pleasing outward appearance with a highly functional interior.

Much of this growth is based on the fact that people want vocational educational programs in their communities to better serve the needs of all students, young and old. Congress has responded to this demand, particularly with the passage of the Vocational Act of 1963 and the Vocational Education Amendments of 1968.

Vocational education might be termed crisis education, since the federal government has turned to vocational education for solving personnel problems in times of both military and economic crises. At such times, educators and lay citizens are likely to reach an early conclusion that social and economic problems can be solved by preparing youths for some type of useful and gainful employment. However, too little effort is made to discover whether the problems are inherent in changing economic and social conditions, or whether vocational education has any relationship to the solution of the problems.

Vocational education is unique in that it was the first, and for a long time the only, federally supported educational program. During the period following the Civil War, when competent workers were needed in agriculture and the mechanical arts, the Morrill Act gave land to the states to establsh agricultural and engineering colleges. When a similar shortage of trained workers in agriculture and industry followed World War I, financial assistance was sent into the secondary schools through the Smith-Hughes Vocational Education Act. Approximately $7 million was to be distributed to the states for support of vocational education in agriculture, trade and industrial education, homemaking, and, later, distributive education. World War II brought the George-Barden Act, to help furnish a fully trained work force, and the War Production Training Act, to provide crash training for war production workers. The Korean conflict necessitated the Nurse Training Act to relieve a critical shortage of nurses.

VOCATIONAL EDUCATION ACT OF 1963

The Vocational Education Act of 1963, the most significant and far-reaching congressional action in the vocational education field, was not the result of a war crisis but of the accumulation of social and economic conditions caused by an unprecedented peacetime economic boom that began between 1956 and 1958 as a result of space exploration. This economic prosperity was the result of scientific and technological industrialization. However, the automation of industry, which had been going on at a startling pace, eliminated scores of jobs and created a need for totally different kinds of employment. The nation was faced with the perplexing situation of widespread unemployment in a booming economy on the one hand and a critical shortage of skilled technicians on the other.

The main factor that brought about the Vocational Education Act of 1963 was the discovery that the unemployment had created an unbelievable amount of poverty in what had been termed an affluent society. A distressing number of poverty pockets were found in the Appalachian coal fields. Government advisers decided that the only real solution to poverty problems was the retraining of workers. This required the extension, expansion, and improvement of vocational education. The recommendations of a panel appointed by President Kennedy to study the situation resulted in the Vocational Education Act, which not only poured vast amounts of money into vocational education, but left the doors wide open for sweeping readjustments and the building of imaginative new programs that involved more than five-sixths of the nation's population.

The act authorized matched grants to the states for assistance in maintaining, extending, and improving existing programs and developing new programs. It also provided funds for part-time employment of needy youths so that they could afford to continue training. It stated specifically that persons of all ages should have access to vocational training or retraining. This meant those still in school, those who completed or dropped out of school, those already in the labor market, and those with any kind of educational handicaps. The training should be part of programs designed to train persons for gainful employment as semiskilled or skilled workers or technicians in recognized occupations. Obviously, this excluded professional training or the preparation for jobs requiring a college degree, but it included preservice and inservice training of vocational and technical teachers. This teacher-training provision and the 10 percent of the funds set aside for research, experimentation, and the development of pilot programs indicated the act's intentions to upgrade vocational education.

Significant amendments to the Vocational Education Act of 1963 were added in 1968. These amendments go a long way toward reordering the original act. Perhaps the most important implication of this legislation was its comprehensiveness: it directed federal funds to a wide variety of services and programs at every level of education. Vocational education had to be considered by the educational community as one of the major missions of the public schools. The 1968 amendments called for the participation of private training sources, and for the use of resources of industry and other employers in making opportunities accessible to all. The legislation called for relating academic work to real-life situations. This fundamental concept was to be taught in the context of occupational preparation orientation.

WHO SHALL BE INVOLVED?

A broad interpretation of the Vocational Education Act with the 1968 amendments would say that vocational education is a must for all people, but discussion here will be concerned mainly with the secondary school phases of the programs. Vocational preparation, a basic objective of terminal or continuing secondary education, has been associated with the middle- and lower-ability students who have pursued courses in vocational agriculture, vocational home economics, distributive education, trades and industry shop classes, and business education.

Unfortunately, vocational education classes have included students who lack either mental or manual skills to participate in such courses successfully. This has been a twofold detriment to vocational education. These students have caused the experiences of the more capable students to be ineffective, and the chances of these low-ability students of getting and holding demanding jobs have been almost nil.

Sights must be raised and service broadened if vocational education is going to fulfill the promises of a golden era. Vocational education must include opportunities for students of all levels of intelligence, capability, and aptitude, and must retain flexibility for rapid change.

The middle- and lower-ability students will continue to form a sizable part of the vocational education field, and they must be fitted with appropriate technical skills for the jobs they are to hold. Determining what skills are necessary is a major educational task that is made difficult by the rapid obsolescence of present industrial processes and the veiled mystery of future ones. A whole new range of programs must be established to prepare the lowest-ability students for unsophisticated service jobs. The number of service jobs available promises to be the economic salvation of these future wage earners. Even for these jobs, however, lack of suitable training or social maladjustment will render such persons useless.

A totally new approach to vocational education will concern the top-level students. An effort must be made to capture the number of capable students who heretofore have left school without completing any useful program. This group includes many who have the ability to enter the highly technical fields but have deferred professional objectives. The secondary schools can provide sophisticated, challenging programs that will prepare these students for technical institutions or junior colleges.

Inclusion of the entire range of secondary youth in the scope of vocational education may help solve problems of dropouts, unemployment, and other social and economic ills. The greatest detriment to success will be the programs' failure to keep pace with new scientific and technological developments.

VOCATIONAL VERSUS GENERAL EDUCATION

Curriculum planners must bridge the dichotomy between vocational education and general education to determine the extent of the vocational education program. General education extremists would practically eliminate any formalized vocational training for secondary school youths (some would also omit it from the baccalaureate program), contending that the best vocational education is a good general education.

Those who oppose the establishment of strong vocational education programs in the school ask what kind of vocational education really makes sense. They hold that automation will render today's skills useless in tomorrow's industrial complex. A common prediction is that job skills will change three times in the life of every worker. Industrial leaders are quoted as urging the schools to leave the learning of technical skills to on-the-job training and to produce students well grounded in the humanities and commercial skills — persons with general intellectual alertness, ability to read and solve problems, and ability to communicate and get along with other people. Studies show that the greatest number of workers lose their jobs in industry through their inability to get along with people rather than their inability to do the work.

The advocates of general education urge curriculum planners to guard general education carefully and to keep vocational education as narrow as possible. They suggest that the purpose of the secondary school is to prepare young people for the fullness of living and that the preparation for vocational proficiency should be left to other institutions and agencies. Naturally, advocates of vocational education do not share this viewpoint, but they must tolerate it so that they can gradually change it and encourage educators to provide for general and liberal concepts in their vocational programs.

SCHOOL ORGANIZATION FOR
VOCATIONAL EDUCATION

In view of the Vocational Education Act, the foregoing discussion of vocational education versus general education may be somewhat academic. With the amount of federal financial assistance being offered and the current social and economic problems, few school districts will withstand the clamor for some type of vocational education. The important question becomes how to organize and house the programs. Educators are sharply divided on this issue.

The Vocational Education Act encourages the establishment of area vocational schools, and the strongest advocates of vocational education believe the special vocational school is the only answer. On the other hand, a strong contingent of educational leaders is dedicated to what Conant called the "really distinctive American school" — the comprehensive secondary school. In this school, vocational education is an integrated part of a comprehensive school program. The choice of school organization is a perplexing problem for curriculum planners, and it demands a careful weighing of evidence before decisions can be made.

A separate vocational school is expensive to build and expensive to operate, but the advocates of such schools are sure that costs can be justified and that programs can be made effective. They hold that a certain amount of comprehensiveness can be maintained in a special vocational school. They point to the large number of these schools in Pennsylvania, Ohio, New Jersey, and New York, where the quality programs of the past decades have originated. The status of the large city schools may influence the thinking of those who do not want to break with the past.

One of the most telling arguments for the separate vocational school comes out of an evaluation of the social status of its students. Vocational school leaders contend that vocational education receives little respect in comprehensive schools. Operating funds are not adequate and there is a glaring lack of administrative and supervisory attention. In too many instances, vocational education facilities are housed in Quonset huts, abandoned storerooms, basements, or isolated wings of the regular school building, and opportunities for participation in the total educational and social program of the school are curtailed. Therefore, vocational students come to be assigned an undesirable status. If the students are already suffering from economic, social, and educational impoverishment, the situation becomes intolerable. Vocational educators do not deny the comprehensive values of the school, but they strongly condemn a situation that makes second-class citizens out of students. A comprehensive program should not come at the expense of a student's self-respect and status among peers.

Whether the new vocational schools, such as the area schools, can acquire a desirable status remains to be seen, but many factors are in their favor. Many of the students will be receiving a technical education that will be far more sophisticated than what former programs offered, and the school population will have a better balance of student ability and achievement. Vocational leaders believe that comprehensiveness can be achieved in a vocational program without merging it with the academic school program. They think such programs should augment and complement each other. The vocational secondary school program should be organized so as to provide a complete range of opportunities for all students to explore and experiment with the different clusters of occupations.

The National Association of Secondary School Principals (NASSP) is on record as favoring the comprehensive high school. According to the NASSP, this type of secondary school provides an opportunity for students from various socioeconomic groups, and with different aptitudes and levels of ability, to live and work together. The publications of the association's Curriculum Committee describe the comprehensive school as one that offers the best structure and content for fulfilling the American ideal of adequate educational opportunities for all youths.

From the foregoing definitions, it may be concluded that the comprehensive school is everything to everybody. This makes it difficult to deny its virtues. Theoretically, it should contain, among other things, a completely functional program of vocational education. In order, then, to identify the advantages of the comprehensive school in relation to vocational education, it is necessary to point out the weakness of separate vocational schools.[1]

Adverse criticism of separate vocational schools can be summarized under the headings of articulation problems, rigidity of curriculum, and unfavorable social relations. The claim is made that a youth is forced to make a commitment too soon in a vocational school. Opportunities for vocational choice should go much beyond fourteen or fifteen years of age, yet once a student has been in a vocational program for a period of time, it is difficult to change courses. If a student returns to the home school, chances of being retarded academically are great. It is equally difficult for an older student to make a late commitment to a vocational school. It is necessary to begin from scratch in shop work, and former academic work is not always applicable. It is possible for these conditions to exist in a comprehensive school, but proponents of a comprehensive school claim that it is far less likely.

One of the most serious criticisms of the vocational school concerns its curriculum. Too frequently, it follows the pattern of the Smith-Hughes Act. This means that at least four periods per day must be devoted to shop work, a plan that does not take into account variability in job requirements or in student capacity or ability. Curricular patterns change slowly, mainly because machinery and equipment are expensive. Yet the rapid development of technology brings quick obsolescence to job requirements and hence to the equipment used in training for these jobs. It is also contended that the vocational school curriculum is too heavily weighted with trade training, considering that trade unions are reluctant to admit graduates to their ranks without apprenticeship.

Minority groups are adverse to vocational schools because of the schools' tendency to de facto segregation. They claim that guidance counselors influence their children to select vocational schools because the counselors continually misunderstand the children's aspi-

---

[1] Carl Larsen Midjaas, "Making the Comprehensive High School Comprehensive," *American Vocational Journal* (January 1975), p. 41.

ration levels. Another type of segregation is caused by the unwarranted idea that the vocational school is the only salvation of low-ability students and prospective dropouts. Thus, the social stigma attached to attending vocational schools becomes one of the most serious handicaps to overcome.

Antagonists, and even many advocates, of separate vocational schools doubt that such schools will survive. Some of the large cities that have had special vocational schools are now turning to comprehensive schools. The administrators still contend that the vocational school is educationally efficient, but they recognize signs of grave social maladjustments that prevent many students from enrolling. For example, after an extensive study of their schools, authorities in one large city found that in spite of good guidance help, many qualified students preferred to remain in their neighborhood high school. Convenience, sentiment, prestige, and family influence affected their choice. Therefore, the authorities concluded that vocational schools were not meeting the needs of most youths, and they turned to the building of extensive vocational programs in comprehensive high schools.

Attempts have been made to reshape the structure of the separate vocational school. Tracks for special technical training have been developed to attract the more able students, attempts have been made to facilitate the flow of students between the academic and vocational schools, and curriculum structures have been altered for technological needs. However, the demonstrated social advantages of community students living together in a community school probably sound the death knell of the separate vocational school as it has been conceived in the past.

VOCATIONAL-TECHNICAL SCHOOLS

The demand for unskilled hands is rapidly diminishing. The complexity of modern jobs calls for greater sophistication of preparation. Service occupations such as health, law enforcement, fire protection, sanitation, pollution control, and education are adding technical classifications constantly. Business occupations in data processing, distribution, transportation, finance, and management are also developing technical categories. The production and manufacturing occupations continue to be centers of automation where only those with technical skills have any chance of survival. The program of the secondary school will continue to furnish terminal preparation for limited-skills positions, but a technical school's program will be needed for these more complicated occupations.

The term *technical school* has many connotations. As used here, it refers to a school that trains youths to be highly skilled artisans and technicians — a community college, a junior college, or a comprehensive secondary school expanded to include the thirteenth and fourteenth years. It is both unfeasible and impractical to provide such training in the usual span of the secondary school years.

Curriculum planners must pay increased attention to articulation, so that students in the comprehensive schools will be prepared to continue their training in a technical school. Preparation should be adequate for both the terminal student in the technical school and the student who plans to continue on toward the baccalaureate degree. This means an added dimension for vocational education at the secondary school level. Spiraling job requirements and the increasing need for breadth of preparation will cause curriculum patterns to be pointed toward post–high school matriculation. This ought to raise the status of vocational education, since most of the students will be "precollege," or at least "pre–junior college" students.

NEEDS OF VOCATIONAL EDUCATION

The Vocational Education Act of 1963 with the 1968 amendments gives vast sums of money for the building of imaginative new vocational programs. The question is, what will be the most effective program?[2]

The task of preparing youths to earn a living remains the primary goal of all education. The secondary school, being the preparatory school, fails in its objective when it permits youths to drop out or graduate without positive evidence of realistic occupational knowledge. The occupational concerns of the student ought to be an inherent part of the school curriculum. In the past, a high school diploma was the passport to satisfactory employment, but many high school graduates are now unemployed. Their preparation is not applicable to the changing world of work.

The task faced by vocational education curriculum planners is both difficult and hazardous because of the inherent problems and the uncertainties of a technological order. The first problem that should be attacked is misguided official attitude. School administrators and their faculties have developed false and distorted ideas about vocational education through a lack of knowledge and understanding of the field. The principal and staff need to take an objective look at the school's obligations for preparing youths to be functionally effective in their social order. The gap between the white-collar worker and the blue-collar worker has narrowed to the point where both are in the same relative area of sophistication. Both need the science and mathe-

[2] Gerald Somers and Kenneth Little, *Vocational Education: Today and Tomorrow* (Madison: University of Wisconsin Press, 1971), pp. 68–72.

matics laboratory; both need the ability to think in problem-solving situations; and both need the ability to get along with other people.

A second problem that detracts from the value of vocational education is the idea that college preparation represents the only real value in education. Students are classified as going to college or not going to college. The not-going-to-college group become second-class citizens — vocational students. Administrators should realize that going to college involves vocational preparation and that college-bound students will enter the labor force. Irreparable damage is done in the secondary school when attention is focused on the college-bound group and equal status is denied all others. If the school is sincere in its desire to meet individual needs, it will expand its view of all vocational obligations, which are equally honorable and equally valuable.

A third problem in vocational education is that employment needs change continuously. A curriculum that does not keep pace can pointlessly waste school funds and disillusion scores of pupils. Certain facts need continual evaluation: local employment statistics are subject to periodic revisions, mobility of the work force on a state and national basis affects job preparation, and the turnover of employment in each occupational area warrants careful attention. Good survey practices call for the involvement of many people beyond the school staff. Help should be enlisted from leaders in business and industry, parents, students, state and national divisions of vocational education, employment bureaus, and placement services. Survey results will call for carefully planned procedures tailored to fit the individual needs of students in each local school area.

Another facet of vocational education that needs increased attention is the work-study program. The Vocational Education Act furnishes financial assistance for the development of such programs. Work-study programs have grown haphazardly in the curriculum for several years. In many instances, they have lacked vitality and any real integration in the vocational preparation programs. Too often, work-study arrangements have been made for students as a means of financial assistance to enable them to stay in school. While this objective is not without value, it should not be a determining factor in deciding which students should be involved in work-study activities. The selection should be based on vocational education objectives and sound educational principles. Work-study programs should be an integral part of job training, furnishing job environmental experience that will enable students to set worthwhile educational goals for themselves.

A NEW LOOK

It is problematic whether there will be a new look in vocational education or whether the old look will just be transferred to a new setting.

However, interesting experiments are being conducted that give promise of new approaches.[3] The concept of vocational education is undergoing a thorough reexamination. Vocational education has been seen as work students do with their hands, but now the career concept is being accepted. Curriculum planners are thinking in terms of providing specialized education for a complete range of academic and career needs. Following are a few examples to illustrate the wide range of unique, attractive, and serviceable facilities that are being constructed in different parts of the country. Space here, of course, limits the illustrations; duplication and variety are almost limitless.

Columbus Metropolitan Career Center

The first phase of the Columbus Center to be completed was the construction of three specialized buildings on a forty-nine-acre site in downtown Columbus, Ohio. It serves the entire metropolitan area with training in such specialties as computer programming, health services, radio and television, and the performing arts. It does not duplicate knowledge and skills students get in their regular high school program, but rather draws out the students' abilities and interests with emphasis on special aptitudes and talents. The center tries to provide a career mix with a cross-section of the real world of professionals, technicians, and skilled workers.

The first phase of the new campus includes buildings to house three occupational training centers — for business, health services, and the performing arts. Probably the most unique feature of the campus is the business education building, designed like a shopping center with the shopping mall as the hub of activities. It is lined with training laboratories for supermarkets, department stores, mass merchandising, cosmetology, fabrics, computer programming, and office work.

The completed campus will serve eleventh- and twelfth-graders attending fourteen public schools in the city and the suburbs. Instruction is organized in clusters, with each cluster broken down into identical curriculum components. The whole center idea is a bold concept in emphasizing the importance of vocational-technical training in the lives of modern students.

Aircraft Maintenance Laboratory

At San Antonio Junior College in Walnut, California, housing the thirteenth and fourteenth grades, is an imposing five-story building

---

[3] Thomas E. Eachus and Dale G. Findley, "Curriculum Up-Date: Vocational Education," The National Association of Secondary School Principals *Bulletin* (April 1975), p. 107.

with twenty-five classrooms and adequate offices connected to a single-story aircraft industry instruction building and lecture hall. The one-story aircraft maintenance technology instruction facility is modeled after typical industrial plants in southern California.

While the aircraft maintenance technology facility is only part of the technology center, it is complete in every aspect. Training is provided in basic electronics, airframe, power plant, and machine techniques. Metallurgy, quality control, and industrial supervision are also included.

Two specially designed areas, called cells, are for tests of reciprocating and jet engines. Students monitor tests with equipment in an acoustically treated control room between the cells. All phases of engine maintenance, control, and repair are part of maintenance laboratory experiences.

The entire aircraft enterprise is part of the technology center of the school. Training in all phases of aircraft operations is available, including air conditioning, heating and refrigeration, plumbing, water treatment, ground school instruction, steward training, climatology, meteorology, navigation, instrument flight, and traffic control.

Admittedly, an aircraft maintenance laboratory is most likely to be located in an aircraft industry center; this program, however, illustrates the efforts of vocational curriculum designers to build realistic programs.

Joseph P. Keefe Technical School

The Joseph P. Keefe Technical School in Framingham, Massachusetts, is philosophically aimed and physically designed to give its students an important choice: whether to prepare for advanced training or for a skilled job immediately after graduation. In either case, the objective is to enter the work force as a skilled, technically trained worker. The school gives the student the opportunity to develop creative potential in a self-directing way in the technical as well as the academic field.

The school plant was designed to meet the special needs of an educational program that offers a mix of academic subjects such as English, mathematics, history, and thirty-one vocational courses including auto mechanics, graphics, electronics, plastics technology, cosmetology, carpentry, metal fabrication, practical nursing, culinary arts, and media technology. Students can select a course of subjects that will prepare them either for a rewarding skilled career after graduation or for college.

The curriculum is based on the most obvious reality — that young people represent a wide range of individual differences. Subject matter thus ranges from functional academic work and skill training to highly demanding courses at the college-preparatory level. The school contains the most up-to-date facilities. Students enrolled in media technology operate a closed-circuit television program within the school. Students enrolled in culinary arts run their own bakery and restaurant, and students studying auto mechanics are prepared to do any kind of auto maintenance work or repair. Although predictions are for an increasing demand for students with technical training, students at this school will continue to have a choice.

Marine Propulsion Technology Program

The marine propulsion program at Florida Keys Community School at Key West is designed to train students as supervisors of marine repair facilities, marina managers, and small-boat officers. The program is divided into three segments: gasoline engine technology, marine diesel technology, and marine propulsion technology.

Students get hands-on training on a majority of gasoline and marine diesel engines. They are also taught salable skills such as the ability to analyze, repair, and demonstrate the condition of a marine engine or accessory. With the expansion of pleasure boating and marine industries, good jobs are available for graduates of the school.

The program was developed to provide broad training experiences in a field that is particularly pertinent in a peninsular state such as Florida, but it is applicable to many other areas of the country.

West Virginia Program

West Virginia has developed a complete vocational education program. The state operates on a county-unit basis, with fifty-five county boards of education. All secondary school youths in West Virginia have access to a vocational-technical school. Some schools are comprehensive; others are either county or area schools.

Two unique features of the West Virginia program are the attention given to training in the coal mining industry and the establishment of a complete FM radio station in one of the schools.

One of the leading industries in West Virginia is coal mining, and state law requires a training program for all prospective miners. Part of the training program is handled by the public schools and part by the respective coal companies. The school portion of the program is centered in the vocational-technical schools.

The West Virginia Legislature mandated that all persons to be employed in underground coal mining operations must be certified as apprentice miners and must complete a required instructional program consisting of eighty clock-hours of classroom and field trip orientation prior to their application for consideration as underground miners.

Instructors for the program are selected by local administrators and must be certified through the Vocational Bureau and meet minimum requirements as a vocational instructor. In particular this requires that the individual complete high school and work as an underground miner for a minimum of six years.

The general course outline is as follows:

1. General Orientation to Mining
2. Introduction to Mine Safety
3. Underground Mine Tour
4. First Aid
5. Recognition and Avoidance of Electrical Hazards
6. General Safety
7. First Aid, Part II
8. Mine Gases and Their Detection
9. Fire Prevention and Control
10. Ventilation and Mine Mapping
11. First Aid, Part III
12. Roof and Roof Control
13. Haulage and Safety Equipment
14. State and Federal Laws and Regulations
15. First Aid, Part IV
16. Miner Operator Rights and Responsibilities
17. Health and Sanitation
18. First Aid, Part V
19. General Safety
20. General Mining Safety
21. First Aid, Part VI
22. Summary and Debriefing

(One may observe from the course outline that an extreme amount of emphasis is put on first aid and safety.

Two interesting projects are connected with the mining training program. At Welch, a deep mine has been constructed for actual experiences, and at Logan, all the surface conditions of a coal mine have been assimilated.

Careers in Radio Broadcasting is a program in operation at Fort Gay High School. Activities are centered around a ten-watt FM public radio station sanctioned by the Federal Communications Commission and maintained by the Wayne County Board of Education.

Objectives of the program include the exploration of a variety of careers in the broadcasting industry, the creation of student awareness of the roles the various careers play in a technological society, the preparation of students to pass third-class FCC tests for licensing, and the exposure of students to the educational programming aspects of radio broadcasting.

Students become involved in all aspects of radio broadcasting. Their duties range from reporting and writing news and community interest stories to maintaining and repairing equipment. The classroom environment is unusual in that students are considered employees of a radio station. Their grade represents their salary, and their salaries are reduced if they do not maintain their skills. The purpose here is to make students realize that they are just one step from the real world.

ADVISORY COMMITTEES

Advisory committees have become an important part of vocational education. The Vocational Act of 1963 and the 1968 amendments require a state advisory committee vested with a great deal of power and responsibility for direction of a total state program. Numerous other local advisory committees are suggested in the legislation; as many as fourteen separate advisory committees may be found in some vocational schools.

Advisory committees can and do contribute to the vocational education programs in a number of ways. In addition to identifying training needs, they can provide information for keeping the program coordinated and information for keeping the instructional program current. They play an important role in the placement of graduates as well as being instrumental in building respect and prestige for vocational education.

Advisory committees can express approval for programs and offer valuable criticism. By involvement in all phases of the continuing activity, an advisory committee can be of inestimable value to vocational education curriculum planners.

RELATION TO CAREER EDUCATION

Some educational authorities would change the image of vocational education by redubbing it *career education*. These authorities claim that students are disenchanted with education that does not lead to a meaningful goal.[4]

---

[4] John F. Jennings, "Emerging Issues in Vocational Education," *American Vocational Education* (September 1975), p. 30.

Enthusiasts for the relevancy of career education say it is not intended as a substitute for vocational education as such, nor is it intended as a substitute for general education or college-preparatory education. In their view, it means all educational experiences geared to preparation for economic independence. Career education should permeate the whole public education program, grades K through 14, and be a part of the curriculum for *all* students. The proponents of career education envision sufficient flexibility to enable the switching of options within a wide range of occupational choices, including the option to go on to college.

Curriculum planners in career education would offer fifteen clusters of occupations, each student having the opportunity to explore three — perhaps in the middle school or junior high school. Specialization in occupational training would be offered in the senior high school and beyond. All students would receive work experiences before graduating or leaving school.

Vocational education curriculum planners propose three models for career education outside the schools. One would be an industry- or employee-based model, one a home-based model, and one a special residential facility–based model. This last model would offer special intensive programs and services for teenagers and adults in residential schools and possible camps.

The goals offered for career education are consistent with those offered for vocational education in general:[5]

1. meeting the personnel needs of society
2. increasing the options available to each student
3. serving as a motivating force to enhance all types of learning

It is a matter of semantics whether the title of vocational education is changed to career education or whether it retains its well-established identity. What is important is that a large segment of educational planning will be directed toward improving skill levels and productivity that will provide job satisfaction for a wider number of youths and would remove some of the class and status considerations that too long have been associated with the world of work.[6] Chapter 15 of this book, which is entirely devoted to career education, stresses that career education should be integrated with all subjects rather than restricted to subjects related to vocational fields.

[5] L. W. Prakken, "National Assessment of Career Education and Occupational Development," *School Shop* (March 1977), pp. 2–4.

[6] Robert E. Campbell, "The Role of Education in the Acquisition of Life-Career Management Skills," *American Vocational Journal* (January 1978), pp. 60–63.

Vocational education is on the threshold of its greatest hour. The schools of the nation are dedicated to the responsibility of providing the best possible education for youth. The influence that social and economic forces exert on the school must finally be resolved into courses, experiences, and programs. A technologically minded society has forced vocational education into a clear perspective, and the implications are explicit for both creative and functional planning. Vocational education planners are faced with the pleasing prospect of infiltrating the school curriculum with their type of education from the early school years to the final stages of adult life.[7] It is a worthy challenge, and it can be a valuable accomplishment.

FUTURE TRENDS

It does not take too much clairvoyance to predict that new types of area vocational schools will be developed, due to financial stimulation offered by the Vocational Educational Act. The type of programs developed in these schools, however, is an open-ended question. In sparsely populated sections, the schools may accommodate students from other schools in the area who will attend technical classes for part of each day, then return to their home school for academic and social experiences.[8] In other situations, students may attend courses requiring from one to six weeks for completion. Most likely, the area schools will specialize in technical training and adult education; they will not serve as the permanent base for the student's entire secondary education. The area vocational schools in urban centers will probably offer highly technical, advanced programs.

Pilot programs in large cities show that youths with impoverished backgrounds frequently show both aptitude and talent when a favorable climate is provided. This favorable climate is augmented when students are able to attend school in their home community with friends and neighbors. U.S. Office of Education statistics show that the secondary school is the last formal schooling for more than four-fifths of the school population. It follows that the comprehensive school is the best type of school organization to meet the many needs of so large a segment of youth.

For a secondary school to be truly comprehensive in meeting the needs of vocational education, it must offer a variety of vocational,

[7] W. G. Conroy, "Secondary Vocational Education Measures Up as Positive Investment," *American Vocational Journal* (November 1976), pp. 44–47.

[8] Paul V. Braden and Paul Krishan, *Occupational Analysis of Educational Planning* (Columbus, Ohio: Charles E. Merrill Books, 1975), p. 118.

technical, and occupational classes to enable students to develop marketable skills. The curriculum must also offer reading-improvement courses and such special services as work experience programs for in-school and out-of-school youth and for on-the-job training.

Guidance programs will take on added significance in a comprehensive school. Since the students do not have to commit themselves at any particular time, they need continuous advice and counsel for vocational preparation. This should affect the dropout rates, because youth will not be bound to an unsatisfactory program or school. Greater flexibility of programming is possible in the large comprehensive school, permitting greater freedom of choice according to the interest, achievement, and readiness of the individual student.

One of the desirable trends in urban areas is the development of regional skill centers. It may be argued that these regional skill centers are sophisticated forms of the regional vocational school. To a certain degree, this is true. Transfer to a regional skill center may be on a full-time basis, but most likely students will remain as members of their home school and attend the skill center on a part-time basis. Planned for students who, through their aptitude and achievement, qualify for high-cost specialization that is not practical in a comprehensive school, the center may include advanced placement and honors programs of a technical, vocational nature. Courses of study involve such subjects as aeronautics, automatic transmissions, cosmetology, data processing, and electronics.

TOPICS FOR STUDY AND DISCUSSION

1. What are the eventual long-term implications of a separate school for vocational students?
2. How will the move toward accountability affect the emphasis on students' entry qualifications?
3. Evaluate the use of modern instructional methods in vocational education classes.
4. How well do conventional letter grades and other forms of student report cards work in shop classes?
5. Advisory boards are required in most grants of federal money. What guidelines should be set up to make them effective?
6. Develop a model for articulation between secondary and postsecondary vocational classes.
7. Is the continuous education idea a pipedream or a reality? Reinforce your answer.
8. It is frequently stated that many pupils who should register for vocational courses in the secondary schools do not. Why?
9. What factors are relevant in a decision about whether there is a dichotomy between vocational education and general education?

10. What is the validity of the view of those who contend that vocational schools force an early vocational choice on youths?
11. Assume that a community had to choose between a vocational school and a junior college. What factors would be relevant in the decision?

SELECTED REFERENCES

Buros, Oscar Krisen. *Vocational Tests and Reviews*. Highland Park, N. J.: The Gryphon Press, 1975.
    This book contains reviews of hundreds of standardized vocational tests. Specific tests are criticized for their usefulness and applicability. In an era of accountability, this material ought to be valuable to vocational curriculum planners and vocational shop and classroom teachers.
Evans, Rupert N. *Foundations of Vocational Education*. New York: Charles E. Merrill Company, 1971.
    This is a refreshing modern treatise on vocational education. It suggests an organizational pattern for vocational education and identifies future trends.
Kimbrell, Grady, and Vineyard, Ben S. *Succeeding in the World of Work*. Bloomington, Ill.: McKnight & McKnight Publishing Company, 1971.
    This is a work-study textbook that brings together the essentials every student needs for analyzing job selections. It deals with the meaning of work and appraises student interests, abilities, and aptitudes.
Maley, Donald. *Cluster Concept in Vocational Education*. Chicago: American Technical Society, 1975.
    Fifteen career education clusters will aid educators, labor representatives, employers, and curriculum consultants. The book shows how vocational education can meet early employability needs, provide broad skills and understandings of a fluctuating labor market, changing industrial work patterns, and increased geographical mobility. Elements of program development and field testing are covered. The author explains the cluster concept, providing a rationale for its use in vocational education. Seven examples of cluster vocational programs are examined. The how-to of organizing, structuring, and preparing teachers for cluster education is explained.
Meyer, Warren C.; Crawford, Lucy C.; and Klaurens, Mary K. *Coordination in Cooperative Vocational Education*. Columbus, Ohio: Charles E. Merrill Books, 1975.
    The principles and procedures of career development are set forth in words and models. In defining cooperative vocational education, the authors rely on the Vocational Education Amendments of 1968. The roles and tasks of a teacher-coordinator are discussed. The book also offers various methods of program evaluation.
Somers, Gerald G., and Little, Kenneth. *Vocational Education: Today and Tomorrow*. Madison: University of Wisconsin Press, 1971.
    This volume deals with the pressing issues confronting vocational educa-

tion. It analyzes the impact of the 1963 Vocational Education Act and the 1968 amendments.

Sugarman, Michael N., and Pautler, Albert J. *Vocational Education for Youth and Adults.* New York: MSS Information Corporation, 1975.

This book contains twenty articles dealing with current issues, concepts, and trends in vocational and technical education. Typical topics include vocational education in postsecondary schools, diversity of curricula, implications for articulation, technical education in the military, programs to aid teacher planning, and occupational curriculum development.

Urban, Stanley J., and Tsuji, Thomas. *The Special Needs Student in Vocational Education.* New York: MSS Information Corporation, 1976.

This volume focuses on ideas and issues related to the general problems of delivering special educational services. It discusses the role of the law in assuring that special needs students receive vocational training. Other areas developed deal with handicapped students, career education, implementation of programs, and many suggestions of sources of assistance for curriculum planners of special needs students.

III

Developments That Cut Across Curriculum Areas

15

Career Education

Preparation for earning a livelihood has always been a basic purpose of schooling. Confusion arises when terms such as *vocational education* or *career education* are applied only to courses in agriculture, industrial education, homemaking, and business education. Career education is a much broader concept. The basic point of view here is that every subject in the curriculum has vocational implications and thus in fact is career education. However, schools need definite, coordinated programs to reach the goal of preparation for employment.

HISTORICAL EMPHASES ON CAREER EDUCATION

The first type of secondary school in the United States, the Latin grammar school imported from Europe, was vocational. Those students who completed the rigorous curriculum were able to obtain positions and a degree of success not open to those who did not. Also, the completion of the curriculum was an essential requirement for admission to the universities. Another type of school, the academy, which originated in the United States shortly before the Revolutionary War, developed in part to provide more practical courses, thus placing increased emphasis on career education. Ultimately, a different institution, called the high school, became the predominant secondary school in the United States. The high school placed even more emphasis on preparation for work.

As the country grew in population and prospered in the latter nineteenth century, there came an accompanying democratization of the high school curriculum. Emphasis on academic courses decreased in favor of more practical subjects. As indicated in detail in Chapter 8, a major thrust for vocational education came during World War I with passage of the national Smith-Hughes Act. In 1917 that program provided the first substantial financial grants to the states for the purposes of developing vocational programs. These measures were particularly useful in the period following World War I as the high school developed into an institution that served the majority of secondary school–age youth for the first time in this country or in any other.

Another significant boost to career education occurred during the 1930s because of the Great Depression. Millions of Americans were out of work, a condition which had a special impact on young people. The emphasis during that time was not only on more practical courses in school but also on national programs to provide what was called work experience. The public high schools now had a widespread competitive educational system called the National Youth Administration, plus educational activities of the Civilian Conservation Corps and a number of other federally subsidized programs.

Those depression-based programs ended when the United States entered World War II in 1940. Career education then aimed directly at winning the war. The education of women for careers, which had received some stimulus during the depression years, now had an all-out emphasis during World War II. Possibly no other single influence brought so many women into career education and the work force.

The 1950s and 1960s, years of postwar prosperity, relatively full employment, and pressures caused by the Soviets' headstart in the development of atomic energy, resulted in a major deemphasis of vocational education. The subjects widely considered most important were science, mathematics, and foreign languages. There was a massive move to place counselors in schools to persuade more students to take training in these three academic areas. At the same time, a period of relatively full employment made career education seem less significant. An exception was an impetus to technical education, but most technical courses were offered in post–high school institutions.

The late 1960's and the 1970s brought another turnabout in secondary education in this country, as jobs became more scarce and the fear of Soviet supremacy in atomic energy seemed less significant. Unemployment became a national specter that, as always, was hardest on the young. Politically, it was time once again to emphasize career education as a solution to a national problem. Today nearly one-half of secondary school students enroll in vocational courses of one kind or another.

You have read already in Chapter 14 a detailed account of the development of vocational education in this country, including the remarkable changes in programs as the complexities of the opportunities for employment increased over the years. This chapter builds on these developments, extending the concepts to all other curricular areas.

ACTION LEARNING

The title of this section might also be called "What's in a Name." Throughout the book are many examples of the use of new names to describe programs that have been urged by innovators for many years. For example, team teaching was once called cooperative teaching. The concept functioned in various forms, such as when a so-called master teacher taught other students or less-trained teachers, who in turn taught all the other students. The "new" concept of continuous progress was commonplace more than a century ago when students left school during the harvest to work on the farms and then returned to school to pick up their studies again. Independent study, another supposedly new concept, has taken many forms over the years, from including the supervision of students in large study halls to the present innovation of lengthening class periods in order to permit the study of a particular subject under the supervision of the teacher in a classroom or resource center.

Even the title of this chapter, "Career Education," is a different term to describe what many years ago was called manual training and domestic science. Those two names aimed to give prestige to the field by adding *science* to preparation for home living and *training* to improve what persons did basically with their hands! The term *vocational education* was emphasized in the early decades of this century as efforts were made to improve on the terms *manual training* and *domestic science*. *Business education* replaced terms like *typing, shorthand,* and *bookkeeping.*

It is only natural, therefore, that in spite of efforts for many years to utilize the community as a learning environment to provide experiences more closely related to the real world of work, individuals now would develop a new name to attract more interest; hence the term *action learning.*

According to the proponents of action learning, for too long a dichotomy has existed in schools between academic and action learning. Of course, learning by doing is an important ingredient of any subject whether it be mathematics, social science, agriculture, or something else. Action learning moves beyond simple, voluntary use of the community. Such simplistic methods as giving credit for what persons learn in the community or recognizing the community as a laboratory are replaced by more systematic involvement of the community and increased recognition that skills are developed best in an arena that is most closely related to the real world where students use the skills.

Certainly, what is called action learning is an essential part of the secondary school curriculum. We have pointed out in our writings for many years that people learn in three areas: school, home, and community. The improvement of the secondary school curriculum requires decisions regarding which of these three environments is the *best* place for teaching and learning any given aspect of the curriculum. Certainly career education provides a natural place to start that rationalization. The use of the term *action learning* may provide the stimulus for those developments; otherwise, it will simply be another educational fad.

RESOLVING CONFLICTS BETWEEN GENERAL EDUCATION AND VOCATIONAL EDUCATION

This brief and, of course, inadequate summary indicates not only the lack of a consistent philosophy of preparation for work as an educational goal in the United States but also highlights the kinds of pressures that influence the curriculum. These external forces exist because schools are a part of the social order, buffeted one way or the other by the various movements and pressures that society exerts.

Career education or preparation for work continues to be impeded by superficial beliefs and attitudes. One myth is that general or liberal education emphasizes *thinking* while vocational or career education stresses *doing.* Although thinking without doing is unproductive and doing without thinking may be suicidal, the dichotomy produces conflicts between the "liberal" subjects of English, social studies, mathematics, science, and foreign language on the one hand and the more pragmatic or vocational subjects of fine arts, practical arts, and physical education on the other.

Another example of illogical thinking and practice is to provide private and public schools with academic curricular emphases in the more favored socioeconomic areas of cities and the nation. Concomitantly, education in the inner city or other less favored regions emphasizes the practical and the vocational. Thus the wealthy have the privilege of thinking and the poor have the responsibility of doing!

Is it possible to break the hold of such indefensible generalizations? We think so. However, school programs need to make a frontal attack on the situation with a number of specific curriculum reforms.

CURRICULUM IMPLICATIONS
OF CAREER EDUCATION

Every school subject is vocational. Therefore, career education is a fundamental purpose of every curriculum area, and every teacher is a vocational instructor. Every person who leaves the secondary school, graduate or nongraduate, needs systematic vocational preparation. Therefore, every school subject must be presented so that students clearly understand the career opportunities that the subject provides as well as its values in their general education. Only then will school programs attack basic societal problems that now force so many people into the ranks of the unemployed and welfare rolls. Such commitment by schools to career education produces a constructive image of institutions that really care and do something positive to help all students.

The achievement of the foregoing goals calls for basic changes in curricular organization. As emphasized in Chapters 2 and 30, carefully conducted studies need to determine what is *essential* for every student to know and perform in each area. Those studies also reveal the subject's potential for hobbies or recreational interests. The third emphasis must be on career possibilities.

What is essential must be determined locally in order to enhance motivation. In this way, the curriculum will include what students need to survive in the world of work, assuming that they remain in the same community. If a particular student's goals definitely include moving out of town, contact with the school system in the new locale will indicate the needs of that area so that proper transitional steps may be initiated.

The school also needs to use every possible method to persuade students to go beyond those minimum requirements to enrich their lives and to make them more interesting and productive human beings. Beyond those two levels, the school program specifically identifies the career opportunities that the subject provides if students learn even more of it. This third level constitutes the school's program in career education; that involves *every subject* in the school.

CAREER EDUCATION IN THE SCHOOL SUBJECTS

The philosophy that career education is an essential part of the curriculum makes work an integral part of a person's total life. It is not simply a means to provide income for survival. Rather, it contributes to the development of the individual and to family relationships. Work experience helps provide young people with meaningful activities that enable them to make positive contributions to society and to a particular job. Because work occupies a central position in life for both young men and young women, finding a career must not be left to chance. Career education can help young people find a better life.

This approach has been difficult because the specialists in the academic subject areas have never adequately highlighted the career education aspects of the subjects that in fact provided careers for them. Another reason is their reluctance to place in an elective category much of what is now required but actually not needed by everyone.

This approach to career education is neither new nor untried. For example, in the 1930s the Chicago secondary schools produced posters, which were displayed prominently in all classrooms, and booklets that provided details about career opportunities open to pupils who studied any particular subject in depth.

A few simple illustrations of this approach to career education suffice to illustrate the concept. Taking as an example the question of what reading skills are *essential* for everyone, the goal might be stated as the fifth-grade level as measured by conventional norm-based tests. Such a minimum would allow students to read the daily newspapers and other materials that are necessary for them to understand what everyone needs to know.

Teachers then constantly need to use various techniques to persuade students to learn to read better than at the essential level. The approach would indicate as specifically as possible the reading skills required for indicated careers. For example, a student going to college to study law obviously would require a much higher reading level and different types of reading competence than someone whose present career goal is to work in a supermarket.

The mathematics needed by everyone is much more limited and varies markedly from what most secondary schools now require for graduation. The study of algebra might provide some interesting hobbies but is scarcely necessary for the great majority of persons in relation to their everyday needs. Of course, algebra and many other levels of mathematics are essential if the career goal is some phase of engineering.

Students do not have to understand all that is required in conventional courses of world history in order to live quite adequate lives.

However, history is a fascinating subject with many opportunities for hobbies and special interests. A few people make their living as historians or people who teach history; other career possibilities in the subject are well known to history teachers.

Much of what is now taught in physical education is not necessary; conversely, some matters in the areas of health, fitness, and recreation are essential and presently ignored or underplayed in many schools. Hobbies and special interests abound in this curricular area. Some people, such as professional athletes and recreational directors, make their living at it; significant career education possibilities exist.

The practical arts are the *only* subjects that have systematically attacked the divisions between what everyone needs to know and to do and what is needed for vocational or career education. Chapter 9 provided in considerable detail numerous examples of what is essential in the area of industrial arts and the many hobbies and careers that may develop as a result of the curriculum in that field.

Every subject area in the curriculum needs to receive systematically the kind of analysis illustrated only superficially in the preceding paragraphs. Moreover, such analyses need to be done in local schools and communities to provide more practical examples for students and teachers. National and state guidelines can help, but local designations increase relevance in the minds of both groups. Until that happens, career education will not attain the status it should have. Rather, it will remain an educational fad to be revived only periodically and sometimes for the wrong reasons. Above all, it will be viewed in the context of an unproductive competitive category: vocational versus academic education.

The need for greatly improved and expanded programs of career education in schools could provide a motivational lever for secondary school curriculum improvement that many schools lack. Curriculum experts certainly could provide the leadership in this movement. The present thrust for improved career education in schools, coupled with the relatively simple efforts that this chapter suggests for any local school faculty, may provide the motivation to involve specialists in more systematic approaches.

SCHOOL, HOME, AND COMMUNITY RELATIONS

This book repeatedly emphasizes the fact that the secondary school curriculum involves not only schools but also homes and communities. Unfortunately, the relationships among these three learning environments have not always been clear in the minds of not only persons who work in schools but also those who work in communities and homes.

Historically, of course, families had the responsibility for educating the young. Since many people believed that not all homes exercised these responsibilities adequately, communities organized schools to complement the work of homes. However, as communities delegated responsibilities to schools, the determination of what should be taught in schools and what should be taught in communities became unclear. The result is that both communities and families turned over too many responsibilities to schools.

The school's responsibility in career education, as with all other educational goals, is to coordinate its own programs effectively with what occurs elsewhere. In the process, persons who work in schools need to recognize the tremendous differences that exist not only among homes and communities but also in the same homes and communities from one time to another. Unless school programs assume responsibility for surveying these factors, there will be no consistency in any locale, whether it be rural, small-town, city, or large urban areas.

Schools systematically should urge parents and guardians to provide children with work experiences around the home. Although it is true that in earlier times some children were exploited by too much work on farms and in factories, that situation seldom exists today. Many parents now overprotect children from work experiences around the house.

Child labor laws also are overly restrictive in protecting young people from employment outside the home. The old saying "all work and no play makes Jack a dull boy (and Jill a dull girl)" needs to emphasize the converse: all play and no work can develop juvenile delinquency and unrealistic attitudes toward what needs to be done in society. The present need for cooperative activities of schools, homes, and communities in preparing children for the world of work is extremely crucial for the success of all three.

Schools need to plan with both management and organized labor in developing the community as a learning environment in career education. The concern must be with all levels of employers, from the one-person operation to the large corporations. In between the two extremes are a great variety of locally owned establishments. Still another dimension includes government operations. The point is that the school needs to involve all kinds of prospective employers and locales for students to obtain work experience and career education.

Beyond these points of view about curricular and locale allocations of career education are a number of other basic considerations. Motivation is an essential ingredient of learning in any subject. In this regard, there are a number of questions to answer prior to planning this program. For example, how is career education related to the present and future lifestyles and goals of the learners? Do students at their present developmental stages really want to know about the world of work, or are they more interested in avoiding it? What rewards for pupils result from working? Is work today really challenging? What future is inherent in the kinds of work open to young people? Who controls the system, and how? What other information about careers do individual students want, or need, to help them cope with the world of work? Unfortunately, in the past most schools have not helped students arrive at constructive answers to these questions.

INDIVIDUAL AND GROUP ACTIVITIES IN SCHOOL

The instructional methods provided elsewhere in this book relate also to career education. As described in Chapter 21, the school program needs to provide motivational experiences in larger groups to stretch the minds of students over the vast opportunities in career education that the school, the community, and the world outside provide. These presentations include not only the use of audio-visual devices but also a variety of personal, live talks by competent persons. Teachers may make some presentations. Employed adults and employers may provide others, as may students who are now engaged in work in the community.

Every presentation should be followed by opportunities for students to react in small groups, as described in Chapter 22. The school then provides continuing opportunities for students to learn more in depth about careers in which they believe they may have potential interests; Chapter 20 describes the process.

The methodology in discovering potential career interests is the same that the school uses in other teaching. School counselors work with teachers to assemble materials relative to career opportunities; types of preparation programs available in the school, the immediate community and elsewhere; part-time job opportunities; salaries and welfare provisions; and other relevant information. Career information centers, placement and follow-up services, employer contacts, and other schoolwide services help students and teachers keep abreast of opportunities and make appropriate contacts.

Data are collected in depth and breadth continuously about the evolving interests, achievements, and difficulties that each student develops and encounters during the school years. These records produce data that are analyzed periodically by the student and his or her teacher-adviser, as described in Chapter 25. These basic data help implement a variety of prescriptive actions that the student follows in developing self-awareness, understanding, appreciations and attitudes, skills, and other competences essential for success.

All these activities aim to develop a student's ability and willingness to make tentative decisions about possible careers. As those decisions approach realization, the school helps the student acquire the information and skills that contribute to employability. The student's progress is monitored by a teacher-adviser who is continuously in contact with the student and with his or her other teachers. All these exploratory and preparatory activities ultimately eventuate in tryout experiences and finally in placement. An extremely close relationship among the school, the home, and employers focuses on what is best for each individual student and what will help her or him develop maximum potential and service to an employer.

The school constantly needs to analyze what it does in relation to what employers need to do. The term *related training* describes the school's responsibilities, while the complementary term *on-the-job training* refers to what the employer provides. These two aspects are coordinated carefully to avoid unnecessary repetition on the one hand or unfortunate gaps on the other.

The third part of the program, home-related training, is usually neglected by both school and community agencies. Parents sometimes not only are confused about what they should do but lack the advantage of knowing what other parents are doing. Their own children may give them inadequate and incorrect information. Thus the school must take responsibility for providing leadership and information in this regard.

SOME CHARACTERISTICS OF CAREER EDUCATION PROGRAMS

The emphasis in this chapter has been on the need for curriculum reform to include career education as an essential part of the secondary school curriculum, a logical continuation of what elementary schools provide. Currently, many persons are saying that this rational development is not enough, that crash programs are needed.

Some writers and speakers properly attack schools for overemphasizing academic subjects. Many youths from poverty-stricken areas need job preparation more than a foundation for college. Those who later decide to go to college will presumably be highly motivated to complete whatever additional preparation is required. However, all students need better preparation for producing goods and rendering services. Schools must face the realities of current economic crises. The real world is center stage with problems of unemployment, underemployment, urban deterioration, warped value systems, crime, and a host of other social and economic ills. To many people, career education seems a panacea.

Key elements of the program include expanded guidance and counseling staffs, more and better information about the world of work, more educational options, development of higher levels of employability and assumption of responsibility for job placement of all students, dropouts as well as graduates.

Such a program obviously requires total commitment by the community. The school no longer exists as a separate entity with a public relations program to tell the community how good its program is. Career education can not be a fad; rather, it must be a continuing, long-range approach to new concepts of increased responsibility for the welfare of all youths in a program fully shared with the community. In the process, the roles of teachers, counselors, and school administrators must change as the roles of students change. As these roles change, so will the materials, the courses, the locales of teaching and learning, and all other aspects of the curriculum.

Any school that plans to improve its program of career education may profit from studying what others are doing. Books, magazines, films and filmstrips, and materials that other schools create may provide ideas and leads. However, a word of warning is in order. Seldom is it wise simply to import programs from other communities. Every school community is unique. The potentials, relationships, and attitudes are local rather than universal. Studies of what others are doing are motivational and suggestive but not necessarily completely importable.

Career education is a never-ending process. The doors of the school should always be open to students of various ages who may want to come back for further advice and other kinds of assistance. Today's schools tend to forget about students after they graduate except for some periodic follow-up activities. The school envisioned in this book has a continuing relationship to aid employability and at the same time serve the people in the school's constituency.

Career education needs to go beyond the guidance department of the school, which hands out pamphlets and puts up posters and brings in some worker in the field to talk to students who *volunteer* to come to a meeting, thus indicating that they already have developed some interest in the field. That process ignores the possibility of interesting students who at the moment do not have any interest.

All students must participate. The motivational presentations and other methods that all departments use have to require the participation of everyone except students already enrolled in advanced work in a given department. Otherwise there is no opportunity to arouse interest that students may not at the moment possess.

Career education needs to rise above the status of an educational fad. Unlike "worthy home membership, better use of leisure time, ethical character" and the four other esteemed goals[1] that have been relatively ineffective in influencing curricula, career education must go beyond catchy phrases and periodic special grants and become in fact an integral part of curriculum improvement in secondary schools.

TOPICS FOR STUDY AND DISCUSSION

1. Unemployment caused either by technological advances, depressed economic conditions, or other factors weigh heavily on young people. An oversupply of teachers may affect you or someone you know. What other causes of unemployment are related to school programs and services and what recommendations do you have to help alleviate the situations?
2. How many school subjects and activities other than the social studies develop programs to foster productive youth employment? Use your own curriculum speciality as an example.
3. Prepare a proposal for improved coordination and cooperation of appropriate agencies in your community to assist youths and adults in locating productive careers.
4. Analyze the factors that made you choose both the broad field of education and your particular specialty. What lessons have you learned that should influence changes in the secondary school curriculum?

SELECTED REFERENCES

"Action Learning." National Association of Secondary School Principals *Bulletin* (November 1974), pp. 1–80.
> Eleven speakers at a conference on the use of the community as a learning environment describe both rationale and experiences in this important aspect of career education. Recommendations are provided by fifty-four conferees from a variety of urban and rural locales.

Bailey, Larry J., and Stadt, Ronald W. *Career Education: New Approaches to Human Development.* Bloomington, Ill.: McKnight & McKnight Publishing Company, 1973.
> Bailey and Stadt provide historical antecedents as well as describe the evolution of career education today. Chapter 5 deals with needs of women and the culturally disadvantaged. Chapter 10 and 11 emphasize curriculum development. Chapter 12 suggests ways to implement change in education.

Frymier, Jack L. *Annehurst Curriculum Classification System.* Chapter four, "Assessing a Learner's Characteristics." West Lafayette, Ind.: Kappa Delta Pi, 1977, pp. 69–103.

---

[1] NEA Commission on the Reorganization of Secondary Education, *Cardinal Principles of Secondary Education* (U. S. Bureau of Education Bulletin No. 35, Washington, D. C., 1918).

This chapter offers a comprehensive treatment of a method for assessing experience, intelligence, motivation, emotion-personality, creativity, and social, verbal, auditory, visual, and motor characteristics and developments — all with implications for career education.

Goldhammer, Keith, and Taylor, Robert E., eds. *Career Education.* Columbus, Ohio: Charles E. Merrill Books, 1972.

A group of persons — including Sidney P. Marland, Jr., then U. S. Commissioner of Education — stress the importance of career education and suggest programs to implement the idea in all aspects of schooling.

Grubb, W. Norton, and Lazerson, John. "Continuities and Fallacies in Career Education." *Harvard Educational Review* (November 1975), pp. 451–474.

Grubb and Lazerson provide a provocative review of the historical antecedents of the movement and give some warnings about the limitations of the movement when the focus is too largely centered on conventional vocational education and a cure-all for today's social and economic problems. They urge more attention to the role of work in society.

Hoyt, Kenneth, et al. *Career Education in the High School.* Salt Lake City: Olympus Publishing Company, 1977.

The authors provide a comprehensive treatment of philosophy and contributions of the movement. Models are given for both junior and senior high school programs, including relations to the subject areas, methodology, and evaluation.

Isaacson, Lee E. *Career Information in Counseling and Teaching.* Boston: Allyn and Bacon, 1971.

This book provides practical information on the scope and classification of occupations plus factors that influence workers and their careers. It shows how to collect and utilize career information and methods to use in schools to arouse interest and help in decision making.

Kapfer, Miriam B. *Behavioral Objectives in Curriculum Development: Selected Readings and Bibliography.* Englewood Cliffs, N. J.: Educational Technology Publications, 1971.

Thirty-eight authorities present pros and cons and examples of the use of better stated purposes in all curricular areas. The book provides practical suggestions for persons interested in almost any aspect of the topic.

Marland, Sidney Percy, Jr. *Career Education: A Proposal for Reform.* New York: McGraw-Hill Book Company, 1974.

This comprehensive treatment by the former U. S. Commissioner of Education provides a comprehensive treatment of purposes and programs.

Ohlsen, Merle M. *Guidance Services in the Modern School,* 2d ed. "Career Development," "Using Tests in Vocational Counseling," and "Placement and Follow-up Services." New York: Harcourt, Brace, Jovanovich, 1974, pp. 304–384.

In addition to descriptions of philosophy, programs, and methods, the book provides an extensive bibliography for persons wishing even more information. Practical suggestions for school programs are given; see particularly pp. 304–384.

Youth. The Seventy-fourth Yearbook of the National Society for the Study of Education, Part I. Chicago: University of Chicago Press, 1975.

"Youth and the Meaning of Work" (pp. 145–160), by Robert J. Havighurst and David Gottleib, and "Youth and Experiential Learning" (pp. 161–193), by Richard Graham, are two superlative statements that describe changes in work and how young people's values about work also are changing. Many examples and references to data document the material in this chapter.

16

Common Learnings, Mini-courses, and Special Projects

The preceding chapter emphasized relationships between career education and the conventional subject areas in a school. That discussion also pointed out the necessity of deciding in each of the major curriculum areas what knowledge, skills, and effective outcomes were *essential* for everyone to possess.

This chapter describes three alternative types of curriculum organization. First, a different point of view from that presented in Chapter 2 regarding essential learnings may produce the concept of "core curriculum," or "common learnings" as indicated in this chapter.

Second, at the level of hobbies and careers as explained in Chapter 15, some schools develop mini-courses to introduce students to selected curricular areas and to encourage further study. Many examples of these courses were given in Part II in connection with the various subject fields. The potential values of mini-courses in curriculum improvement are emphasized here also to show how varied lengths of time, flexible arrangements relating to who teaches the courses, course locations, and the methods of evaluating and reporting student progress can lead to further curriculum improvements in other aspects of the program.

Third, encouraging students to delve even more deeply into certain areas that they select can lead to special projects that are more comprehensive than conventional end-of-unit or term papers. They are studies in depth that will help secondary school students arrive at better decisions than they do now about future plans for higher education and/or career choices.

COMMON LEARNINGS OR CORE PROGRAMS
DEVELOPED AROUND THE NEEDS OF YOUTHS

The idea of a core program of common learnings received much attention in the late 1920s and early 1930s as curriculum experts sought ways to avoid duplications among the subject areas and to relate the total curriculum more closely to what all students need to acquire during their school years. Although elementary schools found this curricular approach easiest to accomplish, a considerable number of secondary schools worked along similar lines.

Pupils in the primary and middle years of schooling usually do not think basically in terms of their needs for English, science, mathematics, social studies, and the other school subjects described in Part II of this book. Do secondary school students need those designations? Some educators believe that these students will be motivated more, understand better, and remember more effectively what they learn if the curriculum is organized in relation to student needs rather than as content that comes basically from the subject specializations in higher education. Another way of stating the philosophy is that elementary and secondary schools should be organized to serve the needs of all youths rather than just to prepare some students for the advanced studies they will need for higher education.

A central emphasis on the common learnings idea in secondary schools occurred in two memorable 1944 publications: a book, *Education for ALL American Youth*,[1] and a briefer booklet[2] based on the book. These documents prescribed separate programs for youths in rural and urban areas. Although the general approach was the same in both locales, differences in application were made because at that time

[1] *Education For ALL American Youth.* Washington, D. C.: National Education Association, Educational Policies Commission, 1944.

[2] *Planning for American Youth: An Educational Program for Youth of Secondary School Age.* Washington, D. C.: National Association of Secondary School Principals, 1944.

more young people lived on farms and small communities than do so today.

The heart of the program was entitled "Ten Imperative Educational Needs of Youth." This statement, following a list of ten imperative needs of society, provided the basis for the development of a great many specific proposals under the heading "Common Learnings." The ten needs are repeated here as a basic reference because generally they are as relevant today as they were more than three decades ago:

1. All youth need to develop salable skills and those understandings and attitudes that make the worker an intelligent and productive participant in economic life. To this end, most youth need supervised work experience as well as education in the skills and knowledge of their occupations.
2. All youth need to develop and maintain good health and physical fitness.
3. All youth need to understand the rights and duties of the citizens of a democratic society, and to be diligent and competent in the performance of their obligations as members of the community and citizens of the state and nation.
4. All youth need to understand the significance of the family for the individual and society and the conditions conducive to successful family life.
5. All youth need to know how to purchase and use goods and services intelligently, understanding both the values received by the consumer and the economic consequences of their acts.
6. All youth need to understand the methods of science, the influence of science on human life, and the main scientific facts concerning the nature of the world and of humanity.
7. All youth need opportunities to develop their capacities to appreciate beauty in literature, art, music, and nature.
8. All youth need to be able to use their leisure time well and to budget it wisely, balancing activities that yield satisfactions to the individual with those that are socially useful.
9. All youth need to develop respect for other persons, to grow in their insight into ethical values and principles, and to be able to live and work cooperatively with others.
10. All youths need to grow in their ability to think rationally, to express their thoughts clearly, and to read and listen with understanding.[3]

The curriculum proposed for the schools in what was called American City was divided into five major areas: personal interests (for the

[3] *Education for ALL American Youth, op. cit.*

junior high school years), individual interests (for the upper years of secondary education), vocational preparation (also for the upper years of secondary education), common learnings, and health and physical fitness (for all years). The curriculum in all these areas except health and physical fitness was to draw from all the subject fields in the school and to be organized around young people's needs and interests.

The curricula in the common learnings courses would consist of experiences that everyone needed, regardless of what occupation was to be followed or where the individual happened to live. The course was to be three hours daily from grades 7 through 10, two hours daily in grades 11 and 12, and one hour daily in grades 13 and 14 (the community college).

Students would develop essential skills in reading, expression, mathematics, and study habits as they learned to give effective expression about and to study the history and development of their own community, state, and nation. They would learn how science has changed the world, how to use mathematics to understand what has happened, and how both these disciplines and others serve them in their daily lives.

In the upper years of the secondary school, the students would study American City at work and how people live, by means of visits, readings, films, talks, and discussions. Problems of family life, labor unions and management, sanitation and community health, consumer spending, and personal problems would help them better understand mathematics, science, social studies, English, and the other school subjects.

They would study how people live in cities and see what various organizations do for youths, how recreation occurs, and how plans are made and carried out to improve the environment. In the process, education for civic competence, leadership, housing and welfare, and general programs of group living and city planning would be understood. Students would come to appreciate how the roots of these problems can be found in national history and literature. Older students would study these problems in a world setting so that in the process they would have learned not only about their own community and nation but about the world as well.

As students participated in these common learnings or unified courses, they would also improve study skills, reading habits, and the like, with remedial help as needed. By tackling big problems that were real to them, students would come to understand other human beings better and ways that each one of them might make a maximum contribution.

The foregoing ideas are taken directly from the booklet *Planning For American Youth.* We refer in some detail to this work because it represents curriculum improvement that common learnings or core programs provide both in content and methods of learning. Obviously, teacher roles change and many other factors contribute to the process.

Although there was much enthusiasm at the time and much study of these approaches by faculty groups, the opposition of subject-matter specialists, especially university professors, was so pronounced and effective that the common learnings program was unable to achieve the success that many persons had envisioned for it. However, the movement is by no means dead.

Many people still believe strongly in the core or common learnings approach. Certainly it has had more impact at the level of middle and junior high rather than at senior high school. At the latter level, the closest approach has come from some of the unified or fusion courses that combine, for example, English and social studies, or mathematics and science. Humanities courses, as described in Part II, draw content from the fine arts, social studies, and English.

MINI-COURSES AS A METHOD FOR ENRICHING THE CURRICULUM

Another approach to secondary school curriculum improvement has become increasingly popular. As indicated previously, the use of mini-courses makes possible the introduction of new materials and diversification of the offering without changing the present program but rather simply by adding to it. Students may complete these mini-courses in specified lengths of time — such as one week, six weeks, two months, or whatever the teacher or department specifies — instead of the usual required semester or year. Also, in many cases it is possible for students to enroll in the courses without the usual restrictions of curriculum sequence or grade level. The conventional approach is to provide fractional credits for these courses, depending on their duration.

Proponents of mini-courses list a number of advantages to this approach to curriculum improvement. Probably the most important single reason is to provide updated and more relevant subject content without changing the existing organization of the curriculum in schools. Basic revisions in curriculum may take several years to complete, whereas mini-courses may be developed in a much shorter length of time and with fewer persons involved.

Teachers have hobbies and special interests, as do students. The mini-course allows teachers to develop courses along those lines, which may not have been included in the conventional curricular offerings. For example, a teacher who is interested in backpacking or some other hobby could organize this activity as an extracurricular activity, which students would have to engage in on weekends or during some other out-of-school time. But the development of a mini-course on the subject legitimizes the activity, giving interested students the opportunity to enroll in the course and receive credit during the regular time that schools are in session on either a half-day or full-time basis. Thus the program recognizes better the diverse interests and talents among both the staff and students.

Students may find that a particular mini-course, or a selection of mini-courses, meets their needs better than a conventional course that is longer and more diverse. Secondary school students should have covered basic skills earlier in their educational programs. If they have not done so, the school program can readily provide remedial work as needed. For example, some mini-courses may require relatively little reading, which is a boon for students with reading difficulties. If a mini-course specifies high levels of some physical skill, unskilled students may elect not to enroll; a conventional course, however, may have required them to perform some physical activities that would have been simply impossible for them.

The mini-course approach to curriculum improvement represents a cutting edge. Since not all teachers need to be committed to a given program nor all students involved in a given activity, it is easier for a school to implement this approach than to make conventional efforts to improve the curriculum.

The number and nature of mini-courses in a given school depends on the talents and interests of both teachers (those regularly employed by the school plus some lay citizens from the community) and students in that particular locality. Therefore, it is impossible to list specific recommendations of courses to be offered. The list that follows — and the illustrations given earlier in discussions of the various curricular areas — merely illustrate some courses that have been developed in some locales. In no sense are these recommendations made for a given school; in fact, some of the courses would be entirely inappropriate for some communities.

Physical education mini-courses, for example, might include badminton, weight training, water games, and horseshoe pitching or shoeing horses. Here are some examples in other curricular areas:

Oriental Cooking and Cultures
Exploring the Geological Past and Present to Observe Wildlife and
    Plant Forms
Basic Survival Techniques and Procedures for Mountainous Areas
Backpacking and Hiking
Camp Counseling
Forestry
Asian Literature
Film Making

Introduction to Anthropology
Learning to be a Politician
Intermediate Bicycling
Advanced Bicycling
Cake Decorating
Making Successful Marriages
Politics and Politicians
Home Electrical Repair
Gardening
Study of Hawaii
Horseback Riding
Individual Projects in Business
Japanese Conversation and Culture
Model Rocketry
Advanced Sailing and Racing
Speed Reading
Earning and Saving Money
Veterinary Science
Personal Automobile Maintenance and Repair
Local Weather Forecasting
Better Boating
Swing Choir
Beginning Bridge
Advanced Bridge
Drawing for Pleasure
Folk Dancing
Tourist French (or Spanish, Italian, or other languages)
Jewelry Making
Guitar Playing
Teaching Younger Children
Personal Grooming

The foregoing list illustrates how mini-courses represent an effort to liberalize and enrich the curriculum. A student can drop a course after one or two weeks if he or she finds it unrealistic, uninteresting, or a waste of time. A student may take more of these courses than would be possible as simply enrichment of conventional courses. A faculty may produce these courses more readily than revise conventional courses. Introducing or abolishing mini-courses is simpler than adding or subtracting units from conventional courses. The provision of mini-courses enables the curriculum to be more responsive to local needs in terms of youth needs, area needs, quality of the staff, and the like. These courses also provide opportunities for the school to experiment with escapes from the traditions of credit, pass/fail, and a wide variety of other recommendations for curriculum development made elsewhere in this book.

Schools use a variety of approaches in introducing mini-courses. We believe that these courses should be continually available; periodic announcements could indicate when a new course will start. Some schools have introduced the mini-course program by stopping all the conventional courses for a week or two so that most students and faculty members are involved in the mini-course approach.

At least one school provides a wide variety of mini-courses for the final six weeks of the conventional school year, a time when students usually become restless. Everyone in the school is able to elect a variety of these courses, the number being limited only by whether the student has completed all requirements in conventional subjects by the end of the second six-week period at the end of the second semester. Incidentally, that requirement itself provides some motivation for students insofar as the regular curriculum is concerned.

Although the cumulative records that the school keeps for each student should include a list of mini-courses completed, approximate time spent, nature of outcomes, and some indication of quality, conventional grades and credits should be avoided. See Chapter 33, pages 498–509, for our recommendations.

SPECIAL PROJECTS, MAINLY INDIVIDUAL

The special projects approach to curriculum improvement is more individualized than the mini-courses described in the preceding section. The mini-course typically involves a group of students; the special project is usually for one, two, or three students working together. The project is more likely to be a direct outgrowth of a conventional course, especially for talented students with avid interests.

Some schools call this type of program independent study. As indicated in Chapter 20, we define independent study quite differently, to include all the activities that students utilize in learning what the school requires of them. Therefore, the concept of special projects is not applied to all students but to those with specific interests and aspirations.

The special project may produce a written or an oral report, an audio or visual production, an exhibit, or a demonstration. The purpose is not only to provide the student with an enriching experience but also to develop a product that may be motivational to other students or contribute to the resources that the school provides for other students interested in that topic. A copy of the project should become a part of the library or other school resources so that it is available to other students. In some instances, the product may merit publication.

The perimeters of the special project are relatively more open than is the case with conventional assignments and independent study activities. Although a special project may be relatively limited and consummated in a short period, here we are referring to longer-term projects that are wider in scope and deeper in exploration and study. Some special projects have occupied more than a year of a student's time, although that is somewhat unusual. The point is that the school's program of special projects should be extremely flexible in these regards.

Here again, a few topics are suggested merely as illustrations and certainly not as specific recommendations. The creative talents of all teachers help to suggest possible special projects to students. Certainly, students should be encouraged to submit their own projects and to make suggestions for further study and investigation and production by other students. Here are some examples:

effects of various environments on the glands of frogs
characteristics of specified emerging African nationals
creative writing: "My Book of Poems"
studies of human behavior based on an analysis of inmates at a state reformatory
analyses of penalties called against the local high school football team during one or more seasons
the effects of the use of calculators on mathematics achievements
developing an advertising campaign and other methods to improve the offering and use of the school cafeteria
creative uses of photographic equipment
comparisons between old and new aspects of English literature
analyses of population changes in this city during the past decade
planning, designing, constructing, and cost analysis of a given piece of furniture
photographic essay of the locale and nature of accidents involving students and teachers in this school
a study of courthouse records to indicate the nature and changes in real estate ownership and development of a given area
writing a play, musical comedy, or other presentation

Again, there can be no prescribed list of activities for all schools in a district or all age levels in a given school. The local program does need to suggest appropriate kinds of activities, the methods for initiating such projects, how the project will be evaluated, what happens to the product in terms of future use by this school or elsewhere, and other suggestions that staff and students decide. Open-ended prescriptions add to creativity in the special projects. Every student should have the opportunity to develop a special project; the emphasis is on diversity rather than specific requirements for all students.

As is the case with common learnings and mini-courses, special projects represent a basic effort to improve the secondary school curriculum without necessarily altering the approach that the curriculum provides in conventional subjects. It is hoped that in the long run, as the curriculum becomes more individualized from the standpoint of both teachers and students, the emphases in this chapter will become incorporated into the regular curriculum of the school rather than being offered only as enrichment, as suggested here. In the meantime, the school program needs to provide motivation, time, resources, guidance, and evaluation for all students to engage in special projects.

TOPICS FOR STUDY AND DISCUSSION

1. Consider the idea of organizing the curriculum around common learnings rather than such conventional subject areas as English, mathematics, and home economics. Then prepare to defend or oppose this approach against the subject-centered idea. The outcome may be a paper, a debate, or a consensus-seeking class discussion.
2. The ten imperative youth needs were developed in the early 1940s. What new needs would you add or which of the original ten may be de-emphasized now?
3. Are mini-courses a good way to improve the curriculum or are they merely an easy way to keep the old curriculum while developing separate new, highly segmented alternatives? Defend your answer.
4. Using the subject you teach regularly or are prepared to teach, provide an optional mini-course on a topic that specially interests you — or that you think would interest students in a given locale. Develop, in at least outline form, the purposes, procedures, and evaluation methods for the course.
5. As a university student or a teacher, you have written term papers and done special projects. Take some one of these efforts as an example for a paper or oral presentation in order to describe the benefits you received from doing it and, if possible, the contributions of your effort to others.
6. What records should schools maintain about the curriculum efforts discussed in this chapter? Should these records be distributed to other institutions and employers along with conventional transcripts of credits? Prepare to argue, discuss, and possibly reach some consensus on these questions.

SELECTED REFERENCES

Alberty, Harold B., and Alberty, Elsie J. *Reorganizing the High School Curriculum,* 3d ed. New York: The Macmillan Company, 1962.

In "Curriculum Designs for General Education," pp. 199–236, these noted authorities on core programs describe time-blocks; correlation of two or more subjects; organization of three or more subjects around themes; organizations around problems, needs, and interests of adolescents; and teacher-student planned activities without reference to formal structure. They also cite arguments for and against core, list research studies, and provide an extensive bibliography.

Frymier, Jack L. *Annehurst Curriculum Classification System*. West Lafayette, Ind.: Kappa Delta Pi, 1977.

Chapters 2 and 3 provide specific steps for selecting materials and programs that can meet individual needs, sometimes by cutting across conventional subject areas, but more often by identifying new content within school subjects.

Guenther, John, and Ridgeway, George C. "Mini-Courses: Promising Alternatives in the Social Studies."

A study in Kansas in 1972 indicated that 28 percent of the state's high schools were offering mini-courses and that many others were planning to do so. Guenther and Ridgeway indicate the reasons.

Howard, Alvin W., and Stombis, George C. *The Junior High and Middle School: Issues and Practices*. Scranton Penna.: Intext Educational Publishers, 1970.

Chapter 13 lists factors that influence design and describes a variety of approaches, including subject-matter, fused, and core approaches, with advantages and disadvantages of each.

Unrue, Glenys G. *Responsive Curriculum Development: Theory and Action*. Berkeley, Calif.: McCutchan Publishing Corporation, 1975.

Part 1 traces theory and action in curriculum development, and Part 2 emphasizes pressures for change that come from changing moral values, concepts of democracy, individual needs, and systems development.

Vars, Gorden F. "Curriculum in Secondary Schools and Colleges." In *A New Look at Progressive Education*, 1972 yearbook. Washington, D. C.: Association for Supervision and Development, 1972.

Vars describes a variety of approaches to curriculum reform, including broad fields, fusion, core, and problem areas. Four lessons from past difficulties are emphasized: more planning, better sets of problem areas and resource units, more use of curriculum specialists, and continuous information to parents and other community members.

17

Extraclass Activities

Relationships between secondary school administrators and their students have undergone many changes in recent years. Student issues regarding school governance, race relations, sexual freedom, and grievance procedures are part of the scene today. Serious problems of communication in these areas are inherent. Authorities in the student activities field are pushing for a wider and better use of student activities as a means of bridging the gap. Some advocate the identity of a "third curriculum" encompassing a variety of student activity programs as a means of accomplishing the goal.

In the evolution of today's system of secondary education, the abundant recreational, athletic, and club activities may well be identified as a third curriculum, with the area of elective subjects as the second curriculum and the required courses as the first curriculum. This identity of a third curriculum may not be too important, but it does call attention to the development and importance of extraclass activities.

The need to define the purposes of student representative organizations is especially important in this time of educational, social, and

301

political change. America's democratic system is rooted in the belief that all citizens who are affected by a system should have a voice in deciding how that system operates. Unfortunately, this belief has not been generally accepted in regard to student activities. Student leaders are pressed on one side by fellow students who accuse them of weak leadership and on the other side by some administrators who deny the need for and the right to any student leadership.

Academic scholarship was the sole purpose for a school's existence, but a dualism developed in American secondary schools. In addition to scholarship activity in the classroom, a whole series of educational activities developed outside the classroom. Some overenthusiastic proponents of extraclass activity even claim that this activity program comes closer to supplying basic educational needs than does the regular academic program.

The origin of the extraclass activity movement probably could be traced to the first time a school administrator became interested in the games students were playing outside the jurisdiction of the school and invited them to bring their activities into the regulated area of the school. Development was rapid, because parents were invited to see their students perform and the students liked the exaltation of having spectators. Teachers became willing sponsors because they enjoyed the break from the formality of the regular classroom.

Status was established for extraclass activities when college directors of admission began to consider them important enough to be listed on secondary school transcripts and employers began to use student participation in extraclass activities as criteria for evaluating potential job success. Both these developments reflect the current feeling that students learn from these activities many things that are important for successful participation in adult life. In particular, they suggest that human relations can be developed better in extraclass activities than in academic classrooms.

In many schools, a student's social status depends on the extent and type of participation in extraclass activities. Students who are in positions of leadership or who participate in prestige clubs have the highest status. In the rapidly developing suburban areas, parents relate their children's social status in school to the social prestige desired by the adult suburbanite. The blue-collar parents encourage their children to grasp the reins of leadership as basic training for quite a different role. Extraclass activities furnish the experiences students from laboring families need for labor leadership roles.

The various terms used to describe extraclass activities illustrate a changing emphasis on their educational importance. One of the most frequent terms used is *extracurricular*. This connotes curricular status, but beyond the realm of the regular curriculum. The term *cocurricular* is also used in many schools. Apparently used to establish equal status for all learning activities, whether inside or outside the classroom, the term suggests a cooperative basis for extended activity beyond the academic classroom. In many situations, curriculum leaders have given regular classroom status to activities that heretofore have been considered outside the curriculum. School bands, choral groups, and orchestras have been scheduled as regular class periods, usually with full academic credit. The school newspaper is the main activity of the secondary school journalism class, and the school annual may be prepared in a regular classroom situation.

The use of the term *extraclass* suggests that everything a student does under the sponsorship of the school is an extension of the classroom. This situation may be the result of a desirable improvement in comprehensiveness — a balance of emphasis on all the student's learning activities. Thus, athletic contests and band concerts become classroom learning situations, and the Latin club is pragmatic evidence of a good language-learning situation.

ISSUES INVOLVED

The expansion or reduction of extraclass activities is one of the issues that continues to trouble secondary school administrators and their faculties. School evaluators stress the importance of these activities and attempt to measure the effectiveness of the school in terms of student participation. The various accrediting associations cite schools for unusual ventures into fields of new activities. It would appear there would be no reason for curtailment of extraclass activities, but this is not an accurate deduction.

Overinvolvement and Underinvolvement

Both overinvolvement and underinvolvement of students are troublesome problems in regulating extraclass activities. So many activities are available that faculty sponsors may compete among themselves for the time of the capable and popular students. These overactive young people are often also carrying a heavy schedule of academic work. Parents complain of overworked, exhausted, and frequently emotionally disturbed children. Church and civic leaders blame the school for their inability to capture students' time for community work. Many schemes have been used to curtail and regulate student participation.[1] The most common one is a simple regulation of the number of activities in which a student is permitted to participate each semester. Some people question such regulations, holding to the oft-repeated statement that it is the busy person who really gets things done. They say participation is a matter of individual needs and should be accompanied by intelligent guidance on the part of the school.

It is possible that underinvolvement is a more serious problem than overinvolvement. Most of the dropout studies show that youths dropping out of school are not participants in extraclass activities. Their school activities are confined to regular classroom work, and continued failure or boredom haunts their lives. It is thought that maladjusted students would find success and interest in the less restrictive boundaries of extraclass experiences. Therefore, school administrators have turned to forced participation through graduation requirements. However, forced participation might remove valuable spontaneity from such activities. Probably the most satisfactory answers to student involvement will come through intelligent guidance and the development of appealing activities.

From the standpoint of the curriculum, the issue of student involvement in extraclass activities may be solved by giving curricular status to many of the activities that have not been considered worthy of regular school time. Rejection of this idea has been a foolish hobgoblin of those who would not temper the sacredness of the so-called solid subjects. A realistic educational objective would be to bring vitality and purpose to all classroom activities and then let these qualities flow over into the extraclass hours.[2] Another aid to greater participation will come through the development of more flexible scheduling, so that the relative values of these activities can be adjusted to their needs.

Meeting the Changing Needs of Society

One of the most critical issues related to extraclass activities concerns the question of whether they can be adjusted to meet the changing needs of society. These changes obviously affect the curriculum. It has been pointed out before that the United States is a highly urbanized, industrial nation with an affluent society pockmarked by racial discord

---

[1] Richard A. Gorton, "Major Problems in Student Activities," in *Responsible Student Involvement* (Washington, D. C.: National Association of Secondary School Principals, 1975), pp. 33–34.

[2] J. Golub, "Going Beyond Motivation to Involvement at the Junior High–Middle School Level," *English Journal* (February 1977), pp. 80–83.

and poverty. Adults in industry are working fewer hours, and unskilled youths are finding work scarce. People who wish to take an active part in society's affairs soon learn they cannot be heard unless they join like-minded individuals in voluntary associations.

Social maturation is occurring earlier than in the past. Former college activities are now part of the high school milieu, and junior high youngsters are having proms and formal dances. A teen-age subculture has developed, exhibiting a wide fascination for fads and offbeat social ventures and alternately worshiping the ridiculous and the serious. It purposely strives to confuse its elders, but it is a force that demands and secures recognition. The commercial entertainment business has been revolutionized to meet its needs: recording of teen-age music has become a multibillion dollar business; motion pictures are slanted to adventure, horror, and sex; and television networks openly admit that their programs for the new season are aimed at the twelve-to-sixteen-year-old group. This teen-age culture, operating on the outer limits of the school program, presents a problem for school planners, but a mistake will be made if the school does not adjust its programs to capitalize on the serious longings this group is covering up with its loud flamboyance.

Youth — idealistic, as always — is in search of a cause. It longs to be heard, struggling against the impersonality of the day and seeking to change its own lot and the lot of others. It suffers from boredom thrust on it by financial security and by the fact that it is not needed in the work stream of the social order. Youth necessarily has been shunted out of the mainstream. It is conscious of the lack of important things to do.

Solutions to the problems of youth are complex, and school officials cannot be blamed for groping, but certain ground rules are evident. The overwhelming success of the Peace Corps suggests that young people want to work at something worthwhile in order to feel necessary and important. The risk of life involved in joining intense racial demonstrations shows a deep-rooted desire to do something for others. Young people constantly struggle to be accepted as partners by adults. Perhaps the aimless frivolity of some of the school's extraclass activities has caused administrators to underestimate the capacity of youth for serious social decisions. They must reevaluate objectives of extraclass activities considering teen-age cultural propensities.

Realistic Evaluation

A third issue in the extraclass field is how to evaluate activities properly. To date, much of the evaluation has been based on opinion rather than controlled research, so many of the claimed benefits are more theoretical than realistic. There is always the possibility of claiming too much on one hand and failing to develop full potential on the other. Character building and leadership development are usually credited to extraclass activities, although this evaluation has not been substantiated. A Texas high school principal, to justify the identification and grouping of football players in physical education classes, says his boys get their start here for professional football contracts. An overzealous dramatics teacher attempts to dominate the life of a budding female actress to the exclusion of parental advice and guidance. The jazz trumpeter in the stage band is filled with delusions of fame and success by his admiring classmates and the unwise forbearance of his band director.

Another phase of the evaluation problem concerns decisions about the extent of the school's extraclass program. Where does the responsibility of the school end and that of the community begin? Is the school performing functions that can be done better by community agencies? Should the school or an outside agency sponsor recreation? Should the school sponsor dances or merely teach students to dance? Is the school attempting to shoulder too much of the responsibility for young people's out-of-school hours? These decisions are especially important if the school's existing program is ineffectual and no other agency has a youth program.

Probably the greatest need for careful analysis of the school's function lies in the area of overstressed athletics and marching bands. In a pedagogical sense, athletics and other performance activities are considered extraclass activities, but the unreasonable emphasis put on these things by some schools raises the question of whether they are educational activities. In those schools they are more of a form of entertainment than of an educational venture. Stressing the importance of having a winning team, excessive firing and hiring of coaches, and overindulgent solicitude toward varsity athletes are all marks of maladjusted educational objectives. School bands are used at athletic contests to provide additional entertainment. In a struggle for a share of the gate receipts, an argument sometimes arises over whether the football team or the band has more entertainment value at the game. Certain communities think so much of the "chamber of commerce value" of the high school band that they raise thousands of dollars to send it across the nation to participate in spectacular parades.

Some educators accept this overemphasis by rationalizing that the activities are good public relations and that the students gain educational travel experience. This is certainly a distorted viewpoint, and it is hard to believe that any serious-minded school leader, who sees extraclass activities as the purposeful extension of regular classroom work, can accept it as a valid educational evaluation. In several states, secondary school principals have banded to form voluntary associations for the purpose of bringing all extraclass activities under centralized control. Accrediting associations also have given these activities added attention. Surveys consistently show that thoughtful patrons are more interested in the basic educational purposes of the school than in public performance display of its students. Could it be that where excessive overemphasis exists, school administrators are being misguided by outspoken minorities?

BASIC AREAS OF ACTIVITIES

Whether activities are made a regular part of the curriculum or whether they remain in the extraclass category, they are usually classified as clubs, student councils, publications, dramatics, and athletics. There are two general types of clubs: those closely allied to the classroom, such as the Future Homemakers' Club (a requirement in the vocational home economics program), and the hobby-type club somewhat removed from the mainstream of classroom work, such as the camera club or the ham radio club. Theoretically, the best purposes of education are served when the club is an extension of classroom learning.

The success of all club work depends on the enthusiasm of the students and the devotion of the faculty sponsors. The two types of clubs call for different types of sponsors and appeal to different types of students. In the associated classroom type of club, the sponsor has inherent capability due to knowledge of the subject and interest in enriching classroom learning. A member of an accrediting team expressed amazement at the extensive activity of one school's Latin club. From a school population of around 1000 pupils, the Latin club enrolled over 250. The club met during the noon hour and membership was entirely voluntary. The secret of the club's success could be found in the outstanding ability of the Latin teacher, whose students were excited about Latin activities both within and without the classroom. It was difficult to discover where one began and the other ended.

The special interest, or hobby, clubs appeal to pupils who desire a less formalized activity. These clubs are usually developed from the expressed interest of students who persuade some faculty member of like interests to sponsor them. It has been said that a successful camera club takes a real "photography nut" for a sponsor. It must also be added that it takes students who are keenly interested in photography. Sometimes financial ability to buy equipment and supplies determines the student's participation, but it is usually more a matter of interest.

Needless to say, securing capable and interested sponsors is a major administrative responsibility. With the coming of negotiated contracts, teachers are demanding compensation for all duties beyond regular classroom instruction. While there is no doubt as to the justification of teachers seeking extra pay for excessive demands made on their time in sponsoring extraclass activities such as clubs, it does tend to remove part of the spontaneity of an informal relationship, and in cases of restricted school finances it will probably reduce the number of clubs a school can support.

From a curricular viewpoint, school clubs should fulfill two objectives. First, they should integrate the educational purposes of the school. Second, they should provide wholesome enjoyment for participants. Criteria for evaluating club activities and sympathetic stimulation of those participating should be administrative objectives.

STUDENT COUNCILS

The student council represents one of the best agencies in the school for putting into practice all the objectives for democratic citizenship. In the opinion of many evaluators, a good student council is one of the best identifications of a good school. It is difficult to understand why any school principal would fail to recognize this, yet in some schools, the principal is either lethargic in backing the council or downright hostile to its existence, claiming that students have no right to interfere in the administration of the school. This must be the mark of administrative insecurity or an autocratically directed school.

In the early days of student participation in school administrative affairs, the term *student government* was used. Unfortunately, students were directly involved in such things as the discipline of their classmates. Elaborate systems of student courts were established, and penalties and fines were levied. This type of participation was doomed from the start. Students should share in the administration of the school, but they should not run the school. Leaders in the student council movement have worked hard to establish the principle of separation of powers between the pupils and the administration. There ought to be mutual understanding and rapport between the council and the principal, and each should know where authority begins and ends.

The function of a student council is to determine the wishes and desires of the student body and make them known to the administration and faculty. This group of elected leaders coordinates extraclass activities, school improvement, and school morale. The council should have extensive authority in determining the operation of student affairs that are outside the classroom but within the jurisdiction of the school — the part of school life that closely resembles community responsibility in the adult neighborhood. Through the student council, students can gain realistic experiencs in procedures of democratic government.

The constitution of the student council should clearly define its powers and responsibilities. Many activities can be given over completely to the council, others can be shared with the faculty, and still others should be out of the council's jurisdiction. The faculty and administration can take pride in the extent to which youths can carry responsibility for their own growth and development. But they must be prepared to help students right themselves if they stumble and fall.

If the student council is to play an important role in the school, the administrator will need to exercise extreme caution in rejecting its recommendations. Of course, this does not mean that recommendations that are clearly illegal or are not in the best interest of the school must be accepted, although discerning which recommendations to accept and which to reject will take a great deal of administrative judgment and wisdom. Administrators should realize that they will probably have to compromise sometimes and, in certain instances, take risks in accepting the recommendations they believe to be impractical. However, frequently the only way the students can appreciate the judgment of the administrator is by being permitted to make their own mistakes.

While it is probably true that some administrators prefer a student council that confines its program to organizing social events, the administrator who is truly interested in capitalizing on and encouraging the interests and skills of students will help them develop a more far-reaching program. This program should have as its main purpose the improvement of the educational and social environment of the school and the community. Included in the program might be the following kinds of activities:

1. conducting remedial classes in a disadvantaged neighborhood
2. refurnishing a community center for youths and adults
3. setting up a city-suburb exchange program
4. meeting with the principal to recommend new courses for the school's curriculum
5. arranging for an after-school series of school lectures on a topical issue
6. developing a form for evaluating class instruction
7. organizing a student-led seminar on contemporary issues for summer school, without grades or credits
8. setting up a corps of student tutors to help slow learners

9. developing student-written individualized learning materials
10. meeting with community leaders to plan for more effective use of community resources
11. meeting with parents to explore school problems as parents perceive them
12. making a proposal to the school board to hire teacher aides

Recent critics of student councils warn of the pitfalls such organizations may encounter. They contend that a homogeneous membership, weak student leadership, and the wrong adviser can culminate in a meaningless program. Membership should reflect all segments of the social order of the school, else the council will be composed of a homogeneous group of the "right" students. Rejection of such a group by many students renders the council impotent. Good leadership is essential but difficult to secure. Unfortunately, leadership characteristics that have been in vogue in the past are detrimental in the present-day student milieu. For example, a good way for a student council leader to become ineffective is to appear too supportive of the school administration. Finally, the right sponsor is vital to the success of a council. He or she certainly should not be an inexperienced teacher, nor the old war-horse type. Neither should this person be one who tries to direct too much. Obviously the sponsor must be able to communicate and be accepted by today's youth.

The success of a student council largely depends on the principal and the faculty. A sympathetic, friendly, and cooperative faculty can give a council so much help and support that success of almost any council venture will be assured. An apathetic, unconcerned faculty, too busy to extend time or effort in support of council projects, can render the organization ineffective in short order. Much of the responsibility for faculty attitude toward the student council rests with the principal. The task is to interpret students' objectives to the teachers and teachers' wishes to the students. He or she can help afford the council the prestige it rightly deserves.

INTERSCHOLASTIC ATHLETICS

As has been mentioned earlier, it is debatable whether interscholastic athletics are any longer an extraclass activity, for they are overemphasized and out of harmony with good educational objectives. However, in the minds of thoughtful educators, athletics in proper perspective should and must remain a truly extraclass activity. Because of the potential for controversy and the magnitude of the problems involved, athletic programs must be directed by those who are willing to make judgments based on sound principles. The extensiveness of an athletic program, including interscholastic athletics, may make the delegation of authority a necessity, but the responsibility for its relation to the total educational program must remain under central administrative control.[3]

Efforts at regulation have probably been greater in athletics than in any other school activity. Objectives and standards have been established, debated, and reestablished. School officials, athletic officials, accrediting associations, special committees, and even government agencies have been active in establishing regulatory principles for conducting athletic contests. Statewide activities commissions, organized and operated by secondary school principals, probably have been the most progressive and most effective agencies operating in this area. Over half the states have established such commissions, which regulate the entire range of extraclass activities involving interscholastic competition. (A complete discussion of these organizations is presented later in the chapter.)

Enthusiastic advocates of interscholastic athletics claim it is one of the best sources for realization of educational objectives because of the intense interest involved and the highly emotional situations that develop. This claim is based, of course, on the supposition that the program is well organized and well conducted. If it is not, the potential for adverse outcomes is equally great. Athletic programs in which students are exploited to entertain the public, advertise and earn money for the school, or enhance the professional reputation of the coach have no place in educational institutions and should not be tolerated.

Sensible and reasonable ground rules can be set up for an athletic program. In the first place, all activities should be conducted as an integral part of the total educational program. Athletics, including interscholastic games, should supplement rather than substitute for a good physical education program. Equal time should be given to each game when planning intramural athletic contests or providing experiences in games such as tennis, golf, bowling, and archery. Administrative control of interscholastic athletics must remain with the central administrator of the school. The physical welfare and safety of participants must be a primary objective; permitting injured or poorly equipped players to take part in games is intolerable. Finally, if good sportsmanship and good citizenship are to be outcomes, rules and regulations of officials and regulatory bodies must meet with cheerful and cooperative compliance.

[3] L. E. Alley, "Athletics in Education: The Double-Edged Sword," *Phi Delta Kappan* (October 1974), pp. 105–109.

Some of the most troublesome problems in the area of athletics have arisen in the junior high schools, where athletic programs have tended to become junior replicas of the high school. The same excesses have entered junior high interscholastic athletics, and damage due to the immaturity of the participants is inestimable. The issue is whether junior high students should be taking part in interscholastic games. Physical education authorities suggest a limited program adapted to the capacities and needs of junior high school boys and girls. Certainly the physical and emotional immaturity of junior high youngsters should be a determining factor in program establishment. Basic objectives of the junior high school are not tolerant of overadulation of varsity athletes and the "hoopla" of championship games.

A new dimension in interscholastic athletics has been created by the government and court regulations that require full eligibility for girls in all sports and physical activities.[4] Most schools are using federal money in some form or another. Such being the case, regulations from the Department of Health, Education, and Welfare clearly state that there shall be no discrimination in regard to sex in participation in any school activities. These regulations are the implementation of Title IX of the Educational Amendments of 1972.

Furthermore, taken as a group, recent court decisions dealing with rules prohibiting girls from participating on boys' athletic teams appear to establish the principle that eligibility rules of schools or state athletic associations that prohibit female athletes of proven athletic ability from competing for a place on boys' teams in noncontact sports violate the equal protection rights of girls where separate interscholastic teams for girls are not maintained. A few state courts have interpreted the federal statutes to include contact sports. Final decisions in this area are unclear.

Many governing bodies for state interscholastic athletics have amended their regulations to permit female participation in all but contact sports. The state of Michigan adopted the following: Female pupils shall be permitted to participate in all noncontact interscholastic athletic activities, including but not limited to archery, badminton, bowling, fencing, golf, gymnastics, riflery, shuffleboard, skiing, swimming, diving, table tennis, track and field, and tennis. Even if the institution does not have a girls' team in any noncontact interscholastic athletic activity, the female must be permitted to compete for a position on the boys' team. Nothing in this subsection may be construed to prevent or interfere with the selection of competing teams solely on the basis of athletic ability.

---

[4] D. E. Arnold, "Compliance with Title IX in Secondary School Physical Education," *Journal of Physical Education and Recreation* (January 1977), pp. 19–22.

Many problems are associated with the entrance of girls into full participation in interscholastic athletics, but most of them are solvable, particularly those dealing with finance and facilities. No longer can secondary school administrators offer as the reason for denial the physiological differences between sexes.

STUDENT PUBLICATIONS

Student publications — the newspaper, the yearbook, and the literary magazine — are among the best examples of activities that should not be classified as extraclass. Formal publications of the students have been made part of the curriculum in many comprehensive schools, and in no sense of the word should they be considered "extra," or outside the regular classroom schedule. When the publications are organized and prepared according to good educational procedures, they fulfill two objectives: they are the vehicles for making practical application of writing skills, and they afford opportunities for vocational exploration that might lead to careers in professional journalism.

The school newspaper can add or detract from the image of the school, depending on whether it publishes lively news or adolescent social trivia, or on whether it is a true representation of student life or a censored product of the faculty sponsor. Surveys of school newspapers show that as high as 80 percent of the news consists of such nonsensical information as what junior girl is dating what senior boy, and who is carrying a secret torch for the football captain of the school. A good school newspaper should have the same credentials as a regular newspaper. It should report the newsworthy activities of the school accurately, and it should reflect the serious thinking of the student body. It should be the voice of leadership for its youthful clientele. The just fate of an unworthy publication is to have its readers lose faith in its purpose or become bored with its stale ideas. Teen-age culture is filled with exciting and intriguing experiences as well as stubborn and baffling problems. The school newspaper should mirror this unsettled growth period.

Student newspapers have been a source of considerable controversy in recent years. They have tended to reflect student unrest through editorial attack on school administration and faculty. Questionable taste in the use of pictures and obscene language has caused administrative problems. In many cases the appearance of an underground student newspaper has been the source of extreme irritation to school authorities.

In some cases where school administrators have used their authority to stop such practices, students have gone to court. Courts have generally upheld student rights to publish material with the following exceptions:

1. *libelous material,* that which may result in defamation of character, such as a statement concerning a person that may unnecessarily expose her or him to hatred or contempt, or which could have a tendency to injure the person professionally
2. *obscene and profane material;* generally the courts have been more restrictive regarding language and pictorial representations of students younger than college age.
3. material that would tend to *incite to disruption* the educational process of the school
4. material that would *clearly endanger the students' health and safety*

If the administrator or the journalism adviser of a school is going to censor some aspect of a student publication, it appears that such censorship should be based on one or more of these four categories.

Some schools publish worthwhile yearbooks. In other schools, however, publishing activities are worthless as educational ventures because they involve too much deleterious assistance from professional publishers and photographers. Frequently, a school selects a publisher for the yearbook on the basis of how much professional help its agent will render the school. Unfortunately, this help often takes the form of unimaginative advice aimed at rendering greater profit to the publishing house. A high degree of tolerance is given to stereotyped material such as the last will and testament and the senior prophecy, and early submission of such material is awarded a discount, since it helps the commercial publisher maintain a balanced work load. The commercial photographer also has a profit motive. If a large number of group shots are included, the photographer guarantees a certain number of dull informals. Of course, the real profit comes from the sale of individual photographs to the seniors. The school's reward is a photographic cut for the yearbook.

The extraclass planners need to reevaluate the publication of the yearbook carefully.[5] The excessive costs of publication, the sterility of educational content, and the lack of opportunities for practical experiences for pupils raise the issue of whether the yearbook actually has educational value. To restore vitality to this publication, students must be made responsible for arrangement of content and imaginative authorship and photography.

[5] Charles E. Savedge, "Is the High School Yearbook in a Critical Era?" National Association of Secondary School Principals *Bulletin* (February 1975), pp. 62–66.

A limited number of schools support a literary magazine. Some of them are exceptionally good, while others suffer from lack of emphasis on the real purpose of such a publication: to provide encouragement for creative writing. Submission of material should not be confined to members of English classes or to seniors. Creativity is the possession of every student. The freshman science pupil as well as the embryonic sportswriter in the sophomore class may come up with youthful literary gems.

SPEECH AND DRAMATIC ACTIVITIES

Valuable dramatic and forensic experiences are gained in the formalized atmosphere of the classroom. Good teachers use these activities to bring variety and enrichment to their classroom learning situation. A certain amount of dramatic flair is inherent in children. The alert teacher, capitalizing on their natural tendency to imitate, to exaggerate, and to dramatize, provides them with opportunities for self-expression, development of imagination, and acquisition of self-confidence. The extension of these opportunities forms the extraclass activities of dramatics and speech.

School plays, dramatic club offerings, and interscholastic speech contests form the central core of dramatic and speech extraclass activities. The school play is a familiar landmark in American education. Its values are relative and depend on the educational objectives involved. Some schools have a reputation for the highly dramatic effectiveness of their plays. This means a finished product is a basic objective, requiring the assignment of leading roles to experienced students with proven dramatic ability. Educational values are associated with a high degree of specialization. In other schools, dramatic excellence is sacrificed by casting eager, inexperienced, and less capable students. The objective here is to afford these experiences to as many students as possible.

A well-balanced dramatic program should meet both objectives. Students of unusual and superior talents should be given every opportunity to further their growth. At the same time, all other students who want to act should not be denied the opportunity. The school should support dramatic clubs of differing purposes and should join the National Thespian Society, a dramatic honorary association for worthy students, whose membership encompasses anyone engaged in dramatic effort — actors, stage hands, electricians, and directors.

Forensic activities have reached a low ebb in some schools. This is regrettable, because lasting values can be gained from organizing thoughts and effectively communicating them. Many people in industry and public life can trace their success to the ability to communicate orally. Concomitant values assigned to public speaking experiences include the development of research attitudes, the ability to organize and retain knowledge, and the ability to develop critical thinking. Authorities in the speech field hope for a resurgence of scholastic speaking activities. Planners of extraclass activities should consider this area carefully.

SUPERVISION AND CONTROL

The direct control of extraclass activities operating within the school is the responsibility of the principal and faculty. Part of the responsibility is delegated and shared with the students. To solve the problems that occur when extraclass activities move off campus, school administrators have formed regulatory bodies. The earliest of these were state athletic associations for the purpose of regulating interscholastic athletic competition. Thirty-four states have already supplanted these single-purpose groups with more inclusive groups for the purpose of regulating all extraclass activities. These organizations are generally known as activities commissions or associations.

The need for more extensive regulation of off-campus extraclass activities partially resulted from the stepped-up activities of high school bands. It is not uncommon for schools to engage in local, district, and state contests to determine the superiority of these musical organizations. They are used extensively for giving students "educational trips" and providing "publicity" for local communities. Not only have high school bands been sent from coast to coast, but in several instances they have been involved in foreign junkets. School authorities, sensing the development of problems beyond the control of local power, turned to voluntary state regulating procedures.[6] It appears logical to include the whole gamut of extraclass activities in the scope of these newly organized activities commissions, although there is no urgent need for regulating many of the less troublesome activities.

The advocates of state voluntary regulating bodies point to the need for united action in any field of endeavor. They contend that the individual school administrator is powerless to withstand local pressures and local snap judgments unless group support is given. Group action is a prerequisite to efficiency, and such action is possible only when members of the group are loyal to its ideals and recognize the value of

[6] Robert L. Ackerly and Ivan B. Gluckman, *The Reasonable Exercise of Authority* (Washington D. C.: National Association of Secondary School Principals, 1976), p. 22.

organization. Policies and regulations must be formulated to insure a degree of equality in competition and to prevent excesses that might be forced on one school to the detriment of all other schools in the group.

Other forms of off-campus regulation of extraclass activities are furnished by professional organizations and accrediting associations. The National Association of Secondary School Principals publishes an annual list of approved contests and activities. The North Central Accrediting Association sanctions this list for its member schools as well as approving the regulations of the various state organizations. It must be emphasized that all organizations operate on a voluntary basis and in no way attempt to absorb or abridge the legal authority of local or state boards of education. They are simply a means of implementing the authority and responsibility delegated to the local school administration. In a larger sense they are the means for providing more abundant and wholesome extraclass experiences for boys and girls.

IDENTIFICATION OF VALUES

Assuming that the student quest for "relevance" is not met in the classroom, there could be experiences in extraclass activities, resulting from student participation in decision making, that could stabilize total school experience. The demarcation between class and extraclass activities is fading in many of the modularly scheduled, independent-learning, mini-coursed secondary schools, but there still are opportunities for students to promote a number of educational activities that are officially sanctioned and relevant to their needs. To assure relevance in extraclass activities, care should be exercised to see that they do not become static from year to year. In a relevant situation, activities are born, flourish, and die each year — responsive, as they should be, to student needs at the time. The future development of extraclass activity will depend on how well school authorities identify and implement the values inherent in these activities. Basically, they are one of the best potentials for establishing good student-teacher relationships. In the informal atmosphere that is characteristic of these activities, a mutual friendship and respect can be developed that enables the teacher to understand the student and the student to recognize the teacher as an ally or friend. This rapport can lead to better overall school morale. Opportunities for better guidance are abundant for a mutual feeling of trust can enable the teacher to gain the student's confidence and learn his or her problems.

Extraclass meetings foster the freedom and informality that is characteristic of adult group meetings. The experience of speaking as a member of the group, the development of leadership roles, and the spontaneous contributions made in an extemporaneous matter prepare the student for similar activities in the adult order.

Extraclass activities provide a vehicle for securing a broad look at possible vocations. Many students develop interests in these areas that lead to the pursuit of a future occupation.

Extraclass activity is probably most valuable as a supplement to regular classroom work. The wise teacher uses it to enrich classwork and motivate students to explore vistas creatively beyond the scope of prescribed classroom hours. The total school program can be enhanced by this extension of the classroom learning situation.

Finally, a major health need can be met in the extraclass area. Mental health leading to a general physical well-being can be developed by broad and varied opportunities for students to participate in stimulating and challenging activities beyond the scope of the classroom. This can lead to a much-improved use of leisure time by both youths and adults.

TOPICS FOR STUDY AND DISCUSSION

1. What criteria should be used in regulating student participation in extraclass activities?
2. How may an extraclass activity be evaluated in terms of its contribution to desirable educational objectives for secondary schools?
3. If the personal social development of the pupil is a major objective in extraclass activity, what type of organizations will best meet this objective?
4. Should the right to participate in extraclass activities be based on minimum grade-point averages or would desirable objectives be achieved through other qualifications?
5. There is considerable evidence in research that school administrators are frequently disenchanted with the so-called activity period in the daily schedule. Analyze the problems involved.
6. There appear to be two desirable conditions for a good extraclass program. The program must be built on the expressed interests of the pupils, and the faculty must be capable of sponsoring activities. What course of action should be followed if one or both of these conditions is lacking?
7. There is a tendency in some schools to curricularize most of the so-called extracurricular activities. Evaluate the pros and cons of such a movement.
8. Some critics contend that varsity athletics have lost most of the desirable characteristics of a purposeful extraclass activity. Propose reasons for such a viewpoint.
9. What safeguards should be placed on the management of funds collected and dispensed in extraclass activities?

10. A secondary school authority in a recent talk said, "In a completely flexible school, there are no *extraclass* activities. Individualized scheduling allows students to meet as a part of the school day for photography, basketball, stamp collecting, chess, or to participate either as a listener or producer of special assembly programs." What do you think?

11. Assess the value of extraclass activities in the quest of youth for viable alternatives to out-of-school social demands.

SELECTED REFERENCES

Allnutt, Benjamin W., et al. "Scholastic Journalism." National Association of Secondary School Principals *Bulletin* (February 1975), p. 89.
This issue of the NASSP *Bulletin* is devoted to extensive coverage of secondary school scholastic journalism programs. Discussions concern the principal's role, the adviser's role, and the value of various publications. One article presents a complete journalism course of an American high school. Other articles explore the financing of publications and clashes between students and administration over what can be published. The resulting court decisions are reviewed, and proposals for future compliance are presented.

Ginsberg, Jill, et al. "Student Councils — Have They Really Changed?" *Student Advocate* (March 1976), p. 2.
This issue of *Student Advocate* has three valuable discussions of material important to curriculum designers of extraclass activities: student councils, the student and the law, and National Honor Society regulations. The material on student councils is the result of a national survey. The profile presented is not too encouraging. For instance, more than 91 percent of student council advisers report that their councils provide only social activities for their students, and only 17 percent of faculties in schools "always" consider the council valuable.

Giroux, Terry, et al. *Responsible Student Involvement*. Washington, D. C.: National Association of Secondary School Principals, 1975.
This is a special volume published by NASSP for secondary school administrators and faculty seeking answers to the problems involved in extraclass activities. Pragmatic programs are proposed in the many areas where relationships between students and administrators are breaking down. Topics presented include the student image, communication improvement, students and the law, control of funds, decision making, school security, and girls in interscholastic athletics.

Goldberg, Enid A. *How to Run a School Newspaper*. Philadelphia: J. B. Lippincott Company, 1970.
The many phases of operating a good school newspaper are discussed. Emphasis is put on proper journalistic procedures, selection of student staff, sound financial procedures, and types of relevant news. The delicate problem of administrative censorship is examined.

Karlin, Muriel S., and Berger, Regina. *The Effective Student Activities Program*. West Nyack, N. Y.: Parker Publishing Company, 1971.

This book analyzes the strengths and weaknesses of an effective student activities program; establishes objectives for administration, faculty, and students; and offers many good suggestions for working with youths in an extraclass setting.

Lane-Palagyi, Addpe. *Successful School Assembly Programs.* West Nyack, N. Y.: Parker Publishing Company, 1971.

Effective assembly programs are a needed factor in a good student activity program. This book offers a great deal of help for harassed secondary school administrators. The changing values of assembly programs are assessed, and suggestions are made for effective procedures.

Lukens, Harold A., and Rayman, Robert. "An Activity Program for the Middle School." *American Secondary Education* (March 1976), p. 1.

Problems concerning activities in the middle school center around areas that have been problems in the junior high school, namely, athletics and musical organizations. Authorities contend that students in the middle and junior high grades think that interscholastic sports should be very limited, with major emphasis going to intramural and individualized physical activity games. Criticism is also noted in the development of large musical groups such as marching bands and traveling choral organizations. This article contains a complete outline for implementing an activities program in the junior high school and the middle school.

Tilles, Roger B. "The Principal and the Law." *Journal of the Michigan Association of Secondary School Administrators* (Fall 1975), p. 58.

This publication contains a section dealing with the principal and student rights and responsibilities. Attention is given to the whole area of due process. Student publications and newspapers are analyzed as to value, management, and trends. Other topics included for curriculum planners' consideration are dress and grooming, married and pregnant students, corporal punishment, school records, fee charging, and alternative activities. The area of administrative liability is given careful treatment.

18

Adult Education

In its broadest sense, adult education includes all educational activities beyond the teen-age years, including college. Discussion here, however, will be centered on the continuing education of the large segment of the population that does not secure a college education. It is true that extensive programs of adult education are found on college campuses and college graduates participate in adult education activities in the community, but this participation is somewhat removed from the continuing education program of the public schools.

THE NEED FOR CONTINUOUS EDUCATION

The need for continuous education is closely allied with employment problems. Technological developments have greatly reduced the number of jobs available to people with limited marketable skills and have made it necessary to retain people for new jobs.

Other problems are perhaps as important as those of employment. Today, citizens must have the ability to make complex decisions; yet 11 million adults are functional illiterates, and too many voters base their decisions on scanty information, prejudiced opinions, and hope for personal favors. Lack of social skills results in tension between peoples of different race, color, and religion. Mounting divorce and crime rates emphasize the problems of unsatisfactory social adjustment. Extended life expectancy and the declining number of necessary work hours greatly extend the amount of leisure time available, but too often the new leisure is more frustrating than rewarding.

The potential enrollment for adult education far exceeds the enrollment possibilities of either elementary or secondary education. This makes it one of the most significant educational movements on the American scene.

DEVELOPMENT OF ADULT EDUCATION

Adult education has developed through a variety of patterns and organizations. In the early stages it was entirely vocational education through trade schools. An extensive network of public and private correspondence schools developed later, and colleges and universities began to include a variety of extension courses. World War II marked the formal and well-organized entrance of the military into the adult education field. Today, part of the military budget is still devoted to the continuous education of service personnel.

Community colleges and vocational schools are the latest developments on statewide scales. Oregon, among other states, offers financial assistance to communities willing to develop schools for continuing education. In Florida, a series of junior colleges have been well established. In addition to the basic two years of college, they provide extensive vocational and technical programs that are terminal. Plans are well under way for a program of continuous education from kindergarten through graduate school at one location.

A series of events have marked the development of the national structure of adult education. The Smith-Hughes Act of 1917 furnished federal funds for extensive vocational agriculture programs — evening classes or other continuing education activities — for adult farmers. Adjustments and extensions of these programs were made by the George-Dean Act of 1936 and the George-Barden Act of 1946.

The latest impetus to the vocational aspects of adult education was furnished by the Vocational Education Act of 1963, which developed out of the growing awareness that vocational education is a tool for the social and economic improvement of underprivileged people. The scope of this act was greatly enlarged by amendments added in 1968.

The first professional recognition of the status of adult education came in 1924, when the National Education Association established the Department of Adult Education. The formation of the Association for Adult Education and the National Home State Council followed in 1926.

The federal government formally entered the adult education field in 1933, when it developed the Federal Emergency Program to provide training for victims of the Great Depression. This involved such programs as the Civilian Conservation Corps, which trained young adults for forest conservation activities. Another federal government activity was the creation of the Armed Forces Institute in 1942. Since its conception, this program has provided for the continued education of thousands of young men and women in the armed forces. Today, part of the military budget is still devoted to the continuous education of service personnel.

The Adult Education Association, formed in 1951, has conceived many of the national programs and plans for adult education. The Fund for Adult Education, which plans and supervises programs, was established the same year. Thus it may be seen that adult education has had much more federal backing than any other form of education. However, good programs of adult education must be state and locally oriented.

Although most of the traceable development of adult education is largely within the framework of educational institutions, curriculum planners must be aware that a number of adult education programs are outside this framework. They may be sponsored by museums, libraries, industrial organizations, labor unions, professional societies, military establishments, hospitals, religious organizations, trade associations, state and local governments, prisons, and a host of political, charitable, social, civic, ethnic, and other community organizations.

PUBLIC SCHOOL INVOLVEMENT

The structure for adult learning is formed in the elementary and secondary schools, and the basic and preparatory training of the regular school program must be articulated to the continuing needs of adult learners. Part of the secondary school curriculum is geared to adult education in the formal school period, and adults may continue to take courses in the postschool years. This is true particularly of the subjects with vocational training aspects, such as vocational agriculture, vocational home economics, and distributive education. Formal classes are conducted within the school, and regular school personnel engage in follow-up activity in the homes, on the farms, and in the communities. Late afternoon and evening classes, allied but not directly associated with the regular school program, are part of the curriculum of many comprehensive secondary schools. Their counterpart may be found in the regular schedule of vocational and technical schools.

Available research indicates that public schools are the major agency for promoting adult education, and the evening school is the main organizational pattern. Evening school enrollments have steadily increased since 1955, and there has been a gradual increase of academic subjects and a decline in vocational subjects. There is little uniformity of curriculum structure, since the needs of students vary greatly.

Little progress has been made in preparing teachers for adult education. The usual procedure is to recruit from the regular day school program. Often, however, these teachers do not adapt themselves well to evening school teaching, even though it offers greater financial remuneration.

ADULT EDUCATION OBJECTIVES

The local curriculum planners must make decisions on vocational stress, terminal emphasis, academic continuation, or preparation for leisure-time pursuits, since immediate objectives for these programs will vary from community to community.

There are, however, at least three broad general objectives that ought to underlie all programs of adult education. The first is enrichment of community living and improvement of the social order. Many adult education activities are in themselves community enrichment. This is particularly true of certain social and cultural ventures such as the creation of art galleries, the development of symphony orchestras, and the organization of various cultural study groups. If adult education is to be community centered and financially supported, this objective is realistic.

A second objective that ought to be inherent in well-planned adult education programs is the fostering of respect for human dignity and personality. This objective involves an all-out effort to reduce racial tensions and criminal activities and to improve community living conditions everywhere.

A third objective concerns the improvement of the citizen's ability to make the intelligent decisions required by the complexities of modern society. This objective is vital in a democratic society.

These objectives, natural extensions of secondary school objectives, attain fruition in adult education. Their refinement, improvement, and application are part of the opportunities of adult education.

BASIC ASSUMPTIONS FOR
CURRICULUM PLANNING

Curriculum planners for adult education can make certain basic assumptions with a reasonable degree of assurance. Research and experience will be needed, of course, to substantiate these assumptions. It can be assumed that adults, like children, can learn, depending on individual ability and experience. The cliché "too old to learn" will not withstand psychological evidence. Learning ability does not change, except in case of brain damage or related physical deterioration. In fact, learning among adults can be enriched by their broad experience and great dedication of purpose. Some of the most productive years can come late in life. Adults, then, can profit from continued education, and the complexities of modern society and technological development make it necessary for citizens to update all their knowledge constantly.

It can also be assumed that adult education is here to stay and that the local community is the focal point for planning and implementation. It is unfortunate if curriculum planners do not articulate adult education with all related divisions of learning.

The final assumption is a word of caution: a minimum of organization is desirable. Adults want purposeful action; organizational intricacies cause them to lose their patience and interest. The longer adults have been away from the formal structure of the average public school, the more they want structure to fit their pattern of living.

INSTRUCTIONAL ACTION POINTERS

In the operation of adult education programs, certain action pointers should be observed. Whether the program is sponsored and operated by a school system or by another community agency, community participation is greatly enhanced by voluntary leadership and association with governmental agencies. In the case of a school-sponsored program, voluntary involvement would be in the area of advisory councils and student leadership activities.

Teachers for evening programs must have patience, skill, and understanding, and they must plan their instruction carefully. Since attendance is not compulsory, students drop out of programs quickly if they do not like the teaching procedures. They resent being "talked down to" as much as they dislike vocabularies that are over their heads. Techniques that will work in other classroom programs are often unsuccessful with adult students.[1] Extensive lecturing, for example, may result in a decline of interest. The program must offer them freedom of choice and freedom in learning development. Above all, its values must be apparent and practical. Student involvement in problem solving is one of the soundest teaching procedures. This means the teacher consults with the student to help identify problems, helps gather data for solutions, furnishes the technical advice needed for the formation of hypotheses, and gives the student ample latitude to reach successful solutions. To a certain degree, the whole realm of adult education should be geared to upgrading intelligent decision-making ability. Decisions in the voting booth, the marketplace, the public forum, and the family circle require greater acumen than ever before. Good citizenship requires ready ability to analyze an issue, study the facts involved, and come to a clear, valid, and unbiased conclusion. Too frequently, the average adult is unaware of the necessity or even the desirability of making a decision.

Adult education programs should help mature people do the intelligent thinking so necessary for solving the ever-increasing political, economic, and social problems. Here again, actual experience is important. Descriptions of the processes and techniques of decision making must be supplemented by realistic experiences.

Any plan of action for adult learning activities should include a word of caution concerning the disturbance of deep-lying prejudices. A frontal attack here can be fatal. This is where the best techniques of nondirective teaching must be used. The teacher must skirt the edges of these prejudices to help the student extend his or her horizon beyond their petty confines. This calls for problem solving of the highest order.

It is very important in adult education to avoid any aura of remedial learning. The concept of a "second-chance" education is not desirable. The pride of adult learners can be hurt if they feel they are compensating for deficiencies of earlier experiences. Learning can be adjusted to the learner's level, however elementary, but the learning activities should be developmental rather than remedial.

It is not feasible to analyze the dropout problem here, but it is important to raise the question of whether the term *dropout* is accurate or deserves the stigma frequently attached to it. Basically, for one reason or another, potential dropouts are maladjusted and disen-

[1] D. R. Weaver, "How to Teach Someone Old Enough to be Your Father," *American Vocational Journal* (December 1976), pp. 43–45.

chanted with their present school. If adult education programs are properly developed in association with the public schools, the dropout will merely become a transfer. The main change in status will be from youth to adult. The dropout's educational program may be different, but it will be continuing.

TRENDS IN THE FIELD

For curriculum planners to solve the numerous problems of adult education, the public must recognize its intrinsic values, and educators must establish coordinated curriculum patterns. The stumbling blocks are diversity of authority and diversity of opinion concerning the field's rationale. While vocational education is important, it should not continue to dominate program planning. Adult education is well beyond the narrow confines of vocational training. It also exceeds the limited academic outline formerly followed.

The general ability level of adult students will continue to rise, and the facilities provided for their use will expand gradually. Differentiation of curriculum and instruction will occur as the body of knowledge about adult needs and abilities increases. Concurrent with these developments will come a clarification of the unique role of adult education.[2]

The trend of learning emphasis in the regular school program will soon affect adult education. As teachers shift their purpose from the transmission of knowledge to the development of capacity to learn, the curriculum will shift from a subject-mastery organization to a learning-skills organization. Teachers will become persons who help students inquire. With this changed concept of education, adult education truly will be continuing education. Everyone will continue to seek new information throughout his or her lifetime.

One of the chief factors in adult education curriculum determination is the point of dissemination. Both public and private agencies are engaged in the development of formal programs. Most of the private agencies are reputable, but the profit motive tends to influence their objectives. Public education is in the best position to establish an educational continuum. Financial support for the entire structure of education will be increased by the involvement of the adult population, and a closer liaison will be established between the secondary school curriculum and the adult education curriculum. It is difficult to envision the "needs" and "wants" of the total post–secondary school popu-

---

[2] Nancy K. Schlossberg, "Career Development in Adults," *American Vocational Journal* (May 1975), pp. 38–39.

lation, ranging as it does from the out-of-school youth interested in pragmatic affairs, such as job improvement, personality improvement, and home building, to the senior citizen to whom cultural and purposeful leisure activities are paramount.[3]

There is evidence that emphasis in all social planning is shifting from the technological aspects to the humanistic aspects. This does not mean a slowdown in technological progress, but rather a stepping up of efforts to help people adjust to the problems of a technological order. This involves continuous adult education for all social groups.

The trend toward the practical and functional will continue. Objectives must include the improvement of public life as well as the improvement of private life through better trained public leaders in business and government affairs.

Adult education leaders must put renewed emphasis on the use of voluntary coordinating groups such as central labor councils, educational federations, ministerial alliances, social welfare agencies, federated men's and women's clubs, trade associations, and other civil agencies supporting programs of adult education. They must also work increasingly with officials of government and leaders of political parties to stimulate the use of educational processes in the performance of legislative, administrative, and judicial responsibilities.

With the fulfillment of the objectives of continuing education will come a better delineation of the responsibilities of childhood education. The basic purpose of the formal school years should be to provide the skills and knowledge necessary for life pursuits. If it is achieved, then adult education will enable its students to utilize these educational processes throughout their lives.

CONTINUING EDUCATION

It may be noted throughout this discussion that emphasis has been on continuing education. This concept has slowly replaced the more limited concept of adult education. Continued education is necessary for minimum competence as a citizen, and more specialized education is necessary for positions of responsibility.

The greatest problem in the field of continuing education is how to benefit all citizens. In the past, adult education has been too much of a process of educating the educated. Little success has been achieved in reaching those with less than an eighth-grade education, those over

[3] R. E. Reber, "Some Key Principles for Guiding Adult Education," *Adult Leadership* (December 1976), pp. 117–118.

fifty-five years of age, those from lower socioeconomic levels, and those from certain ethnic and cultural groups. These groups must be reached if the concept of continued education for all citizens is to be meaningful.

The acceptance of the concept of continuing education for all people may cause some curriculum planners to start scurrying about for new formulas and new procedures. This is not necessary. While the problems may be somewhat different in scope, the basic learning techniques remain the same. Subject matter probably will continue to be diverse, encompassing such subjects as literacy training, professional and technical education, religion, personal development, speed reading, sewing, woodworking, literature, music, and the arts. Activities will continue to involve correspondence study, apprenticeship, on-the-job training, internship in classes, discussion groups, conferences, lecture series, and community forums. Teaching will still be done by lectures, panels, forums, demonstrations, projects, discussions, teaching machines, and workshops.

COMMUNITY EDUCATION/COMMUNITY SCHOOL

A promising new development on the American educational scene is a rediscovery of the importance of integrating the entire community with the formal learning process. As has been stated before, modern America is experiencing myriad social problems. The accelerated rate of change, the trend toward urbanization, modern technological advances, and the sheer magnitude and complexity of modern institutions have created a fragmentation of the basic elements that create and constitute the community. Those elements consist mainly of communication and the sharing of common problems. A new meaning has been given to community education; the institution identified with the process is the community school. Where the community education concept is accepted, a new dimension is given to adult education.

The responsibilities for the design and development of continuous learning reside in all major institutions of society and at all levels of the formal and informal educational systems. Every institution shares responsibility for fostering lifelong learning and developing a commitment to self-education. What the school does depends on what churches, families, employers, and government do or do not do to reinforce the motivation and the opportunities for people to learn.

Many labels have been used to describe lifelong learning. It is variously called continuing education, adult education, career education, informal education, and recurrent education. These labels, however, can create false impressions because they are related almost exclusively to the adult population. Lifelong learning is more accurately described as the totality of learning that takes place during a person's life.

The acceptance of learning and education as continuous and lifelong processes, rather than a series of terminal behaviors and unrelated experiences, is a basic part of the philosophical foundation of community education. One of the basic components of a community education program is providing a delivery system and community process that involves all ages and addresses all "cradle-to-grave" learning needs and desires.

The types of activities and programs go beyond what many traditional elementary and secondary education personnel consider the formal education domain. Providing a broad range of programs and learning opportunities, compared with providing specifically defined or structured learning content for educational processes, is a major distinguishing factor between community education and traditional K–12 education. The elementary or secondary community school is used as a vehicle to launch programs of early childhood education, extended day education, youth enrichment, adult education, leisure and recreation, senior citizen activities, as well as many other programs that are dimensions of lifelong learning and enrichment.

Community educators do not just organize classes, activities, and specialized community activities. They facilitate the interaction process for defining and assessing needs; assist in finding the resources to meet these needs; and help people decide what is important to themselves and their communities.

Adult education curriculum coordinators seeking information on the community education/community school concept may find it through the National Community Education Association and more than sixty university centers for community education development. The Mott Foundation in Flint, Michigan, sponsors the National Center for Community Education and the Flint Community Schools. Program models may be found in Tulsa, Oklahoma; Blue Springs, Missouri; Wellston, Missouri; Independence, Missouri; and Longview Community College, Kansas City, Missouri.

Community education's proponents do not promise that it will solve all the problems of education or the many and complex situations arising from the American social, political, and economic scene. They believe, however, that community education can make a difference if people perceive the concept in its totality and modify existing educational organizations' structures to accommodate these new dimensions and directions.

TOPICS FOR STUDY AND DISCUSSION

1. It has been said that education does not change very much, that it only acquires new labels. Does this statement apply to renaming adult education as continuous education?
2. How can adult education contribute to community enrichment?
3. The solution of major social problems is frequently considered the task of education. What is the role of adult education in this assignment?
4. Is it realistic to leave the implementation of many adult education activities to so-called volunteer personnel?
5. Assess the role of the various levels of government in financing, coordinating, and planning programs of adult education.
6. In the past, much of adult education was associated with vocational education. Was this because vocational education met the needs of adults for continuing education or because it furnished salable skills to the unemployed?
7. Enumerate the probable future trends in adult education in view of the ever-increasing life span. Will these trends affect secondary education?

SELECTED REFERENCES

Bergenin, Paul. *A Philosophy for Adult Education.* New York: Seabury Press, 1971.
This book presents a stimulating and concise analysis of what one adult educator believes should be the ideas, principles, and goals that structure adult education in a democratic society.
Community School: Sharing the Space and the Action. New York: Educational Facilities Laboratory, 1975.
This report outlines the history of the community school movement and analyzes the principles and methods by which these complexes have been built. Fifty working examples of joint architecture and planning are presented. The report relates the different ways cities and communities have gone about developing centers and gives a glimpse of the future in terms of the most recent community school programs.
Hall, Clyde W. "Adult Education Upgrade." *American Vocational Journal* (February 1975), pp. 84–86.
This article is a review of an address made in the Adult Education Department sessions at the American Vocational Education convention. It discusses the different value systems of different sets of adults. The management skills needed by leadership personnel are noted, and the role of the area vocational school adult education program is well delineated. Attrition rates are identified and suggestions are made for improvement. The article closes with major recommendations for adult education update.
Lassey, William R. *Leadership and Social Change.* Iowa City: University Associates, 1971.

This book provides a collection of papers carefully integrated with introductory chapters emphasizing leadership in terms of communications, organizational change, community change, and small-group structure.

Logsdon, James D., et al. "The Principal's Responsibilities in Community Education." National Association of Secondary School Principals *Bulletin* (November 1975), pp. 1–71.

This is one of a series of eleven articles. In addition to a discussion of the principal's responsibility in community education, other articles are devoted to conceptual framework, administrative alternatives, daytime and evening programs, innovative processes, and research studies. A closer look at the meaning, development, and current status of the community education movement is taken. Basic tenets and misconceptions are thoroughly explored.

IV
Options in the Curriculum

19

Overcoming Barriers in the Setting

Secondary schools in the United States have always received criticism. However, the forces today are somewhat different and more influential than in the past. Blacks, Chicanos, and other ethnic groups often find the curriculum out of touch with their needs. Some believe that their schools are influenced too much by white, suburban mores. Yet in many cases, when these persons move from inner cities to more affluent suburban areas because they have achieved better jobs and higher incomes, they exert influence for even more emphasis on conventional, college-preparatory programs.

The solution lies in getting rid of, once and forever, the idea that all schools in any given school district, county, or state need to have the same kinds of curriculum offerings and methods of teaching and learning. Moreover, uniform requirements for everyone within one school should be limited much more than they are now. The confusion of uniformity with equality of educational opportunities has plagued secondary schools in this country from the very beginning. That situation came naturally as the colonizers brought their traditions to a new world.

Some persons want to maintain the status quo. They vigorously resent and oppose changes that may threaten their control over the lives of other persons. For example, they sometimes label the elimination of failure or the threat of failure in schools as a Communist threat designed to undermine the character of this society. In the opinion of the ultraconservative, increased diversity of curricular offerings represents a type of socialism and therefore should be avoided.

The problem with some teachers is that they do not see much need for curriculum improvement. They successfully completed high school and a university with a major, or at least a minor, in the subject or subjects they teach. They like it the way it is. It is difficult for them to understand why some or possibly most of their students do not feel the same way.

Is there something in your subject or the way you teach it for a young person whose life outside school is in a ghetto, a small, rural town, or a sophisticated city or suburb? What about the worries, the defeats, the hopes that these students bring to their classes? Does the present curriculum content help as much as it could? What about the present methods of teaching and how the school organizes the setting for learning? Are there barriers in the setting?

Improving curriculum or anything else requires an analysis of the forces that now maintain the status quo. Some persons blame inept or frightened school administrators. Others place the blame on poor teacher preparation, conservative communities, old buildings, lack of funds, regulations of state departments of education and regional accrediting associations, the universities, and so on. Although most of these factors are indeed straw men, they seem both convenient and dangerous to many people. Actually, recent court decisions and legislative enactments are giving more local responsibility to educators who want to take further steps to individualize learning and professionalize teaching.

Curriculum improvement requires resolving issues and answering questions that confront anyone who plans to make changes. You were directed in Part I of this book to some issues and questions. Parts II and III provided information about developments and issues in the various curriculum content areas. Now we discuss in more detail how content may be organized, some methods of teaching and learning, school schedules, educational facilities, and a number of structural matters. The educational setting may either enhance curriculum improvement or stand in its way.

First, we discuss some barriers. Barriers to curriculum improvement include certain concepts of school organization, the use of space and time, school regulations adopted for administrative convenience, and the limitations of partial changes in school programs.

THE SELF-SUFFICIENT CLASSROOM

Today's conventional secondary schools schedule about twenty-five to thirty-five students with one teacher for five periods a week, usually at the same time each day, in what is regarded as a self-sufficient class room. Most teacher and learner activities occur in that setting, supplemented only by study halls, libraries, laboratories in some subjects, and homework. This self-sufficient classroom inhibits many of the newer concepts of instruction in the various subject fields. Providing a variety of learning opportunities both inside and outside the school building makes any subject potentially more interesting to the learners.

Chapters 20, 21, and 22 describe how learning activities may be categorized under three headings: independent study, large-group instruction, and small-group discussion. On an average, teachers in self-sufficient classrooms spend almost half their time lecturing, presenting, demonstrating, showing films, and giving tests — activities for which the size of the group is irrelevant as long as each student can see and hear well. Independent study occurs, but it is difficult to accomplish in this setting because the materials are limited, the students do not have adequate space, and the time is limited by standard periods. Small-group discussion as described in Chapter 22 is also difficult because the number of students is too large.

Every student and teacher in a school should have access to some thirty different kinds of supplies and equipment, not counting specialized laboratory equipment. Good teaching techniques involve books and other printed materials; overhead, film, and slide projectors of various types; tape and disk recorders and playback equipment, television and video tape equipment, and so on. The absence of any of this equipment limits the opportunities of both the student and the teacher.

Of course, it is unrealistic to suggest that all classrooms have this equipment. The cost of such a program would be prohibitive even in an affluent society, and students would find it difficult to move about with all that material in one room. Moreover, experience shows that even if the equipment were provided, teachers would not use much of it.

Probably the greatest shortcoming of the self-sufficient classroom, from the students' point of view, is that students are limited by whatever competences their one teacher possesses. Teachers also are restricted. Because the room can accommodate only twenty-five to thirty-five students, educational economics requires that teachers be scheduled into these rooms five to six hours per day, twenty-five to thirty hours per week. Expected to perform most of the teaching services for a given group, the teacher often provides services for which he or she is less competent than some other teachers in the same building, doing tasks of personal interest instead of others, lacking technical devices to enliven teaching, and performing many clerical and custodial activities for students.

UNIFORMITY IN TIME ARRANGEMENTS

Today's school typically schedules classes into standard-length periods for all subjects and activities. Once it has been decided how long periods should be — forty, forty-five, or fifty minutes or some other length of time — classes meet for that time, usually at the same time each day. Such an arrangement provides a situation in which a student can think about science for only forty-five minutes, then stop thinking about science in order to think about history or physical education for an equally short time. The home economics teacher selects recipes that can be completed in forty-five minutes, including getting materials out and putting them back. The length of the class should be determined by the teachers and students, not by an electric clock in the school office. (Chapter 25 describes a number of ways in which schedules are made flexible so that teachers and learners can make decisions about the use of time.)

THE MULTIPURPOSE CLASSROOM

Excepting rooms for science, fine and practical arts, and physical education, schools tend to build look-alike classrooms that are multipurpose in their conception. An English room looks like a mathematics room except for a few superficial decorations. Everything is supposed to happen in the same room — large-group instruction, small-group discussion, and independent study.

Because they are multipurpose, these rooms are unnecessarily expensive. Proportionately twice as many students could be put in the same space for large-group instruction and 50 percent more for small-group discussion than are allocated according to present requirements in multipurpose classrooms. However, the most important fault in these multipurpose rooms is that the cost of equipping each one adequately is prohibitive, as indicated earlier in this chapter. For example, designing a room to serve as gymnasium, auditorium, and study hall creates compromises that detract from the potential effectiveness of the space.

Some newer schools attempt to push the multiservice idea even further by using movable walls. The theory is that such an arrangement will encourage team teaching. If four classrooms are arranged in a huge square with movable interior walls, one of the four teachers makes a presentation to the total enrollment of the four classrooms when the walls are pushed back. Then the walls are closed and each teacher takes her or his original class for small-group discussion and independent study. However, the seating arrangement is not good for large-group instruction and the smaller rooms are not appropriate either for small-group discussions or for independent study.

THE EDIFICE COMPLEX

Some communities tend to build monuments for schools rather than facilities primarily designed to improve the quality of teaching and learning. The building itself costs too much in relation to the money spent on supplies and equipment. An immediate goal might be to spend 25 percent less on the building and to use that amount of money to provide better aids to teaching and learning.

Whether caused by the "edifice complex" or not, another glaring weakness of school buildings is the failure to provide teachers with adequate places to work — an office with some privacy, meeting rooms, and places where instructional materials may be prepared. Clerks and instructional assistants also need adequate space. Including a separate classroom for each teacher is needlessly expensive. (Chapter 28 suggests other ways to improve educational facilities.)

ADMINISTRATIVE CONVENIENCE

The rules and regulations that school administrators and the public consider necessary for a "smooth-running school" often form another barrier to curriculum improvement. Many of these regulations are designed to free the administration from decision making, since they apply to all persons without exception and can be interpreted by clerks. But individual differences among students and teachers are difficult to recognize by the application of uniform rules and regulations. Illustrative of the regulations are the following: using standardized tests to classify students into ability groups; applying standardized admission policies to graduates of other schools or of elementary schools; resorting to letter-grade requirements for participation in athletics or other extraclass activities or admission to some school subjects; adopting standard rules regarding when a student may leave school or graduate; reducing a student's grade arbitrarily in relation to the number of days of unexcused absence accumulated during a grading period.

Comparable rules may militate against the professionalization of teaching: uniform salary policies, uniform teaching loads, uniform rules for providing clerical assistance, uniform class sizes, and so on. Many standards of state education departments and regional accrediting associations fall in the same category; for example, requiring all classes to meet 200 minutes per week, enrolling no more than thirty students in a class, requiring a given number of books in the library per pupil enrolled, and so on.

The quality of education in a school is not measured by decibles of sound or silence. Clearing the corridors of students except during massive changes at five-minute intermissions between class periods has little virtue per se. Administrative convenience may get in the way of curriculum improvement.

LIMITED TIME FOR TEACHERS
TO WORK ON CURRICULUM

Teachers require much more time during the school year than they now have available to improve the curriculum in the various ways that we propose. No one has established a precise figure of how much time is required. As a start, we propose five hours per week times the number of teachers in the school. Some teachers will spend more time than others.

All departments need to decide what content is required, what is desirable for students who develop hobbies or special interests in the field, and what is necessary for those who envision a career in the area. In spite of some interest over the years in such designations, very little has been done to accomplish the separations that those purposes require.

Teachers also need time to prepare guidesheets and worksheets or some form of learning packages to direct and stimulate students to do more complete and creative independent study. Such materials need to be largely self-directing, self-motivating, self-pacing, and self-evaluating. Even though teachers may consult banks of behavioral objectives, learning packages, textbooks and other learning materials, and a variety of externally prepared examinations, these materials need to be further tailored for the local situation.

Teachers also need time for obtaining feedback from the learning and work centers to help diagnose the needs for further curriculum changes. They need time for conferences with each other and with consultants who may be brought to the school to help them. They need time to evaluate the total curriculum.

Our experiences suggest that this time needs to be available to teachers during the school year rather than on an occasional afternoon or day. A school that individually schedules teachers and students can provide more time for some teachers at certain periods during the year as needed. We find that the quality of teacher productivity is better during the year than in the summer when they are not in close contact with learners and the program.

A school system has two basic alternatives in providing teachers with time to work on curriculum. One option is to hire extra teachers, an alternative that is costly and mostly unnecessary. The other alternative, the one we recommend, is to provide differentiated staffing as suggested in Chapter 26. Of course, there are good reasons for such staffing changes that go beyond providing teachers with more time to work on curriculum. A school can achieve the goal largely within existing revenues.

CONTINUED ACCEPTANCE OF OTHER QUESTIONABLE PROCEDURES

Schools today remain overly oriented to group methods. Such dedication constantly gets in the way of individualization applied to both students and teachers. Uniformity is confused with democracy. As a result, the school tries to treat all students and teachers alike instead of concentrating on the individual differences among both groups in an effort to help each one attain maximum development.

The curriculum goal is to develop the best possible program for each student under constant monitoring and with the processes of diagnosis, prescriptions, implementations, and evaluations. The method requires that each student have a teacher-adviser as described on page 407, someone who really knows each one of them and can do something constructive to improve interests and talents.

Curriculum evaluation needs to get away from the practice of comparing what a given school offers in relation to other schools in the district, the state, or some other region. The concern in program evaluation is whether a given school has a better curriculum today than a year or five years ago. The practice of comparing one school with another must be abandoned because cultural levels, economic levels, parental aspirations, and other factors associated with economic status make such comparisons unreliable and invalid.

Other assumptions about schools get in the way of constructively seeking ways to improve the curriculum. These widely held beliefs about quality education have little or no support in research findings. As a teacher or school administrator, ask yourself whether you accept the following generalizations as essential for improving the curriculum:

1. Schools would be better if classes were smaller.
2. Teachers should continue to spend one-third or more of their time doing clerical duties.
3. Schools would be better if there were fewer supervisors and administrators.
4. The excellence of a school is directly proportional to the amount of money spent per pupil.
5. Academic subjects are more important than the fine arts, practical arts, and physical education.
6. Of all the academic subjects, none is more important than English.
7. Education should be located in places called school buildings with only incidental attention to the community and to homes as learning environments.
8. The threat of failure is the most important motivational device.
9. Students learn best when teachers talk to them to explain matters and to tell them what they must learn.
10. The most important way to improve schools for inner-city youth is to place more emphasis on reading.
11. Students should be placed arbitrarily in remedial subjects, even if they have no motivation for learning them.
12. Learning by doing is appropriate mainly in physical education, fine arts, and practical subjects.
13. Students learn best when they are grouped heterogeneously in classes of twenty-five or fewer.
14. Students learn best while listening to teachers talk 50 to 75 percent of the time that classes are in session.

The past two decades have demonstrated that curriculum innovations are possible. When those changes are carefully conceived and well developed, student attendance improves and discipline cases are reduced. Students also become more creative, teachers are more productive, and supervisors are more effective; those outcomes do not result from simple changes but rather from comprehensive alterations in what all three groups do.

Periodically, after a period of curriculum innovations, the conservative forces combine to attack the whole idea of change. Their favorite phase is "back to the basics." Of course, there usually is some difficulty in defining the term *basics* — and rightly so. Throughout this book, we have tried to help you think constructively about what the essential outcomes of schooling are for *everyone,* so that you may plan better for secondary school curriculum improvement.

INADEQUATE PLANNING OF CHANGES

Well-meaning teachers and administrators, in the very process of innovating and experimenting in their schools, may create barriers to further curriculum improvement. For instance, they may fail to recognize that a systems approach is essential in educational change. A language laboratory imposed on a conventional system of teaching a foreign language produces only partial gains, or in some cases actually impairs the effectiveness of language teaching. Failure to understand that television is only one form of large-group instruction and that it cannot substitute for small-group discussion or independent study constitutes another failure to recognize the systems approach.

Learning outcomes will not improve if team teaching merely means that occasionally two or more teachers put their classes together for large-group instruction and then return to their conventional classes. Such arrangements fail to accept the notion, expressed in Chapter 1, that changing one part of the instructional system requires changing all the others related to it.

Educational change should involve reeducating teachers. If they continue to teach as they did in conventional classrooms, no particular benefit to themselves or to their students will result. Methods for evaluating student progress must also change, as explained in Chapter 32.

No one philosophy of the curriculum or one method of schooling may dominate secondary education. Even within a single school, there must be a wide variety of options available to students. The way to avoid the pendulum complex in curriculum improvement — that is, swinging from one extreme to the other — is to recognize that both extremes and a variety of gradations in between are conceivably good for some students and some teachers in any school. The chapters that follow indicate the kinds of options that secondary schools need to provide.

TOPICS FOR STUDY AND DISCUSSION

1. Select a school problem, such as how to develop more student responsibility for learning or conduct, how to improve attendance or discipline, or how to reduce the number of dropouts. How do present school policies

affect the problem? What changes in policies or procedures would lead to improvement?

2. Considering an educational innovation, such as television, language laboratories, computer-assisted instruction, or programmed learning, answer the questions listed in topic 1.
3. Interview several teachers to discover the special interests of each, the self-images (what they think they do best or least well), and their ideas for improving schools. Analyze their responses in writing your report.
4. Do the same as in topic 3, but interview students instead.
5. Some persons today believe that the barriers listed in this chapter are so immovable that the only solution is to create new institutions, such as "free schools" or "schools without walls." Prepare to argue for or against such proposals.

SELECTED REFERENCES

Baroni, Rev. Geno C. "The Inner City: A New Challenge to Catholic High Schools." In *Catholic Education in Contemporary American Society*. Washington, D. C.: The National Catholic Educational Association, NCEA Bulletin (August 1967), pp. 108–116.

This article presents the problems schools face in larger cities and suggests remedial steps.

Bishop, Lloyd K. *Individualizing Educational Systems*. New York: Harper & Row, 1971, pp. 175–221.

This chapter emphasizes the student as a coparticipant in the educational enterprise and suggests strategies for involving students in school programs.

Cay, Donald F. *Curriculum: Design for Learning*. Indianapolis: The Bobbs-Merrill Company, 1966, pp. 136–153.

This chapter discusses problems related to time, money, materials, and teacher personnel.

Goodlad, John I., and Klein, Francis M. *Behind the Classroom Door*. Worthington, Ohio: Charles A. Jones Publishing Company, 1970.

Goodlad and Klein show how teachers resist educational changes and suggest constructive measures.

Hickerson, Nathaniel. *Education for Alienation*. Englewood Cliffs, N. J.: Prentice-Hall, 1966, pp. 73–98.

These three chapters emphasize thirteen curriculum changes needed to provide better education for the economically deprived.

Manlove, Donald C., and Beggs, David W. III. *Flexible Scheduling Using the IndiFlexS Model*. Bloomington: Indiana University Press, 1967, pp. 29–39 and 64–78.

These two chapters discuss some myths that should be destroyed and the need for new professional roles for teachers.

Mann, Dale. "The Politics of Changing Schools." National Association of Secondary School Principals *Bulletin* (May 1977), pp. 57–66.

Changing the curriculum or other aspects of schooling in light of present developments requires updated understandings of the power structures that control schools, new techniques of persuasion, and persistence.

Woods, Thomas E. *The Administration of Educational Innovation.* Eugene: University of Oregon Bureau of Educational Research, 1967, pp. 33–41.

This chapter describes several inherent "barriers to change" that inhibit educational innovations and suggests constructive actions.

20

Students Learn
with Alternatives:
Independent Study

A considerable number of today's students are turned off by the curriculum content and the methods that schools use. They spend time at school because that is where some of the "action" is. Sometimes they express their dislike by means of violence and vandalism. They resent being told too often what they must do and when and how they must do it. Schools handle the problem all too frequently by suspending students, blaming parents, calling in the police, allowing students to leave school at earlier ages or with fewer requirements, and taking a number of other steps to cope with these problems rather than finding constructive solutions.

One solution is to increase the amount of time and diversify the methods and contents of what we call independent study. As this chapter will make evident, we define the term to mean something different from what it did in the past.

How much time is our own? Usually we work with other people. Even our recreation involves many group activities. Yet, everyone needs opportunities to learn and do things his or her own way, to develop personal special interests and talents, and to be creative. Without these opportunities and responsibilities, identity is lost in a mass of group functions.

What a person does independently determines a unique personality and helps maintain good mental health. The result may also be major contributions to the general welfare.

The effective school challenges each pupil to manifest higher levels of intellectual inquiry and creativity. It provides opportunities to study and to work apart from the mass. The conventional school, however, schedules most of a student's time into group activities in classes, study halls, laboratories, and other workrooms, and mass examinations and the application of competitive group standards often reward conformity. Such group assignments may deny individual students needed opportunities for independent study and investigation and sometimes bore them with needless repetitiveness or worry them with unnecessary frustrations.

Children in kindergarten and the first grade work independently for a considerable portion of the day even in conventional schools. Unfortunately, as the children grow older, the school structures more and more of their time in groups under relatively close teacher supervision.

THE MEANING OF INDEPENDENT STUDY

Independent study can be defined as the activities in which students engage when their teachers stop talking. Its purpose is to give each individual the opportunity to develop unique talents and interests to the highest possible degree. That is why personal learning activities constitute the central function of education — the heart of the school.

Independent study has two dimensions for most learners. First, they must master the minimum essential knowledge, skills, and other values required in the subject. Teacher presentations tell them what these essentials are and how to attain them. This aspect of education was called *basic education* in Chapter 2. The second level of independent study provides for enriching knowledge and skills, referred to in Chapter 2 as *depth education*. Here students manifest their special interests and talents.

Independent study may be an individual activity or it may involve two or more students working together. A group of learners with similar needs for remedial work may work in a specially equipped laboratory, or an advanced group with special interests may cooperate in a project. In any case, the emphasis remains on the individual, who has been placed in a learning situation where he or she may succeed and contribute to others as well as to personal development.

Independent study takes different forms. In one school, students who were failing every subject in the conventional program were assembled in a room to work with motors. The school provided many types of motors — sewing machine, vacuum sweeper, automotive, and others — and some were brought to school by the students themselves. Competent teachers helped them increase their knowledge of motors. When some of them wanted more information, a reading specialist helped them improve their reading so they could learn more. They also learned about motors by listening to taped information and by looking at films. Ultimately, some of the students wrote reports on what they were doing.

In another school, a senior spent twenty-two hours per week doing original research in the school's biology laboratory, involving equipment he designed especially on the basis of extensive reading and conferences with experts in and outside the school. The student did most of this work outside the conventional thirty-hour school week, but some school time was available to him in the school's flexible schedule.

In an effective school, most students may spent approximately twelve hours of the usual thirty-hour school week in independent study.[1] Many students will spend additional time in subject fields in which they are competent and have particular interests. Ultimately, 60 percent or more of a pupil's time may be spent in independent study. That goal will result from more effective "teacher talk" as described in Chapter 21 and "student talk" as proposed in Chapter 22. The combination of a different school schedule, cooperative professional decisions by teachers and counselors, appropriate attendance and reporting procedures, and new evaluation techniques should be established to encourage and to govern personalized independent study. The types of independent study can be illustrated by considering the variety of places in a school where they occur.

LOCATION OF INDEPENDENT STUDY

Five different areas within the school are recommended for independent study locations. Organization of the areas and the degree to which they are separate from each other depend on the size of the school and the degree of staff commitment. Since there are many ways to provide these facilities in new or old buildings, the spaces are de-

[1] J. Lloyd Trump, *Images of the Future — A New Approach to the Secondary School* (Washington, D. C.: National Association of Secondary School Principals, 1959), pp. 8–9.

scribed in general terms. The five areas are the library, resource centers, special help areas, small-group conference areas, relaxation rooms, and restriction zones. There are also out-of-school study spaces.

Although the basic concern of this book is curriculum improvement, we emphasize the importance of diversity in spaces for independent study. Conventional school spaces are too uniform to provide a setting to develop the maximum degree of skills and self-reliance that students need when they leave the school building and the program housed there. The description of the spaces provides further insights into the concept.

Library

The central library serves two basic functions in independent study. First, it provides a quiet place where pupils who prefer that type of environment may work. Second, it provides a storehouse for printed, recorded, and visual materials that students use while doing more sophisticated research. The library is headquarters for the librarian and assistants, who also help supervise the resource centers, usually located elsewhere. Because the library is complemented by resource centers, the size of the space and the number of books, recordings, and visual materials stored there are smaller than the published standards for school libraries usually recommend.

The arrangement described here does not minimize the importance of the library and the librarian. Quite the contrary, both have strategic roles to play in the independent study program. Many students need at times the quiet and the resources that the library provides, as well as the services of the librarian; but they do not need these services all the time.

Resource Centers

These special learning areas, essential for every school subject, have two parts. First, there is the *study area,* where students read, write, listen, view, think, and at times talk with others briefly. Second, there is the *workroom,* where the staff keeps the "tools of the trade" of the particular subject, such as the gymnasium, the art room, the foods laboratory, or the social science workroom. In larger schools there are advantages in having separate resource centers for each of the subject areas. Smaller schools may combine the subjects into fewer centers. The two facilities for each center are located near each other.

The study area includes ten or twelve individual study carrels with walls approximately five feet high. Nearby shelves carry a wide variety of reading materials frequently used by most students in the particular subject. A simple coding system makes it easy for them to find and replace the materials. Another part of the room has tape, disk, and video players and a stock of frequently used recorded materials. Recordings of all large-group presentations and of selected small-group discussion sessions are provided. Some of the recordings are prepared by local teachers or outside consultants for students of different ability and interest levels; others are purchased from commercial sources; some are made by students themselves. As in the case of printed materials, recordings are coded simply.

In another section of the room, screens are mounted on the walls, and magazine-fed 8-mm motion picture projectors, 16-mm sound projectors, and filmstrip and slide projectors are available. Students use earphones so that they do not bother those engaged in different activities. The resource center also houses programmed instruction materials and self-teaching exercises prepared by the staff or purchased commercially to help students learn the basic facts and skills in the subject.

Some schools provide computerized carrels or electronically equipped centers where students may select and work with materials located elsewhere in the school or outside the school. Special programs for remedial, average, and advanced instruction are provided.

The study area of the resource center is noisier than the library. Students move about a good deal and occasionally talk to each other, interrupting what they are doing to discuss an important topic. The atmosphere is still somewhat subdued, however, like the quiet area of an office away from the noisy machines.

The other part of the resource center, which we may call the workroom, is a noisier place. Let us consider several examples. Good social science instruction includes student surveys and studies in the school and community with consequent need to tabulate the collected data — so calculating machines are available in the social science workroom. The workroom also provides typewriters for writing reports, duplicating machines, and equipment for making maps, charts, and the like. A teletype machine brings the students the latest information on economics, international affairs, and other local and regional happenings.

Science workrooms include supplies and equipment found in the conventional school's science laboratories, but the emphasis is different. The equipment is more portable, and special facilities are provided for more extended and extensive experiments. Of course, the biggest difference between today's science laboratory and the resource center envisioned is that science students also have a room in which they can read, write, view, and think with the science materials at their fingertips.

The physical education workroom differs from today's gymnasium. The emphasis is on activities that students may engage in individually or in very small groups — activities similar to those that they may use for recreation and physical fitness at home or on a fifty-foot lot. The size and shape of the physical education workroom is not dictated by the dimensions of a basketball court. Provision for basketball is in an entirely different room. Adjacent to the physical education workroom is a place where students may read, view, listen, write, and think about health, recreation, and physical fitness with appropriate materials readily available.

The foreign language workroom includes recording and listening equipment to test students' ability to pronounce and speak and to understand the speech of others. The resource center also houses materials in the language for pupils to read, write, listen to, and view.

Special Help Areas

In addition to the resource centers that meet the needs of most learners, the school needs to provide regularly for those with special interests and needs. The teacher or instructional assistant in the resource centers is responsible for a considerable number of students at a given time. A student who has difficulty may have to wait too long for assistance or the facilities in the resource center may be inadequate. The school facilities also need to include special help area(s) where students who need temporary assistance or a more involved remedial program in any curriculum field can obtain the assistance immediately. The special help we describe requires the assistance of a competent teacher with interest and preparation in the subject field. That teacher will decide when the learner may profitably return to the other resource centers.

Another example of an area with a different purpose is a special help room, where a school places a group of students, some with behavioral problems and others with remedial needs. A carefully selected teacher and some assistants are in charge. The number of assistants depends on the number of students and the kinds of help needed. The situation may be compared with the one-room school of former days (a few still exist) where one teacher taught all subjects to elementary school pupils. In the present situation, however, the students are scheduled out of the room for such special subjects as practical arts, fine arts, physical education, and other studies that require special facilities present elsewhere in the building or in the community.

The teacher in charge becomes the personal adviser for the students assigned to this room, helping each one to discover and develop the talents and interests that each one possesses, as limited as these might be, or to attain the degree of self-control that students need to function in the regular school program. These students have serious problems, more difficult to resolve than those described later in the discussion of "restriction zones."

Small-group Conference Areas

Spaces are required where students may gather in small groups of three or four to discuss their projects, exchange ideas, make suggestions for further investigation, engage in preliminary evaluation of their efforts, and work together in other ways. Frequently, a group of students will ask a teacher to sit in on a discussion to make suggestions, help solve a knotty problem, or plan future activities.

Students may gather around a table in the school cafeteria for this purpose. Similarly, tables and chairs may be placed in an ordinary classroom or on a patio or in a room near the library. Of course, the noise level of the area may be relatively high because the room is usually full of students talking.

Relaxation Area

Students spend 40 percent or more of their time in independent study, and this time will increase as teacher presentations and study materials become more sophisticated. They need to relax for a few minutes from time to time, for learning is more effective when periods of concentrated s udy are interspersed with different activities. In the conventional school, howev r, the learners are denied this privilege. Teachers go to the faculty lounge and other staff members take coffee breaks, but the students are supposed to work rigorously all day long except for the brief respite between periods. Even then, teachers are often assigned to corridor duty to make certain that the students do not relax too much!

In an innovative school, the relaxation area is usually a part of the cafeteria. Students may purchase soft drinks or light refreshments at snack bars that are open all day. However, students are not pressured to make purchases; they can bring their own sandwiches if they like.

The young people can talk about school work if they wish, but most often they talk about out-of-school activities and events. Students do not spend more than fifteen or twenty minutes in the relaxation area; some of them may use it more or less. Those who abuse the privilege, of course, have it removed.

Restriction Zone

The fifth area for independent study is the study hall of the typical secondary school. True, the conventional study hall is on its way out and has already disappeared from many schools. As a place for all students to study (in many schools the only place besides the library), it was poor. Students lacked materials and adequate supervision and were not allowed to converse. A small study hall is needed as a part of the total independent study program, but its function is now changed.

The school assigns a person to a study hall when actions in the other study areas testify to the fact that he or she has not developed sufficient responsibility for learning. Temporarily, the staff withdraws the privilege of working in the library, the resource centers, the small-group study area, or the relaxation room. The study hall is a place of complete silence. It is supervised by a teacher who helps students become ready to return to the other independent study areas.

The study hall is a general facility serving all the subjects in the school; therefore, the student has to bring materials just as in today's conventional school. Study halls have dictionaries and a set of encyclopedias, but that is about all. The school goal should be to have no more than 1 to 3 percent of the total school enrollment assigned to a restriction zone. If more than 3 percent or so are assigned, there is a clear indication that teacher presentations (see Chapter 21) are faulty or the school has inadequate independent study facilities.

Most educators rebel at the thought of a restriction zone. However, there are always students who interfere with others who want to work constructively, and schools that fail to provide this emergency control have to send a constant stream of offenders to the school offices. Even enlightened societies still have jails or corrective institutions.

Out-of-school Study Spaces

Independent study occurs outside school as well as inside. The kind of activities and the number of hours per week varies. Some of the study may be similar to the conventional school's homework, but the as-

signments should emphasize minimum requirements rather than pre-
scribing in advance a given number of problems to work, the pages to
write, or the books to read.

Some out-of-school study may occur in factories, shops, offices, and
other places where students are acquiring work experience. The school
develops independent study spaces cooperatively with local employers, social agencies, government agencies, and others. Study also
occurs in museums and institutes. This kind of independent study
makes the community school concept a reality.

The rule of thumb that the school uses in determining when a student
is scheduled for independent study away from the building is quite
simple. She or he studies in the community or even at a greater dis-
tance away from the school whenever the physical setting, the materials, and the instructional assistant are better than in the school. An
important consideration is that adequate arrangements exist in the
locale away from the school for supervising the experience and providing reports of the student's progress back to the school.

SUPERVISION OF INDEPENDENT STUDY

Teachers should seek to minimize association with students during
independent study, in contrast to what occurs during supervised
study in conventional classrooms. In a large resource center, a professional teacher should be present to help as needed; in smaller study
areas, the teacher may be in a nearby office and be on call as needed.
In place of the teachers, carefully selected, qualified instruction assistants may supervise the study spaces. These adult assistants need at
least a college minor in the subject represented by the various workrooms and should know the subject well enough to answer many questions and to refer a student to a professional teacher when a specialized type of assistance is needed. Homemakers interested in part-time
work, advanced college students, and retired teachers are usually
available.

When the independent study occurs away from the school in an
office, shop, store, or wherever, the instruction assistant is an employee
jointly selected by the manager or employer or other person in charge
of the institution in cooperation with the head of the department in the
school or the teacher of the subject. This joint supervision is another
factor bridging the gap between the school program and the world
outside.

The instruction assistant is there primarily to maintain order (a simple matter, usually), to recommend any student who needs to be transferred to the restriction zone, to keep the machines and books in usable

condition, and to provide other assistance as needed. The person is under the cooperative supervision of the head of the teaching team in the subject area and the school librarian.

Students are scheduled into the workrooms, and appropriate records are maintained so that the school and the parents know where they are and in general what they are doing. They leave the workrooms only with the permission of the instruction assistant in charge. The atmosphere of the workrooms must be relaxed, yet businesslike. Students may confer as long as they do not abuse the privilege. In some schools, those who have earned the privilege may, with parental consent, come and go as they wish among the independent study centers. This "open-campus" concept is an ideal toward which all schools may strive.

NEW DIRECTIONS

School personnel must become more sophisticated in assigning students to various types of independent study, recognizing the individual's past records, potential talents, and special interests (see Chapters 21 and 25). Program success also requires effective evaluation of such diverse student projects as a model, a new discovery, an exposition, the solution of a problem, a proposed reclassification of data or species, a poem, a musical composition, a new tool, a product, or a survey (see Chapters 32 and 33).

Both dimensions of independent study — the essential learnings and the opportunity for creative and depth efforts — are for all students. This reiteration emphasizes a concept that schools often neglect. Teachers readily conclude that independent study is meant only for the talented few. All students need to learn the required content with as much freedom as possible from constant supervision and help. All students need to follow their special interests and talents even though some of them achieve mediocre results in relation to others — a contrast that teachers should refrain from highlighting.

Immature young people are highly conscious of the values placed by a school on different types of activities. Superior presentations may motivate students, and exciting discussions may stimulate them, but they will consider independent study an unwarranted luxury if the school emphasizes the marks on factual examinations. The school that places high value on the quality and quantity of independent study when it appraises and reports individual progress will reap the benefits of superior work by students.

The school should send parents, colleges, employers, and the general public an analysis of the total productivity of its student body in independent study, as well as examples of excellent individual pupil activity. This reporting creates a special image of educational priorities.

The teacher's goal is to become increasingly dispensable. The expectation is for all students to grow in self-analysis, self-correction, and self-direction, for the quality of the student's independent study reflects the quality of the teaching. Every student failure in independent study should challenge the teacher to help him or her succeed next time; it should not be an excuse to resort to the easier route of more teacher domination and control. Independent study is the ultimate educational objective.

TOPICS FOR STUDY AND DISCUSSION

1. Consider some division or unit in a course you now teach or are preparing to teach. List and define the essential concepts to be learned by all students.
2. Take the same example as in topic 1. Suggest one or more depth studies or potentially creative activities that might be profitable for (a) low achievers, (b) average students, (c) high achievers.
3. Plan a learning resources center for your subject area, indicating kinds of materials and their location.
4. Develop a set of guidelines to help instruction assistants supervise students in one or more of the places where independent study occurs.
5. Your visit to a learning resources center shows that almost all students are reading textbooks or encyclopedias or copying materials from them to complete reports. What steps do you take to make independent study more productive?

SELECTED REFERENCES

Alexander, William M., and Hines, Vince A. *Independent Study in Secondary Schools.* Cooperative Research Project No. 2969. Gainesville, Fla.: University of Florida, 1966. Multilithed.

This book reports on visits to thirty-six schools having innovative independent study programs. Purposes, curriculum areas, pupils served, types of studies, teacher activities, facilities, and evaluation are described.

Beggs, David W. III, and Buffie, Edward G., eds. *Independent Study.* Bloomington: Indiana University Press, 1965.

Twelve authors describe junior and senior high school programs and procedures.

Berman, Louise M. *New Priorities in the Curriculum.* Columbus, Ohio: Charles E. Merrill Books, 1968.

The author's suggestions for curriculum development, especially as summarized in hypotheses at the end of each chapter, are valuable guides to anyone developing materials for pupils to use in their independent study.

Davis, Harold S. *Independent Study — An Annotated Bibliography.* Cleveland: Educational Research Council of America, 1966.

This pamphlet lists 150 books and pamphlets relating to different aspects of the subject.

Ellsworth, Ralph E., and Wagner, Hobert D. *The School Library: Facilities for Study in the Secondary School.* New York: Educational Facilities Laboratories, 1963.

This book describes a variety of existing and proposed facilities designed to enhance the contributions of the library resource center for college and secondary school programs.

Fisher, D. L. "When Students Choose and Use 15 Times." *Educational Leadership* (December 1973), pp. 267–270.

Fisher describes how independent study operates in a Detroit, Michigan, middle school.

Howard, Alvin W. and Stoumbis, George C. *The Junior High and Middle School: Issues and Practices.* Scranton, Penna.: Intext Educational Publishers, 1970.

Chapter 18, "Independent Study," shows how this program operates, with younger students listing advantages and problems.

Libraries in Secondary Schools — A New Look. National Association of Secondary School Principals *Bulletin* (January 1966).

Sixteen writers redefine the library's role as a resource center.

McClosky, Mildred G., ed. *Teaching Strategies and Classroom Realities.* Englewood Cliffs, N. J.: Prentice-Hall, 1971, pp. 143–174.

Part IV of this book describes human resources for independent study that most schools utilize very little or ineffectively. Eight authors give examples in most curriculum areas.

Popham, W. James, and Baker, Eva J. *Establishing Instructional Goals,* v-130, and *Planning an Instructional Sequence,* v-k38. Englewood Cliffs, N. J.: Prentice-Hall, 1970.

These two self-instruction books will help teachers understand and plan better programs of independent study.

Sizer, Theodore R. *Places for Learning — Places for Joy: Speculations on American School Reform.* Cambridge, Mass.: Harvard University Press, 1973.

Sizer emphasizes the need for broader school programs for students of all ages, with much independent study, and continuous progress arrangements.

Trump, J. Lloyd. "Independent Study: The Schools." *The Encyclopedia of Education,* vol. 4, pp. 557–562. New York: The Free Press, 1971.

This article provides further details and includes additional bibliography.

Watkins, Robert. "Independent Study Projects: Practical Considerations." *The Clearing House* (September 1975), pp. 44–46.

Based on five years of successful experience in a school, the author lists ten imperatives, emphasizing the importance of careful planning and supervision.

21

Motivating Students in Larger Groups

The significance of motivation in curriculum improvement is emphasized throughout this book. A particular segment of curriculum content may be motivational for some students and exactly the opposite for others. That fact causes us to stress the need for more diversity in content than most schools provide now. A similar statement may be made regarding evaluation systems, locales of learning, and all the other topics included in this book.

This chapter emphasizes yet another method to motivate learners. The focus here is on what may be termed teacher-talk. However, the concept goes beyond that activity to include all forms of presentations. The focus is on how these activities bear on the need for an enriching curriculum and thus inhibit or enhance learning. Also introduced is the concept that a variety of settings are utilized. The conventional term *mass media* is expanded to include what we call large-group instruction. These motivational presentations are done on a departmental basis. They should be open to all students whether or not they are at the time involved in that department's curriculum.

For the purpose of these motivational presentations, we would combine the subject areas listed in Parts II and III into the following eight departments (plus a ninth, religion, in parochial schools): English, fine arts, health-fitness-recreation (different term for physical education), mathematics, other languages (foreign), practical arts, science, and social studies.

Reading a book, magazine, or newspaper, watching television, listening to radio and recordings, going to a movie, and attending a lecture are examples of participation in large-group instruction. What a person hears and sees in these activities frequently becomes the subject of discussions with other persons (usually in groups of two to six) and often motivates the individual to seek more understanding of the subject in independent study in libraries, bookstores, museums, or elsewhere.

Every school has large-group instruction. The trouble is that it is wastefully done in classes of twenty to thirty, is teacher dominated, and often is not motivational. Typically, teachers talk, show films, play records, give demonstrations, and otherwise make presentations for about one-half the time that their classes meet. The learner is physically passive, except for taking notes. However, each one can and should react mentally to what is seen and heard, noting the matters he or she wishes to discuss with colleagues or to study in an appropriate setting. Ideally, presentations should be followed by specially planned independent study and by student-centered discussions in groups of fifteen or fewer. Unfortunately, many conventional classes do not include either activity.

One other point to keep in mind is that when teachers talk or present materials, the size of the class or audience does not matter as long as each pupil can see and hear well. Motivational experiences in larger groups as a part of the instructional system refer to presentations provided either by teachers or by some other persons or by media. We recommend that in a typical month with one departmental presentation per week, the three presenters might be a teacher, a student or group of students, and someone or several persons from the community. The fourth presentation might be audio-visual, with a teacher available to highlight the program. Such a balance is easier for the department because it means that each staff member has only one presentation per month even though the department resumes responsibility for developing the total program.

The key to success is whether the presentations actually provide a motivational experience that not only holds the interest of most students but also stimulates later discussions among them and more productive independent study. There is nothing unique about this proposal. These kinds of presentations occur regularly in all schools in all subjects and at all grade levels.

PURPOSES OF LARGE-GROUP INSTRUCTION

Three goals must guide large-group instruction. First, the presentation should be *motivational*, arousing student interest in learning more about the subject. Second, it should be *informational*, providing facts, ideas, and points of view *not otherwise readily available* to students. Third, it should be *directional*, suggesting activities for students to do following the presentation. Failure to aim for these three goals — or adding materials that go beyond them — detracts from the effectiveness of the presentation.

Motivation

Determining who should teach the large group or whether to use a film are crucial matters in motivating pupils. The basic criterion is to select the best teacher for a given topic to work with a specific group of students. However, if someone in the community, or a film or television program, has more to offer than any local teacher, that person or the film or TV program should be used, with the best available local teacher complementing the presentation. Remember, the basic purpose of large-group instruction is to place students in contact with the *best possible* teaching for the particular topic.

The presentation is like the appetizer that stimulates interest in, and prepares the body for, an excellent meal. Unfortunately, teachers sometimes act as if it is the main course of the banquet — they overstuff their listeners, who then want no more of it or develop indigestion. In contrast, the good teacher whets the pupil's appetite by providing only a part of the poem, problem, or experiment — then tells the learners how to obtain more.

Other factors that influence motivation, discussed in Chapter 2, can highlight the importance of planning and preparing for large-group instruction.

Information

Some people object to large-group instruction because it reminds them of experiences they had with certain college professors who failed to

understand that large-group instruction should provide information
not readily available elsewhere. For example, a professor may have
lectured from the same notes used in preparing a textbook that students were required to purchase.

If large-group instruction covers content similar to that which
students are expected to acquire through independent study, they will
be bored by the large-group presentation and develop various schemes
to avoid listening or be less interested in pursuing the subject in their
independent study. On the other hand, if it is used creatively, the large-
group presentation can provide a more current interpretation of history
or scientific data, develop an interpretation quite different from the
conventional book or recordings, or cover materials not available to the
pupils in the local independent study resource areas.

Teachers must avoid the tendency to cover the subject, topic by
topic. Making that mistake causes all sorts of trouble. For example,
teachers then indicate that independent study is locked into what is
currently presented to the large group. That assumption is incorrect.
The new information may relate to a topic that some students studied
previously — stressing the need to revise what they learned. The
presentation may be current with or anticipate the independent study
of other learners. Remember, the teacher does not need to cover the
course orally. The goal is for the students to cover the course requirements — and for them to enjoy the process as much as possible.

Direction

A presentation is incomplete without the third aspect of large-group
instruction — the assignment. Students must be told what they need to
know and how they may learn it. Such structuring does not inhibit
creativity. Quite the contrary, it provides the foundation for new concepts and leaves open-ended a variety of directions in which students
may go. These assignments are sometimes given orally, but preferably
they are on printed or duplicated guidesheets and worksheets. A physically present teacher thus supplements the instruction given by a film,
a television program, or a community expert.

HOW TO PREPARE PRESENTATIONS

The preparation of a large-group presentation requires careful study
and creativity, as well as considerable time and energy. The teacher
must assess the group's past achievement and interest in the topic. Some
teachers think they can teach more efficiently by dividing students into
groups based on the extent of their knowledge of the subject to be dis-

cussed. Of course, that procedure requires more teacher time, and there is no evidence to support the contention that more learning results. Students must be able to relate new material to what they already know. That reduces the necessity for pure memorization, thus enhancing interest and conceptualization.

Other important considerations when preparing presentations include using simple explanations, using clever illustrations, developing meaningful relationships, raising thought-provoking issues that will encourage small-group discussion and suggest topics for independent study, and occasionally using questions that may be answered by group response. However, teachers should avoid asking factual questions of individuals, a practice common in conventional classrooms. The teacher's goal is to find out whether all students understand the subject, not just one student. Moreover, the answers given by the individuals do not provide effective discussion.

A competent, experienced teacher may spend ten or more hours preparing a single presentation to be given for the first time. Later presentations on the same topic may require less time as materials are revised and updated.

The proper use of clerks and instruction assistants may reduce preparation time and facilitate presentations. Instruction assistants can check on needed data, prepare visual aids, and help supervise students. Clerks can prepare mats and stencils, check attendance, distribute and collect supplies, and keep files and records.

LOGISTIC ARRANGEMENTS

An overhead projector and sound system are essential in a large-group room, for each student must see and hear as well as possible. Facilities for presenting films, slides, television, and recordings are also needed. The best rooms provide integrated media systems so the presenter can vary the performance by pushing buttons or signaling an operator. Ideally, the rooms should be air-conditioned, for year-round control of temperature, humidity, and air circulation; windowless, for better light regulation; and carpeted, for better acoustic control. Electronic reaction buttons in front of student listeners have been used to indicate their failure to grasp new ideas; however, raising hands as a signal is less expensive.

The number of students included in a group depends on the size of the school, the enrollment in a given subject, the kinds of facilities available, and the personal opinion of the teacher-presenter. Millions of people simultaneously view a television presentation. Thousands of persons gather in a stadium to watch a game or listen to a lecture. Little research has been done on the effects of the size of the audience on the listener's comprehension, but it appears that the size of the audience does not matter as long as each person can see and hear well. Many teachers prefer to limit the size of groups to approximately 150 so the groups can be somewhat more homogeneous according to past achievement. However, the need for such homogeneity has not been demonstrated in research. Diverse populations read newspapers and watch television simultaneously, with each person getting his or her own degree of stimulation and content from the presentation. Obviously, large student groups produce greater economies in the use of teacher time and energy, outside community consultants, and building space.

The optimum length for a period of large-group instruction is unknown. Even small children, including those with relatively low ability, watch television hour after hour without losing interest and gain some understanding from the experience. The subject of the presentation, the audio-visual aids used, the effectiveness of the teacher, the opinion of the teacher, and the air-conditioning of the room are among the factors that must be considered when scheduling the period. Most junior and senior high school teachers prefer a period of approximately thirty minutes for large-group instruction. If the school has no regularly scheduled intermissions, this means approximately twenty-five minutes for the presentation. On the other hand, some schools operate effectively with sixty-minute large-group instruction periods while others argue in favor of shorter periods.

How many large-group presentations to schedule per week is another open question. The answer depends on an analysis of what the school hopes to accomplish in large groups, in small groups, and through independent study. The teachers in the teaching team must base decisions on their best professional judgment, and all discussions must be subject to change on the basis of personal preference and investigation. We believe one meeting per week is sufficient to accomplish the three functions of large groups.

Large-group instruction is being carried on effectively in all the subject areas. For example, physical education calls for the same teaching-learning analysis as history, mathematics, music, or agriculture. Obviously, in every subject, teachers need to talk or show films, and students need time to learn through personal experience and to discuss with each other what they have learned. The large group is an important ingredient in the process.

OTHER LARGE-GROUP ACTIVITIES

Students working on programmed instruction devices (usually programmed textbooks) can work in large groups under the supervision of instruction assistants, with a professional teacher available for consultation when needed. This process saves teacher time and energy. Written examinations can also be administered effectively in large groups supervised by instruction assistants. Thus, testing procedures can be standardized more in the large group than they could be when the tests were given in numerous small groups. Of course, other forms of evaluation (see Chapters 32 and 33) require different arrangements.

TOPICS FOR STUDY AND DISCUSSION

1. Select a topic or unit in the subject you teach or plan to teach. Then plan a presentation that will motivate learners, give information not readily available to them, and provide a diversified assignment as indicated in this chapter. Your plan should be a general outline, sufficiently detailed so you can discuss it with your colleagues.
2. Many teachers are not artists. Perhaps you also lack those skills. However, you need to communicate to an artist on your staff the ideas you have for a visual you will use on the overhead projector. Using the outline you developed in topic 1, sketch one or more proposed visuals.
3. Using your plan for topic 1, go to a visual aids catalog and list possible films, filmstrips, slides, and recordings that you might use in your presentation. If possible, preview one or more of them with your colleagues.
4. Write a proposal for constructing a space, or remodeling an existing space, as a facility for large-group instruction. Consider such matters as size of room, seating arrangements, facilities for the instructor, and equipment.
5. Assume you are involved in a discussion with a colleague or have just finished an article in which the "lecture system" of instruction is deplored. Prepare an answer showing the differences between large-group instruction as described in this chapter and a lecture course you experienced in college.

SELECTED REFERENCES

Bair, Medill, and Woodward, Richard G. *Team Teaching in Action*. Boston: Houghton Mifflin Company, 1964, pp. 122–153.
    Although concerned with elementary school work, the basic principles and suggestions here relate to secondary teaching.
Beggs, David W. III. *Decatur-Lakeview High School*. Englewood Cliffs, N. J.: Prentice-Hall, 1964, pp. 114–122.
    This chapter emphasizes reasons, preparation, methods, and other aspects of large-group work.
Davis, Harold S. *Illuminate Your Lecture*. Cleveland: Educational Research Council of Greater Cleveland, 1964.
    This pamphlet presents the basic principles for using the overhead projector in large-group instruction.

Hoover, Kenneth H. *Learning and Teaching in the Secondary School,* 3d ed. Boston: Allyn and Bacon, 1972, pp. 451–477.

This chapter describes procedures for imparting knowledge and information.

McLeish, John. *The Psychology of Teaching Methods.* The Seventy-fifth Yearbook of the National Society for the Study of Education. "The Lecture Method." Chicago: The University of Chicago Press, 1976, pp. 252–301.

Although the purposes here differ from some aspects of the lecture method as described by McLeish, the chapter updates the research and provides useful suggestions for improving motivational presentations.

Peterson, Carl H. *Effective Team Teaching.* West Nyack, N. Y.: Parker Publishing Company, 1966, pp. 75–100.

This chapter gives criteria for large-group instruction, techniques and some specific examples.

Schultz, Morton J. *The Teacher and Overhead Projection.* Englewood Cliffs, N. J.: Prentice-Hall, 1965, pp. 1–30.

These two chapters offer practical suggestions for improving large-group instruction. The book's remaining 210 pages are divided into chapters for each of the curriculum-content areas.

22

Reaction and Interaction in Smaller Groups of Students or Teachers

We emphasize small groups in this book because the needs for such groups are ignored in most other books and in most schools. Separating content and methodology harms both concepts.

Both teachers and students need to understand how to organize small groups for specifically stated purposes, how to make the groups function well, and how to evaluate group processes as well as how the group environment affects the individuals in it. Since most teachers receive relatively little preparation for these activities, the school's supervisory group themselves need to use proper techniques in working with teachers involved in curriculum-improvement projects. Teachers can then in turn help students along similar lines.

Specially planned educational programs involving small-group discussions are essential to a good school curriculum. The conventional class or faculty meeting is too large for these learning experiences. Dividing a class into two or three subgroups, or holding buzz sessions, is not a good substitute for regular discussion groups of fifteen or so persons because a teacher or other leader can assist only one of the groups at a time while the other groups lack teacher supervision.

Moreover, as far as students are concerned, the makeup of the groups tends to remain fairly constant, limited by the twenty-five to thirty people assigned to the class. In contrast, the students in small-group discussion classes may be changed periodically to produce better results. And the teacher in those classes plays a role quite different from that performed in the conventional classroom.

Life would be incomplete without the discussions that every individual holds with other persons in small groups. New acquaintances and friendships develop in such meetings, and the conversations help to clarify ideas, stimulate further inquiry, and persuade others to accept beliefs.

Small-group discussions also provide essential education for citizenship in a democracy. Students must learn to discuss controversial matters, to communicate effectively, to listen to and respect the opinions of others, and to deal with people whose backgrounds and interests differ from their own. The discussions use and reinforce some of the knowledge gained in large groups and in independent study — they help young people crystallize values and attitudes.

These regularly scheduled discussion groups differ from the various-sized groups that the school creates, that develop out of independent study, or that are established for therapy or counseling purposes. The staff is constantly alert to the desirability of organizing groups of students who have common needs or other goals. As indicated in Chapter 20, there are many groups of various sizes that meet with teachers or sometimes by themselves when their independent study develops along similar lines. The basic aim is related to a specific subject. The small groups described in this chapter have different purposes.

One special purpose is for students to react to the motivational experiences that the school provides in larger than usual groups as described in Chapter 21. Such reactions not only may increase the motivation resulting from the larger experiences but also may provide the staff with feedback about the effectiveness of the large-group presentations. Of course, teachers also are present to answer questions or clear up misunderstandings that the presentations stimulated. Teachers also may help students improve their discussion skills and observe behavior that suggests the need for systematic instructions in the techniques of small-group discussion.

PREPARATION FOR SMALL-GROUP DISCUSSION

Few teachers and students have had adequate training and experience to achieve maximum benefit from small-group discussions. Most of them do not know how to discuss effectively. The oral quizzing erroneously called classroom discussion that occupies much time in conventional classrooms must be forgotten if small-group discussion is to fulfill its purpose.

Teachers must learn to handle the role of listener, adviser, and co-participant. They must also be acquainted with sociometry and behavioral psychology. Once they themselves understand the processes involved in discussion, they can teach their students.

Before actually participating in discussions, students may learn the principles involved through large-group instruction and independent study. Large-group instruction may describe and illustrate the roles each member of a small-group discussion may play (leader, recorder, observer, or consultant) and the many functions of group members (initiating, questioning, elaborating, arguing for, opposing, challenging, blocking, harmonizing, ignoring, keeping silent, entertaining, summarizing, seeking consensus, and evaluating). Pamphlets describing small-group discussion may be placed in the independent study areas. Audio or video tape recordings of small group discussion sessions illustrating good and bad procedures may also be placed in the resource centers so that students may listen to them and react.

Of course, the learning is best when individuals themselves practice various roles in a small-group discussion that is evaluated afterward by other young people and by their leader. It is difficult to teach people to express ideas effectively, to listen, to point up issues, to seek consensus, to identify differences, and to respect each other in the process. But students and instructors worry too much about the group's not covering a predetermined body of subject matter. Teachers constantly must seek a constructive balance between correcting too many errors and letting mistakes go by, between too much control and too much permissiveness, too much structure and too much freedom of choice of topics, and so on. The middle-of-the-road approach with occasional deviations may be the best solution.

GROUP CONSTITUENCY AND MEETING ARRANGEMENTS

Experiences of schools with small groups, and research in group process, indicate that the desirable size for a group is about fifteen participants. That number provides opportunities to become actively involved in discussion during a reasonable period. A group of fewer than fifteen is unnecessarily small and expensive to staff. Remember, the purpose here is to obtain reactions, teach oral communications skills, and improve relations, not to cover the subject or to provide group therapy.

One small-group discussion per week for each departmental area is sufficient in most cases. Most schools believe that about thirty minutes is a desirable length for these group discussions.

Every school subject can profit from a discussion group. Physical education groups may meet to discuss health, physical fitness, and recreation. Mathematics groups may discuss the application of quantitative thinking to personal, community, and world problems. An English group may relate the content of reading to school issues. The world of work may be discussed by a vocational or practical arts group. A French group may discuss *in French* a political development in France that affects other countries. Imaginative teachers and students never lack content for discussions.

Teachers and counselors should determine the makeup of groups, changing the composition as frequently as necessary. For example, if teachers observe that two or three students are dominating the discussion in a given group, they could transfer them to a group containing stronger student discussants. Both groups might benefit from this transfer, and the new group might have beneficial effects on the transferred students.

Groups are composed on a variety of other bases, such as friendships, emotional maturity, sex, quality of past school work in the subject, special interests, and vocational or educational goals. Counseling records, interest inventories, teacher opinions, sociometry, school records, and other appropriate data are utilized in making original assignments of students to groups and in changing group composition. Teachers, counselors, and supervisors meet to exchange information and ideas about ameliorative arrangements for different individuals and groups.

GROUP ORGANIZATION

Whether the group in a school is a number of teachers developing curriculum tasks that need attention or a group of students organized for any of the purposes stated earlier in this book, the development of specific skills will help. What follows here is a brief summary of the organization and the skills necessary to foster this area of curriculum improvement. The emphasis is on helping students function better in small groups. However, the same requirements apply to groups of teachers with whatever tasks they select to work on.

Four persons with specialized roles facilitate small-group discussion. A *leader* helps guide the discussion. A *recorder* keeps an account of what the group discusses. An *observer* constructively criticizes the discussion. A *consultant* provides information that the group needs.

The Leader

One of the issues that divide teachers of small groups is whether students originally should be selected as leaders or whether the teacher should serve that role. The arguments pro and con are quite obvious. If a teacher is unwilling to relinquish the leadership role, it may be better never to assume it. On the other hand, much can be said for a teacher's assuming leadership for the first two or three meetings of the group to provide an example of how a leader should relate to the group. Natural leadership can emerge from the group in that brief time, so that the teacher can relinquish leadership to another person within two or three sessions. The teacher then alternates between the roles of group observer and consultant, sharing both roles with students.

The first task of the group leader, student or teacher, is to help the group decide on the issues it wishes to discuss, clarify the issues, and plan procedures. During the discussion, the leader tries to involve as many of the group members as possible. For example, noting that some members are not participating, he or she may raise a question regarding what the group is missing by not knowing what the others are thinking. The leader may even call on some of them for expressions or assistance. If the group departs from the subject of the discussion, the leader tells them what is happening and asks the group to decide whether they want to turn to a new topic or continue discussing the original one. If the discussion is going badly, the leader calls on the group observer for reactions on why the discussion is not going well. Periodically, the leader calls on the recorder to summarize the discussion to date or may call on the consultant for clarification or for more adequate information. The leader also helps the group to keep in mind the time limits on their meeting and to focus their discussion more sharply. All in all, the leader aims to help individual members, and the group as a whole, to become more effective and efficient in their discussions.

The Recorder

One member of the group is appointed recorder. The job is to keep a record of the content of the discussion so that he or she can report to the group on request. Since the group is interested more in *what* was said than in *who* said it, it is unnecessary to record the names of persons making contributions. The recorder notes the areas of agreement and disagreement, rather than everything that was said by each person. Usually the recorder provides a summary of the discussion at the close of the period, but she or he may be called on anytime a report is needed.

The Observer

One student, in addition to the teacher, is asked to serve as a group observer. This person does not participate regularly in the discussion in order to concentrate on what is happening. A tally of who participates in the discussion may be kept so the observer can report whether some persons, perhaps including the leader, are monopolizing the group time or if some are not contributing. The teacher may supplement this record by keeping a qualitative record for other purposes. A plus (+) designates a helpful contribution, a negative (−) marks a useless, incorrect, or interrupting comment, and a zero (0) indicates remarks that neither help nor hinder. This scheme helps evaluate individual and group progress in discussion skills.

The observer analyzes why the group is being particularly successful or is having difficulties in discussing a given issue. When called on by the group leader, the observer raises questions with the group on points of evaluation, trying to help the group grow in the quality of their discussion rather than serving as a conventional teacher scolding some people and praising others for what they say.

Students need the observer's report regularly. For example, assume that a discussion group in English has been talking about problems associated with *work*. They have been reading poems, essays, short stories, and novels about *work* as one unit in the course, but not one pupil in the discussion group has referred to anything he or she has read on the subject during the unit. In critiquing the discussion, the observer might question the omission. Or noting that at least three times during the discussion students said, "I have went," he or she might point out that while that expression communicates the idea, it is incorrect grammatically, and that society tends to lower its estimation of the person who fails to use the correct form, "I have gone."

Common sense keeps the observer from too many or too frequent criticisms that would appear to nag the group too much. On the other hand, failure to point out important shortcomings abrogates the teacher's role. The teacher-observer typically reports near the end of the discussion but might do so anytime. The report usually raises questions for discussion rather than pontificates.

The Consultant

The teacher, a student member of the group, or someone specially invited to meet with the group for a given discussion, may serve as a consultant. The purpose is to provide specific information and experience that other members of the group may not have, but not to make a speech or monopolize the discussion. A teacher sometimes finds this role difficult because as consultant he or she must not set too high a level for the discussion or allow personal domination of the group because of status. On the other hand, if a teacher or other consultant hears a group member making an error that could misdirect the discussion, the consultant is responsible for correcting that information. Deciding whether the error really matters is a difficult task that tests the consultant's ability to help students learn to discuss effectively.

Periodically, the teacher meets with the leader, recorder, and observer of a new group to help them grow in their various responsibilities. The teacher may suggest to the student leader some provocative questions for discussion. However, too many such questions may become a crutch rather than a challenge to the students' creativity. The teacher also talks to the members of the group, helping them understand what they are doing as individuals and as a group. They must analyze the member who contributes little, who talks too much, who constantly gets the group off the subject, who asks irrelevant questions, or who irritates by being antagonistic constantly. Conversely, the group should recognize especially helpful members who bring desirable information at the right time, summarize the discussion, help clarify issues, and help noncooperative group members become cooperative.

RELATIONSHIPS TO LARGE GROUPS AND INDEPENDENT STUDY

When attending small-group meetings, the teacher must guard against the temptation to lecture, to quiz the pupils, or to feel the small group must cover everything presented in the large group or learned in independent study. The teacher may, however, observe matters that need to be presented more effectively in large-group instruction. Listening to the discussion may help appraise the quality of independent study. The teacher may help stimulate independent study through small-group discussions by scheduling occasional brief reports from students engaging in exciting projects. Thus the teacher insures planned relationships among all three of the basic phases of the instructional system.

Our experience leads to the recommendation that the small groups should be scheduled as soon as possible after the large groups. The reactions brought from the large groups are more intense, thus contributing to the effectiveness of the discussion. Also the teacher meeting with the small group can view the discussion as a sounding board to help colleagues appraise and possibly change the content or the approaches used in the scheduled presentations to other large groups. Moreover, as students realize that they will have a regular opportunity to react to the large groups in the small-group discussions, they approach both experiences with a sharper focus.

OVERCOMING BARRIERS

Our experiences during the past several years in working with the curriculum in both conventional and innovative schools underscores more than ever the need for systematic instruction in small groups. Students should understand and practice better relationships with their peers as well as with teachers, parents, and other older persons. Although some spectacular publicity and some unfortunate experiences in ill-conceived encounter groups have turned off some people, the fact remains that school programs tend to ignore this all-important aspect of humanizing educational programs.

If you as a teacher or administrator have not been prepared adequately by your university programs to organize and conduct these groups in productive ways, the school needs to provide in-service programs to help you attain the necessary attitudes and skills. As in all other aspects of teaching, experience is an essential ingredient in learning how to do it. Practice sessions with professional colleagues, with competent supervision, is an excellent way to start.

TOPICS FOR STUDY AND DISCUSSION

1. Talk about some subject with your colleagues, recording the complete discussion on tape. Play back the recording several times to analyze various roles: member, leader, recorder, observer, consultant. Also, evaluate the quality of the different comments with a +, −, 0 scale.
2. Record a discussion involving students and a teacher. Analyze and evaluate it as you did for topic 1.
3. Take a curriculum unit or segment in the subject you teach or are preparing to teach. List some topics that would provoke effective discussion.
4. Prepare one or more instruments to measure interpersonal relationships among students or among a group of colleagues. Plot the relationships on a chart. Your question might be, If you had an opportunity to sit with three of your classmates (or of the faculty or of the department) around a table to discuss (list the topic), who would you prefer to have in the group?

SELECTED REFERENCES

Benne, Kenneth D., and Muntyan, Bozidar. *Human Relations in Curriculum Change.* New York: The Dryden Press, 1951, pp. 66–139 and 154–192.
These pages have many practical suggestions to help teachers and prin-

cipals understand the roles of group members and help groups improve their operation.

Bradford, Leland Powers, ed. *Group Development*. Selected Reading Series One. Washington, D. C.: National Training Laboratories, 1961.

This book consists of an introduction to the field of group process, consisting of twelve articles by different authors on such topics as group dynamics and the individual, functional roles of group members, and feedback and group self-evaluation.

―――. *T-Group Theory and Laboratory Method*. New York: John Wiley & Sons, 1964, pp. 336–394 and 452–486.

Robert Blake and Murray Horwitz show how to analyze and improve group action and to resolve conflicts; Mathew Miles relates the T-Group to the classroom; and Leland Bradford and others look to the future.

Gall, Meredith D., and Gall, Joyce P. *The Psychology of Teaching Methods*. The Seventy-fifth Yearbook of the National Society for the Study of Education. "The Discussion Method." Chicago: The University of Chicago Press, 1976, pp. 166–216.

The second and fourth sections deal especially with interaction groups; however, the entire chapter is helpful in understanding the purposes and methods of discussion in small groups. Some reports of recent research are included.

Glatthorn, Allan A. *Learning in the Small Group*. Melbourne, Fla.: Institute for Development of Educational Activities, 1966.

This pamphlet includes descriptions of small-group discussion as well as special groups for independent study.

Hoover, Kenneth H. *Learning and Teaching in the Secondary School*, 3d ed. Boston: Allyn and Bacon, 1972, pp. 273–313 and 478–509.

These chapters provide suggestions in the areas of group dynamics, including teacher and student roles in groups, behavioral objectives, and methods of recording and evaluating participation.

Rogers, Carl. *Carl Rogers on Encounter Groups*. New York: Harper & Row, 1970.

This reference is for teachers to understand a particular type of group activity.

Schmuck, Richard, and Schmuck, Patricia. *Group Process in the Classroom*, 2nd ed. Dubuque, Ia.: Wm. C. Brown Company Publishers, 1975.

Theoretical analysis and practical suggestions are provided to help teachers and other school leaders develop better group climates through the application of group dynamics.

Solomon, Lawrence, and Berzon, William, eds. *New Perspectives on Encounter Groups*. San Francisco: Jossey-Bass, 1972.

Twenty-four chapters by different authors cover topics relative to encounter and other types of groups. Theoretical and research reports are provided. The central theme is how learning groups are improved through the use of group dynamics. Theory and research information is provided, along with specific examples from schools.

―――. *A Humanistic Psychology of Education — Making the School Everybody's House*. Palo Alto, Calif.: National Press Books, 1974, pp. 70–90 and 169–231.

The latter part of Chapter 4 discusses different types of groups with special emphasis on the applications of group dynamics to school programs. Chapter 5 focuses on the climate of learning groups, providing background theories plus practical applications in schools. Both chapters provide suggestions for further reading.

23

Technical Devices
in an Instructional System

Audio-visual devices have spread from wealthy suburbia to the ghetto. Transistor radios and TV sets join with street sounds, CB broadcasters and receivers, and loudspeakers on streets and inside buildings to influence our lives. The sounds and sights also dominate the schools. However, the audio and visual media often are not utilized adequately or well in the instructional process; the printed page and handwriting still dominate most teaching and learning.

Audio-visual aids have been available for educational use during much of the twentieth century. More than four decades ago there were heated discussions on the potential role of radio in education. Speeches were made and articles written on various sides of the subject. Some feared that the monster, radio, might replace the teacher in the classroom; others discussed dangers of introducing a technical device into the teacher-learner relationship, making it less personal. School administrators worried about how difficult it was to schedule the broadcasts with existing classes. Certain educational philosophers warned against developing national networks for teaching all the classrooms of the country at the same time, with resultant thought control. Others considered radio an opportunity to bring to all students of the country the best teaching that could be found. The arguments *for* radio approximated those given today in favor of television and other technical devices.

What happened as a result of all these discussions? Though students occasionally listened to radio broadcasts or produced some themselves, radio never became an integral part of the curriculum.

Most teachers today have only a few more instructional aids than teachers had three or more decades ago. The exhibits at educational conventions and advertisements in educational periodicals testify to the variety of available films, filmstrips, slides, projectors, recorders, radio and television receivers and transmitters, automated reading devices, programmed textbooks and machines, books and other printed materials, pictures, flannel board, and numerous other audio-visual devices. A few schools are experimenting with computer-assisted instruction.

Recently, cheaper and simpler recorders and listening devices using tapes in cassettes have become more common in classrooms, resource centers, libraries, and other study and work areas. Learning packages may include recorded directions, explanations and tests to accompany, or in addition to, printed materials. Even small children use cassette recorders effectively. Older students increasingly are using video tape recorders to prepare programs. Film making excites many students, providing wide variations in quality and creativity.

There is no shortage of "hardware" (the machines) or "software" (the programs). However, technical devices still play a limited role in the total instructional system, for not enough people are trained to use them properly. The one exception to this statement are the hand-held calculators that even some elementary school teachers allow students to use. Of course, some others believe that these devices will produce mathematical illiterates.

PREPARATION FOR USE

Curriculum content and methodology that fail to include technical devices are sterile indeed. However, these technical aids require effective settings and trained personnel in order to accomplish the high purposes for which they have been devised.

The overhead projector currently is probably the most widely used of the newer technical aids to teaching. However, teachers often write on the overhead visuals the same way they write on a blackboard. That activity is not a very exciting adjunct to teaching. They should avoid merely writing outlines and make more effective use of symbolic materials to stimulate creativity, use different colors to emphasize ideas, and develop other imaginative approaches to arouse student interest and make better assignments.

Tape recorders are also used ineffectively. For example, a tape recording need not merely repeat instructions that students already have available in their textbooks, but rather may present information not readily available elsewhere. The list of suggestions for using technical devices could be extended, but such lists are available in numerous other publications.

Students also must learn to use technical devices to best advantage. They have been taught to read but have not been taught to view and to listen. For example, there is little evidence that they obtain maximum benefit from many excellent out-of-school radio and television programs.

The three components of large-group instruction explained in Chapter 21 may be used to improve students' viewing and listening habits both in school and outside. They also need training in how to operate the various devices, how to know when they are not working properly, and where to go for help. Systematic programs of evaluation will enable teachers to know how well students are using the materials available to them.

TEACHER USE

Technical devices are used when they can provide a needed service better than a physically present teacher can, when they complement a teacher's presentation, or when they save time and energy for teachers through adequate substitute performance. Therefore, teachers use technical devices in large-group instruction, to help them to motivate, to inform, and to make the assignment. The devices are also available to pupils for use in their independent study.

The need to use these devices in physical and instructional settings that are economical, effective, and feasible provides one of the more significant arguments against the conventional classroom with one teacher and thirty students. Every classroom has to be darkened. If the school has only one projector someone has to bring it to the classroom from a storage place — or if each classroom has one, it is unused much of the time. The school has to develop a variety of procedures for scheduling, delivering, picking up, and operating equipment in widely separated spaces.

Confronted by a number of technical devices, the creative teacher carefully studies the goals he or she has in mind for large-group instruction or independent study, then selects the media that will produce the optimum result. The qualities of simplicity, economy, and effectiveness affect the decision. A film may be quite costly in comparison to slides, and the majority of materials in the subject to be covered may not require motion. Sound films are more expensive than silent films; in some instances, the sound track is not essential. A teacher may be able to get across a concept better with an overhead projector than with a fleeting television program. The immediacy of television may be superior to the film that, like a book, may have become dated. A recording without a picture may stimulate creativity more than a film or slide, which relays a specific image to the mind. On another occasion, a picture is essential for understanding.

Technical devices help teachers become more professional. Teaching is the only profession that remains largely in the handwork era. The teacher's voice, printed materials, handwritten instructions, and a chalkboard are the usual tools of a teacher's trade. The arguments about teachers versus machines are ridiculous. The professional constantly seeks ways in which technical devices can help. The teacher determines what to do personally and what the technical tool can do either with or without help, and then instructs students in how to select and use the best technical aids to enhance their learning.

STUDENT USE

In some respects the most promising development in recent times concerning technical devices is their use in resource centers, workrooms, and libraries. A group of students gathered around a projector or a recorder, stopping the equipment at will in order to discuss an idea generated by the film or recording, presents a highly desirable image of curriculum in motion. Also desirable are the programmed instruction devices that make individual pacing possible. This technique represents a curriculum improvement over the uniform pace provided by the standard textbooks in which teacher assignments tend to keep the students all working together, unduly pushing some and holding back others.

Students learn to use technical devices by observation in large-group instruction and practice during independent study. The instruction assistants help them locate materials, teach them to operate the equipment, and assist them in translating ideas and reports into audio or visual forms.

Some schools now provide relatively elaborate dial-access systems that enable learners individually or in groups to call onto a screen and/or into a speaker a variety of films, video and audio tapes, and filmstrips that are stored in a materials center or library. A few schools have computer terminals for contacting distant sources of information. Telephone systems are used to listen to lectures and for asking questions of authorities located at distant places. All these technical devices add breadth and depth to the curriculum when integrated into the learning system.

Besides gaining information from technical devices, students also learn to express their own ideas through such devices — they are not limited to written or spoken reports. For example, a set of slides or a filmstrip about safety in the school (developed as a result of a survey of school accidents and how they might have been prevented) is a good independent study project. The product may be used later as part of a large-group presentation under the direction of a teacher. Advanced students can be trained to prepare programmed materials for beginners or for those having learning difficulties. Those preparing the materials will benefit as much as the pupils who will use them. At other times, students may prepare charts and graphs, some of which may be illuminated by overhead or slide projection, for a brief presentation to be followed by discussion in small groups.

THE SYSTEM

Technical devices used as an adjunct to otherwise conventional instruction rather than as an integral part of a totally changed system will produce disappointing results. The vast majority of experiments comparing educational television with conventional teaching reveal no statistically significant gains or losses in pupil learning as measured by standardized or typical teacher-made tests. The same findings often result in studies involving the use of language laboratories or programmed instruction devices. Where there are significant differences, usually in one-fourth to one-third of the studies, the majority of cases report favorable results for programs using the new devices, probably a result of the typical Hawthorne, or halo, effect that favors experimental groups.

The television and programmed learning proponents must recognize that their medium is merely one of numerous forms of large-group instruction, with all the potential and the limitations of such presentations. (See Chapter 21.) They must also realize that their medium cannot fulfill its true potential if the administration does not change aspects of the program that constitute effective roadblocks to success. Failure to understand the purposes of large-group instruction and to change teaching and learning methods in independent study and small-group discussion, scheduling, and content, makes the resultant research on television and other devices no more meaningful than the large number of class-size studies conducted in numerous countries for many years.

All aspects of the curriculum system must be related if the results of the new devices are to be favorable. Consider, for example, the use of technical devices in foreign language instruction. In large groups, technical devices or someone who has been to the country may provide students with cultural backgrounds of the country whose language they are learning. The teacher or someone from the community who speaks the language can illustrate basic grammatical forms and vocabulary information. Grammar and vocabulary may then be studied by individual students using programmed devices, slides, or filmstrips showing still pictures of the narrated motion pictures seen in the large groups. Work in the language laboratories with tape recorders may then improve pronunciation of the language and review vocabulary and grammar. Recorded lessons can also be made available for students to study at home with their own phonographs or tape recorders.

Small-group discussion provides the setting for practicing conversational ability in the foreign language. So do individual study groups of two to four pupils meeting around a table if at least one of the pupils is reasonably fluent in the language. All aspects of the system are related to each other through the instruction of teachers and by the sequence of the activities of students. Curriculum development requires that all persons involved plan how to use technical devices effectively.

MATERIALS PREPARATION

A study of catalogs reveals a tremendous quantity of commercially prepared audio-visual materials. Teachers must supplement those materials with a considerable number of visuals and recordings made locally, because a film or television program prepared for national use often needs to be complemented for maximum use in the local setting. The school must provide material and personnel to help teachers prepare these additional audio-visual aids.

The place where technical devices are prepared may be called an instructional materials center. Although a city or county system may provide a centralized center, each school needs its own center to complement the services of the centralized location. The teacher roughs out an idea; the personnel of the materials center translate the idea into an effective technical device to aid the teacher. Instruction assistants do the research needed to prepare a visual or recording, artists or technicians prepare the end product, and clerks store the materials and keep records.

THE SETTING

Technical devices lose their effectiveness when students cannot see and hear well. Yet, strange as it may seem, experience in visiting thousands of classrooms indicates that large numbers of teachers fail to appreciate the importance of the arrangements for seeing and hearing. Television sets are not adjusted properly; screens are placed incorrectly; sound address systems are inadequate; light control is not sufficient to insure good visibility; sound fidelity is poor; distractions bother students working on programmed material. These faults are easy to remedy and should receive immediate and continuing attention. Students can help. Teachers need to be sensitive to the needs.

Screens and television sets should be placed as near the ceiling as possible and tilted forward to minimize keystone effects and to provide better visibility for all students. That arrangement is especially important if the student seating is on a flat, level floor. Remember also to place screens in partially lighted rooms with the screen's back to the light source in order to gain more visibility. To gain better sound distribution and quality, scatter a number of speakers throughout the room instead of using one or two speakers in the front of the room. Provide chest microphones so that teachers may move around while speaking. Pay attention to the importance of light control, ventilation, acoustical control, and the other features of good facilities described in Chapter 27.

RELATIONSHIPS WITH OUT-OF-SCHOOL
LISTENING AND VIEWING

Unfortunately, most teachers and school programs neglect, even ignore, the impact of students' out-of-school listening and viewing. Students often spend more time with television, radio, and motion pictures at home or with other students than they spend in school buildings. Teachers often ignore this aspect of learning because they regard much of it as overly commercial and because some is irrelevant to school work. However, not all of it is that way. Some programs would be extremely useful if the school itself made plans for systematic use of these media.

Someone in each school department with commitment and allocated time should regularly analyze the program schedules for each upcoming week on television and radio and in local entertainment centers. That person, knowledgeable about current and long-range departmental studies, should prepare annotated listings, and with the help of appropriate colleagues, recommendations for students to follow. Both Public Broadcasting System and commercial programs should be included as well as private and commercial entertainments in the community. Such efforts will not only enrich the school curriculum but also in the long run have an ameliorative effect on what happens on the media outside school.

TOPICS FOR STUDY AND DISCUSSION

1. Plan an overhead projector visual to go with some presentation that you might make in the course you teach or plan to teach.
2. Outline plans for a locally made filmstrip on a topic such as the following: how to avoid accidental injury in the school or on the grounds; gaining work experience in this community; local historical sites; architecture in our town.
3. Assume an annual school budget of ten dollars per pupil for audio-visual aids. Show how you would spend the money and defend your choices.
4. Considering a given subject, what audio-visual aids would you list as having highest priority for improving pupil learning?
5. Since technical devices provide optional learning strategies in addition to reading and writing, plan an experiment where individual students learn by increased, or even total, use of viewing and listening programs.
6. Evolve some guidelines for incorporating the use of technical devices in a learning package.
7. Analyze the commercial and Public Broadcast System television programs for a current week. Which of these programs seem relevant for school use to enrich the curriculum in subjects you specify?

SELECTED REFERENCES

Burke, Richard C., ed. *Instructional Television.* Bloomington: Indiana University Press, 1971, pp. 57–85.
    Chapter 5, "The Television Teacher," describes techniques useful in large-group instruction.
Bushnell, Don D., and Allen, Dwight W., eds. *The Computer in American Education.* New York: John Wiley & Sons, 1967, pp. 59–107.
    Don Bushnell discusses simulation and gaming, information retrieval, and the production and evaluation of curriculum materials. Karl Zim reviews systems and current projects involving computer-assisted instruction.
Davis, Harold S., ed. *Instructional Media Center.* Bloomington: Indiana University Press, 1971.
    Fourteen writers describe various centers for elementary, junior high,

and senior high schools for pupil and teacher use, examining theory and successful operations, and giving instructions and further references.

Elles, Allan B. *The Use and Misuse of Computers in Education.* New York: McGraw-Hill Book Company, 1974.

Three procedures are emphasized: use computers for procedural matters where specific instructions are possible; constantly evaluate the outcomes; and do not rely too much on computer specialists.

Ely, Donald P., and Gerloach, Vernon S. *Teaching and Media: A Systematic Approach.* Englewood Cliffs, N. J.: Prentice-Hall, 1971.

This book relates classroom objectives to the selection and use of media.

Garner, W. Lee. *Programed Instruction.* New York: The Center for Applied Research in Education, 1966.

After giving the reasons for programming, the author describes various types of programs, shows their applications in education, and explains how to train programmers and how to make programs. The final chapters relate programmed instruction to computers and look to future developments.

Gordon, George N. *Educational Television.* New York: The Center for Applied Research in Education, 1965.

This volume gives historical perspective and examines the reasons for, present status of, and effectiveness of instructional television. It speculates about the future of open-circuit and closed-circuit installations.

Green, Allan C., ed. *Educational Facilities with New Media.* Washington, D. C.: National Education Association, Department of Educational Technology, 1966, pp. A-1–A-42.

Report A presents a comprehensive account of new media as they relate to educational innovations.

Kaimann, Richard A., and Marker, Robert W., eds. *Educational Data Processing: New Dimensions and Prospects.* Boston: Houghton Mifflin Company, 1967.

This book presents statements from numerous experts on systems theory and analysis, information systems, computerized guidance and instruction, simulation in teaching and administration, and other aspects of data processing. It shows how this new and rapidly changing field will revolutionize curriculum development.

McClosky, Mildred G., ed. *Teaching Strategies and Classroom Realities.* Englewood Cliffs, N. J.: Prentice-Hall, 1971.

Fourteen authors write about ways to use pictures, overhead projectors, recorders, music, advertisements, and student-produced films to liven up and improve teaching and learning.

McLuhan, Marshall, and Fiore, Quentin. *The Medium Is the Massage.* New York: Bantam Books, 1967.

This volume states that technology is reshaping every aspect of life, calling for a new kind of education that "must shift from instruction . . . to discovery . . . to the recognition of the language of forms."

24

The Nongraded, Continuous Progress School

Is there really anything new under the sun? One of the educational innovations of the past two decades is the idea that learning should not be organized on a basis of months or years or grades. The idea of measuring what a person knows in terms of how many years spent attending classes in the subject has suddenly become repugnant to many people, although most schools still are organized that way.

More than a century ago, many students in the United States did not attend school regularly. Someone learning to read, write, and compute could leave school to work (or for some other reason), then return and resume where he or she had left off. Administrators did not have to consider whether the student should be put into the third grade or the sixth because that classification was unknown. About a century ago, however, as schools become larger, a scheme for dividing pupils into different classes or rooms became necessary. A graded system was imported from Germany in the middle 1800s.

The system of grades, like the Carnegie unit and many other quantitative administrative procedures to simplify decision making, was imported or developed locally by state departments of education and regional accrediting agencies. Colleges needed standards for determining who should be admitted to college and for evaluating secondary school courses. Secondary school administrators needed easily administered methods for determining when pupils should enter their schools, how much progress they were making, and when they should be permitted to graduate.

Needless to say, quantitative standards tend to bring rigidity to school administration and to teaching, making it difficult to treat the differences among students effectively. Content must be compressed or expanded into standard-length courses that meet a given number of minutes per week for one semester, one year, or some other specified period. Curriculum revision relates directly to the grade structure, or the lack of it, in any middle, junior high, or senior high school .

The practice of ungrading schools, especially the primary grades, started to receive considerable attention in this country about a quarter of a century ago, when a number of studies revealed the ineffectiveness in many cases of making failing pupils repeat a grade. Other problems arose when brighter pupils were pushed ahead by "skipping" a grade.

The use of ungraded primary classes proved successful in reducing failure, because many slow children, allowed to stay with their classmates, were able to increase the tempo of their achievement during subsequent years and catch up with the others. The ungrading of the 1930s and 1940s, however, failed to consider adequately such other potential improvements as curriculum reorganization, newer teaching and learning methods, changes in the organization of instruction, and the various extraschool influences that create differences among school students.

EXISTING PLANS

A number of plans are used today to permit students to progress at different rates of speed. In some places, secondary schools classify students on the basis of ability or achievement, tempered by teacher judgment, and select special content to fit the needs of each group. That procedure contrasts with the conventional program that arbitrarily organizes courses called English 8 or English 10, French 1 or French 2, or Sophomore Physical Education — and then tries to fit students into them.

Other schools have adopted a track system, so that low-ability students do not have to compete unsuccessfully with higher-ability students, but may graduate with considerably less achievement in the lowest track. Different types of diplomas sometimes are given to students to show which track system they went through in high school. Such programs require basic changes in curriculum content, teaching methods, and evaluation. A disadvantage of this system is that students from less favored homes, or from some national or racial groups, tend to cluster in certain tracks. Also, teachers sometimes dislike working day after day with students in lower tracks.

Another issue relative to nongrading concerns horizontal or vertical enrichment of curriculum content. Some educators feel that students should be permitted to take advanced or additional courses so that they may graduate from high school in less time and go on to college. Those opposing that practice want all students to spend six years in the program between elementary and higher education. They believe higher-ability students can benefit simply by taking more courses and engaging in special projects in regular courses — projects not expected of less able students. A compromise approach is the Advanced Placement Program, where students remain in the secondary school while taking college-level courses with the expectation that they will be given credit for those courses when they enroll in college.

Other nongrading procedures are being followed in some schools. A small high school may cycle its required courses. Instead of offering world history, U.S. history, and problems of democracy every year, one of the courses is offered each year to all students. Everyone in a given course, regardless of age, works in a group appropriate for her or him. Correspondence courses supplement the curriculum when necessary for pupils who transfer into the school during the year and find that the course they need is not offered at the time they need it.

Other schools divide courses into segments designed for pupils of varied talents. Teachers observe individual progress in each segment to determine which subsequent materials are appropriate. The purpose is to place students in situations where they can succeed. Independent study time and the facilities for learning activities are increased. One school varies this pattern by organizing all courses into eight-week units. Each junior high school student chooses the unit and study activities desired for the next eight weeks. A teacher-adviser approves the choice.

Although each of the foregoing proposals has some merit and is better than the conventional graded program, none of them represents the ultimate goal. A truly nongraded school is one that has gone far beyond eliminating annual promotions, grouping students subject by subject on the basis of achievement, or making local curriculum revisions that contribute to a nongraded approach. Each of the foregoing may be the first step toward a nongraded program. (Other first steps will be described in Chapter 30.)

For maximum curriculum improvement, the nongraded school must use team teaching, flexible scheduling, technical devices, and the teaching-learning methods described in earlier chapters that dealt with independent study, large-group instruction, and small-group discussion. It must also adapt to the socioeconomic, political, cultural, and other characteristics of the areas where its students live. Students in a large city are different from those in the rural Midwest, and students in a community overwhelmed by poverty require a different curriculum than those in an affluent area. The nongraded school negates student frustration because it lessens the pressures for conformity. Students are comfortable with a peer group with whom success is a distinct possibility. The nongraded school enhances the possibility of individualized learning.

DETERMINING CONTENT

As indicated in Chapter 2, curriculum developers need to determine what content is *essential* for all educable persons. That content consists of the skills, knowledge, concepts, and attitudes in every area of human knowledge that are regarded as necessary for all persons in any particular society.

Educators must also determine what additional material is *desirable* and what is *enriching* — desirable for the average students and enriching for the talented, those who are likely to be the leaders in the schools of today and the society of tomorrow.

National experts may determine the content that is essential, desirable, and enriching for all persons regardless of where the school is located. The content is the *basic education* of all persons and may become, in fact, a national curriculum. State and regional agencies may supplement that curriculum to provide for particular local needs and interests. The faculty of the local school then will add to the state and regional curriculum content.

A second curriculum task is to arrange the required content logically and sequentially in relation to what is known about child growth and development. The schools group and regroup pupils on the basis of individual progress through this material. Each child should cover the entire content, starting when school is first entered and finishing near the end of the compulsory education age. Much of the content can be programmed through texts and machines. Someday students will progress through it individually by means of computer-assisted instruction.

The third curriculum task requires the development of a program of *depth education* at all levels and for all subject areas. Whether a student completes the elementary school (including kindergarten) and secondary school in fewer than thirteen years is a matter for professional decision. Making that decision wisely, however, assumes the availability of a broad program of depth education that aims to stimulate creativity on the part of all students, not merely the most able and the most creative. When a school administration considers it desirable for all students to remain in secondary school the same number of years, teachers and counselors can provide enrichment programs for the students who might otherwise complete the average program of depth education too early. Incidentally, someday that policy will change!

The charts on pages 390–393 illustrate how curriculum content for the nongraded school might be developed in the areas of social science and home economics. The charts are illustrative rather than definitive. The most able scholars in the subject disciplines working with the most able scholars in child growth and in the behavioral sciences must develop the actual content, updating and revising it constantly on the basis of experience and research.

Some readers may object to the emphasis here on subject disciplines in contrast to what has been variously called core, common learnings, life adjustment, or general education, wherein subject matter is organized around general themes or purposes. However, the subject discipline approach helps students understand the various subjects as such, in order to comprehend books and lectures better and to make advanced educational or vocational decisions. Teaching teams can cut across subject lines by pointing out areas where the subjects relate closely. Ultimately, the integration of subject content occurs in the minds of individuals as they discover relationships and develop generalizations.

ARRANGING CONTENT FOR CONTINUOUS PROGRESS

The curriculum goal here is to arrange content so that each student can proceed at an individual pace with appropriate learning strategies, a variety of options open, and emphasis on self-appraisal. The materials also need to provide for individual diagnosis and direction. Although teachers and assistants are available to help, the emphasis is on increasing responsibilities for learners.

Various arrangements can foster the foregoing goals. The self-contained classroom places responsibility for monitoring on one teacher. The future doubtless will see more of this monitoring done by computer-assisted instruction. In the meantime, teachers and other professionals are producing a variety of aids, which bear such names as learning packages, UNIPAKS, Individually Prescribed Instruction (IPI), and guidesheets and worksheets.

The essential developmental steps in all these materials include:

1. stating the concepts, skills, appreciations, and other goals that the student is to achieve
2. listing the specific subconcept(s) and other aims in this particular segment
3. defining in behavioral terms specifically what is to occur and how the learner will know that the goals have been achieved
4. providing a pretest so the learner knows what already has been achieved and what remains to be accomplished
5. indicating a variety of learning strategies that may be followed: read what, do what, listen to what, view what, take a field trip where, and the like
6. including self-tests to enable the learner to know when the required outcomes have been accomplished
7. telling the learner whom to see when he or she has difficulties
8. indicating the teacher (or instructional assistant) who will administer evaluation and check results
9. providing three alternatives when the learner finishes the required, prescribed program:
   a. go on to the next required segment
   b. go into greater depth: more of the same or similar
   c. create; "do your own thing"

The three options at the close of each segment are extremely important. Without those three alternatives, individualized learning does not occur. The departmental curriculum goal is to interest each pupil in the second or third choices. However, the department competes with all others in this regard. The student decides which course to follow with the help of teachers in all the departments and his or her personal teacher-adviser (see Chapters 25 and 26).

CONTINUOUS PROGRESS AND THE YEAR-ROUND SCHOOL

A current interest is to utilize educational facilities more effectively by extending their use longer hours each day and for more days in the year, perhaps ultimately for every day including Saturdays and Sundays, all the months. Unless the continuous progress concept is incorporated in these plans, some unfortunate side effects may occur. For

PROPOSED SOCIAL SCIENCE CURRICULUM MODEL (Recommended Pattern for All School Subject Areas)

Present Grade Equivalent	Age	Subject Emphases	Basic Education for All — Topics	Depth Education for Some
Primary				
K	5	All: Selected terms and concepts from all seven social science subject areas	Seasons, holidays, places and names in the news, value and use of money, families and neighborhood	Very little at this point. Students work briefly on special interest topics within their "home base" room or in a resource area
1	6		People in selected lands (e.g., Japan, India, Nigeria, Australia, France, Brazil, and Canada) — how they live, their governments, their geography — in relation to ours	
2	7		Effects of geography (environmental factors) on producers and consumers, transportation and communication, cultural patterns, social relations	
3	8	History Geography	Local, state, and regional history and geography	
Middle				
4	9	History	United States history and geography	From time to time, to explore personal talents and interests and to motivate others, some students make limited studies of selected aspects of these sub-
5	10	Geography History Anthropology	Human development from prehistoric to modern times showing intercultural influences, the flow of history, and general time relationships	
6	11	History Political Science	Struggle for power and search for peace (contemporary scene with a perspective from experiences of the past)	
7	12	Economics Sociology	Economic and social relations (e.g., food, clothing, shelter, exchange, urban and rural	

jects — usually in the social science laboratory

		Subject	Content	Level of Essential Knowledge	Level of Desirable Knowledge	Level of Enriching Knowledge
				Level 1	Level 2	Level 3
8	13	History Political Science History	life, social groups) — contemporary and in the past Government institutions and services (local, state, national, international) — rights, responsibilities, and security for individuals and groups — contemporary and in the past			
9	14	History Philosophy Psychology	Beauty in the arts, world religions, value patterns, personal and group adjustments (social psychology) — contemporary and in the past			
10	15		United States civilization up to 1900 — review and reinforcement of historical, geographic, socioeconomic, political, anthropological, and scientific forces that have shaped this country, with emphasis on the interplay of forces	Individual or 2–3 students spend 25–50 hours per year on some topic or project	Individual or group works several hours per week for several months	Individual or group studies 10–25 hours per week
11	16	All	United States civilization to the present			
12	17		Problem solving and action — weekly presentations, discussions, and actions on topics of current significance			
Secondary						
Adult Education						

Note: During K–3 (Primary period), "home base" teachers do most of the teaching, with social science teachers assisting and making some presentations in a team-teaching relationship. Programs for grade 4 and above are taught by social science teachers in teaching teams, using large-group instruction for presentations, films, television, and the like; small-group discussion for personal interaction, problem solving, and communication skills; and independent study in social science laboratories. Schools are nongraded.

PROPOSED HOME ECONOMICS CURRICULUM MODEL (For Discussion Only)

	Present Grade Equivalent	Age	Basic Education for All	Depth Education for Some
Primary	K	5	Planned study, informal in treatment, of such topics as family and human relations, care of clothing, respect for others, consequences of acts, problem solving, group planning, personal responsibility for beauty in home and school	Very little at this point
	1	6		
	2	7		
	3	8		
Middle	4	9	Personal and family health	From time to time, some students make special, but limited, studies of selected phases of these subjects to explore their personal talents and interests and to motivate other students
	5	10	Food habits and practices Care and selection of clothing Care of home and surroundings	
	6	11	Safety and sanitation, table manners, duties of family members	
	7	12	Personal and family finances The arts in the home, clothing, etc.	

	Level 1	Level 2	Level 3
	Student spends 25–50 hours on some topic, e.g., survey of housing, or food habits in India	Group works for a semester on some topic, e.g., planning and furnishing a new home, or health and home nursing	Rigorous course, e.g., foods, clothing, child study, principles of design, or consumer economics
	Level of Essential Knowledge	*Level of Desirable Knowledge*	*Level of Enriching Knowledge*

Secondary

8	13	Food and nutrition
9	14	Clothing and textiles
10	15	Home management
11	16	Child study and family relations
12	17	Review, reinforcement, and updating: special presentations, discussions, and independent study

Adult Education

Note: During K–3 (Primary period), "home base" teachers do most of the teaching, with home economics teachers assisting and making some presentations in a team-teaching relationship. Programs for grade 4 and above are taught by home economics teachers in teaching teams.

example, the school schedule might schedule different holidays for different children in the same family under some of the programs. One proposal is to have some students attend school for 45 days and then take a required 15-day vacation. This program simply divides the conventional school year into four 45-day segments instead of the conventional two 90-day semesters or one 180-day year with the usual three-month summer holiday. The curriculum task in such a program is ignored.

The individualized curriculum with self-directing, self-pacing, self-motivating (with a variety of learning strategies and options), and self-evaluating materials provides a more satisfactory solution to better utilization of educational facilities and human resources. The necessary school regulation is that a student may drop in and out of school at times that are convenient for the entire family and that are good for each student personally. The only requirement is that each must attend school a minimum of 180 days per year. If a student is interested and if the family and school counselors approve, he or she may attend more than 180 days each year and complete the secondary school in fewer calendar years. Policies also may allow a student to stay in the home community longer and take more subjects than the school requires for graduation. In this case, the school may decide to charge a special tuition for such an expanded program.

The continuous progress concept permits more extensive work experience and/or travel during the secondary school years than is possible in the conventional school, and at times when the student is especially interested or needs the experience, as family and school counselors approve. The next chapter presents more alternatives in flexible scheduling.

TOPICS FOR STUDY AND DISCUSSION

1. Take a unit or segment of a course you now teach or plan to teach. List the facts, concepts, skills, and other content that are essential, desirable, and enriching for pupils, as defined in this chapter.
2. Consider the subject area that interests you most. Make a chart comparable to the one on pages 390–393.
3. After consulting the readings for this chapter, prepare to defend the concept of nongrading by listing all the potential advantages. Or, take the opposite point of view.
4. Analyze in greater detail than is provided in this chapter the other aspects of content, teaching methods, and school structure that need to change along with the development of a nongraded program.
5. What are the implications of the continuous progress concept for the year-round school, early graduation from high school, or work-study programs?

SELECTED REFERENCES

Beggs, David W. III, and Buffie, Edward G., eds. *Nongraded Schools in Action*. Bloomington: Indiana University Press, 1967.
Twenty-five authors write about elementary and secondary programs. Part I includes the historical perspectives, basic organizational concepts, procedures for starting, methods of evaluation, and a look ahead. Part II describes programs in specific schools; Chapters 17, 18, and 19 concern high schools. A selected, annotated bibliography suggests further readings.

Brown, Bartley Frank. *The Appropriate Placement School: A Sophisticated Nongraded Curriculum*. West Nyack, N. Y.: Parker Publishing Co., 1965.
Chapters 6 and 7, respectively, describe junior and senior high school multiphased programs. Two other chapters present a curriculum for dropouts and disadvantaged youths.

————. *The Nongraded High School*. Englewood Cliffs, N. J.: Prentice-Hall, 1963.
This author gives reasons for nongrading. He describes the flexibility it brings, and the concept-centered curriculum, the changes in evaluation, and the public relations program it requires. He tells the story of Melbourne, Florida, High School, where he was principal.

Curtis, Thomas E., and Bidwell, Wilma W. *Curriculum and Instruction for Emerging Adolescents*. Reading, Mass.: Addison-Wesley Publishing Co., 1977.
Chapter 14, "Organization for Learning," describes the nongraded organization in junior high and middle schools.

Howard, Alvin W., and Stoumbis, George C. *The Junior High and Middle School: Issues and Practices*. Scranton, Penna.: Intext Educational Publishers, 1970.
Chapter 17, "Flexible Scheduling, Team Teaching, and Nongraded Schools," describes the application of these concepts to early secondary education, with pros and cons.

Jenkins, John M. *Curriculum Development in Nongraded Schools*. Bloomington: Indiana University Press, 1972, pp. 135–167.
An author with considerable leadership experience in nongraded schools explains an organizational pattern involving "phasing," proposes a model, and describes in some detail the preparation, use, and evaluation of learning packages.

Miller, Richard I., ed. *The Nongraded School*. New York: Harper & Row, 1967, pp. 72–154.
C. Robert Blackmon and Richard I. Miller summarize the reasons for the nongraded school movement. Most of the material in these two chapters relates to intermediate and secondary schools.

Worner, Roger. *Designing Curriculum for Educational Accountability: From Continuous Progress Education Through PPBS*. New York: Random House, New York: Random House, 1973.
This book emphasizes the continuous progress concept as a way to relate input to output in learning. The school needs to provide better identification and sequencing of concepts and skills that students need to learn so each one may achieve maximum achievement. Teachers play key roles in the process in each school.

25

Individualized Scheduling, Accountability, and Teacher Advisers

The schedule of classes or group meetings reflects the current educational philosophy, or possibly merely the tradition, of the school. The time arrangements specified in the schedule enhance or inhibit curriculum improvement. The schedule may encourage depth study or it may keep students from caring deeply about any subject. It may encourage a broad, general education including the fine and practical arts or it may keep those subjects away from most students in the upper secondary school years. It may give teachers variety and free them for curriculum planning and development, or it may keep them in a daily routine that saps their energies. Attention to the schedule has high priority in curriculum improvement.

New mechanical aids available to the schedule maker are stimulating a desirable interest in flexible scheduling. However, we must disassociate speed from the concept of flexible scheduling. Electronic data-processing equipment may be used to do faster what should not be done at all; namely, facilitate and freeze a conventional school schedule. Doubtless, electronic aids can help students and teachers use their time better, but concentration on machines may well delay achieving the kind of flexibility that is needed. Since everyone has the same amount of time, the question is how to use it to best advantage.

The goal of the schedule is to give teachers and students as much freedom as is reasonable in the use of time, space, and numbers of persons, as well as content for instruction. The following are worthwhile objectives:

1.   The class schedule may be changed daily, or at least frequently, on the basis of teacher requests.
2.   Each studen:, under competent direction and with appropriate controls, may make choices regarding his or her part in the established schedule.
3.   Conflicts are reduced to a minimum.
4.   Teacher and student loads permit both maximum professionalization of teaching and maximum individualization of learning opportunities.
5.   The school know what its students and teachers are doing and where they are.
6.   The whole scheme is financially feasible and logistically operational.

The best way to achieve the foregoing goals is to implement the role of the teacher adviser. The progress of each student in the school is monitored by personal contacts and systematic reports. Not to be confused with what homeroom teachers or professional counselors have done in the past, this approach as described later in this chapter is an essential ingredient in a humane, individualized, and well-controlled school. When the program of monitoring is well done, the school curriculum becomes the servant of the students and staff rather than the master of them all. Likewise, time, that unstretchable commodity, is better utilized.

STEPS TOWARD FLEXIBLE SCHEDULING

One of the basic reasons for changing schedules is to make possible a number of different institutional arrangements for education. For example, principals and teachers, understandably dissatisfied with the rigidity of today's schedules, may conclude that some courses need more time than others or that some classes need to meet less often, but for longer periods of time on certain days. Such considerations may lead to the "modular concept" of flexible scheduling. Instead of the conventional forty-five- or fifty-five-minute periods, the schools adopt a fifteen-, twenty-, or thirty-minute module, or period length, so that instead of six periods per day, the school schedule includes twelve, sixteen, or twenty-four periods in a day. The school then schedules various subjects for a different number of modules, sometimes the same number each day in the week. A degree of flexibility results, but once the change is made, the new schedule can become almost as rigid as the one it replaced. Some examples of modular and other flexible schedules are shown on the following pages.

Some schools vary their schedule by rotating periods, sometimes of different lengths, or even by rotating special schedules on different days. This system is often chosen when a school that has been following conventional curricular organization patterns wishes to make it possible for a student to take six or seven subjects instead of the conventional five or six. The subjects are scheduled to meet four times a week instead of five; they are scheduled on a floating basis to fill out the five-day week, and some periods are made longer than others. Although this change is sometimes called flexible scheduling, the new

15-MINUTE MODULES — SAME SCHEDULE EVERY DAY

Time	Subject
8:00 8:15 8:30 8:45	Mathematics
9:00	Speech Correction
9:15 9:30 9:45 10:00 10:15	Science
10:30 10:45	Music
11:00 11:15 11:30	Spanish
11:45	Music Practice
12:00 etc.	Lunch

50-MINUTE MODULES — TWO-HOUR CLASSES, MONDAY THROUGH THURSDAY; ONE-HOUR CLASSES, FRIDAY

Time	Monday	Tuesday	Wed.–Thurs.	Friday
8:00 9:00	Biology	Geometry	Same as Mon.–Tues.	Biology English
10:00 11:00	English	French	Same as Mon.–Tues.	French Geometry
12:00		Lunch and Activities		
1:00 2:00	Physical Ed.	Study or Elective	Same as Mon.–Tues.	Phys. Ed. Stu./Ele.

program also can become quite rigid and actually contributes relatively little to the improved use of time by students and teachers.

Still another arrangement is represented by a variety of team-teaching approaches. According to one form, six teachers are responsible for 180 students for a 2-hour block of time each day. Teachers and students may divide their time among large-group instruction, small-group discussion, and independent study. All the students may watch a film for 18 minutes, then separate into groups so that 90 students attend a supplementary presentation by one of the teachers. Four groups of 15 each discuss with 4 other teachers, and the remaining 30 students go to a library or workroom for independent study under the supervision of the sixth teacher. The new arrangements may last for thirty-six minutes, or any other specified time, so long as the total 2-hour block is maintained. Then the students are rearranged so that all have small-group work and independent study. Obviously, this approach represents a more flexible use of time, space, and student groupings than is possible in a conventional organized school. But again, flexibility is limited, this time by the 2-hour block.

A few schools organize instruction almost completely on the team-teaching basis, with large-group, small-group, and independent study arrangements. Such schools achieve still more flexibility in scheduling by using a modular approach. Large classes of 100 or more pupils in a given subject may be scheduled for two 20-minute modules (40 minutes) twice a week. Seminar-size groups of 15 or fewer students in the same subject area are scheduled for two modules, twice a week, at different times in the day from the large group and possibly on different days in the week. Independent study in each subject is scheduled for each student, depending on interests and talents, for 3, 4, or more consecutive modules on different days in the week.

ROTATION OF CLASSES—STANDARD PERIODS

Time	Monday	Tuesday	Wednes-day	Thursday	Friday
8:00	1	1	1	1	2
9:00	2	2	2	3	3
10:00	3	3	4	4	4
11:00	4	5	5	5	5
12:00			LUNCH		
12:30	6	6	6	6	7
1:30	7	7	7	Special	Special

Note: Numbers indicate different subjects.

Though schools using that approach usually change the independent study of their students at will, they often hold quite systematically to the scheduled time for large-group instruction and small-group discussion. The conventional idea (not based on research) that an English class must meet 5 days per week, 50 minutes per day, at the same hour of the day, with one teacher in charge, may merely be replaced by the equally unsubstantiated concept that English must meet twice per week, 40 minutes per time, in classes of 120, with the best teaching available and once a week, for 40 minutes, in classes of 15, with a

ROTATION OF CLASSES — PERIODS VARY IN LENGTH

Time	Monday	Tuesday	Wednes-day	Thursday	Friday
8:55–10:26	1	2	4	5	6
10:30–11:26	2	4	5	6	1
11:30–12:26	3	3	3	3	3
12:26–1:04			LUNCH		
1:04–2:30	4	5	6	1	2
2.34–3:30	5	6	1	2	4

Note: Numbers indicate different subjects.

TEAM TEACHING — BLOCK OF TIME	
Time	*Monday through Friday*
8:00 9:00	3 U. S. History & 3 English teachers schedule 180 junior students as they deem desirable
10:00	Planning Period for Team
11:00	Conventional Classes
12:00	Lunch
12:30 1:30	Same as first period but with different students, e.g., sophomores
2:30	Planning Period for Team

teacher in charge of each class. The new schedule says, in effect, that English requires 120 minutes of group instruction per week, plus whatever time (80 minutes or more) the staff determines is necessary for independent study by pupils in English resource centers or the library. The staff becomes so enamored with these arrangements that the

TEAM TEACHING — MODULAR APPROACH

Time	*Monday*	*Tuesday*	*Wednesday*
8:20 8:40	History LG	English LG	History LG
9:00 9:20	French Sem	French LG	French Lab
9:40 10:00	History Sem	Homemaking LG	English Sem
10:20 10:40 11:00 11:20	PE	Science Sem ——— Homemaking Lab	PE
11:40 12:00	Math LG		Math LG
12:20		LUNCH	
Etc.	Humanities RC	Typing LG	Science RC

LG — Large-Group Instruction; Sem — Small-Group Discussion; Lab — Laboratory; RC — Resource Center–Independent Study "flexible schedule" becomes rigidly established. This is especially possible if the schedule is made with expensive data-processing equipment. More research is needed to determine better the time requirements of different teaching and learning activities.

EXAMPLES OF SUCCESSFUL PROGRAMS

Several schools have initiated their own programs that successfully provide for flexible daily schedule changes by teachers and students. Individual members of teaching teams determine three days in advance which pupils they need to teach, in what size groups, for what length of time, in what places, and with what technological aids. Then they prepare job specification forms containing this information and turn them in to their team leaders.

The team leaders and a clerk assemble to make a master schedule that includes what students "must" follow for the day. The master schedule is then duplicated and made available to the students and their advisers. In a daily twenty-minute meeting, with the advice and consent of the individual's adviser, each student plans a schedule, filling in personal choices for the considerable amount of time open to him or her. The student may choose to spend time in independent study in the art room, science laboratory, or library. The adviser either approves or rejects this decision. The student then makes out a personal copy, one for the office, one for the adviser, and one for parents. The schedule is developed mainly by hand. Doubtless, mechanical aids could simplify the process by helping to avoid conflicts and other problems that arise and by saving time for both students and teachers. It should be noted, however, that the concepts of schedule making come first and the machines that facilitate the process come second.

Another school constructed a new building without including a program clock or bell system. Instead, teachers meet daily in grade-level teams to change the schedule at will. This program and others like it in some ways represent an advancement over the block-of-time schedule described on page 401. The larger the number of teachers, the larger the number of students, and the greater the amount of time they are brought together, the more flexible teachers and students can be in using the time.

The diagram on page 403 illustrates such a schedule, showing how various groups might be assigned during a given week. All 360 students involved are assembled in one place on Tuesday for a thirty-five-minute mathematics test. Science teachers have scheduled three-hour field trips on Monday, Wednesday, Thursday, and Friday for 90 students each day. Orchestra rehearsal for 90 students occupies eighty

PARTIAL SCHEDULE FOR ONE WEEK

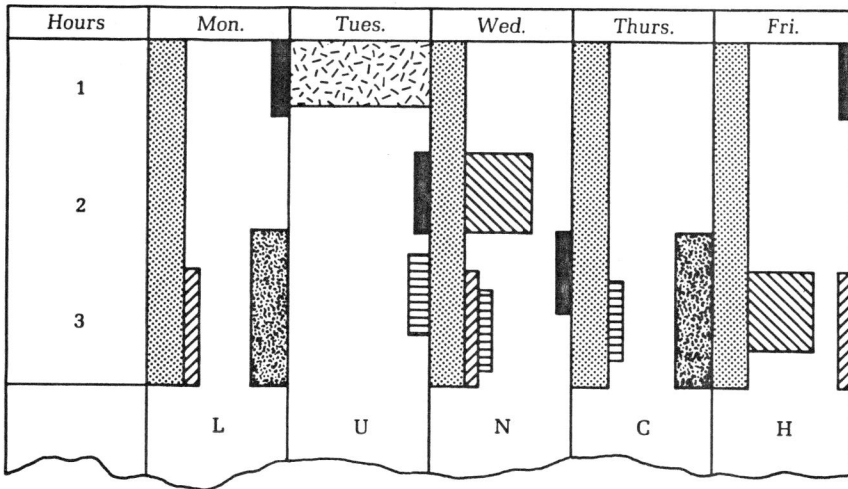

Hours	Mon.	Tues.	Wed.	Thurs.	Fri.
1					
2					
3	L	U	N	C	H

Code

History (180 students—40 minutes)

Science field trip (90 students—3 hours)

Remedial reading (20 students—1 hour)

Orchestra (90 students—80 minutes)

Vocal ensemble (24 students—40 minutes)

Mathematics test (360 students—35 minutes)

English (15 students—40 minutes)

The schedule also includes many groups not shown, and students spend much time in independent study in all subject areas.

minutes Monday and Thursday. A 24-student vocal ensemble practices for forty minutes on three days. The 360 students are divided in half for large-group presentations in history on Wednesday and Friday. Small-group discussion sessions, remedial reading groups, independent study, and other groups are similarly scheduled.

Still another school has devised a "priority period" to give teachers and pupils control over time. They have reduced the number of class periods per week from five to four to provide free periods for students and teachers. Each group uses these periods for what they regard as high-priority activities. A teacher may take a group of students for remedial work. A student may spend time in the music room, shop, or science laboratory. Data-processing cards avoid conflicts and provide class lists to check attendance during the priority periods. A next step might reduce class meetings to three times per week — one large group and two small groups or two large groups and one small group.

Will this school and others following similar or even more imaginative practices fall back into a rigid schedule? Such a development is possible but certainly less probable than in the case of the approaches described earlier in this chapter. Further use of automated instruction devices (teaching textbooks and machines) and the development of computer-assisted instructional systems will encourage further individualization of instruction and consequently more individual scheduling.

Flexible scheduling ultimately depends on the reorganization of curriculum content into a nongraded sequence, an increase of time for independent study, and a decrease of group activities, both large and small. The flexible schedule that we envision provides one large-group and one small-group motivational presentation for a reaction discussion for each pupil once per week in each of the eight general areas of knowledge — nine in parochial schools.[1] All other time in the school week is for study and work experiences. These three activities were described in Chapters 20, 21, and 22. Each school will make its own decision about the length and frequency of the large and small groups that we recommend. Our experience is that about thirty minutes per week in each activity in all the areas is preferred; however, much more needs to be known about the potential in such activities. The balance of the school week is for independent study under supervision.

The schedule presented on page 405 represents what we call *individualized scheduling*.

These developments represent a level of sophistication not yet achieved in most schools. In the meantime, scheduling continues to be a knotty problem — even with computers to help. The stake that teachers have in the flexible schedule may be the force that pushes the balance in favor of student choices in the use of time. Both groups have much to gain.

HUMANISM AND ACCOUNTABILITY

Individualized scheduling aims to make a school more humane, more individualized for students and teachers, and to facilitate accountability of both groups. The goal is to provide students with a

[1] English, fine arts, health-fitness-recreation (physical education), mathematics, other cultures (foreign languages), practical arts (including vocational), religion, science, social studies.

MONDAY	TUESDAY	WEDNESDAY	THURSDAY	FRIDAY
A	DAILY MEETING WITH TEACHER-ADVISER			
1 *				
2 **ENGLISH	PRACTICAL ARTS	SOCIAL SCIENCE	FINE ARTS	SCIENCE
3 ***English	Practical Arts	Social Science	Fine Arts	Science
4		MATHEMATICS		
5		Mathematics		
6 L	U	N	C	H
7				
8				
9				
10				HEALTH, FITNESS, RECREATION
11				Health, Fitness, Recreation
12				
13	OTHER CULTURES			
14	Other Cultures			

   * Independent study—supervised study/work
  ** Large-group instruction—motivational experience sessions
*** Small-group discussion—reaction groups

curriculum environment that encourages self-exploration, decision making, and learning in an environment best suited for each one of them. Each student's teacher adviser helps accomplish that goal by varying the time, locale, and learning strategies available. A school with the humane emphasis keeps the students in touch with all curriculum areas by means of motivational presentations and reaction discussions, as described in Chapters 21 and 22. Alternatives for study and in the use of time were outlined in Chapters 20, 22, and 24. The individualized schedule as described earlier in this chapter facilitates the process.

Accountability involves much more than how a school spends money and how those funds produce gains or losses on standardized tests.

Accountability also involves questions about how and where students spend time and what the alternatives in curriculum content and settings do to each one of them in the school. Accountability also involves different concepts of evaluation, as we shall see in Chapters 32 and 33.

The conventional school realizes accountability by placing each student in a class of about thirty, five or six periods per day, and assumes accountability by the classroom teacher as long as each student attends the class with some degree of regularity and conforms sufficiently to the curriculum provided there both in content and teaching-learning methods.

KEY ROLES OF TEACHER ADVISERS

Individualized scheduling transfers basic accountability for each student to a teacher adviser, although it holds the different departments responsible for a curriculum that provides options and for the monitoring of progress, or lack of it, while the student is studying and working in the various resource centers inside and outside the school. The teacher adviser, unlike the classroom teachers in a conventional school, through the process of individualized scheduling and the reports received from all the supervisors of study and work centers, now sees the student as a total human being, *educationally speaking.* This central responsibility for each one, vis-à-vis the divided responsibility among a number of classroom teachers or with a professional counselor who makes out programs for 300 or more students (too many for individual monitoring), is the concept we urge.

The teacher adviser exercises this curricular responsibility in the following manner. When a student first comes to the school, he or she is assigned to a teacher adviser. The teacher adviser works with that student as long as the student remains in the school unless a deliberate change is made. The adviser schedules the independent study time on the same day(s) that the office schedules the student's large and small groups in order to produce a reasonably balanced use of the school's facilities. The teacher adviser's part-time secretary keeps tallies and informs the office.

When a student wants to change the schedule, the availability of space must be determined. The procedure is to obtain from the supervisor of the area either a YES or NO form with the hours and place noted and properly signed. If a NO form is given, that fact is noted by the teacher adviser and the blank is sent to the building administrator in the school office so action may be taken to provide more space when a number of such NO forms are received. Of course, if the student has a YES form and the teacher adviser approves, the teacher adviser's secretary changes the schedule.

The method that the teacher adviser uses is the process of diagnosis–prescription–implementation–evaluation in a continuing sequence. The goal, of course, is to help each student discover personal interests and talents in a systematic way that holds promise for present and future hobbies, interests, and careers. Evaluative data sent to the teacher adviser by other teachers in the school or the community who are in contact with the adviser's students are diagnosed cooperatively by the teacher adviser and the student for whom the data are provided. The two cooperate in developing some alternative prescriptions, one of which is selected for implementation. Parents and guardians are involved with the process as needed. The final decision is then implemented as described in the preceding paragraph. After the implementation, more evaluative data are collected in a continuing effort to help the individual student capitalize on personal talents and interests.

References at the end of this chapter provide more information about the selection of teacher advisers, their relationships with the school's professional counselors, and other related considerations. Certainly the creation of this new position — not to be confused with conventional homeroom programs — is a key element in the school's efforts to improve accountability and humaneness.

Attendance is checked at irregular times in the various areas of the school and elsewhere where students are scheduled to be. Instruction assistants in the study and work areas periodically report progress or lack of it to the teacher advisers, who then discuss with advisees the possible need for further schedule changes affecting time and locations.

We cite the foregoing procedures to show the importance of developing accountability while permitting individualized scheduling. Too much permissiveness gets in the way of accountability just as too much structure gets in the way of humaneness; both extremes show that the school really does not care about the individuals in it.

TOPICS FOR STUDY AND DISCUSSION

1. Hold a brainstorming discussion on the ideal secondary school schedule. What do you and your colleagues recommend in order to return the control over time to teachers and pupils?

2. Prepare a statement defending or objecting to a current regulation of your state education department or regional accrediting agency that specifies a given number of minutes per week for a selected course or subject.

3. As a teacher, what would you do if you had more time free from scheduled contacts with groups of students?

4. Is the individualized scheduling program described at the end of this chapter the ultimate goal in a humanized school? Why or why not?

5. List ways in which a teacher adviser functions differently than a typical homeroom teacher.

SELECTED REFERENCES

Bush, Robert N., and Allen, Dwight W. *A New Design for High School Education Assuming a Flexible Schedule.* New York: McGraw-Hill Book Company, 1964.
> This book describes factors to consider in developing a flexible schedule.

Howard, Alvin W., and Stoumbis, George C. *The Junior High and Middle School: Issues and Practices.* Scranton, Penna.: Intext Educational Publishers, 1970, pp. 381–412.
> Chapter 17, "Flexible Scheduling, Team Teaching, and Nongraded Schools," describes the application of these concepts to early secondary education, with pros and cons.

Manlove, Donald C., and Beggs, David W. III. *Flexible Scheduling Using the IndiFlexS Model.* Bloomington: Indiana University Press, 1965.
> This volume relates quality education to flexible scheduling. It shows how staff and students are involved and explains how to make best use of facilities and equipment. It proposes a specific program for putting the data together and developing the schedule.

Murphy, Judith, and Sutter, Robert. *School Scheduling by Computer: The Story of GASP.* New York: Educational Facilities Laboratories, 1964.
> This pamphlet describes one of the major projects using MIT consultants and computers and tells how it operated in several schools.

Ohlsen, Merle M. *Guidance Services in the Modern School,* 2d ed. New York: Harcourt Brace Jovanovich, 1974.
> In addition to descriptions of philosophy, programs, and methods, this book provides an extensive bibliography for persons wishing even more information. Practical suggestions for school programs are given. See particularly pages 304–384.

Sciara, Frank J., and Jantz, Richard K., eds. *Accountability in American Education.* Boston: Allyn and Bacon, 1972, pp. 8–41.
> This portion of the book emphasizes the significance of program changes for improved accountability.

Swenson, Gardner, and Keys, Donald. *Providing for Flexibility in Scheduling and Instruction.* Englewood Cliffs, N. J.: Prentice-Hall, 1966.
> The mechanics for making different schedules each day instead of once a semester or year are discussed. Teachers and students have considerable control over their own time in a program involving large and small groups and independent study.

Trump, J. Lloyd. *A School for Everyone.* Reston, Va.: National Association of Secondary School Principals, 1977, pp. 31–46.
> Chapter 3, "Helping Each Student," provides detailed information on providing teacher advisers and counselors, as well as their functions, in various-sized schools.

26

Team Teaching and Improved Staff Utilization

Local, area, and national teacher organizations have brought significant gains to teachers in many ways in the areas of higher salaries and improved working conditions. Teacher salaries in this country for generations have constituted a national disgrace because they were so low in comparison with other professional groups. Some of the welfare provisions in the negotiated agreements also were long overdue. However, two areas frequently covered in working agreements have practically nothing to do with improving the quality of teaching and learning outcomes for students. One of these is class size and the other concerns the amount of time teachers spend on the premises without considering how that time is spent.

Helping teachers to find more time for curriculum improvement and to utilize that time more effectively must be a major concern of school administrators as well as the teachers themselves. What teachers do, the organizational setting in which they function, and the way each one best utilizes personal skills are crucial matters not only in the improvement of curriculum and methods of teaching and learning but also in the satisfactions that teachers derive from the situation.

PROFESSIONAL TEACHERS

The further professionalization of teaching concerns not only the professional concepts held by teachers themselves, but also the understanding that others hold of teaching as a profession. The professional concept requires that teachers have enough time and the proper facilities for such activities as preparing for their professional tasks, keeping up-to-date, conferring frequently with colleagues, conducting research and innovations, improving the curriculum, and developing better evaluation of what they do and what their pupils accomplish. Specifying what professional teachers need to do themselves and what may be done by assistants and technical devices constitutes another ingredient of professional development. Certainly, each professional person needs the opportunity to do what he or she is most interested in and able to do. Also, the professional should have the opportunity to improve income on the basis of what is done rather than be inhibited by uniform standards applied indiscriminately to all teachers.

Team teaching aims to develop these requisites for the professionalization of teachers — as well as for improved learning for individual students. Its goals are to recognize better the individual differences among teachers and to utilize better the special competences of each person.

WHAT TEAM TEACHING IS

The term *team teaching* applies to an arrangement in which two or more teachers and their assistants, taking advantage of their respective skills, plan, instruct, and evaluate in one or more subject areas a group of elementary or secondary students equivalent in size to two or more conventional classes, using a variety of technical aids to teaching and learning through large-group instruction, small-group discussion, and independent study. If one of the foregoing ingredients is missing, the result is *not* team teaching. It may be "cooperative teaching," "rotation of teaching," "utilization of teacher aides," or something else — but it is not team teaching.

The members of a given team may come from one subject department or grade level in the school or from several subject or grade areas. Although present research does not favor one kind of team over the other, we prefer teams that cut across subject lines. Such teams tend to plan instruction that better recognizes the interrelatedness of subject content. (In this regard, teaming has some of the same objectives as the core or common learnings curricular approaches.) Teachers still work primarily in their specialties, even with special interests within their subject fields, but they benefit from working in group activities with colleagues in other fields. Of course, we have seen excellent as well as ineffective teams of all types. The organization itself does not produce the goals of team teaching.

A team preferably includes older, more experienced teachers as well as beginners and less experienced ones, each benefiting from contact with the others. The team should select a leader to preside at planning and evaluation sessions. However, formalizing this position too much, or paying extra salary to the leader, may inhibit the achievement of team-teaching goals. The position of team leader is not analogous to that of a department head.

WHAT TEAM TEACHING IS NOT

Early attempts to initiate team teaching may involve practices that do not harmonize with the definition in the preceding paragraphs. Though we do not wish to discourage persons who may find no other way to develop what they call team teaching, we must point out the shortcomings in such procedures.

Team teaching is not, for example, a procedure whereby three teachers and 90 students come together occasionally for a presentation to the total group and then return to their respective classes of 30. This simple variation of class size is not likely to produce any more gains for teachers or learners than the hundreds of class-size studies conducted in this country and in others for many years have demonstrated in their reports.

Team teaching does not mean rearranging standard-sized classes of 30 into independent study groups and classes of 15 or 120 without changing what teachers and students do. What teachers today call class discussion is inappropriate for large or small groups. Similarly, a small-group session is largely wasted if teachers continue to conduct oral quizzes or lectures. And productive independent study involves more for students than doing conventional homework or merely reading books and filling in blanks.

Team teaching is not limited to either secondary or elementary students. Nor is it confined to the academically able or the highly motivated. It is not a system that is appropriate only for some subjects; rather, it works well in all of them since the principles of teaching and learning are similar.

Above all, team teaching is not a fad to be engaged in simply because others are doing it, or as a temporary expedient to solve a building space problem or financial difficulties because a referendum did not pass. Team teaching is not a superficial arrangement for educators who have not thought deeply about how to improve educational quality.

The foregoing negations emphasize the essential need to plan team teaching carefully. The way schools so frequently conduct what is called team teaching will not produce gains, as research studies show. It can and should be a basic, broad-scoped educational reorganization to develop improved conditions for teaching and learning that are necessary for better achieving the major educational goals. If it is less than that, those who plan and direct the program should take another look and try again. Limited concepts of team teaching will produce limited gains.

Compromises between ideal and realistic programs may be made, but when those compromises are approved there should be an accompanying plan for reaching the necessary goals over a period of years.

PROVIDING ASSISTANCE TO
PROFESSIONAL TEACHERS

A basic purpose of team teaching emphasizes the truly professional role of the teacher; therefore, a team needs the help of general aides, clerks, and instruction assistants. These assistants are sometimes called auxiliary personnel in education.

Actually, general aides are not usually assigned to specific teams because their functions may be schoolwide. Unlike clerks or instruction assistants, they do not possess specific educational qualifications. They are employed to assist in such tasks as supervising playgrounds and cafeterias, taking tickets, sorting materials, and supervising games, assemblies, or school dances.

Clerical assistants type and duplicate materials, keep records, assist in supervising large groups, take attendance, pass out materials, check objective tests, and so forth.

Instruction assistants are qualified in a given subject area, although they usually do not possess the certification requirements of professional teachers. Typically, the instruction assistant has at least a college minor in the subject area of the team to which he or she is attached. Tasks include helping to assemble materials, supervising independent study workrooms, and assisting with evaluation. There are three major sources of instruction assistants: homemakers, advanced college students, and retired teachers. They are employed on an hourly basis — usually ten to twenty hours per week. They do some of their work at home or in libraries or museums.

The number of such assistants was recommended in a 1959 publication.[1] The hours needed per week of the three kinds of assistants in relation to the number of teachers in a school is as follows: instruction assistants — twenty; clerical assistants — ten; general aides — five. These figures came from an analysis of the subprofessional activities that teachers perform in conventional schools. The curricular importance of these aides arises from the need for additional qualified adults to provide needed assistance for pupils engaged in independent study and to provide teachers with more time to produce instructional materials for student use.

Special consultants provide another type of assistance. Someone in the community who is better qualified than any member of the teaching team to make a presentation on a particular subject is invited to do so. Both a visual and a sound record should be made of the presentation so that the material is available for further use without asking the consultant to return repeatedly. The team should assemble a file of available consultants with appropriate notations regarding specialized competences. The PTA, student council, or service club may take a census of the community to prepare the file.

The school selects the four types of assistants as carefully as teachers. Since they have essential tasks to do, they must be competent to do them. (Some assistants will become professional teachers.) They need to be paid employees rather than voluntary workers so the school has legal control over them. Also, that arrangement enables school officials to give the assistants legal responsibility for supervising students — as is done in the case of office clerks, custodians, bus drivers, and other school employees.

OTHER CHANGES THAT FACILITATE TEAM TEACHING

Team teaching requires a number of other provisions. Instructional reorganization, including changed teacher roles, and curricular organization affect team teaching. The teams must determine which purposes are served best by large-group instruction, small-group discussion, and independent study (see Chapters 20, 21, and 22) and decide *who* will do *what* in the altered organizational program. The nongraded concept discussed in Chapter 24 enables the team to plan and

---

[1] J. Lloyd Trump, *Images of the Future — A New Approach to the Secondary School* (Washington, D. C.: National Association of Secondary School Principals, 1959), pp. 15–22.

supervise learning experiences more effectively than through the conventional approaches of track systems, homogeneous groupings, and similar developments that have accompanied the graded curricular organization.

Wide use of technical devices to aid teaching and learning is essential. (See Chapter 23.) Without technical aids, a large-group presentation may be no better than the lectures that teachers now give in conventional classes. Independent study will resemble today's homework unless printed materials are supplemented with extensive projection and recording devices, programmed materials, and the specialized tools of the subject that students can operate and use themselves.

Another requisite is a flexible schedule. Team members will decide not only who does what with which groups of students, but also *when* and for *how long*. Instead of rigid time arrangements in secondary schools fostered by the concept of the self-contained, or self-sufficient, classroom, time varies with the purposes of teaching and learning, as described in Chapter 25. Unless teachers and students control time for their respective purposes, new procedures are needlessly inhibited.

Evaluation methods different from those techniques now typical in conventional classrooms are also essential. Chapter 33 will show how evaluation varies with instructional organizations and purposes.

The school administration and board of education policies respecting expenditures of school funds need to be altered for team teaching, as described in Chapter 27. The preservice education of teachers should be reorganized and supervisory programs should be initiated to help teachers change and improve their teaching roles, as discussed in Chapter 28.

HOW THE TEAM OPERATES

Teams operate in much the same manner whether their members come from one subject area or cut across two or more subject fields. Nor is the number of members important. The three requirements for any team, whatever its organization, are that the members plan together, teach together, and evaluate together.

The team meets frequently to discuss a variety of topics. The following questions and answers illustrate subjects that may arise at such meetings and decisions that may be made.

What content will be presented to large groups of students, by whom, and how? Each member will teach the content he or she can handle best. What visuals or records will be helpful? Ideas are "roughed out" so the instruction assistant–artist can make or assemble the aids. Who will observe the presentation? There is no need for all team members to attend, but one person might. The school principal is a good selection. That staff member may join the presenter in leading an evaluative discussion at the team meeting the next day. How is the independent study program progressing? (Instruction assistants may join the team for this discussion.) Some team member should plan systematic observations in the study areas to obtain answers to questions raised in team discussions. What instructional purposes will we evaluate at this time? What data will we collect? What observations will we make? The team will assign responsibilities to different members and also involve appropriate colleagues outside the team. (More suggestions abcut evaluation and feedback will be provided in Chapters 32 and 33.) Why are small-group discussions less effective than anticipated? What needs to be done? What distinctive overt pupil behavior has been observed — or should be studied? What remedial steps are needed?

To get answers, the team uses its own resources and draws on consultants. The school principal and assistant principal meet regularly with teaching teams. So do the school librarian, counselors, and other staff members who have something to contribute. Incidentally, principals, librarians, counselors, and others benefit from these regularly scheduled meetings, for they get out of their offices and become involved in the main stream of instruction.

The team focuses on the processes of teaching and learning, on instructional content, and on learning aids rather than on the performance of its members. They recognize that mistakes will be made. Criticisms are given freely, openly, honestly, tastefully, and professionally. Always there are constructive efforts to find solutions to problems. The old saying "two minds are better than one" is the basis of team teaching.

Team personnel may change from time to time. The goal is to use the talents of each teacher to the individual's best advantage and for the team's maximum success. Flexibility in team membership should be a staff commitment.

Continuous evaluation of team procedures as well as student gains is essential. Are the creative talents of teachers stimulated? Are staff interests utilized? Are better facilities being developed? Is instruction improving? Is curriculum content more effective? The team will study many other comparable questions. Failure to do so inevitably leads to frustration. Incidentally, taping team sessions is helpful.

The team must have time for the foregoing activities. The team member's *average* weekly schedule need include no more than one or two large-group presentations and a dozen small-group discussion sessions. Experience indicates that teachers need to spend more than half the conventional school week, fifteen to twenty hours, on preparation, team meetings, individual and special group student conferences, and evaluation.

A team that operates below the standards set here will be less successful than it could be. Therefore, the team must work constantly with school administrators to improve the conditions under which it functions. Team teaching then will achieve its potential for curriculum improvement.

HOW IMPORTANT IS THE NAME?

The term *team teaching* came into prominence in the late 1950s. Of course, the concept is much older than that. The important matter is that teachers need to work cooperatively, each doing what he or she enjoys most and does best. A corollary is that students have contacts with more teachers so each one may find the most stimulating and helpful instructors, not having to contend for a semester or year with one who may or may not be the best for him or her. Some students relate even better to some teacher aides.

As long as schools organize the curriculum along subject lines, the departmental team will be the common approach. The relatively slow developments in the directions of core curriculum or common learnings suggest that interdepartmental teams are not practical immediately. Certainly, team teaching of this nature should not be the tool to achieve what curriculum developers have been unable to accomplish on a wide front. Thus most schools today, especially senior high schools, have departmental teams.

Whether cooperation as urged in this chapter is called team teaching does not matter so much as the acceptance of the concept. We believe schools will be better for teachers and students as more cooperative efforts occur. The determination of how much better is the subject of Chapter 32.

TOPICS FOR STUDY AND DISCUSSION

1. Stage a mock team meeting. The topic might be planning a large-group presentation, evaluating the use of resource centers (or whatever you decide). Then ask your colleagues or members of your university class to criticize the session.
2. List what you believe are the most important advantages in team teaching as compared with conventional teaching. Do the same for the most important difficulties.
3. Take some instructional topic in the course you teach or plan to teach. Then plan how you would survey the community to discover adults who

might contribute their time or materials to help students learn the topic. What forms would you use? How would you conduct the survey? What records would you keep?

4. Read about one or more team projects as described in some educational periodical. (See "Team Teaching" in *Education Index*.) How might the project have been made more successful?

5. Some people argue that differentiated staffing including the use of a variety of assistants is the most important single ingredient in furthering the concepts of individualized learning and professionalized teaching. Argue for or against that statement.

SELECTED REFERENCES

Anderson, Robert H. *Teaching in a World of Change.* New York: Harcourt, Brace & World, 1966, pp. 71–108.
>Concise statements of antecedents, rationale, types, practices, and evaluation of team teaching are included.

Armstrong, David G. "Team Teaching and Academic Achievement." *Review of Educational Research* (Winter 1977), pp. 65–86.
>A comprehensive review of the extensive research, with special emphasis on studies in secondary schools, leads to further questions. An excellent bibliography is provided.

Beggs, David W. III, ed. *Team Teaching — Bold New Venture.* Bloomington: Indiana University Press, 1965.
>Twelve experienced teachers and administrators describe team teaching in various subjects and grades.

Caldwell, Bruce G. *Differentiated Staffing — The Key to Effective School Organization.* New York: The Center for Applied Research in Education, 1973.
>Personal experiences in Temple City, California, help the author describe one system of differentiated staffing with advantages and some problems. Read especially Chapter 1 for background, Chapter 8 for problems, and Chapter 12 for a summary and personal advice.

Curtis, Thomas E., and Bidwell, Wilma W. *Curriculum and Instruction for Emerging Adolescents.* Reading, Ma.: Addison-Wesley Publishing Company, 1977, pp. 284–293.
>The authors describe various types of teams and the methods used in middle and junior high schools.

Davis, Harold S. *How to Organize an Effective Team Teaching Program.* Englewood Cliffs, N. J.: Prentice-Hall, 1966.
>This pamphlet describes team teaching in selected elementary and secondary schools and tells how to implement the new procedures.

———. *Team Teaching — A Selected Annotated Bibliography.* Cleveland: Educational Research Council of America, 1967.
>This pamphlet provides general references for secondary and elementary schools plus articles under the major subject-matter headings.

Georgiades, William. *How Good Is Your School?* Reston, Va.: National Association of Secondary School Principals, 1978.

> This book summarizes the methodology and some of the findings in program evaluation used in NASSP's Model Schools Project, 1969–75. The kinds of data reported here are important for all schools in arriving at prescriptions for changes.

Heller, Melvin P. *Team Teaching.* Dayton, Ohio: National Catholic Educational Association, 1967.

> This pamphlet answers questions about team teaching and provides practical suggestions for planning, conducting, and evaluating a program.

————. "Team Teaching — Professionalism for Professionals." *Catholic High School Quarterly Bulletin* (January 1966).

> This pamphlet lists advantages and guidelines and includes charts for evaluating team teaching.

Hoover, Kenneth H. *Learning and Teaching in the Secondary School,* 2d ed. Boston: Allyn and Bacon, 1968, pp. 328–348.

> The author provides suggestions of methods that teaching teams use.

Howard, Alvin W., and Stoumbis, George C. *The Junior High and Middle School: Issues and Practices.* Scranton, Penna.: Intext Educational Publishers, 1970, pp. 381–412.

> Chapter 17, "Flexible Scheduling, Team Teaching, and Nongraded Schools," describes the application of these concepts to early secondary education, with pros and cons.

Lewis, James, Jr. *Differentiating the Teaching Staff.* West Nyack, N. Y.: Parker Publishing Company, 1972.

> Using differentiated staffing as a central theme, the author also discusses teacher training, flexible scheduling, individualizing instruction, remodeling schools, accountability, and evaluating effectiveness.

Olivero, James L., and Buffie, Edward G. *Educational Manpower.* Bloomington: Indiana University Press, 1970.

> The writers summarize a diversity of approaches to defining personnel roles in instruction, along with attention to accountability.

Noar, Gertrude. *Teacher Aides at Work.* Washington, D. C.: National Education Association, Commission on Teacher Education and Professional Standards, 1967.

> The author reports on-the-spot impressions from visiting teacher aides at work in various parts of the United States.

Peterson, Carl H. *Effective Team Teaching: The Easton Area High School Program.* West Nyack, N. Y.: Parker Publishing Company, 1966, pp. 1–32, 121–161, and 177–197.

> These six chapters describe one school's program to illustrate reasons for team teaching. They explain how to initiate and carry on a program and how to overcome "common team teaching problems." They suggest ways to use resource people, and methods for conducting accelerated projects.

27

Humane Environments for Teaching and Learning

Providing better facilities constitutes a basic challenge in curriculum improvement. Whether the environment is humane has little to do with how new it is, how much it costs, how many machines it includes, how many acres of ground surround a school building, how large it is, or even where it is located. All these features can make the environment more or less humane, however, depending on how the program utilizes the environment as a vital part of the curriculum.

The term *educational facilities* refers to school moneys available for educational purposes, to the school building and grounds, and to the supplies and equipment that the school uses in instruction. The allocation of school money enhances or inhibits curriculum improvement.

That educational funds always are inadequate is axiomatic. Therefore, administrative decisions about allocating money are crucial to curriculum improvement. For example, better priorities are needed. The building shell contributes little to curriculum improvement; the critical aspect is found in the teaching tools and learning aids. Money saved on the former can be spent more advantageously on the latter.

Teachers and school administrators must be more active in planning new buildings and remodeling existing ones in order to save money for curriculum improvement.

Today's school buildings often are unnecessarily costly, reflecting too much the residential architectural styles of the times. For example, because some people had fascinating views from their houses, architects fostered the concept of a picture window. It became so popular that many houses without exciting views also were given picture windows. Transferred to schools, the concept produced great glass walls. The questions are: Do glass walls enhance or inhibit the educational programs they contain? Are they more or less expensive to install and maintain than other, educationally more desirable walls? What answers other than yes or no influence curriculum improvement?

Let us consider another illustration. Many families resented the narrow lots that are associated with city living. When they moved to suburbs, where land was cheaper, they sought new architectural forms to go with the land. Architects brought them the concept of the ranch house, or the rambler, as it is sometimes called. So their houses had fewer floor levels and spread out over the land. This style was then transferred to suburban and city schools. Since land was cheaper in the country, it became stylish to build suburban schools with twenty, forty, or even more acres of land surrounding them. Do these sprawled-out buildings and the rolling hills surrounding them contribute to or get in the way of achieving educational goals?

Architects do not deserve all the blame for today's costly and often inefficient school buildings and grounds. Often, they cannot obtain imaginative educational specifications from teachers and educational administrators, who may simply look at what other schools are building and then follow the current styles. Some architects like this procedure because they do not have to come up with as many new forms, new calculations, and new risks. It is easier to follow the common mold than to be creative.

What is a school building for? Dr. Harold Gores, first president of Educational Facilities Laboratories, reminded us that the building itself inherently serves two purposes: to maintain an inside climate that is better than the outside climate for comfort and maximum human efficiency, and to keep insects, birds, and animals out of the way. Beyond those minimum essentials, a school building takes its cues from what teachers and their pupils want to do inside the building — how they want to live educationally. Too many buildings get in the way of curriculum improvement. Even the best buildings provide little more than a neutral influence. What can the building do positively to facilitate the teaching-learning process?

THE CURRICULUM AND THE BUILDING

This book presents two basic curricular emphases. First, it supports the comprehensive middle school and junior and senior high school idea that requires a wide diversity of subject offerings available to all youths in one center. Second, it says that students learn best through a combination of independent study, large-group instruction, and small-group discussion with sequentially arranged content designed to produce maximum development for all students no matter how they differ. The school building must provide places where students can carry on appropriate learning activities for all subject areas and places where teachers and their assistants can plan, prepare, conduct, and evaluate those activities.

Chapters 20, 21, and 22 described the spaces necessary for independent study and the rooms suitable for large-group instruction and small-group discussion. Here are some guidelines for including those spaces in new buildings or for remodeling old buildings to meet instructional needs.

Resource Centers

You will recall that learning resource centers for students are needed in all subject areas. Each of the resource centers has two parts: the place where students read, listen, view, think, and write and the place where they work with the specialized "tools of the trade" in that subject area.

Let us assume that facilities are being planned for 1,200 students who will spend 40 percent or more of their time in a variety of independent study activities. The practical arts area, for example, needs a room in which boys and girls can read, listen, view, think, and write, plus specialized laboratories in food, clothing, electronics, machine shops, woodworking, agriculture, and whatever other areas seem appropriate in the local community. The equipment will be portable or easily moved to provide flexibility among the various curricular areas. The fine arts area also will provide a room for reading, viewing, and the like, plus a variety of small rooms in which individuals and small groups may practice vocal and instrumental music; specialized workrooms for ceramics, metals, and the like; and larger rooms for orchestra, band, large vocal groups, and varied art activities, depending on the nature of the local program.

Arrangements in the academic subjects will be comparable to those just described. Regardless of the size of the school building, the independent study areas constitute its major floor area.

Some classrooms in conventional schools can be readily changed to provide the reading, listening, and viewing areas. Others can be remodeled to provide many of the laboratories and workrooms. A first step is to remove student desks or, at least, take most of them out and place the rest around the perimeter of the room. Substitute tables and chairs. Carpeting helps both acoustically and aesthetically.

Other Areas for Independent Study

Chapter 20 described other kinds of spaces for independent study. The library is one of them. In a school with 1,200 students, the central library should provide seating in carrels with quasi-privacy for reading, thinking, and writing. A new library should avoid tables in the reading room and older libraries should replace them with carrels as rapidly as possible. Adolescents are especially interested in each other and look around constantly as others walk by or as noises occur. Carrels with dividers that extend to the sides, beyond the desks and chairs, tend to minimize these distractions. Comfortable lounge-type chairs are needed for students who wish only to read. The library should also provide listening booths and a viewing area that will accommodate up to thirty students each. Dial-access systems enable users to contact a variety of materials as needed for work in various subjects. The library also needs an informal area where students sit on the carpeted floor or on cushions to read and discuss.

The school cafeteria can provide most of the places for the three other kinds of independent study arrangements — conference workrooms, strictly supervised areas, and recreation rooms. An operable wall can divide the cafeteria into the recreation and work areas, each of which might accommodate forty students seated around tables in groups of two to six or seven. In an older school, the supervised area may be a conventional classroom that will house the fifteen to thirty students that will be assigned there.

A new school building should provide separate rooms for these three activities. One room is the student lounge with an automated snack service. A second room has various sizes of tables to seat two, four, or eight persons for conferences. The third room has tables and desks for students needing close supervision. Each of these three rooms should accommodate about forty people.

Older buildings can be carpeted, remodeled, painted (sometimes by students), and relighted to become cheerful, useful spaces. Sometimes students feel more ownership in an older building that they have helped renew.

Area for Large-group Instruction
and Small-group Discussion

All subject fields may use the same spaces for large-group instruction and small-group discussion. Assuming large-group instruction in all subjects, a building for 1,200 students can use six spaces, each accommodating up to 150 students, with operable walls that can be opened to create larger spaces as needed. Such an arrangement provides considerable flexibility in the use of spaces. Four spaces, for example, may be combined into an auditorium that will seat 600 for concerts, plays, community gatherings, and the like. The other two spaces may be combined for a "theater-in-the-round" arrangement to seat 300. In older school buildings, a wall may be removed between two conventional classrooms to provide a large-group instruction space that will easily handle 120 students.

Assuming small-group discussion classes in each subject, a school of 1,200 will need about twenty rooms for small-group discussion. Each room, about 250 square feet in area, should contain a table with sixteen chairs ranged around it. Three such rooms can be made from a conventional classroom in an older building.

Precisely how many large and small rooms and how many independent study spaces a school needs depends on the current decisions of the staff about teaching and learning. If only some of the staff are prepared to depart from conventional practices when the school moves into a new building, the building needs conventional classrooms plus enough large and small rooms and independent study areas to take care of the innovative teachers' needs. Requirements may be estimated easily. The important consideration is to provide walls that may be changed economically as teacher ideas change. A school can justify operable walls between classrooms only if those walls are as acoustically satisfactory as and more economical than other walls. If they are not, the school should use the kind of walls that can be taken out later as needed. Most schools are likely to find that the three places for operable walls are the auditorium, cafeteria, and gymnasium.

A school building should never be finished. It must be constantly remodeled and improved so that it can best serve the ever-changing educational needs of learners and teachers.

Teachers' Work Spaces

An essential facility, and one that is often inadequate in today's schools, is a place for teachers to plan, to prepare materials, to evaluate, and to confer with colleagues, assistants, pupils, and visitors. Classroom space, often wastefully utilized for those purposes, is usually poorly equipped.

Curriculum improvement requires that each teacher has an office with some privacy. The area should also provide working space for instruction assistants and clerks as well as for artists, research assistants, and other specialized personnel that may be involved in preparing teaching aids. Soundproof recording studios are required in this area, as are photographic darkrooms and other places to prepare visuals and duplicated materials. Two or three small conference rooms, a lounge, and a dining room are also needed.

SOME SPECIAL CONSIDERATIONS

School buildings need to be compact to facilitate movement from one part to another, and elevators or escalators should be provided for those teachers and young people who should not climb stairs. Compact design also makes year-round air conditioning economical. Even in areas where the outside temperature is reasonably comfortable, the humidity control that air conditioning provides makes a school building a fresher and more stimulating teaching and learning environment, because it takes care of excess humidity and the stuffiness created by large numbers of people in one space.

Both light and sound control are important in planning new buildings or remodeling old ones. Glass should be used in a school building only when it enhances the educational program. It interferes with the effectiveness of light, sound, and temperature control in all large-group instruction and small-group discussion areas; therefore, no glass should be provided in those spaces. On the other hand, independent study areas for students and work areas for teachers are enhanced by small windows so that they can look outside, rest their eyes, and relax for a moment. Such "vision strips" are quite small and do not interfere greatly with light, sound, and temperature control. Incidentally, glass should not be used on inside spaces in a building because the views distract students from work.

The amount of artificial light and the type of fixtures vary in different parts of the building. Standard regulations are obviously impossible, for the task determines the requirements. Variable controls are needed in large-group areas. Less light is needed in small-group discussion spaces than in the work spaces of the independent study rooms. Some study areas need high-intensity light and others more diffused light. The use of appropriate colors in walls and furnishings adds variety to visual experiences. Color dynamics suggests cool colors in sunny areas, warm colors in darker places, and often a variety of colors in one room.

Sound control is essential. Carpeting quiets independent study areas used for reading, listening, viewing, thinking, and writing. It also helps acoustics in large-group instruction areas. Acoustical treatment of walls and ceilings is, of course, assumed.

Corridor and lobby spaces in schools are about as expensive as classroom space and contribute little to the educative process. Imaginative architects can and should produce school buildings that reduce this wasteful corridor space to a minimum; some buildings almost eliminate corridors. Flexible schedules can reduce concentrations of travel in corridors. In many instances, traffic from one independent study space to another can be incorporated into the rooms themselves.

School buildings should be beautiful places that reflect a concern for the artistic in everyday living. If there is a beautiful view outside the building, a strategically placed picture window can reveal and highlight that view while the opaque walls shut out undesirable scenes. Carefully placed fountains and gardens in inner courts can add beauty inexpensively. Strategic use of different building materials, color, and the like may also create an atmosphere of beauty without adding greatly to construction costs. The creative ingenuity of architects is needed here. Today's schools in many cases are unnecessarily drab and ugly.

SUPPLIES AND EQUIPMENT

The typical industrial building today spends only 25 percent of the total capital outlay for the structure, while 75 percent of the outlay goes to the equipment and the tools of the trade inside the building. Strangely enough, school buildings reverse those figures. Three-fourths of the cost goes into the building shell, and only one-fourth into the all-important instructional tools and supplies. That ratio makes no sense when we recall that the building shell contributes little to the teaching-learning process other than temperature control and freedom from insects!

Chapter 23 emphasizes the wide variety of technical devices needed in schools. The future will see new aids to teaching and learning only dreamed about today. Efficient use of these devices, however, requires that they be placed in strategic locations in the school rather than being scattered about the classrooms as they are in most of today's buildings.

THE USE OF AVAILABLE MONEY

Money allocated to curriculum improvement may be used to produce change or it may be used as an excuse to maintain existing procedures and policies. Educational moneys are valuable only to the extent that they produce better conditions for learning and teaching and better results.

How may a school use available money differently to produce a better educational product? Several ways to save money are obvious. Teachers now spend about one-third of their time in activities that can be done as well, and in most cases better, by clerks and instruction assistants. Clerks cost about half what teachers cost. Part-time instruction assistants usually cost only slightly more per hour than clerks do. It is also reasonable to estimate that another one-third of what teachers are doing now could be done by pupils themselves under the supervision of the less costly instruction assistants, and with the aid of technical devices. Since instructional costs constitute the major portion of any educational operational budget, the savings may be considerable.

A school can also save money through more efficient use of technical devices. For example, if teachers in conventional schools use overhead projectors frequently, they may want one of these devices for each classroom. However, the use of projectors only in large-group instruction reduces the number required for a given school building.

Large-group instruction saves money while it saves teacher time and energy. Obviously, it costs less to teach a lesson once to 120 students than it does to teach it four times to groups of 30. Today's teachers spend almost half their time in conventional classrooms with 25 to 30 students in activities that may be done just as effectively in large groups.

Earlier in this chapter reference was made to certain economies in school building construction. Compact buildings with year-round air conditioning usually cost less per square foot to construct than do conventional school buildings without air conditioning. A glass wall is more expensive to construct, to maintain, and to repair than masonary or wooden walls. Making usable educational space out of corridors and lobbies, which occupy such a prominent place in today's schools, is another economy. Broadly distributed decorative materials can be eliminated in order to provide selected beauty spots with more dramatic emphasis.

However, not all changes necessary for curriculum improvement will save money. Some of the changes suggested in this book will cost more than the present practices. For example, the proposal is made that about 20 percent of the students' school week should be spent in small-group discussion, in classes of fifteen as contrasted to today's conventional classes of twenty-five to thirty. For that portion of the school week the instructional costs in teachers' salaries are doubled. Also, the hours that teachers are scheduled with students must be reduced, the proposal being that not more than fifteen hours per week should be spent with student groups. Today's teachers have no more than five hours per week away from student groups, some even less than that. This change in the teaching load costs more money. Additional technical devices are required in independent study areas.

Experience to date is that the costs and the savings represented by the proposed changes just about balance each other. Of course, other factors may enter the picture. For example, holding school all year round may cost more because more students than in today's schools receive an expanded education. Teacher salaries have increased markedly during recent years, but they still are not as high as they should be for the level of professional services demanded of teachers.

Today's schools spend something like 0.02 percent of the school budget on research and development — much less than business provides for the same purpose. Raising that amount to one or two cents out of every dollar is not unreasonable.

The basic consideration in the use of available money is to relate financial input to educational output. Chapter 33 discusses in detail what is meant by educational output. Although it may never be possible to screen every educational dollar in relation to its impact on student learning, professional workers and board of education members must keep that goal uppermost in their minds. When a proposal for spending educational funds is made, a corresponding proposal should be made to evaluate, after a reasonable period of time (for example, one, two, or five years later), what effects the added funds or the reduced funds have on conditions of learning, the professionalization of teaching, the individualization of learning, and the resultant quality of gains for each person. An analysis of this nature guarantees more consistent curriculum improvement than almost any other policy that the board of education might adopt, because it strikes at the very heart of the school's life.

The word *accountability* occurs frequently in current literature. The term has many meanings: measuring and relating student and teacher output to changes in expenditures for schooling; testing the effects of different methods and material; analyzing various types of building structures; scheduling students into facilities for learning in addition to or in lieu of school buildings; utilizing facilities for more hours and months in the year; and analyzing many other input and output relationships. Further discussion of this topic occurs in Part V. Certainly, the more effective use of educational facilities can facilitate secondary school curriculum improvement.

DECLINING ENROLLMENTS AND UNUSED SPACE

Secondary school enrollments are declining nationwide because of birthrate reductions in the 1960s. Not so many spaces for students are now required. Mobility of populations also creates vacancies in some areas and overcrowding in others. Some districts have closed some schools and others experience only partially occupied ones. The question is what to do with vacant spaces and buildings.

Here are some possibilities as recommended recently by Harold B. Gores of Educational Facilities Laboratories, Inc.: provide shuffleboards for the use of older citizens as well as other facilities for them and other people who could use the building for recreational and educational purposes; use surplus space as places for special activities that should have been provided in the first place for a complete school environment; involve community persons in discussions to find out the needs of all the people, not just the children. Some examples might be socially useful activities housed in the school building; space for a community health center; preschool, child care, or senior citizen centers; an occupational center where students can secure the skills that may facilitate their quick entry into the job market; and spaces to handle the overflow of paperwork from, say, city hall, local courts, offices of United Fund agencies, public library branches, and museums.

Other uses would call for outright rental to the private sector. Recognizing that public institutions tend to be nervous in the presence of private, for-profit corporations, and also that laws in some places may preclude the renting of public property, the possibilities need to be considered because policies and laws can change. Even if the whole building becomes excess yet is structurally sound, the building must be kept in use by somebody instead of being boarded up and mothballed, which preserves neither the building nor the real estate values of the neighborhood.

The best way to protect property is to fill it with people. For example, some communities have converted a high school to a center for personnel training, adult basic education, and community recreation; relinquished a large high school building to the city for adult education, a private school, and a senior citizen center; and used an abandoned junior high school to become a community school center with administrative offices. Another surplus high school became a junior college; another was turned over to the city for public recreation; and yet another high school building was sold to an entrepreneur who recycled it to become a shopping center, private offices, and housing for the elderly. These examples do not solve the problem in a given locale, but they may suggest alternatives to consider.[1]

The emphases in this chapter are that curriculum improvement is enhanced or limited by the school's policies and procedures in constructing and utilizing environments for teaching and learning. To omit these needs from a book on curriculum betterment would be a grievous fault. Conversely, to write about facilities without considering curriculum needs would be equally useless.

TOPICS FOR STUDY AND DISCUSSION

1. Select some school building problem, for example, how to eliminate or greatly reduce corridor space, how to provide independent study space in your subject field, or how to remodel an existing school facility in your subject. Prepare some rough drawings (you are not an architect) and present these to your colleagues for discussion.
2. Locate in the library a plan of a proposed school building or one recently constructed. Criticize the facilities that relate to teaching and learning in your subject field or one that interests you.
3. Analyze a portion of the budget — your subject field, for example — or the total school budget of the place where you work or some place you know. How could some of the money be spent differently to produce curriculum improvement? Defend your proposal in a paper or oral discussion.
4. The proposal has been made to locate a senior high school in a densely populated location in the central area of the city. The first two floors would be leased for offices and small business operations — to provide both revenue for the school and work experience for students. Various surfaces, including plastic grass, on the roof and some upper story areas will provide physical fitness and recreation areas for students. Prepare arguments for or against this kind of school.
5. Develop a presentation to show how the use of the community rather than the school building as a setting for some aspects of the curriculum could save money and building facilities.
6. What are some consequences, based on functional analyses, of these three educational philosophies of curriculum: open, closed, a combination of the two?

[1] Harold B. Gores, "Declining Enrollment and Options for Unused Space," National Association of Secondary School Principals *Bulletin* (May 1976), pp. 92–97.

SELECTED REFERENCES

Divisible Auditoriums. New York: Educational Facilities Laboratories, 1966.
This pamphlet illustrates several methods of dividing auditoriums to produce better utilization, with special emphasis on acoustics.

The Education Park: Report to the School District of Philadelphia. Wilton, Conn.: Corde Corporation, 1967.
This multilithed report gives reasons for and methods of combining primary, intermediate, and secondary schools in various locations to facilitate articulation, racial integration, and educational innovations.

Green, Allan C., ed. *Educational Facilities with New Media.* Washington, D. C.: National Education Association, Department of Educational Technology, 1966, pp. C-1–C-55.
This report provides data on lighting, climate, acoustics, furniture, and other equipment.

High School: The Process and the Place. New York: Educational Facilities Laboratories, 1972.
This little book defines the concept of school facilities, special values in the school environment, and how to manage a "live" environment. This beautifully written and illustrated document relates the humane and facilities factors unusually well.

The High School Auditorium: Six Designs for Renewal. New York: Educational Facilities Laboratories, 1967.
This book shows how to renovate little-used auditoriums in old and middle-aged schools to accommodate contemporary educational programs.

New Life for Old Schools. Chicago: Research Council of the Great Cities Program, 1965.
Several architects and educators from a dozen large cities discuss plans for updating school buildings.

New Schools for New Education. New York: Educational Facilities Laboratories, 1961.
A report of a conference of architects and educators at the University of Michigan, where plans were proposed and discussed for schools to serve the "Trump Plan."

Schneider, Raymond C. *Space for Teachers.* New York: Educational Facilities Laboratories, 1961.
This pamphlet shows imaginative illustrations of places for teachers to plan and work.

Three High Schools Revisited: Andrews, McPherson, and Nova. New York: Educational Facilities Laboratories, 1967.
This booklet, from the series "Profiles of Significant Schools," shows how innovative schools are using specially designed buildings. Separate publications on the three schools were issued several years earlier when the buildings were first opened; this report shows their strengths and limitations.

V
Procedures for Curriculum Improvement

28

Organizing for Change

Many individuals and organizations are involved in curriculum change: principals, teachers, students, parents, taxpayers, government officials, university staff members, foundations, businesses and industries, labor organizations, and civic groups of various types. As leader of the school, the secondary school principal must exercise that responsibility with knowledge and vigor. The principal and the teachers in the school need to understand their own motivations as well as those of each of the foregoing groups.

Selfish interests are understandable. Sometimes such concerns benefit students, sometimes not. Considerations for the general welfare must come first.

THE PRINCIPLE OF ACCOUNTABILITY

Basic to change is an understanding of the consequences of alternative decisions for curriculum improvement. Requiring content that some

432

neither want nor need shows a lack of accountability, as does the failure of the program to schedule students into the best learning environments in the school or community that are appropriate for given tasks. Not analyzing the consequences of any procedure in relation to expenditures and quality of learning also violates the principle of accountability. So, in connection with the curriculum or any other aspect of schooling, the individuals involved need constantly to relate expenditures in effort, time, money (including all facilities), and personnel to productivity in terms of the stated purposes. Accountability is crucial; this factor applies to the variety of people and programs involved in curriculum improvement.

Most teachers enter the profession because of a deep-seated commitment toward helping young people become better people. However, teachers are also people, with the usual drives to succeed, to live well, to feel that their talents are utilized properly, to protect their security, and to avoid unnecessary hard work. Those who plan curricular changes must help teachers understand how the new program will affect each of those drives.

Students, more than any other group, have the largest personal stakes in curriculum change. The principal and other persons involved should provide them regularly with information that will give assurance that they are learning as much as, and in most instances more than, they did under the former program. The students rightfully need confidence that they will be able to get into the colleges to which they may reasonably aspire, that they will be better prepared for their chosen vocations, and that their present lives in school will be more stimulating and rewarding.

Parents want the same assurances for their children. When any alteration in the school program is being planned, they must be told how the changes will help students achieve each of the appropriate goals.

Taxpayers want to know if the changes are going to be expensive. If the costs go up, they need assurance that the new program is worth what it costs. School administrators sometimes ignore the relationship between financial input and educational output, but that is not a defensible business policy.

Civic groups are also concerned with curriculum improvement. They want to be proud of their schools when they write letters to their friends in other communities or when people from other places come to visit them. Community pride cannot be ignored.

Employers in business and industry want assurances that the graduates of the new program will be better employees than the graduates of the program it replaced. Organized labor wants to be sure that the graduates of the new program will be more employable and that, other factors being equal, they will fare better if they graduate from the changed curriculum.

Representatives of government agencies also enter the picture. If the school is one of several in a city or county school system, the central administrative and supervisory staff will want to know how their services will be utilized in the new program. The system may exert pressures for uniformity among all schools. A given school must carefully describe the reasons for being different, the methods of change, the manner of evaluation, and the financial implications.

Since state education agencies are responsible for maintaining standards throughout the state, they establish a number of quantitative measures of excellence that all schools are expected to achieve. The state officials check school reports carefully and on occasion visit schools to make certain that the quantitative aspects are obeyed. If the change proposed in a given school violates one or more of these quantitative standards, the school should report the change in advance and request permission to be released from existing standards. It should also specify how the program may be evaluated by state authorities.

If the school receives federal aid, there are bound to be certain restrictions on how that aid is used. A school planning a change that violates some existing federal standard must clarify the situation before putting the change into effect. Increasingly, government agencies and educational foundations are making funds available for curriculum innovations. If a school wishes to obtain a grant, it must plan a program that is in harmony with the grant's specifications. Of course, the availability of grants does not mean that schools should practice only innovations that are likely to be supported, but they should be aware of the types of fundable programs presently available and the procedures for applying to participate in them. A school planning to change should check various governmental and foundation interests if it wishes to obtain financial support for a given experiment or demonstration. Perhaps an existing school interest may be adapted to the programs that foundations or government agencies are promoting.

Universities and other higher educational institutions play specific roles in secondary school changes. Some innovations affect secondary school–university relationships — marking systems, course outlines, or procedures for reporting the school's estimate of students' ability to succeed in the university. School authorities should correspond or meet personally with admissions officers and other appropriate university representatives when planning revised programs for reporting and evaluating the competence of students who will go to the university. Administrators often invite university personnel to serve as consultants to the school in planning changes, reeducating teachers for the changes, collecting materials, and evaluating the results. The close working relationship that can develop between the schools and the universities from this practice is a major bonus factor in organizing for change, but it will not occur unless specific efforts are made by teachers and the school principal.

The first responsibility in organizing for change is to conceptualize an educational system that will serve individual students better and will raise the professional standards of teaching. These goals have been described in detail in earlier sections of this volume. Inconsistent or inadequate concepts of educational systems can plague schools and cause inefficient and ineffective instruction even in innovative programs. Language laboratories have been installed in some schools largely because government funds were available and other schools were doing it — with the result that the laboratories were only partially or uncertainly used. Some schools engage in team teaching because it is prestigious or fashionable. Then they practice only large-group instruction, or fail to give the teachers common time together to plan and to evaluate, or to do other things that show inadequate or incomplete understanding of the purposes of team teaching.

Before making an innovation, the principal and the staff involved in the change should prepare specific answers to such questions as the following: What do we believe? How do the various aspects of the new educational program relate to our concepts of the educational provisions necessary for individual students? Is this a carefully planned program of action that includes changes over several years? Are our educational specifications sharply drawn? What kinds of help do we need and from whom? How do we propose to evaluate the effects of the changes on students, teachers, and other concerned individuals? What will the changes cost?

The principal, administrative assistants, and teachers in each school must bear prime responsibility for providing viable answers to the foregoing questions. They must analyze carefully in their plans and progress reports what effects are anticipated and are happening. The principle of accountability with accurate and understandable reports must replace the glossy kinds of public relations releases that can produce creditability gaps. Everyone must understand that change does not come easily or quickly. Everyone must also understand and know what is occurring as much as possible.

DEVELOPING READINESS FOR CHANGE

To effect a change, the principal and the central planning committee must have the cooperation of the various groups mentioned in the first section of this chapter; therefore, they should see to it that the groups are ready to change. They may develop such readiness through a variety of approaches. It is difficult to make specific suggestions that will work in every school; the recommendations that follow have been utilized in various places with success.

Teachers and principals often capitalize on events outside the school, using them as a psychological lever to encourage change. For example, a group of critics may deplore the accomplishments of the students in the so-called fundamentals of reading, writing, spelling, computing, and the like. So the school undertakes a study of the need for changes in these areas and proposes a number of alterations that it believes will help the situation. Patriotic groups may complain that citizens do not know the nation's history, so the school takes a constructive approach to improve instruction in this subject. A successful space program by a competing nation may provide the lever to reassess science and mathematics programs. Problems in the economic world may stimulate work in the social sciences; so may political and social problems. A national program to combat poverty may lead to a reexamination of selected aspects of the school's programs.

Other procedures that may stimulate interest in curriculum improvement include studies to determine why dropouts leave school and what happens to them when they leave, and follow-up studies of graduates, analyzing their success or failure in colleges and in employment. Studies of attendance and disciplinary problems may point the way to increased guidance services, and they may also focus on needed changes in the curriculum.

Studies in each of the curriculum areas may be undertaken to ascertain what the teachers in that particular area believe their programs should be like. In separate studies, students, parents, and employers may be asked the same question about goals. What people *think the program should be* may then be compared and contrasted with the program *as it actually exists* to reveal reasons for change. For example, what is the purpose of the health, physical education, and recreation program in the school? Is it to produce professional athletes, to serve as community entertainment, or to improve physical fitness? Are these purposes necessarily opposed to each other?

Another approach to developing readiness for change involves the principles of teaching and learning described earlier. The principal, or the teacher considered best for the task, makes a large-group presentation at a meeting of faculty, PTA, a civic club, a women's organization, or the like. (Occasionally, an entire oral presentation may be best; at other times a film may be more motivational than a live presentation. However, a combination of live and audio-visual presentations is usually most effective.) The school provides additional materials for individuals to read, view, or hear on their own. Small groups are then organized to discuss and clarify ideas and to make reports. In other words, the principal uses the same approach to teaching others that he or she expects teachers to use effectively with their pupils.

Here is a specific illustration. Suppose the principal believes that team teaching would be a desirable change in the school. For most of one school year faculty meetings are used to present various films and filmstrips on team teaching. Outside speakers with team teaching experience talk with the group. A collection of books, pamphlets, and filmstrips on team teaching in the professional library encourages teachers to examine these materials in their own independent study prior to discussions at grade or departmental levels. The small-group discussions produce questions, which the principal answers in subsequent large-group meetings. Toward the end of the year, the principal finds out which teachers want to become involved in a demonstration-experiment on team teaching the following year. The next step is to prepare the teachers for the changes they plan to undertake.

FURTHER EDUCATION OF TEACHERS INVOLVED IN CHANGE

The teachers who will be involved in a new team-teaching system, along with their instruction assistants and clerks, should attend a summer workshop for two weeks, or preferably one month. During the workshop, they prepare materials and practice large-group instruction with volunteer students who criticize and make suggestions. The teachers also produce assignments for productive independent study and organize small groups of students for discussion sessions. At discussions, one of the teachers acts as the teacher-leader and the others sit outside the circle as observers. Later, the groups meet for critique sessions. The goal of those sessions is to produce plans and materials that teachers may use for at least the first month of the school year. Of course, the teachers benefit from the confidence they acquire in this "learning-by-doing" activity.

Incidentally, young people usually volunteer their services happily for these summer sessions. They feel important when they help teachers in a new enterprise. The use of school facilities for swimming or hobbies plus some light refreshments are sufficient material rewards.

Before starting the new system, the principal makes all the appropriate administrative changes needed to give the innovation a chance to succeed. A different kind of schedule is necessary, for the teachers need adequate time to plan together, to prepare materials, to evaluate their work, and to consult with individual students. Changes in room arrangements are also needed, and a variety of materials for teacher use and for independent study must be provided. Before beginning the experiment, the school must prepare attractive, explanatory brochures and distribute them to all the groups mentioned in the opening of this chapter. The basic purpose of the publications is to acquaint everyone with the nature of the project under way. The brochures should not be burdened with too much statistical material, nor should they be over-involved with historical backgrounds and quotations from authorities. The story should be told simply and directly. Line drawings and charts may be added to emphasize certain points.

Professional help in developing a brochure is usually necessary, since the training of most teachers and principals has not included preparing effective materials of this nature. Someone with journalistic training may take what others have written and remove excess or unclear verbiage. There is no magic length for brochures, but they will usually be ten to twenty pages long if they are to be widely read. There should be a good deal of open space so that the casual reader is not overwhelmed by the printed material but should be able to complete the booklet in fifteen to twenty minutes. Remember, the purpose of the brochure is not to tell the whole story, but rather to whet the reader's interest and to provide a general understanding of what is taking place at the school.

ADMINISTRATIVE POLICIES DURING THE YEAR

The changes undertaken also need to be publicized throughout the year by competent writers and speakers. The experimentation to date should be described as effectively as possible in newspapers, on local radio and television, by means of slides and tapes, and if more funds are available, through professionally produced filmstrips and films.

Periodically, the school should issue carefully written summaries of what is happening as a result of the changes that have been made. The reports should contain illustrations and data showing the effects of the changes, plus statements by students and teachers concerning their reactions to what is happening. The report should honestly describe unsolved problems as well as accomplishments.

Staff members not immediately involved in the experimentation may be suspicious and, in some cases, defensive about their failure to be involved in the studies. Psychologists call them the "out-group." They must be kept informed about what is going on and what is being accomplished, and they must be encouraged and helped to plan studies for themselves. They may decide to join the "in-group" (persons immediately involved) next year. If so, they will be prepared at a summer workshop.

The most important matter of all during the first year of change is close supervision of the teachers involved in the new program. The principal must change personal priorities about how to spend time and energy. He or she needs to delegate responsibility for the cafeteria, the bus routes, routine discipline and attendance, conventional public relations, service club responsibilities, custodial care of the building, and comparable tasks to administrative assistants specially trained and employed for tho~e tasks. The principal has to concentrate on the improvement of instruction, working with the groups involved in change. Teachers do not change their teaching methods easily, nor do students change their learning habits easily. To facilitate the process, the principal must ask many different questions, help find answers, point out things that are being done incorrectly, and suggest how to improve procedures. Evaluation continually has high priority.

THE PRINCIPAL'S RESPONSIBILITY

We trust that this chapter has not destroyed the desire for change by making the task appear too complicated. The barriers to curriculum improvement have been enunciated elsewhere in this volume. Removing those barriers requires creative imagination, commitment, and hard work by the principal and other professional colleagues. In the final analysis, the principal bears the awesome responsibility of organizing for change to improve the curriculum. Effective results require broad involvement with strong leadership — and an open mind for new ideas and procedures.

We emphasize the central role of the principal in the change process because she or he is in the best position to see the total picture of the school — and is there in charge. The superintendent and colleagues in the central office, or university consultants and state education department supervisors, may help mightily but they are not there in the school all the time. They do not know the youths, the teachers, and the community as well as the principal does, if he or she does the job well. A teacher may innovate in the classroom, but the principal's administrative restrictions will limit effectiveness if he or she opposes the changes. Conversely, the principal may stimulate curriculum improvement by changes in scheduling, facilities, evaluation, and other instructional matters. Organizing for change requires active leadership by the school principal. Others will go along when they understand the advantages for them.

Three recent publications contain many specific proposals for changing schools.[1] A common thread runs through all these publications: changing a school is like teaching. The head of the school, along with department heads, committees of teachers, or any others with supervisory responsibilities, needs to use sound methods in changing the program and the responsibilities of the personnel involved.

Motivation for change comes from the collection of data about how existing programs operate and the results such efforts produce. How do these data relate to what students, teachers, other people, and the program really need? The collection of data is a prerequisite to diagnostic procedures that produce a variety of possible prescriptions for improvement. Then, as we have indicated repeatedly in this volume, decisions are made about what changes to implement with concurrent plans to evaluate the outcomes. The resultant data lead to rediagnosis and the other steps in the continuing efforts to change the program to improve outcomes.

Organizing for change is crucial. Curriculum improvement will occur to the degree that the foregoing steps are implemented accurately.

TOPICS FOR STUDY AND DISCUSSION

1. What needs to be done to improve the curriculum in the school where you work, or one that you know? A scientifically conducted needs assessment would help more, but you can start by sampling the opinions of some students, teachers, parents, other taxpayers, employers, representatives of government agencies, university personnel, and others.
2. Consider some educational change that you believe is desirable. Then analyze why people such as those mentioned in topic 1 are likely to oppose the change. Why are they content with the situation that you want to change?
3. Either using your analysis for topic 1 or taking a different educational change, plan a strategy to neutralize the opposition so they may be willing to accept constructive suggestions to individualize learning or professionalize teaching.
4. Select some change that you or others are advocating and analyze the potential effects of the change on teachers and students.
5. Select some local, state, national, or world development that currently is in the headlines or on TV or radio. What, if anything, does the development require of schools? Present a case for or against change in teaching or learning methods.

---

[1] J. Lloyd Trump and William Georgiades, *How to Change Your School;* Reston, Va.: The National Association of Secondary School Principals, 1978, pp. 1–70, and "Curriculum Planning and Change," National Association of Secondary School Principals *Bulletin* (October 1977), pp. 1–79.

6. From ten current articles in one or two educational journals, select two articles that have the best and the worst style and presentation. Prepare an analysis of your reasons for choosing the two articles.

SELECTED REFERENCES

Anderson, Vernon E. *Curriculum Guidelines in an Era of Change.* New York: The Ronald Press Company, 1969.

    This paperback provides practical suggestions for developing a rationale for curriculum changes.

Frymier, Jack R., and Hawn, Horace C. *Curriculum Improvement for Better Schools.* Worthington, Ohio: Charles A. Jones Publishing Company, 1970, pp. 19–49 and 237–251.

    These three chapters provide practical suggestions for planning and conducting curriculum improvement projects in schools.

Georgiades, William. *How Good Is Your School?* Reston, Va.: The National Association of Secondary School Principals, 1978.

Goodlad, John I. *The Dynamics of Educational Change: Toward Responsive Schools.* New York: McGraw-Hill Book Company, 1975.

    Although the ideas were generated mainly by working with eighteen elementary schools, the principles are relevant to secondary schools as well. The final chapter describes Goodlad's model for change.

Lessinger, Leon M. *Every Kid a Winner: Accountability in Education.* New York: Simon and Schuster, 1970.

    See especially Chapters 1 and 2, which show the importance of linking learning to costs and suggest changing assumptions about education and improved management techniques.

Tanner, Daniel. *Secondary Curriculum.* New York: The Macmillan Company, 1971, pp. 403–435.

    This chapter provides a model for curriculum change along with brief descriptions of some innovative proposals.

Tye, Kenneth, and Novotney, J. *Schools in Transition: The Practitioner as Change Agent.* New York: McGraw-Hill Book Company, 1974.

    The authors suggest ways to overcome obstacles that teachers and principals face in their efforts to improve schools.

Unruh, Adolph, and Turner, Harold E. *Supervision for Change and Innovation.* Boston: Houghton Mifflin Company, 1970, pp. 236–275.

    The authors describe plans for building a rationale, developing a support system, and implementing a program.

Van Til, William, ed. *Curriculum: Quest for Relevance.* Boston: Houghton Mifflin Company, 1971.

    Fifteen writers, including Wilhelms, Havighurst, Robinson, Krutch, Doll, Crosby, and Shane, write about new approaches, new subjects, priorities, relations between humanism and technology, and how to change.

Watson, Goodwin, ed. *Concepts for Social Change.* Washington, D. C.: National Education Association, National Training Laboratories, 1967.

    The editor and nine other authors explore in depth factors that cause resistance to change and suggest remedial actions.

29

Developing and Supporting Experimentation

A good school system should have established procedures for studying curriculum to discover areas where changes are desirable. It is not advocated, however, that change must always be going on or that there should never be periods of stability.[1] Change for the sake of change is a foolish premise. Only after extensive study to determine need for change should it be contemplated. The improvement of the curriculum of any school should be a continuing process, and administrators must constantly evaluate its purpose, suitability, and effectiveness. Unfortunately, that is not always done; therefore curriculum movements have been developed to encourage necessary curriculum changes. These movements, under such labels as *curriculum revision* and *curriculum reform,* are usually the result of changing social or technological conditions. Many of the new subject-matter programs are associated with curriculum-reform movements.

---

[1] Kimball L. Howes, "Pathways and Pitfalls in Introducing Change," National Association of Secondary School Principals *Bulletin* (April 1976), pp. 43–51.

Schools must establish guidelines for essential curriculum change. As suggested above, there should be a genuine need for change based on the relationship of the total educational function to community expectation and capabilities. Technical requirements, such as the information needed, schedules to be followed, and facilities for communication, must be considered, and boundaries must be defined.

The involvement of professional personnel is an important consideration. At one time it was thought that all people in the school system should be included — administrators, supervisors, teachers, students, and lay citizens. It was contended that the success of any curriculum venture depended on total involvement. That point of view has been greatly modified, because it has become obvious that some of the school personnel are neither qualified nor interested in curriculum improvement. They would rather not be bothered and frequently resent the extra effort and time such demanding tasks involve.

Personnel for specialized curriculum study must be carefully selected according to capability, interest, and dedication. Provisions for released time or extra compensation are not only desirable but absolutely necessary. This is particularly true for classroom teachers.

Each person in the study should be assigned a function, for such questions as *who makes decisions* and *at what point* are very relevant to success. The cooperative involvement of teachers, administrators, and supervisors must be part of an overall plan. The best procedures for curriculum study will have a carefully selected central committee with definite assignments and tacit understanding that all resources of the school system are available on call.

Changes in the curriculum can result from many causes, planned or unplanned. Most changes resulting from social or technological pressures are usually unplanned, but an alert school administrator will provide for more orderly processes by a continuing evaluation of the present program and frequent development of new curriculum guides. Important benefits can be achieved in situations where curriculum workers are encouraged to "brainstorm" or "go off into the blue." Provisions for the innovators and those possessing imaginative creativity are basic to curriculum improvement.

ESTABLISHING PRIORITIES

Deciding what problem to study first is difficult, because the contemporary curriculum relates to so many aspects of today's social and intellectual life. Each curriculum area holds numerous problems and unanswered questions. Polling of teachers, supervisors, or administrators does little to clarify the issue since their choice of significant problems is limited to the scope of their teaching level or operational area and to their personal strengths and weaknesses.

The establishment of priorities will depend on the objectives of the proposed studies, which in turn depend on the social and cultural objectives of education and the behavioral objectives desired in students. Decisions will also result from an evaluation of the present curriculum design in comparison to the desired outcomes of new designs. It is a question, of course, whether curriculum leaders should constantly strive toward developing new curricula and teaching techniques or whether efforts should be directed toward evolution and refinement of the existing enterprise. It is deceptively simple to say that both should be continuous processes.

Another basis for establishing priorities in curriculum work is the availability of research. Experimentation may be necessary if applicable research is not readily available. Intelligent curriculum decisions require careful evaluation of possible consequences, awareness of available resources and personnel, and clear insight into avenues of appropriate action.

EXPERIMENTATION

The basis for scientific knowledge is established by observation. Sometimes an investigator merely records happenings as they are, but more often he or she creates conditions for a specific purpose. When that is done, the investigation can be called an experiment. How much real experimentation goes on in education is open to question. The testing of a hypothesis against an established practice requires patience and skill. Too often, the educator falls back on opinion that is highly colored by established prejudices.

Much of the ferment in the subject-matter fields is said to be experimental. Thus, the new mathematics was often described as experimental, but the term was probably misapplied in this field. Changes in mathematics resulted for the most part from scholars and teachers coming together to discuss shortcomings in existent programs and to establish directions for change. New materials were prepared and various school systems were asked to try the new materials and report on their usefulness. On the basis of reports, programs were revised, and the new mathematics curricula gradually developed. Rather than true experimentation, it was a trial-and-error process of implementing and refining an initial set of assumptions.

It is impossible to have true experimentation without alternatives. If an attempt is made to measure the value of new subject-matter procedures, alternatives must be created within the field, so that investigators, using comparable evaluation techniques, can experiment with different means to obtain similar ends. Comparing "old" and "new" subject-matter materials is difficult because of the absence of comparable educational objectives and precise measuring instruments that are appropriate for both.

A barrier to experimental work within public schools is the fact that public school officials feel a reasonable responsibility to their conservative patrons, who get satisfaction from a moderately stable curriculum that can be identified and defended. If experimentation suggests the attempting of new ventures, it must have built-in prestige and respectability. School officials are likely to take care that the risk of experimentation is not too great and that definite limitations are imposed.

Since local curriculum leaders are restrained from any widespread experimentation, most of that kind of activity is conducted by outside investigators who merely borrow students to test their theories. They promise a comprehensive report, and local leaders try to assess it in terms of local curriculum improvement. Even then, the board of education is sometimes reluctant to release students for enough time to do real experimentation.

Regardless of the problems involved, it behooves those responsible for improving the curriculum to place experimentation high on their list of objectives. Opinions, prejudices, or guesses will not suffice in keeping a school program abreast of constantly changing social and technological conditions. The answers must be found by carefully planned experimentation. The best types of experimentation will result when a fixed set of objectives has been established and basically different approaches are used to obtain these objectives.

Experimentation is needed in the development of curricular sequences from the bottom up instead of from the top down in order to explore the possibilities of relating longitudinal subject-matter sequences to the learning processes of students. It is also needed to compare patterns organized around single subjects with patterns combining several related subjects. There is constant need for the development of evaluating materials — especially materials that can be used with students from divergent cultural groups and disadvantaged environments.

Educators engaged in curriculum work can engage in specialized experimentation; many good documents on the subject are available with clear, concise directions. Study of these materials will reveal that planning for an experiment usually involves the following steps:

1. statement of purpose
   a. question to be answered
   b. hypotheses to be listed

    c. estimated effects
    d. population to which conclusions will apply
2. description of experiment
    a. treatment to be followed
    b. range of experiment and number of factors involved
    c. type of measurement to be used and accuracy of measurement
    d. experimental design to be used
3. conclusions to be drawn
    a. analysis of variance
    b. tabular forms of results
    c. control of errors and level of significance
    d. possible outcomes
    e. testing of hypothesis against results

EXAMPLES OF EXPERIMENTATION

Curriculum planners are frequently confronted with situations that require decisions concerning school organization and course arrangement. Some examples are whether to change the present school organization to include middle schools and whether to rearrange the curriculum of the high schools to include mini-courses. At least three alternatives might be used in securing information as a basis for making decisions in such matters. First, the educational theorist could be consulted. Then there are the experiences of other educators who have made such moves. Finally, the wise school administrator may elect to have curriculum planners set up experimental situations for obtaining first-hand information.

Assume that the school administrator is confronted with the problem of alienated youth. From observation, he or she knows that the behavior of these youngsters will find expressions of discontent either in action and involvement or in withdrawal and failure. The hypothesis is that given a sufficient number of alternatives, most students elect involvement. The middle school might offer involvement opportunities for younger children, and mini-courses in the high school might bring a series of alternatives for older boys and girls. The prudent school administrator probably will elect to implement such ideas by controlled experimentation rather than take a chance on starting a great number of changes without reasonable assurance of success.

A brief assessment of the middle school idea might be cogent at this point. The real mission of the middle school is to meet the needs of children ready to cross over the threshold into early adolescence.[2] The physiological and psychological needs are sharply perceived at this time. Identified with this period is the stereotypical adolescent boy, hyperactive and awkward, and the quickly maturing girl who is confused or ashamed of her rapidly developing physical characteristics. These youngsters are often in a state of confusion, conflict, and instability. Recognizing this, curriculum planners for the middle school provide experiences that are particularly helpful to boys and girls in solving problems of this age. Such educational experiences are quite different from those sophisticated and frequently stilted experiences that follow in the later secondary years. Building the curriculum of the middle school offers opportunities for experimentation with open classrooms, ungraded sequences, and a wide variety of individualized learning experiences.

An assessment of the mini-course concept also might be interesting. Mini-courses, as the name implies, are compacted experiences in shorter periods of time. They enable secondary schools to offer a wider variety of prime-interest, short-term courses that may be either within or outside the available curricular structure. The possibilities of such courses are limitless in offering alternatives for frustrated youths. Regular members of the teaching faculty, students themselves, or members of the community may have special skills that can be incorporated into the teaching of mini-courses. Segments of regular curriculum courses may be subdivided at any point. Periods of three, six, and nine weeks are popular time arrangements. Integration of subject matter from various fields offers intriguing possibilities. Mini-courses fit well into programs that are flexibly scheduled. Such schedules usually offer blocks of unstructured time, and students welcome the possibility of encompassing this time with interesting and often exciting experiences.

RESEARCH

Research will be treated here as the accumulation of experimental results that affect curriculum planning. The research process will be evaluated as it affects educational objectives.[3] Many problems concern

[2] James Rodgers, "Setting the School's Goals and Priorities," *American Secondary Education* (June 1976), pp. 45–47.

[3] Ellis B. Page, David Jarjoura, and Charles Konopka, "Curriculum Design Through Operations Research," *American Education Research Journal* (Winter 1976), pp. 31–49.

the availability and use of educational research. Those who stress the need for more research in education contend that it is paper-thin in many areas, especially in areas involving the nonlearner and the socially underprivileged.

The paradox in that situation is that the educational leader feels the lack of time to keep up with the voluminous amount of research being completed, and is constantly being chided for failure to benefit from available research. The curriculum worker feels a certain insecurity because of an inability to prevent the widening gap between completed research and its application to curriculum problems.

The use of research poses several problems. It is necessary to select areas where good research has already been validated and decide how to use it in solving practical curriculum problems. Research must be applied in practice, not merely in theory. It is of little value to have a sophisticated, comprehensive curriculum plan in theory and continue to tolerate obsolete practices in the classroom. Another problem is the apparent lack of communication between the researcher and the curriculum worker. The period from 1970 to the present has brought a wealth of new ideas through experimentation and research, but it has not been marked by extensive innovations in learning procedures. Much of this research deals with the disadvantaged student. For example, the knowledgeable researcher has had evidence for some time that students disadvantaged by their environment can be taught by methods that minimize differences in learning and motivation between them and the more advantaged; yet curriculum planners have not been using those methods.

There is a certain amount of honest doubt about the value of educational research. Many scholars take a dim view of the untested evidence-gathering techniques used by educational researchers. They are critical of the use of questionnaires, self-inventories, and methodologies of statistics. They also raise serious questions about the normative and the historical method of much educational research. They point to the lack of reliable information in such crucial areas as learning rates and attitudes, motivations, quality of instruction, and evaluation of teacher competence. Criticism is further leveled at the efforts of educational researchers to apply scientific measuring techniques to people engaged in value-directed activities. This pinpoints the most baffling problem of educational research: how to get valid results despite the multiplicity of interdependent factors affecting human behavior.

The inability to control variables places limitations on educational research. It means the use of single factors, single instruments, and single dimensions. It necessitates the labeling of certain variables as independent of other variables. It causes the researcher to find justification in the rules of theoretical systems. Failure to control variables means that each system is governed by inherent laws and the assumptions that explain these laws. The concepts postulated and defined by the theory are the variables contained in the system. These variables behave according to the rules or laws of the system or according to the hypothesis proposed. Laws and hypotheses provide for conjecture about the regularities of the interrelationships between the variables. Thus, it may be deduced that if the concepts used in a research design are part of the same theoretical system, they can be fruitfully manipulated in varying relationships to each other, and the conclusions or results will be generalizable to other situations in which the same or analogous systems of concepts or variables are to be found.

Despite the criticism leveled at educational research, there is ample proof of its value and justification for its use. It must be assumed that education has the properties of a rational enterprise that is anchored to a clearly comprehensive and objectively derived framework. The properties of good research are present if the research is based on the three accepted stages that characterize inquiry in any field. First, the problem is analyzed to discern basic elements. Second, a survey embracing observation, description, and classification is made. Third, a theory is deductively formulated. In the theory process, inferences are added to facts in order to obtain concepts and testable hypotheses. Research technology within the field of education is not yet comparable to the level of technology in the physical realm, but constant refinement has brought it much closer to that level. Using mathematical thinking, borrowing analytical techniques from the field of agriculture, and developing realistic applications, educational research is growing toward maturity.

It is true that education is a victim of unsubstantiated and conflicting theories as well as a host of unwarranted generalizations, but even the physical sciences are not entirely free from this egocentric tendency of human beings. It is not necessary for every educator to become a research worker; neither is it necessary for the research worker to oversimplify results to make them palatable to the educator; but it is unfortunate if research methods and results are so esoteric that professional people cannot comprehend them. Educational progress depends on the finding of intelligent and valid answers. It is the task of all concerned to harmonize their efforts to that end.

The concept of "research and development" may make experimentation more acceptable. The aim is to seek better ways of teaching and learning. If experimentation is carefully conceived and the results properly analyzed, curriculum development will improve.

RESPONSIBILITY FOR
CURRICULUM EXPERIMENTATION

The responsibility for directing curriculum experimentation will vary according to local conditions. The complexity of the task calls for well-trained people, the availability of whom will affect the amount of reputable experimenting that takes place. In the large school systems, curriculum directors are trained researchers. Where the curriculum director has adequate assistance, the sponsoring of experimentation will be one of the basic assignments. In smaller schools, where trained curriculum workers are not available, the responsibility will probably fall on the principals and teachers.

The principal of a school is the direct representative of the superintendent and the school board. He or she coordinates pupil-personnel services, student activities, and building maintenance, and is also responsible for requisitioning books and supplies, controlling facilities, providing transportation, budgeting funds allocated to the building, and fostering a high morale within the teaching corps and staff. In brief, the principal carries the direct responsibility for providing a good environment for learning. This includes, of course, the direct responsibility for curriculum improvement within the jurisdiction. If responsibility for experimentation is not delegated, the principal must have time to handle it personally. There are inherent advantages in having the principal participate directly in curriculum processes: it brings closer relationships to faculty and pupils with involvement in the things that are most important. The ability to be a good instructional leader is a basic characteristic of a good principal.

The classroom teacher is a pivotal person in educational experimentation. The teacher furnishes a practical approach to shaping the research project and is frequently involved in the laboratory aspects of the situation. Care must be exercised in the involvement of classroom teachers. They tend to be conservative and frequently make decisions based on what has been successful for them rather than implementing the objectives of the experiment. Participation should never be forced. Some teachers are willing and capable, but others have neither the desire nor the ability to participate.

Classroom teachers participating in experimentation must be given released time from classroom duties or extra compensation for hours beyond their regular assignment.[4] An overworked, tired teacher cannot maintain the fervent, optimistic attitude necessary for good experi-

---

[4] Robert L. McGinty and Theodore A. Eisenberg, "Encouraging Classroom Research," *Journal of the Michigan Association of Secondary School Principals* (Summer 1975), pp. 21–26.

mentation. A project of any magnitude will require extensive in-service training of teachers involved.[5]

The best type of curriculum experimentation germinates within the school curriculum process. Involvement may go beyond the school to include lay citizens, college personnel, and certain types of specialists, but the basic responsibility for inauguration and direction of the experiment should rest with the local school administration. When faced with that obligation, school administrators sometimes take extreme positions that disrupt the promotion of good educational research. Some see in it the opportunity for professional aggrandizement and jump on the bandwagon of every opportunity to experiment or innovate. They rush in to accept and promote new ideas even before they are tested. When these hastily adopted curriculum schemes fail to work out, the would-be innovators are disillusioned or they rush off to embrace another equally ambiguous innovation. In contrast to the opportunist is the reluctant conservative who resists change of any kind. Neither extreme produces sound curriculum improvement.

RESEARCH THROUGH FOUNDATION, STATE, AND FEDERAL GRANTS

Many schools throughout the nation are participating in research projects sponsored either by foundation grants or grants from the several federal and state education acts. Unfortunately, too few of these projects originate within the local school systems. The format of the research project is devised by investigators of an outside agency who have a hypothesis to test. They focus attention on a rather narrow area of a problem of interest to themselves, using the schools as their field-testing laboratory. Although local school authorities may be furnished with the tabulated results of the experiment, it frequently is of no relevant value. Local school leaders should become involved in research projects of their own and seek foundation support. Patterns of research demonstrated by outside project agents may be emulated by local research designers.

The entrance of federal and state governments into extensive support of education has brought abundant opportunities for curriculum study and development. Through several legislative acts, grants are available for the building and evaluation of educational programs — including programs that are experimental and innovative. Efficient utilization of such grants calls for educational sagacity from local school administrators.

[5] W. R. Duke, "Development Research in Education," *Education Canada* (Spring 1977), pp. 12–16.

EXPERIMENTAL ATTITUDE

Experimentation is a healthy activity in any enterprise. It may be true that research is not the cure-all for every problem faced by practical educators, but it will provide many of the answers. Educators must be willing to test the results of research and to put into practice the best of tested innovations. It is their task to view the school's program of learning as an ever-evolving and surely improvable situation.

An intelligent attitude toward experimentation ought to be basic in educational planning and policy.[6] This means securing capable researchers, providing them with facilities, authorizing them to proceed, and then maintaining a close working relationship between them and all concerned with curriculum decision making.

Educational research must be utilized. If experimentation is an acceptable procedure in a school system, then every effort should be made to use the results to effect curriculum improvement. Progress is not made by those who stand by unwilling to go through the painful procedures of change. Nor is it made by those who resist change because of predetermined decisions that new ideas will not work. Satisfying rewards can come to those who dare to innovate. Real curriculum improvement can come from intelligent use of research, plus careful program planning and skillful implementation of creative ideas.

TOPICS FOR STUDY AND DISCUSSION

1. Analyze the relationship between stability and stagnation in curriculum development.
2. Weigh the values in curriculum changes originating in current processes and those suggested by "experts."
3. What responsibility does the secondary school principal hold for planning curriculum research activities?
4. Evaluate the vulnerability of educational research in relation to decision making in curriculum planning.
5. Many private agencies are engaged in educational experimentation and research. Develop a monologue on the feasibility of school systems employing such agencies to do their research.
6. A school system in a large metropolitan center has a curriculum research team. A small Midwestern school system makes its principal and teachers responsible for research. Compare and evaluate the two policies.
7. Educational grants are being awarded by the federal government to school systems that show extensive innovations in curriculum planning. Analyze the soundness of this procedure.

[6] H. Howe, "What's Wrong with Research in Education," *Today's Education* (September 1976), pp. 27–29.

8. Prepare a research paper that will substantiate the hypothesis that the purposes now being advocated for the middle school are the same as those advocated for the first junior high schools.
9. Postulate: mini-courses—viable or faddish?

SELECTED REFERENCES

Borich, Gary D. *Evaluating Educational Programs and Products*. Englewood Cliffs, N. J.: Educational Technology Publications, 1974.
  This book is largely for curriculum people working on problems of program evaluation on the research-and-development level. Program evaluation is a comparatively new endeavor in education. This volume points to the emergence of program evaluation as a viable, valid activity that can have a long-term influence on future educational developments. There is a focus on specific methods and techniques that evaluators have found useful.
Brown, George L., et al. *The Live Classroom*. New York: Viking Press, 1975.
  Contributors to this book comment on confluent experiences in two ways. First, a number of theoretical articles examine the implications of these experiences. In each article the authors conclude that problems arise from excessive reliance on either rationality or emotions as to the primary vehicle for reaching truth. The second type of commentary is practical, consisting of first-person accounts by teachers of how they created confluence in teaching literature, mathematics, and science.
Ellis, Allan B. *The Use and Misuse of Computers in Education*. New York: McGraw-Hill Book Company, 1974.
  There is no doubt that computers have extended the educational researcher's ability to handle almost unlimited data, but as the author contends, many users of computers are more interested in quantity than quality. An extensive description of the development and growth of the NEEDS (New England Educational Data Systems) project serves as the author's example of how the computer can be used successfully in schools. The book can be of value to the uninitiated educator as well as to one who already has an understanding of computers.
Kauffman, Draper L., Jr. *Teaching the Future: A Guide to Future-Oriented Education*. Palm Springs, Calif.: ETC Publications, 1976.
  Topics range from introducing the future and types of forecasting to more complex exercises such as use of Cross Impact Matrix. The suggested activities are interesting and show ways for stimulating learning. This book is valuable for curriculum planners who wish to futurize teaching. Ideas are presented for development of future-oriented strategies.
Keppel, Geoffrey. *Design and Analysis*. Englewood Cliffs, N.J.: Prentice-Hall, 1973.
  This handbook is a simple exposition of experimental design and the analysis of variance. All topics are demonstrated with completely worked-out numerical examples. The book covers comparisons among treatment means, two or more factor experiments, repeated measures, analysis of

covariance, and randomized blocks. There is a particularly good treatment of multiple comparisons. This volume should be on the bookshelf of secondary school curriculum designers who would improve the secondary school curriculum through research.

Kerlinger, Fred N. *Foundations of Behavioral Research*. New York: Holt, Rinehart and Winston, 1973.

This is a book about scientific behavioral research. Above everything else, it aims to convey the quality of research in general, and the behavioral sciences and education in particular. A large part of the book is focused on abstract conceptual and technical matters, but behind the discussion is the conviction that research is a deeply absorbing and vitally interesting business. One of the main uses the secondary school curriculum planner can make of this volume is to get a grasp of the intimate and often difficult relations between a research problem and the design and methodology of its solution.

Ovard, Glen F. "The Practitioner's Guide to Research." National Association of Secondary School Principals *Bulletin* (March 1974), pp. 113–118.

This article gives a good description of an actual research project that covered several years (1963–1970) in a large high school. The central purpose of the research was to create a system by which students could be rescheduled daily. Procedural steps used to develop the research are described. The characteristics of the daily demand computer schedules are listed. In the implications drawn, curriculum planners will find answers on how to use valuable research.

Pallante, James J. "The Delphi Technique for Forecasting and Goal-Setting." National Association of Secondary School Principals *Bulletin* (March 1976), pp. 86–89.

The author, working with secondary school administrators, is convinced that the research instrument described here could be used successfully in secondary school. The Delphi Technique is a method for systematic solicitation and collation of expert opinions. It is applicable whenever policies and plans have to be based on informed judgments. The author emphasizes the fact that the Delphi Technique is a potential tool for secondary school researchers in their forecasting and goal-setting concerns.

30

Some First Steps in Curriculum Improvement

Any person can do something to improve curriculum even though the preceding chapters emphasize the central role of the school principal in the process. Anyone — university student or professor, secondary school teacher, superintendent or central school office supervisor, state education agency staff member, architect, equipment manufacturer or sales representative, PTA member or other layperson — may take positive action. This chapter describes how to proceed in five areas: teaching methods, curriculum content, organizational matters, educational facilities, and local studies. The order is not fixed since any one may be the right starting point in improving a particular curriculum in a given situation.

FOUR IMPERATIVES TO IMPROVE TEACHING METHODS

Regardless of whether a given school is organized on the basis of one teacher per classroom with thirty students in it, more or less, or whether the school has already embarked on innovations such as team teaching, flexible scheduling, independent study, television instruction, or programmed learning, the following four imperatives apply. Similarly, whether or not the school has revised its curriculum content recently, the same four imperatives can improve teaching and learning in any school regardless of its location or the kind of students it serves.

A representative of a university or a state education agency can note the degree to which these four imperatives are being followed when visiting classrooms. A teacher can work in the direction of the suggested changes — starting immediately in any setting. A principal or other supervisor can use these four imperatives as guides on what to observe and what kinds of questions to ask teachers. Teaching teams or individual teachers can use these four areas for immediate self-appraisal.

Improving curriculum content without simultaneously improving methods of teaching produces frustrations and disappointing results. The reserve is true also. Here then are four imperatives that we regard as basic. Although we recognize that others might be listed, these four can be readily followed in any school with relatively little outside help.

The First Imperative: To Change the Nature and Amount of Teacher Presentations

We refer here to what teachers do when they talk to groups of students. As indicated earlier in this book, the studies show that teachers spend almost one-half the time classes are in session talking to students. They talk personally or they talk via a film, recording, or television program. We remind you that there are only three reasons why teachers should talk to groups.

The first reason is to motivate. Motivation requires that the teacher talk with such commitment, and in such an intriguing manner that the students will want to learn. The second reason is to present information that is not readily available elsewhere. A never-ending teaching task is to decide what information to talk about and what to leave for the students to find out for themselves. The third reason is to give an assignment. Elsewhere in this volume we have emphasized the necessity of telling students, orally and in writing, exactly what they are expected to know and how to go about learning it.

This appropriate talking done by teachers should occupy no more than one-third of the time that students devote to the subject. Actually, we would recommend reducing the amount to about 10 percent — or about one twenty-five-minute session per week — whether teaching is done in conventional classes with thirty students or in large-group instruction.

The Second Imperative: To Change
the Nature of Independent Study

The facilities for independent study in any classroom can be improved almost immediately by asking students to bring printed materials from home. The quality and quantity of the magazines, newspapers, mail-order catalogues, and so on, may vary, but there is something in every home that can be brought to school to help develop a reading resource area in every subject. Professional and trade magazines are useful to suggest careers. Incidentally, that procedure is an important step in removing the gap between the real world outside the school and the *artificial* world that the school tends to create inside itself. Breaking down that wall, figuratively speaking, is especially important for the so-called disadvantaged youth, but it is also significant for everyone. Teachers and others may also donate items to the resource area, and the school may purchase a variety of paperbacks and other materials. The resource area should include study material related to all the interests and abilities represented in the student body. In addition to printed materials, classrooms need a variety of other items, such as slides, records, and programmed materials, for students to view, to listen to, and to work with.

Whether the school uses a corner of each classroom for the materials or has elaborate resource centers and other independent study facilities (see Chapter 20), the students should be able to engage in independent study for at least one-half of the time they are scheduled in their classes. We would recommend increasing the proportion of time to 60 to 80 percent a week, with much more time spent in interaction among pupils and with the teacher, helping each other, and in self-evaluation.

The Third Imperative: To Provide
for Small-group Discussion

If the class is a conventional one with thirty students or so, the teacher needs to divide the class into three subgroups for small-group discussion. The techniques for these discussions are described in Chapter 22. Even though the teacher cannot be with each group full time, he or she can go from one group to the other to observe how the discussion is progressing and to make suggestions for improving it. Moreover, trained student assistants can perform the evaluations of small-group discussion described in Chapter 32. A teacher in a conventional class can regroup the students on the basis of evaluative records of discussion. Sociometric techniques help guide them in improving interpersonal relationships.

The important considerations are (1) that the teachers train the students for small-group discussion, give them the opportunity to engage in it, and make proper evaluation and (2) that students have 10 to 12 percent of class time per week for this activity. Students in every school subject should have time to react to teacher presentations and discuss the implications of their studies in that field — and to learn how to talk and to listen.

The Fourth Imperative: To Change the Methods of Evaluation

A teacher in any classroom can alter three practices almost immediately: oral quizzes, oversimplified report cards with multipurpose, single-letter grades, and constant comparisons between the individual student and the group he or she is in at the moment. Oral quizzes (called classroom recitation) waste time and may produce bad side effects. Conventional reports to students and parents fail to show what students actually know and can do, the quality of their independent study, the changes in what they do and the resultant products, and how they compare with others on carefully selected norm-based and criterion-referenced instruments. The evaluation process needs to emphasize changes for each student in relation to previous accomplishments, rather than comparisons with other students in a particular group.

Such changes are possible when the purposes of the subjects taught are defined in terms that a teacher can quantify, measure, and report — and students and others can understand. Evaluation thus emphasizes a positive thrust for each student regardless of how he or she compares with others at a given time and place.

To make these changes, the teachers at each grade or department level should meet to discuss and agree on procedures that all will follow. Principals and other supervisors can help by joining these discussions and by making the necessary administrative changes. University students can observe the changes being made; their professors can work with schools to implement the changes; and representatives of city and state education departments can help develop the public's understanding of the changes.

The foregoing four changes that we regard as imperatives may be made in any classroom. They are also required in connection with educational innovations as described in Part IV. Thus teachers and principals may prepare for team teaching, educational television, independent study, and other curriculum improvements by immediately starting with the four imperatives in their present situations.

ANALYSIS OF CURRICULUM CONTENT

Here are some first steps that a staff may take in any school to improve curriculum content. After each teacher has read about the issues and developments in the subject areas of most concern (see Parts II and III), discussions are made about which development to consider *first* to improve particular courses or parts of them. The teacher then can decide how to resolve for the time being the issues that are presented. Each teacher can do this work for his or her own teaching, or a group of teachers in a school or in a school system can do it for all subjects. The goal is to describe the purposes of the teaching and then to compare the present situation with what it should be.

A *second* analysis that can be done immediately in any school is to decide what content is *essential*, what is *desirable*, and what is *enriching* for students in that particular school community. It is true that in the final analysis such decisions need to be made through careful study by curriculum experts in the various subject fields, but preliminary efforts may be made by any teacher or group of teachers in any school.

The goal is to eliminate unnecessary curriculum content that takes so much time for pupils to learn that the pupils lack both time and energy to engage in what we have termed *depth education*. For example, we believe that a careful answer to the question, What facts in United States history are essential for loyalty and good citizenship? might produce a reduction of one-third to one-half in required content. Not all students need to become professional historians. An analogous situation exists in all subjects. With the time and effort saved, students would be able to follow their special interests and talents. Teachers would help by listing the required content and by suggesting topics for special projects by interested individuals.

A *third* kind of curriculum analysis that any school may begin with involves relating content to the activities of students and teachers. Three basic questions need to be answered: (1) what instructional content and purposes may students of different interests and talents learn and accomplish largely by themselves — if they have the time, the space, the desire, and special assistants and devices to help them? (2) What content and purposes require motivation, explanation, demonstration, or other types of presentations by a competent teacher who is physically present or by television, films, recordings, or programmed instruction devices? (3) What content and purposes require personal interaction among learners and between learners and a teacher? Such an analysis of any unit or division of a course, as well as the total course, can lead to better understanding by teachers and others of the need for independent study arrangements, large-group instruction, and small-group discussion. The analysis will help improve curriculum in any class regardless of its organization.

Failure to conduct these analyses inevitably leads to disappointment in curriculum improvement. Human and financial resources largely are wasted when content is merely reshuffled or enlarged without questioning about necessity, relevance, and methodology.

THE QUANTITY APPROACH — SHIFTING PEOPLE AND THINGS

Not long ago a principal reported the following example of an immediate change that occurred in the school. On the opening day of school, in spite of some earlier checks, the bell system was out of order. The principal announced that since teachers and students knew the time schedule of the school, they could simply watch the clocks and their personal timepieces. The situation was so relaxed that both teachers and students came to the office suggesting that the bells be turned off even after the repairs were made. A vote by the students and faculty confirmed that the overwhelming majority wished to eliminate the bell system. After several months, further evaluation revealed no desire to resume the bells. There was much less tardiness, and a more relaxed atmosphere existed. Whether comparable results would happen in other schools may be determined only through experimentation. The point is that any school, at any time, regardless of whether it has a flexible schedule, can experiment with turning off the bells.

The chapter on flexible scheduling described some other procedures that any school may undertake without extended preparation. A group of any number of teachers, a group of thirty or more students, and a quantity of time greater than forty minutes may be combined in new relationships. This arrangement is sometimes called "block of time." Such a change permits a variety of innovations that may affect only a small proportion of the total faculty and students while the remaining part of the school is relatively undisturbed. As pointed out in Chapter 25, the greater the number of teachers, students, and minutes assembled in the new arrangements, the more flexible teachers and students may become in what they do. The point is that this change can be made almost immediately in almost any school without upsetting the rest of the school.

CHANGING HALLS AND WALLS

Lobby and corridor space is largely unused in most schools except for a few minutes at the beginning of each school day, during the intermissions between classes, and at the close of each day. It is economically wasteful to leave this space unused for so much of the time. After all, it costs as much to heat and clean this space as it does to maintain the classroom space that is being used all day long. The challenge is to find some use for it.

In some schools, large lobbies have been converted into areas for large-group instruction. The first group that uses the space in the morning arranges the portable chairs and lapboards in the appropriate locations. The last group in the afternoon moves the chairs back against the walls. A permanent screen has been installed for use with various types of projectors and the necessary sound equipment has been provided.

Corridors may be used for independent study by building carrels along the walls. If the corridors are particularly narrow, the carrel walls may be placed on hinges so that they can be folded back at the end of the period to facilitate student movement. However, most corridors in most schools are larger than they need to be. A study of student traffic may reveal corridor space that can be made into independent study areas without damaging students' movement. More permanent wiring can then be installed to facilitate the use of listening and viewing devices as well as reading materials.

Cafeterias are often unused during much of the school day. A little remodeling can convert a cafeteria into a large-group instruction area, into places for small-group discussion, or into areas for independent study. Similarly, schools have remodeled spaces formerly used as study halls into areas for large-group instruction or independent study.

Some schools build new additions just like the old buildings. More imaginative schools decide to make the new addition into resource centers for independent study. The major consideration is whether the remodeling or the new addition is to be more of the same, or whether the alteration will facilitate curriculum improvement.

ARE YOU ASKING THE RIGHT QUESTIONS?

Critics of curriculum content, methods, and organization are found among all kinds of people. There are those who would *add* to the curriculum. They ask, for example, why the school does not teach more American history, or place more emphasis on what they call the fundamentals of written expression, or give special emphasis to other matters that interest them or their particular group. Others would *subtract* from the curriculum. They urge the school to discontinue driver education, home economics, problems of democracy, or some other content they do not like. Still other critics would make only *moderate alterations*. They propose a reduction of class size in all subjects, or a rear-

rangement of the topics in the world history course, or seven periods
in the school day instead of six. The trouble with all three types of
critics is that they are not asking the right questions. They need to
consider more fundamental matters that get in the way of curriculum
improvement as presented in Chapter 19.

What are the right questions? Since asking the right questions is an
essential prelude to effective discussions and research studies, here
are seventeen questions that should be raised:

1. *Does the school measure educational output (student gains) in
relation to financial input (school expenditures)?* When teachers, administrators, or persons in state or federal agencies request extra funds,
they should justify these funds by listing the anticipated improvement
in learning outcomes for *students.* What gains are expected to result
from the expenditures and *specifically* how will these gains be measured? Remember, any educational goal can be quantified.

2. *What are the school's present financial situations; the levels of
of staff morale; the status of student achievements, abilities, and interests; and the records of school leaves (graduates and dropouts) at
work and in further education?* Every school has an essential need for
data for future comparisons with the effects of curriculum changes of
one kind or another. Lacking those data, it is impossible to know precisely what effects the changes have produced.

3. *What portion of the local school budget is spent on research and
development of new curriculum content, new teaching methods,
changed organizations of instruction, and different evaluation techniques?* What should the proportion be? Commercial enterprises recognize that bankruptcy is avoided only by spending substantial amounts
of money on research and development. Study the financial reports of
outstandingly successful corporations and compare what they spend
for research and development with what schools in the local community are spending in proportion to the total budgets. Should your
school continue to be less concerned about research and development
than successful industries?

4. *What portion of the local school budget is spent on new instruction materials — in comparison to allocations for higher salaries, improvements in the building, and other matters not immediately related
to improved student learning?* This question does not imply that
teachers should not be paid high enough salaries to permit them to live
as well as professional workers in other fields. Nor does it imply that
school buildings should not be attractive places where teachers and
learners can work. The fact remains, however, that many items in
school budgets do not directly affect student learning. What priorities
are needed for future expenditures in your community?

5. *How much money does the school spend on further education of*

the staff to use new curriculum methods? How much does it spend on supervision? And what techniques to improve teaching do school officials use? Here again, comparisons with industrial procedures are relevant. Whenever an industry devises a new product or new procedures, pilot operations are established and workers are trained to operate effectively in the pilot situation. If the pilot operation succeeds, then the industry prepares all workers involved in the new process or product, using the best techniques known to industrial management. Unfortunately, in many instances teachers are expected to learn new techniques on their own time, at the end of a long day or during holidays — often without the benefit of a pilot project.

6. *How does the school recognize individual differences in talents and interests among teachers in assigning what teachers are expected to do?* The special competences of individual teachers should be utilized effectively. Schools that assign uniform workloads and salary schedules, that utilize standard certification requirements, that expect all teachers to supervise extraclass assignments, and the like, violate this principle.

7. *What steps are taken to provide teachers with more time during the school day to prepare better, to keep up-to-date, to confer with professional colleagues, to improve evaluation techniques and reporting, and to work as needed with individual students?* Successful medical practitioners set aside time for these activities. So do practitioners in other professions. One way schools can give teachers more time for such tasks is to assign them fewer classes per day rather than fewer students per class. What is your local situation in this regard?

8. *Has the school applied the techniques of job analysis to the teaching staff in order to discover what teachers must do themselves and what may be done more economically and efficiently by machines?* In an age of technology, teachers still do most things by hand. Industries that do not keep up with the times go bankrupt. There is no question of replacing teachers, but rather of replacing some things that teachers now do that are unproductive and waste their time and energy.

9. *How much work are teachers doing now that could be done well by less costly clerks?* Clerks are trained to type, to duplicate materials, to file, to keep records, to prepare reports, and the like; most teachers are not prepared for these activities.

10. *How much work are teachers doing that could be done by part-time instruction assistants; that is, persons with some preparation in the teacher's subject field or grade level, but not as much as is required for certification as a teacher?* As indicated in Chapter 26, instruction assistants are often homemakers, advanced college students, or retired teachers. They may help teachers to prepare materials, to supervise independent study, and to evaluate some aspects of learning.

11.   *What are teachers doing now for students that they could do for themselves — if the students had the time, the places, and the materials they need for independent study?* As indicated elsewhere in this volume, independent study arrangements can save teachers time and energy for more essential tasks while giving students more experience in learning by doing and responsibility for their own learning — both desirable educational goals.

12.   *How does the school principal spend time?* What are the highest priorities? What should they be? What help does he or she need? School principals spend much time and energy on the schedule, the cafeteria, school bus routes, custodial chores, disciplinary actions, perfunctory telephone calls and visits, talks with sales representatives, community activities, service clubs, and the like. All these tasks have to be done, but do they have to be done by the principal, who in the final analysis is most responsible for curriculum improvement?

13.   *What other services does the school provide to help improve, support, and administer local educational programs?* For example, what use does the school make of university consultants, specialists in the school system's central office, community experts, state department personnel, and others who could help? What special financial grants has the school applied for and received from foundations, state education agencies, industrial concerns, or the federal government?

14.   *Have steps been taken in all subject fields to plan essential curriculum content and to arrange the content logically and sequentially from the kindergarten through the twelfth grade or through completion of general education?* There may be unnecessary or unplanned repetitiveness in curriculum content, for example, offering United States history several times during the thirteen years without changing the approaches or sequence of content.

15.   *How do plans for new buildings or the remodeling of older buildings reflect current educational methods and proposed innovations?* Chapter 27 had much to say about new developments in existing educational facilities and how to plan for an uncertain future.

16.   *Does the school have one-, two-, or five-year plans for the improvement of curriculum content, teaching, and learning?* Not everything can be accomplished at once, but a start is essential. Moreover, the school needs to think through some reasonable goals for future outcomes. A set of priorities is essential for planning.

17.   *How effectively do the school personnel present their present program and their future needs to external decision-making bodies?* Legally, schools may have to depend on other agencies for financial support. The board of education theoretically and practically represents current citizen thinking about education. State education agencies, regional accrediting bodies, federal education agencies, and

university admissions officers present standards that the school must follow or else the school must make appeals for relaxation of those standards. Does the school plan its proposals well, explaining the need for the changes and describing how they will be effected and evaluated? Does the school utilize a variety of mass media in telling its story? Are the students and faculty sufficiently informed so that they can answer questions about curriculum improvements?

The fact that some schools are more productive than others is no accident. Those schools always have dynamic leadership by a succession of able principals who work effectively with their staffs and the community. They analyze the barriers to curriculum improvement and find ways to overcome or move around the difficulties. Whatever the situation, some improvements can be made.

RELATING CURRICULUM IMPROVEMENT
TO OTHER CHANGES IN SCHOOLS

We deliberately define *curriculum* broadly to include more than content. Also involved are the methods of learning and teaching, where they occur, how to evaluate pupil progress and the total program, changes in the personnel for instruction, guidance, and supervision-administration, and such structural matters as time, numbers, spaces, money, and the provision of options or alternatives. The three major curricular aspects — program, people, and structure — are so interrelated that none may be improved without affecting the others. Failure to recognize that basic fact has caused many potential improvements to fail or else be less effective than their proponents had hoped.

Foundations and governments have expended much money to stimulate educational changes, but with frustrating results. Personnel likewise have expended time and energy with few more outcomes than the exhilaration that innovations produce. The remedy is three concepts of change: (1) recognition of interrelatedness, (2) application of consistent principles of teaching and learning to the change process, and (3) patience.

Interrelatedness

After the staff members decide to make a certain curriculum change, they need to analyze all the related alterations and then decide what portions of the student body and the staff are to be included. One alternative would be to involve a group of students, a group of teachers with a differentiated staff, a block of time, several subjects, and a system of evaluation. The rest of the school would operate in a conventional manner. Another alternative could be to involve all students and teachers with a partially differentiated staff, operate with some simple form of flexible scheduling — for example, twenty-five-minute periods instead of fifty — divide a semester into two nine-week terms with mini-courses that would be completed in one-half a semester. Also, by reducing the time spent and changing the methods in conventional classes — for example, meeting two or three days a week instead of five — the program could provide learners with more time for independent study. Conventional report cards could be augmented with some descriptions of behavioral and performance progress. Later and gradually, these changes would be expanded to produce the more comprehensive changes described in this book.

The Change Process

The application of sound principles of teaching and learning to the change process requires first the development of motivation. Presentations and reaction discussions that develop reasons for change may encourage the staff to study the possibilities of change. Interested people then can use faculty resource centers to read, write, listen, and view in order to understand the concepts and procedures. The school and community become learning laboratories where teachers and students experience change through learning by doing.

The process includes diagnosing the needs for change, developing prescriptions, trying alternatives, and evaluating results to provide feedback for planning further improvements. Teachers and students then observe how the changes affect the conditions for teaching and learning and analyze the results. Consultants may help, but the basic responsibilities are with local personnel as they learn the new techniques. The principal and support staffs help organize, supervise, and evaluate the whole process. A variety of meetings, discussions, and publications keep the public informed and solicit active participation.

Patience

No knowledgeable person ever has said that it is easy to improve the curriculum in this broad context. The process is long and involved. Gains are measured yearly, but significant productivity may require five or more years. In the meantime, during the period when significant differences may be difficult to achieve, patience is a virtue. At the same time, a reasonable amount of impatience helps stimulate everyone to work at the tasks. Secondary school curriculum improvement is needed. Many schools have experienced the proposals and procedures described in this book.

TOPICS FOR STUDY AND DISCUSSION

1. This chapter presents many "first steps" toward curriculum improvement. Based on experiences in your present school — or one you know — select one or two of these steps that seem most realistic to you in that setting. Based on your study of this book and additional reading, propose a plan of action.
2. Take an approach similar to that described in topic 1 and engage in some long-range planning. What steps seem appropriate for each of the next five years? List the steps and prepare a brief statement defending your selection.
3. Which steps in this chapter seem to you to be entirely inappropriate? Why?

SELECTED REFERENCES

Cay, Donald F. *Curriculum: Design for Learning.* Indianapolis: The Bobbs-Merrill Company, 1966, pp. 167–176.
   The pages cited propose some immediate tasks for better curricula.
Clark, Leonard H., et al. *The American Secondary School Curriculum.* New York: The Macmillan Company, 1965, pp. 394–420.
   Chapter 18 provides a brief, clear summary of current educational changes. The survey could help workers in a local school or community consider which changes deserve highest priority in their situation.
Fallon, Berlie J., comp. and ed. *Fifty States Innovate to Improve Their Schools.* Bloomington, Ind., Phi Delta Kappa, 1967.
   The author catalogs and annotates 1,001 "innovations" in all fifty states. The index identifies schools, states, types of innovations, and bases of support. Although significant innovations and notable schools are omitted because of inadequate local and state reporting, what is given may broaden the perspectives of readers.
Gordon, Edmund W., and Wilkerson, Doxey A. *Compensatory Education for the Disadvantaged, Programs and Practices: Preschool through College.* New York: College Entrance Examination Board, 1966.
   Chapters 1, 4, and 5 deal more especially with curricula and secondary-age youth. Pages 198–299 include a directory of "Compensatory Practices" listed by states and grade level.
Trump, J. Lloyd and Georgiades, William. *How to Change Your School.* Reston, Va.: The National Association of Secondary School Principals, 1978.
   The authors describe in detail their proposals for change and the methods to use. The recommendations come from their experiences in a national project supported partly by the Danforth Foundation.

Verduin, John R., Jr. *Cooperative Curriculum Improvement*. Englewood Cliffs, N. J.: Prentice-Hall, 1967, pp. 72–137.

   This section proposes methods and techniques for a cooperative approach to curriculum improvement and uses Cassopolis, Michigan, as a case study. Note the "Self-Evaluation Form for Public School Curriculum" in the appendix.

Watson, Goodwin, ed. *Change in School Systems*. Washington, D. C.: National Education Association, National Training Laboratories, 1967.

   The editor and six other authors present strategies for changing schools. The discussion on "change-agents" and "self-renewing schools" are especially important in relation to curriculum improvement.

31

Acknowledging and Coping with Some Obstacles

Improving the curriculum requires changes. Anyone who challenges the status quo must accept the burden of proof. This chapter deals with some forces that resist change and suggests some constructive alternatives.

PEOPLE AND BELIEFS THAT TEND TO OPPOSE CURRICULUM CHANGE

The list of barriers to curriculum change presented here certainly is not all-inclusive. Moreover, we do not claim that all individuals or groups mentioned oppose change, or that all the beliefs are universal. What we do believe is that every point is significant and must be understood by anyone who would improve the curriculum.

Obviously, each of the following items merits more explanation and discussion than space permits. Later in the chapter, we present some suggestions for coping with the potential opposition. The critics are arranged in groups. We emphasize again the diversity of beliefs within and among the various categories because not all persons agree or disagree.

Professors.   Many university professors view secondary school enrollees not only as potential students in their classes, but even as future professional writers, speakers, historians, lovers of Elizabethan literature, scientists, engineers, musicians, athletes, and so on. Some of these professors write the textbooks that secondary school students are required to study, so they have a personal financial interest. They oppose limiting the content, concepts, and skills to the relatively small minimum that is *essential* for all students to know in the subject as separate from the levels of hobbies and careers as described in Chapters 2, 24, and elsewhere in this book.

Teachers.   Some teachers have the same kinds of beliefs and special interests as the specialists and writers in the universities and therefore oppose curriculum changes for many of the same reasons. Most teachers tend to teach as they were taught. This trait of emulating behavior places a straitjacket on the learner whose excellence is judged on ability to memorize, repeat, and replicate teacher behavior. Thus, the whole institutionalized procedure becomes a closed circle.

For the most part, teachers deal with minds, personalities, and aspirations that are much younger than their own. Our culture and most if not all others place parents, priests, and teachers on pedestals; the young are expected to respect, obey, and believe them. Teachers come to accept this respect and obedience as a fair and accurate appraisal of their competence. The cult of infallibility mitigates against change.

Some teachers are reluctant to include current materials in the curriculum. The daily newspapers, current magazines, and radio and television programs deal with issues and materials that are relevant and important to many students not only for motivational purposes but also to update science, statistics, music, writing, history, and so on. Such teachers may be uninformed or feel insecure with these materials.

Closely related to the preceding points are a number of conventional beliefs and practices in schools that constitute false pedagogy. Years ago, research indicated that brief periods of rest among the times spent in learning skills and memorization were desirable; however, conventional schools schedule fifty-minute periods, five-minute intermissions, and rest only at noon and at the end of the day. Stimulus-response and memorization are low in the hierarchy of mental processes; yet those are the major activities that constitute most of the school's program and the highest part of the reward system for students. The recitation methods commonly used by teachers often result in a student's hearing wrong answers as well as right ones; some remember the wrong they hear, failing to distinguish between the two. These malpractices illustrate only a few that might be cited.

Teacher organizations — or at least some of their leaders and/or influential members — see proposed curriculum changes as threats. Fewer teachers may be required. There may be the necessity to spend more time in training or continuing education. A conflict arises between "people and machines." Differentiated staffing could change teachers' roles. Long-time slogans that have maintained a positive relationship between the quality of learning and higher salaries and smaller classes are questioned.

Principals. Some secondary school principals and their assistants, as well as some subject supervisors in central offices of school systems, have developed a sense of security in present practices and/or enjoy the prestige, the community limelight, the extracurricular activities, and other benefits of their present comfortable positions. Also, some of them feel insecure in attempting to work with teachers and the community in the areas of improving methods of teaching and learning, updating and refining curriculum content, individualizing evaluation with more emphasis on the affective domain, and other curricular aspects.

Students. Conformist-type students who have succeeded reasonably well in conventional schools that reward memorization, good attendance, and approved behavior may be afraid of the decision making, creativity, increased personal responsibility, application of what has been learned in new situations, and other additional outcomes that the improved curriculum requires.

As a matter of fact, most secondary school students appear less interested in changing the curriculum than in doing something about administrative rules and regulations. Most of their opposition concerns rules of attendance, dress, conduct, participation in extracurricular activities, use of cars, and the like. Seldom do they mount attacks on what subjects are required, what electives are available, and where learning is to occur.

Lay individuals and groups. Extreme "rightists" and other neo-believers of the same type regard change as Marxist- or Communist-inspired. They use, often out of context, such terms as *child centered, progressive education, permissive, undisciplined, free, watered down, ultraliberal,* and so on, without bothering to read, listen, or get the facts.

Extreme "leftists" and other disillusioned skeptics see no good in any proposal that they have not originated or that can be incorporated into an existing institution. They want to throw everything away as they oppose small or evolutionary changes. They are intolerant in their ridicules of efforts to alter the system.

Smiling, agreeable, "do-gooders" agree that most prcposals to improve curriculum are appropriate — but not *now*. They present many reasons: the time is not quite ripe; there needs to be some more research *done by others;* there is currently a shortage of money (or something else); we need a foundation or government grant, we need a new school building; and so forth.

Some adults in the community oppose all programs that they consider needlessly expensive and not universally necessary. Illustrations of the latter include: high school (elementary education alone should be compulsory and publicly financed); content beyond basic English, arithmetic, U.S. history, and a little science; fancy buildings; higher salaries for professionally trained teachers and administrators; and guidance counselors.

Certain people are frustrated and angry at something in society and take out their feelings on the school programs. Their aggressions involve such matters as school consolidation, high taxes (federal as well as local), rebellious youth, drugs, and liberal politicians. Others dislike some teacher, administrator, or board member, someone who runs the PTA, or some person in the local or national scene with ideas about improving schools. Sometimes parents fight each other through their child or the school program.

Persons inside and outside the school whose learning philosophy emphasizes memorization and conformity as opposed to the cultivation of the higher mental processes, creativity, and the like fail to recognize the importance of broad educational objectives in the cognitive, skill, and affective domains.

Schools and external bodies.   Education as a profession is highly institutionalized. A prime purpose of institutions is to maintain the status quo, to prevent significant change, or at least to consider change as a threat. Learning, on the other hand, can never be institutionalized. Thus a major obstacle to the improvement of learning is the institution itself, the school. The paradox is that institutionalized education that professes an aim to change people is unwilling to change itself. Evaluations thus do little more than evaluate the instruments of measure and not the alleged purposes of the evaluation.

Some people, both inside and outside the school, vocally support curriculum improvement but fail to join the effort because they are sure the "state" will not permit the needed changes. Neither will the requirements of universities, and regional accrediting associations, the superintendent and/or board of education, the taxpayers, or a host of other "straw people" that they conjure up to help them rationalize their lack of aggressive participation in efforts to change.

We said earlier that the list of people and forces that oppose or inhibit curriculum improvement was long. Certainly, this presentation does not encompass all the traditional and conservative factors. It is nevertheless illustrative and imposing. The question is, What can be done?

WHAT MAY BE EASIEST TO CHANGE IN SCHOOLS?

There are no certain guides to selecting the particular aspects of curriculum improvement that will be easiest to achieve in a given school. You may wish to consider some experiences that one of us encountered recently in working with a group of schools that had volunteered to seek curriculum improvement through working toward a prescribed model, similar to what has been described in Part IV. However, as we have mentioned repeatedly in this book, every school has distinct qualities that make it somewhat unique; therefore, what was experienced in other schools may or may not fit a given situation.

The following extract, taken directly from a report in the *Bulletin,* a monthly publication of the National Association of Secondary School Principals, indicates what was most easily achieved by this reasonably representative group of schools along with what was most difficult to achieve and what was possible in only a few of the schools.[1]

MOST EASILY ACHIEVED ASPECTS OF THE PRESCRIBED MODEL
1. *The teacher adviser.* Schools found it easy and productive to have each student assigned to a teacher adviser. Working with the students in developing their programs, changing classes, changing locales of study, and a host of other matters, teacher advisers can handle for a relatively small number of students what professional counselors dealing with 300 or more students simply do not have the time to do. Someone in the school really knew each student and could do something to help.
2. *Providing options.* Schools learned how to give some students much responsibility for their own projects and development while scheduling other students into relatively conventional

---

[1] J. Lloyd Trump and William Georgiades, "What Happened and What Did Not Happen in the Model Schools," National Association of Secondary School Principals *Bulletin* (May 1977), pp. 73–78.

restricted programs in the same school. Advisers also learned how to select those students who could be scheduled into the community while others needed to be kept under the watchful eye of teachers while they worked in the schools. Some students were placed in relatively closed, supervised rooms with little movement, while other students were able to make many choices in methods and locales of study. Options were provided in all aspects of the proposed model for both teachers and students. As a matter of fact, one of the project schools was listed in the first widely distributed book on alternative schools.

3. *Developing materials.* We have no count of the number of learning packages and other self-directing materials that teachers in these schools developed. The number of packages in some of the schools ran into the hundreds. Moreover, as experience in developing packages occurred, teachers became more sophisticated in developing them so that the quality constantly improved. This work in the development of curriculum and methods of study represented a significant gain for these schools. Many schools outside the project also benefited from studying these learning packages as well as other materials and curriculum changes that the staffs produced.

4. *Curriculum revision through mini-courses.* While the idea of mini-courses is not new, the flexibility that the model included gave the schools an opportunity to develop hundreds of small courses, many of them in areas not previously included in the curriculum. These schools provided more choices in curriculum than conventional schools offer. The number of these mini-courses is in the hundreds.

   It is interesting to note that one school in the project operated for the last six weeks in the school year entirely on the basis of mini-courses for all other students whose teacher advisers certified that they had completed the regular courses, required or elective, which the students were studying during the preceding five-sixths of the school year. Such a practice was not recommended in the model but could serve as a transitional device in curriculum improvement.

5. *Providing better spaces in existing buildings.* The schools in the project accomplished mini-remodeling to provide better places for independent study, larger areas for motivational presentations to groups of 50 or more, and special small spaces for discussion groups of about 15 students. Corridors were utilized better, supplies were stored more effectively to provide other spaces for students to study and to work, and temporary buildings were better utilized. The better use of the community

took some students away from the schools so that buildings were less crowded. When there was overcrowding in one of the schools, temporary structures were planned and built specifically to accommodate large and small groups and independent study.

6. *Making schedules more flexible.* Conventional standard periods and the ringing of loud bells were replaced in many schools by more reliance on clocks with occasional buzzer reminders so that large groups could meet for 30 minutes, small groups for 30 minutes, and to allow more time than usual for independent study. Thus, schools provided more varieties in the use of time than do conventional six-period days. Teachers also had more flexible schedules that enabled them to find more time for holding individual conferences with students, working on cur ·culum, and the like.

7. *Increased use of the community as a learning resource.* Practically all of the schools were able to utilize better what has become in some ways a current educational fad, namely, having students spend more time in the community. This is sometimes called "action learning." The increased amount of time for independent study, flexible schedules, and the help of teacher advisers all contributed to students' making improved and more frequent decisions about what could be learned better in the community than in the school.

8. *Program evaluation.* With the aid of the central staff of the Model Schools Project, the employment of a variety of consultants, and the cooperation of rۦgional accrediting associations and state departments of education, the schools utilized more imaginative methods of answering the question, "How good is your school?" Accrediting associations readily released the schools from traditional requirements and accepted the criteria that the schools themselves developed. State departments of education also were extremely helpful. Our project staff developed a variety of measuring instruments which were used by the schools to measure program changes and values.

9. *Evaluating and reporting pupil progress.* The schools found it advantageous to supplement conventional letter grades with a variety of more informative measures. A number of schools developed completely new report forms for students and parents. Such forms provided more information of a meaningful nature than conventional A, B, C, D, F grades indicate. The process was easy but at times some individuals in the community objected. Then schools told parents the equivalent in conventional grades on a request basis.

10. *The supervisory-management team.*   Most schools reorganized their administrative teams so that the principal was available about three-fourths of the time for instructional leadership. Other persons saw salesmen, arranged athletic schedules, policed the corridors, took care of the physical plant, etc., so principals left their offices more to be where teaching and learning occur.

WHAT MSP REQUIREMENTS WERE MOST DIFFICULT TO ACHIEVE?

None of the following difficulties completely stopped progress in all of the schools. On the other hand, some schools made little or no progress in overcoming their difficulties and abandoned what they had agreed to do. Conversely, the fact that some schools were able to accomplish the goals indicates realistic possibilities. These goals continue to challenge school leadership everywhere.

1. *Differentiated staffing, both for teaching and supervising.*   The differentiated staffing that the proposed model called for was a necessary ingredient to provide teachers with essential time to work on curriculum and evaluation and to perform a number of other professional tasks that teachers only have limited time to do in conventional schools. In the early days of the project, differentiated staffing as recommended in the model was implemented in most schools in the project. Teachers were enthusiastic about the gains that they achieved. The same was true with the supervisory-management changes that the model proposed.

   However, during the time of the project, teacher associations that had been active in fostering differentiated staffing changed policies drastically in the interest of increasing salaries and other welfare benefits for teachers. Moreover, during the same period of time it became apparent that there would be a surplus of teachers rather than a shortage that had plagued the profession for the two previous decades.

   In the first year or two of the project a number of schools had employed numerous instructional assistants, clerical aides and general aides as the model prescribed. Then teachers had time to develop program materials, improve evaluations, advise students, and perform other highly professional tasks. As the project went on, this changed in many of the schools as teacher organizations developed different attitudes. Reduction in assistants made it difficult for teachers to do all of the professional planning that the model required.

Today there is an oversupply of teachers in many fields. The project directors have favored without question increased teacher salaries and better welfare provisions. Our records along these lines can be well documented. On the other hand, along with increased salaries, there needs to be redefinition of teacher roles and differentiated staffing concepts consistent with the model. There is some indication at the present time that teacher organizations will return to earlier interest in these matters as well as welfare provisions.

2. *Implementing the total model.* The unique characteristics of the NASSP Model was that it prescribed changes in *all* aspects of schooling. This requirement contrasts with most other innovative efforts which sought to change only one or two aspects of the school. Every school in the project was able to implement some features of the model. However, not one school completely implemented all of them. Several made broad progress.

The proposals in the model were neither new nor untried. In fact, they grew out of experiences that we had had in a number of other projects, in the case of the senior director more than four decades.

Although educational programs have improved over the years, the changes have been minor. Various small projects, supported by federal and foundation funds, lacked effective relationships to other aspects of school programs which, by and large, remain unchanged. Whether this problem will ever be overcome is uncertain. All we know is that it took unusually effective leadership and support of central administration and community to make progress toward the total model. Such support was inadequate in most of the schools.

3. *Explaining the rationale and practices of the model.* The staff prepared audiotapes, slides, films, articles, and a variety of other devices to help schools understand and to explain the model to their constituencies. However, in many cases the schools were reluctant or unable to do so. Perhaps the project directors had difficulties in communication.

Conventional schools in their public relations aim to highlight the successes of students and staff and to cover up shortcomings or outright failures. The same tendency affected most of the schools in this project. Schools are always favorite targets of persons who are unhappy about their tax bills, crime in the community, and many other features that the mass media exploit. Good news is not interesting to many persons; bad news appeals to many. Therefore, the media emphasize bad news and only occasionally report good news.

Certainly it is a difficult and time-consuming task to go out into the community, block by block, to answer questions of persons who do not come to parent-teacher or other meetings or read materials that schools prepare. So, in spite of the fact that only two schools were attacked vigorously by extreme rightist organizations, most of the schools found difficulties or lacked the time to explain the rationale.

4. *Lack of sound research.* Although the project conducted a number of studies and employed specialists of one type or another, and the schools themselves did the same, the resulting data do not provide "sure guidelines" for further improvements. There are many intangibles. When and why does a school conduct research? Is research designed to show the need for further changes or to underscore the early successes of small changes? Will the dichotomy between pure and action research ever be resolved? These questions were not answered adequately in this project nor have they been answered in others.

WHAT WAS POSSIBLE FOR ONLY SOME SCHOOLS?

The preceding section indicated some answers to this question. We mention only two others.

1. *Considerable extension of learning environments.* There are three places where students learn: school, community, and home. All three environments need to be utilized simultaneously, and in more productive ways. Only a few schools in the project were able effectively to expand improvements in all three learning environments. Conventional schools have the same failures.

2. *The continuous progress ideal.* One of the prescriptions in the model was that students should proceed at individual rates of speed when completing course, graduation, and other requirements. Only a few of the schools successfully attacked this problem in ways that resulted in students completing programs in shorter or longer periods of time than in conventional schools.

During the time the Model Schools Project was operating, there were unfortunate and overly simplistic proposals by some persons and groups that secondary education be dramatically reduced since some students were not gaining much from it anyway. Such proposals do have an adverse effect on the Model Schools Project.

On the other hand, a few schools made it possible for students to complete their high school education in varying lengths of time. In fact, it was possible to enter or graduate at any time during the year. Such approaches require almost complete implementation of the proposals in the model. Only a few schools were able to make progress toward the total model, and, therefore, were able to implement the continuous progress ideal.

CONSTRUCTIVE STEPS TO COPE WITH OBSTACLES

Here again, we must emphasize that the suggestions that follow are not the only ones that may serve to help a committed staff cope with the foregoing forces. Each group needs to analyze the obstacles in a given situation, make plans and decisions, take actions, evaluate the consequences, select alternatives, continue the evaluations, and work constructively along these lines in continuing efforts over a number of years. Patience alone does not improve the curriculum, but it is a necessary part of the process. We enumerate a number of suggestions for your consideration and guidance.

1. Recognize that the presence of obstacles constitutes the basis of proposing improvements; we are happy because they exist. There will be neither change nor new ideas without the challenges of unhappy, discontented, frustrated, antagonistic people. The first step, therefore, is to understand the motives of the various individuals and groups. Thus in every school community, the staff who wishes to promote changes needs to analyze carefully the forces that operate, using the possibilities listed earlier in the chapter as a starting point.

2. The second step is to neutralize the forces that cause individuals or groups to take specified positions. We need to understand *why* people act as they do. They will not move in the direction that we think is desirable unless what they regard as pressures are removed. Will people lose jobs, will the changes raise taxes, will youths protest more? If the answers are affirmative, what compensating factors can you devise that might offset these forces or others that propel people in one direction or another? The point is that until a state of instability is created in the proper direction, people will not move as you want them to.

3. In Chapter 32 we emphasized the necessity of collecting more data and presenting more evaluative feedback to various individuals and groups in terms that they understand. In a sense, this requirement means that proponents of curriculum change must accept a responsibility that opponents and skeptics often do not: to collect much more data and to express ideas more simply, directly, patiently, and honestly than usually is the case.

4. The foregoing techniques emphasize the need for accountability, a concept we have emphasized frequently in this volume, especially in Chapters 25, 30, and 33. We need to show how we would spend funds

more wisely, better utilize the talents of teachers, provide better learning environments for students, develop a more relevant curriculum, and operate schools more effectively.

5. Take advantage of the current emphasis that politicians, educators, journalists, and other opinion makers in our society are urging. As one example, a current thrust is for more attention to career education. There is nothing new in the concept of work experience, utilization of community resources, and year-round schools. However, an alert person who wants to improve the curriculum can suggest how learning more English, mathematics, art, or anything else actually opens up more career opportunities. In the process, you can differentiate between *essential* content for everyday living, content for hobbies or special interest, and content for careers.

What will be the emphases next year and the years after that? Alert curriculum workers accept these slogans, old as they may be, and take advantage of the situation. Thus they enlist the support of the opinion makers in the interests of better curriculum.

6. Create options. When you want to change some program in a school, keep the old program as an available option for students and parents who oppose the change. There are different teaching and learning styles and also differences among students and teachers in the speed with which they adapt to changes. For example, when a school changes to a more comprehensive program for appraising and reporting pupil progress, as described in Chapter 33, we recommend keeping the ABCDF system as an option for students and parents who request that information.

If the new system is better, the old will gradually disappear. Some students work better under close supervision while others work better in an open learning environment; the school should provide options as we recommended. The provision of options helps facilitate the change process while reducing the effectiveness of the opposition to change.

7. Provide an environment where people can easily help each other. One example of how this goal may be achieved is making a classroom into an office space for teachers. Even though partitions may provide some privacy, the teachers talk together more and soon are working together to plan and evaluate programs. The principal who uses the faculty meeting as a forum for personal lectures and announcements and seldom leaves the office to mingle and work with teachers violates this suggestion.

8. As parents and other aides come to the school to work with teachers and students, the school creates a better environment for creating community understanding than the typical PTA meeting develops.

Part VI of this book — the concluding section — indicates how enlightened and practical forms of evaluation not only of the total program of the school but also of the growth of individual students may be used to stimulate curriculum improvement in the future. In the long run, these approaches, when carefully considered and carried out, may be the best source of curriculum improvement.

TOPICS FOR STUDY AND DISCUSSION

1. Select a topic that you would like to see emphasized more in curriculum improvement. Then write a paper or prepare a presentation to analyze the forces that would oppose the change.
2. Using a similar procedure, make a presentation showing how you might neutralize the opposition and capitalize on positive, supportive forces.
3. Take any chapter in the book and devise a series of options or alternative practices that you might provide in a school during a period of curriculum improvement.
4. Indicate some illustrative evaluation techniques that could be used to measure the effectiveness of the optional programs described or developed in topic 3.
5. Read more widely in the literature on change either in the field of education or outside it in order to suggest some techniques in addition to those listed in this chapter.

SELECTED REFERENCES

Bent, Rudyard K., and Unruh, Adolph. *Secondary School Curriculum.* Lexington, Mass.: D. C. Heath and Company, 1969, pp. 201–227.
>   Chapter 9 describes curriculum influences, needed changes, pressures and restrictions, and the influences of organizations, laws, textbooks, and foreign education. Traditional cultural values are also analyzed briefly.

Clark, Charles H. *Brainstorming.* Garden City, N. Y.: Doubleday & Company, 1958.
>   This is a classic treatment, simply and practically written, of the techniques of stimulating creative discussion.

Foster, Marcus A. *Making Schools Work.* Philadelphia: The Westminster Press, 1971.
>   This practical book, written in a popular style, hits hard on such topics as leadership style, what's happening, relevance, working with minorities, retooling, and the school as a social force.

Illich, Ivan. *Deschooling Society.* New York: Harper & Row, 1971.
>   This controversial book may provide suggestions for coping with problems even though the author vigorously attacks the concept of organized schools as they exist and are controlled.

Martin, John Henry, and Harrison, Charles H. *Free to Learn: Unlocking and Ungrading American Education.* Englewood Cliffs, N. J.: Prentice- Hall, 1972.

Martin and Harrison present a design for community education with a Family Health Center, a Community Arts Center, a Career Education Center, a Community Guidance and Education Center, and many other features, all developed and managed by an education assembly. These developments would get away from the school board, the graded school, and the other characteristics of present-day education that keep innovations from succeeding in both elementary and secondary schools.

McClure, Robert M., ed. *The Curriculum: Retrospect and Prospect*. Fifty-second Yearbook of the National Society for the Study of Education, Part 1. Chicago: University of Chicago Press, 1971, pp. 219–259.

Ole Sand, in Chapter 9, analyzes forces that support and restrain curriculum change, proposes strategies for change, and forecasts some developments in the 1970s. Frank J. Estvan, in Chapter 10, emphasizes how self-discovery and realism influence how youths react and are involved in curriculum development. Both authors provide specific suggestions and illustrative programs.

Trump, J. Lloyd, and Georgiades, William. "The NASSP Model School Action Program." National Association of Secondary School Principals *Bulletin* (May 1972), pp. 116–126.

This article discusses some "myths of change," simple steps, widely publicized, that show how difficult it is to change curriculum and then describes how some schools are progressing in the task.

VI
Evaluation and Further Progress

32

Needed Stress and Changes in Program Evaluation

Knowing whether a school is a good school, whether a teacher is a good teacher, whether students are learning what they should be learning, and whether a curricular change is better than what it replaced are such fundamental factors in good curriculum development that no one may brush them aside lightly. Yet finding imaginative and comprehensive answers to those questions has plagued curriculum planners for generations. This chapter explains why and provides some positive guidelines for moving ahead.

A SCHOOL'S EXCELLENCE

For years, those who would determine the educational quality of a given school asked questions to get specific answers. The last turn of the century brought some answers that stand in the way of much of the curriculum improvement suggested in this volume. For example, the answer to whether a given subject or course was acceptable became "if

484

it meets 200 minutes per week." That answer is called the Carnegie unit. The answer to how a school might limit the number of subjects taken by students at one time and yet provide good curriculum with differentiation produced the required-elective system.

The decades since the turn of the century have produced many comparable questions and equally inhibiting answers enforced by state education departments and regional accrediting associations.

Here are some illustrations: When has a student completed secondary education? The answer: When he or she has accumulated sixteen units of credit with two majors and two minors. What is the minimum time a student may spend in secondary education? Until the age of sixteen (or whatever particular age is specified in a given state). What is the optimum length of a school year? 178 days (or some other arbitrary figure). What constitutes a good library? Spending X (the figure varies from time to time and in different places) dollars per pupil per year for new books, or having X number of books per pupil, or X square feet of space per pupil. What setting insures quality instruction? A teacher-pupil ratio of 1:27 with no class larger than 35. How can one achieve excellent pupil personnel services? Provide one counselor for each 250 students.

Of course, the list of questions and the expected quantitative answers could be extended. Provisions are made to rate a school on each of numerous criteria; then the ratings are averaged to obtain the quantitative measures of school excellence. The question is whether such techniques really answer the question of school excellence. Research does not support any of these measures as being better than minor modifications of the numbers one way or the other.

Earlier in this century, educators in the United States placed much credence on the system of inspectorial visits to measure school excellence. A representative of the county, city, or state educational agency paid an unannounced visit to a school, roamed the classrooms with pencil and notebook in hand, and prepared a report evaluating individual teachers and the school. That system remains highly regarded in some other countries. However, lacking confidence in the judgment of one person, school systems in this country have turned to cooperative evaluation, where a group visits and appraises the school. But the question still remains, What criteria are used?

Periodically, someone proposes that we use national examinations to measure school excellence. Such examinations, externally prepared, long have been traditional in many other countries. Here again there are gnawing questions. Do the examinations measure the most important educational goals? Are they administered uniformly? Can school excellence be measured by the average rank of a school's students on the latest College Entrance Examination Board test, the average rank of students on some state or national achievement test, the number of scholarship winners in the school, or any other comparable achievement? Is it right to compare schools whose students come from different social, economic, or cultural backgrounds? Can these matters be equated to produce common measures of excellence?

At the time of this writing, those questions were being raised more frequently than ever before. A continuing decline in pupil achievement on national norms of a number of measuring devices, including the Scholastic Achievement Test and others in the areas of reading and mathematics skills, has raised many questions, as indicated in detail in Chapter 3. As usual, superficial thinkers and seekers for easy solutions immediately blamed poor teaching in the schools and changed emphases in the curriculum. Another superficial attack is to criticize the test makers themselves for making the tests more difficult or possibly more irrelevant.

More enlightened educators who understand the relationships between the schools and society find more helpful explanations for the decline, but unfortunately, in many cases they fail to provide constructive solutions to the problem. Several years ago, when a national concern existed about mathematics and science as a part of national defense, students were caught up in the movement and studied harder and performed better in those fields.

On the other hand, when young people, influenced by their parents and forces outside the school, become disillusioned with society as it now exists, their unrest is reflected in a number of other ways. Their attitudes toward schooling, choices of subjects, aspirations, and, of course, their achievement on norm-based tests are affected adversely by emphases different from what the students themselves believe important. The decision, therefore, is whether to change the tests, change the schools, or both. We favor changing both.

Throughout this book, we provide numerous proposals for curriculum improvement. The suggestions show how programs would differ; how students, teachers, and supervisor-managers would perform differently; and how locales for teaching and learning and methods would change. We repeatedly stress the importance of measuring the effects of the changes, along with some of the difficulties involved.

The determination of school excellence is complex. Unfortunately, schools sometimes swear by certain techniques even though their value has not been proved by research. Questions that always need to be answered are, Good in comparison to what? or, On what basis? Standardized test scores alone do not indicate quality of teaching and learning; they should not be used to define excellence. Nor does a high ranking on some particular list of evaluative criteria demonstrate superiority. Following every regulation of some external agency does not guarantee quality.

One difficulty is that people sometimes accept simple answers in their efforts to accomplish specified goals. For example, a few years ago, one professional organization issued a statement titled "Grading the Public Schools." With praise and blame they listed the top state in the union, the bottom state in the union, and the national average on such items as number of students per teacher, percentage of enrolled students attending daily, percentage of eighth-grade enrollment that graduate from high school, per capita state expenditures for public education, and a number of other statistics.

An extremely useless practice, in terms of measuring school excellence, is to equate quality with per-student expenditures or median salaries paid to instru~tional personnel. Some recent court decisions and many writings have continued to fall into that trap. In one major city, for example, a court ruled that the per-student expenditure must be equalized in all the city's schools in order to provide equality of learning for all. Since some schools had more older teachers with higher salaries, the school system had to change teachers around quickly to meet the court order. No attention was paid to curriculum development, methods of teaching and learning, or related matters that bear on educational quality.

Comparative data such as those identified in the preceding paragraphs may be useful to school administrators in convincing the board of education and the public that more funds are needed for education, that a new course should be added to the curriculum, that the library should be remodeled, and the like. However, the items in isolation, or even in a statistically derived combination, do not measure the quality of teaching and learning in a school. Quantitative data are essential in high school evaluation, but they should not be considered ends in themselves. If they are, they may stand in the way of needed curriculum improvements. Moreover, such practices contribute to the lack of faith in present accountability practices in schools, thus producing a credibility gap in taxpayers' minds.

Evaluation of the total school program concerns the effectiveness of what the school *does,* rather than what the school *possesses.* Major emphasis should be on the degree to which the specific objectives of secondary education (derived from national experts and modified for the local setting) are being realized. The school must decide which objectives to measure and what evaluation techniques to use. The next chapter describes how to make that decision. The effectiveness of various resources (financial, human, and material) that the school uses should be appraised in terms of their effects on student learning. The crucial matter in determining excellence is to examine the way the school develops optimum conditions for learning.

TEACHER EFFECTIVENESS

Generations of educators have struggled with the problem of determining teacher excellence. Practically every conceivable scheme has been tried, and all have been found inadequate in one way or another.

Some years ago, statewide evaluation schemes sometimes involved granting "success grades" to teachers on the basis of county testing programs. Each teacher was graded on students' scores made on year-end tests compared with those of others in the county. The success grade was even a factor in determining the teacher's salary for the next year. Ignored were such matters as socioeconomic and cultural differences from one community to another, variables in supplies and equipment for teaching in the different schools, the reliability and validity of the tests, and a variety of other factors. Teachers adapted to the system. For example, one of them raised his success grade seven points by teaching for the test.

Many schools have used teacher-rating schemes. Both the rates and the systems themselves have been proved ineffective. The human rater is subject to criticism on the basis of both reliability and validity of judgments. The rating scheme used may have the wrong priorities or teaching concepts. Moreover, since rating is done periodically, the times that the rater visits the classroom may be unusually good or unusually inopportune in terms of the total teaching-learning process.

Other schools measure teacher effectiveness by systematic observations of classroom behavior of teachers and students. Characteristic actions of so-called good and poor teachers are noted by trained observers, who spend considerable time in classrooms and then report their findings to the appropriate administrative and supervisory officials. Obviously, these tasks require a tremendous amount of time by highly trained observers with carefully defined plans for recording the right information.

Some school systems use examinations to evaluate preservice and in-service teachers. State, regional, and national norms are set up as the basis for individual and group comparisons. The question is, Are superior teachers also superior test performers? Tests and scales are used to determine teacher attitudes, values, interests, adjustment, personality, and other characteristics. Still other instruments measure social interaction between teacher and students and among learners in the classroom.

Through the years there has been no lack of interest and expenditure of energy and money on the evaluation of teachers. Today's techniques for measuring effectiveness are increasingly sophisticated. The problem is that all the foregoing methods ignore the educational setting in which teachers are forced to work by local school policies. Working conditions and policies that ignore individual differences among teachers reward the conformist or the average person at the expense of the creative, especially talented teacher or the person with a peculiar weakness.

One teacher may be stimulated by the opportunity to work with technical devices while another may be seriously frightened by them. A given teacher may be successful with small groups of students but quite ineffective with larger groups. This illustrative list might be extended. Before a school may evaluate teachers effectively, the conditions of work for each person must be optimal so that each may realize personal maximum potential and conversely not reveal personal weaknesses.

A first step that a school should take to improve teacher effectiveness is to develop behavioral objectives for the teaching staff and criteria for judging the various performances. A necessary adjunct is to recognize that all teachers are not expected to have the same tasks; therefore, they are not judged on a single set of behavioral goals. Criterion-referenced items are applied to the particular performance that the system expects of a given individual.

The process used is old in theory but relatively rare in systematic practice. The supervisor works with an individual teacher to diagnose difficulties or problems that stand in the way of improvement. One or more potentially useful prescriptive actions are then selected cooperatively, and put into practice, and the results are evaluated in performance terms. The process is repeated as needed in a continuous search for improved performance and outcomes.

STUDENTS' GOALS

Schools measure learning by a variety of standardized and local tests. The use of both types of tests has grown phenomenally in recent years.

Standardized Tests

Most school officials actually know too little about their students. Typically, school records list attendance, grades, age, height, weight, family data, one or two group IQ scores, some achievement test scores, and an interest inventory. Such data provide incomplete and sometimes unreliable bases for deciding who shall go to what colleges, who is ready for what employment, and the like. Faced with student and parental pressures, the principal and counselors employ such measures as the *Scholastic Aptitude, Primary Mental Abilities, General Aptitude Test Battery,* and comparable instruments that yield scores. All these tests have been criticized at one time or another for their failure to measure what the school is attempting to accomplish or for representing social, economic, and cultural biases over which the local school has little control.

Forward-looking admissions officers and employers quickly point out that they use criteria other than tests for selecting students. But they too are handicapped by not knowing the students well. Local school teachers and counselors know students much better, but they do not systematically record what they know. Motivation, personal responsibility, sudden changes in goals, traumatic experiences, and other factors — alone or in combination — force new interpretations and change the predictive value of test scores. Until schools possess more information and communicate their data and recommendations meaningfully to colleges and employers, some very important mistakes are likely to be made because of too little information and too much reliance on the little that is available.

Standardized tests can help determine the quality of learning if they measure the right outcomes. Teachers state their instructional purposes quite easily, but they encounter difficulties in describing and evaluating objectives that involve changes in student behavior. For example, while English teachers attempt to teach literary appreciation, the absence of a reliable method for measuring student differences in the appreciation of "good" literature has forced them to use tests that mainly measure literary knowledge. Similar problems abound in all subject areas.

However, taking behavioral changes into consideration does not in itself solve the problem of better evaluation. For example, one of the major publishers acquired the rights to publish an excellent test that measured well the ability of students to interpret data — an objective in a number of courses. So few schools purchased the test that business economics required discontinuing the sale. Teachers either are more interested in whether students *know* some materials than in whether they *interpret* wisely, or else they lack confidence in measuring devices.

Think, moreover, of how little interest schools have in evaluating such goals as the following: growth of individual student responsibility for learning, development of habits and skills of intellectual inquiry, acquisition of competence in critical thinking, ability to communicate accurately and persuasively with other persons, and growth in creativity. Yet the measurement of how well these goals are achieved is a more important indication of individual student progress and general school excellence than such data from conventional tests now in use.

Procedures for administering standardized tests vary greatly among schools. True, instructions for giving tests are specific, but frequently they are not followed accurately. Use of different days of the week, hours in the day, or times of the year can affect test scores. Increased use of television with video tape recordings could result in the application of more uniform standards for administration and thus help alleviate the problem of obtaining comparisons among students from a variety of schools. Until more television facilities are available, most schools could use audio tape recordings.

Doubtless there are advantages in the United States system of producing tests that compete on the open market with the aim of measuring similar educational outcomes. Not only is this system in harmony with the American free-enterprise scheme, but also in the opinion of some persons, it obviates the use of a single, all-powerful "national" examination. But there are defects in this system. Students are mobile; schools often have to compare a student's previous record in a former school with different tests given locally. Further development of equivalency tables for the various tests might save students from taking more tests than are necessary. The alternative is a national assessment of basic education objectives.

Tests are better today than ever before, but the authors still include too many poor questions or items. Test makers need to be even more concerned than now about constantly seeking better ways of doing things. The test business apparently is a good and profitable undertaking. New types of measuring instruments are needed to assist nongraded programs, independent study, stimulation of creativity, self-appraisal and the like.

Locally Prepared Tests

Locally prepared tests constitute another measure of learning. However, teachers often spend much time and energy in producing, giving, and marking poor tests. Too often the teacher-made tests represent a competitive guessing game between teachers and their students that frequently focuses on the less important educational goals. The tests typically fail to provide for immediate reinforcement of learning, do not direct learning toward logical next steps, and do not measure desirable behavioral changes. Moreover, such tests lack demonstrated reliability and validity for measuring what they purport to measure. The alternative has been to turn to standardized, commercially available achievement tests, which either do not measure all the teachers' objectives or else unduly influence what teachers include in their instructional programs.

Local, teacher-made tests seem to encourage student cheating. Teachers blame moral laxity, parental pressures for high grades, competition for college admission, and the like. The real difficulty is that the tests emphasize memory skills and isolated facts. A French teacher, for example, is more interested in "catching" student differences in memorizing vocabulary or the content of a story than in teaching facility in speaking and reading — so the test is a competitive exercise of doubtful value. The students are tempted to cheat in order to beat the system, and the teachers try to outguess the students. The resultant tests are poor, often based on outmoded goals of teaching and learning. They emphasize the development of memorization rather than the higher mental processes.

Another problem concerns the methods for reporting progress to the students, their employers, or to the colleges they expect to attend. Teachers, principals, school counselors, and some college admissions officers like to reduce their descriptions of student learnings to single-letter-grade systems.

Principals and teachers question what grades to give students in advanced placement or special-track programs. They worry because an A grade does not mean the same in track 4 as in track 2, or because class rank does not mean the same in a small school in Iowa as it does in suburban Oak Park. No wonder some parents in suburban Washington, D. C., recently demanded that the board of education remove their children from the school's gifted classes so they would receive higher grades in the poorer competition of average classes and stand a better chance of getting into the college of their choice.

Evaluation needs to consider at least three general areas of individual achievement: (1) what students *know* and *can* do; (2) the extent of change in carefully defined student behaviors; and (3) the quality of what students do while engaged in independent study with a minimum of faculty supervision. Attempting to pull all the data that measure individual accomplishments in all these areas into one multipurpose grade is an educational crime. So is the calculation of a standard formula for college admission, or for promotion, for graduation, for admittance to kindergarten, for eligibility for athletics or the student council, or for a number of other similar practices now followed by educators who oversimplify professional evaluation and reporting.

INDIVIDUALIZING EVALUATION

Individualizing learning requires that evaluation also be individualized. Three typical practices found in schools obstruct their goal: the oral quizzing, called recitation or, erroneously, class discussion; combining all aspects of achievement into one grade; and constantly comparing the individual student with the group to which he or she is assigned.

Oral questioning to discover students' knowledge of essential facts is a waste of time for both teachers and students; moreover, it is not a good way to find out if the students know what they are supposed to know. The time that teachers and learners spend in oral quizzing and answering varies from class to class, with the average being about twenty minutes per period. The teachers could use that time better for preparation, conferences, evaluation, and other professional activities. The students could use the time more advantageously in their own independent study.

The recitation plays into the hands of the academically able, verbal, extrovert student; others are needlessly embarrassed. The small-group setting in which pupils are selected according to present ability to express ideas orally is a much better setting for teachers to appraise individual progress, and programmed materials and objective written quizzes are more efficient than an oral quiz for finding out what each one knows of the essential facts of a course.

The second practice to change in order to individualize evaluation is to move away from the multipurpose grade. Besides oversimplifying reports, making them less meaningful both to students and parents, the single letter grade fails to record individual differences in accomplishment. A student with less knowledge than others may be more creative; one with poor attitude, attendance, and self-control may have high achievement in knowledge; another may memorize well but be weak in making application to new situations. The school needs to appraise and report the various goals separately.

The third evaluation policy required is to emphasize the individual's accomplishments in relation to his or her own past record, not in relation to others in the student's immediate group, for that group may not be typical. A high-ranking student may develop laxity with mediocre competition and have difficulties when moved to a situation where the general level is higher. Conversely, the student at the bottom of the group may work very hard and improve but still receive a D—, or unsatisfactory grade, because of remaining low in comparison to the others. Effective competition with one's own past record is the best guarantee of effective competition with the group.

EVALUATING CHANGE

Someone has said that innovators are not evaluators. The converse of that statement also is true. In many cases, evaluators are not innovators. These two statements summarize the problems we face in evaluating educational changes. Basically, what is needed is to understand the relationships between the stated purposes of an educational change, such as team teaching, and how to evaluate or judge the extent to which the purposes are being realized.

Let us examine some purposes of team teaching — some more legitimate than others — that have implications for evaluation. For example, an article appeared some time ago in an educational journal in which a principal indicated that his school initiated team teaching because the plant was so overcrowded that they would have been forced to go on a double-session program if some other arrangements were not made. Double sessions were opposed by both pupils and parents. However, they discovered a well-known fact, namely, that the combination of large-group instruction, small-group discussion, and independent study in a team situation could accommodate a considerably larger number of students than the conventional system could in the same building space. So they instituted that educational change. The principal reported that nearly every parent, teacher, and student approved. Since conservation of building space was the only reason for team teaching in that school, the evaluation was very simple. Team teaching succeeded because more students occupied the available space and they did not resort to a double session. Apparently they were not interested in measuring other potential team-teaching outcomes.

If team teaching is initiated to develop more personal responsibility for learning among students, evaluation needs to go beyond giving standardized or locally developed achievement tests. What the pupils do during their independent study inside and outside the school must be analyzed as suggested in Chapter 33. Or if team teaching aims to encourage more and better reading, the evaluation goes beyond giving standardized reading tests, to include records of *how much* reading and *what kind* of reading students did before and now do after team teaching.

The point is that evaluation must be related to the specific purposes of any change or innovation. Hazy purposes bring hazy evaluation. Using wrong or inadequate measuring instruments to evaluate well-defined purposes is equally out of focus. Chapter 33 illustrates the constructive action that is needed. The emphasis is on stating the purposes of change in behavioral terms and developing criterion measures of the performance that ensues.

EVALUATION IN A CHANGING SOCIETY

A chapter on changes in methods of program evaluation would be incomplete without reference to the problems that schools face in determining how well they are doing in relation to past performance. Repeatedly in this volume we stress the view that school programs inevitably reflect the social, economic, and political mores of the times. Program evaluation that ignores those factors lacks validity.

The arguments still persist, even though there is little reason for that situation, that schools have a responsibility as well as the ability to influence society, that education may in fact create a new social order. The idea that such a possibility exists has caused school programs all sorts of difficulties throughout history. Some educationists appear to accept the idea that schools can change society, possibly because it gives them a sense of power as well as a reason for existence. As a matter of fact, that premise is wrong. Schools have always reflected the mores of the society in which they exist and which in fact create the schools and maintains them. School programs, properly developed, can help students and others in their communities learn how to be constructively critical of the society in which they exist, but they certainly cannot by themselves as institutions change society.

This point is repeated here for emphasis. All sorts of special groups continuously try to influence the curriculum in order to reach their own particular goals. The temptation to accept these responsibilities is great but must constantly be avoided.

The question is whether the curriculum is in fact producing students who are aware of what is going on, know how to analyze situations based on the collection of adequate evidence, and to arrive at personal solutions for constructive action. Educational programs make that contribution, as evidenced by what the graduates in any community do to create a better world. The schools have done their part. The methodology of constructive change is a program responsibility; determining what change is desirable is beyond the scope of the program.

What we are emphasizing is that the schools cannot be blamed for drugs, crime in the streets, thievery and dishonesty in government and business, and the many other problems that abound. Many of these developments were discussed in earlier chapters of the book, especially Chapter 13. The emphasis here is on evaluation of school programs: what can and cannot be done.

TOPICS FOR STUDY AND DISCUSSION

1. A newspaper article recently indicated that a neighboring school produced six finalists in the last national competition for merit scholarship winners. Your school produced none. One of your school patrons has just called to ask, "Why isn't our school as good as theirs?" What is your answer?

2. What do you believe is the best quantifiable criterion for judging curriculum excellence? Be prepared to defend your answer in a group discussion.

3. If the educational setting affects teacher excellence, what improvement in the setting should have highest priority in a school you know in order to achieve a better quality of teaching?

4. Taking the subject you teach, or one in which you are especially interested, list the goals you would use to evaluate students in your school in comparison with those in other schools of the city, county, state, or nation. Perhaps your answer is none. In either case, defend your conclusion in a paper or discussion.

5. With your colleagues, discuss how to improve the system of reporting student progress to parents.

SELECTED REFERENCES

Anderson, Scarvia B.; Ball, Samuel; Murphy, Richard T.; and associates. *Encyclopedia of Educational Evaluation,* San Francisco: Jossey-Bass, 1975.
> The 452 pages constitute a comprehensive reference for evaluation models with purposes, designs, social contexts, approaches, analyses, and interpretations. The index and bibliography are also useful in developing programs.

Findley, Warren G., ed. *The Impact and Improvement of School Testing Programs.* Sixty-second Yearbook of the National Society for the Study of Education, Part 2. Chicago: University of Chicago Press, 1963, pp. 163–210.
> Max D. Engelhart and John M. Beck discuss how tests have developed over the years and present nine recommendations for improvement. Ralph W. Tyler writes about the problems and effects of external testing and offers constructive suggestions for coping with pressures caused by the programs.

Goodlad, John I. *Facing the Future.* New York: McGraw-Hill Book Company, 1976, pp. 149–161.
> In Chapter 10, "Perspective on Accountability," the author suggests why this approach has little promise for improving educational procedures and outcomes.

Hoffman, Banesh. *The Tyranny of Testing.* New York: Crowell-Collier Press, 1962.
> This book is a controversial classic in pointing out the evils in conventional testing programs. It describes weaknesses in various tests and testing procedures.

Howard, Eugene. "Can Accountability Improve Secondary Education?" *Educational Leadership* (May 1976), pp. 595–600.
> A strong argument is made for considering aspects for improving schools beyond the conventional accountability syndrome so popular today.

Invitational Conference on Testing Problems. Princeton, N. J.: Educational Testing Service, 1957.
> This is the report of the 1966 conference, a program that has been sponsored annually for more than a quarter-century. Pages 3–60 contain six lectures relating to educational innovations and evaluation.

Mager, Robert F. *Measuring Instructional Intent*. Belmont, Calif.: Fearon Publishers, 1973.

This author, whose book on preparing behavioral objectives was widely used in the 1960s, has written a teaching book to help readers learn how to relate test items more closely to instructional goals.

Merrill, M. David, ed. *Instructional Design: Readings*. Englewood Cliffs, N. J.: Prentice-Hall, 1971, pp. 327–374.

Part V deals with the criterion-referenced measurement plus conditions and criteria, thus providing the reader with both theoretical and practical bases for developing better evaluative techniques and instruments.

Popham, W. James, ed. *Evaluation in Education*. Berkeley, Calif.: McCutchan Publishing Corporation, 1974.

Nine authors present views on a variety of evaluation procedures ranging from purposes, variety of approaches, standardized tests, and criterion-referenced measurement to such matters as cost analysis and matrix sampling. The last chapter emphasizes the uses of evaluative data to improve programs.

Saylor, J. Galen, and Alexander, William M. *Planning Curriculum of Schools*. New York: Holt, Rinehart, and Winston, 1974, pp. 297–346.

The authors provide further details on the nature of evaluation as applied to content, instruction, and the program of evaluation itself.

Shane, Harold G. *Curriculum Change Toward the 21st Century*. Washington, D. C.: National Education Association, 1977.

This report of NEA's Bicentennial Committee emphasizes a need to look to the future. The seven cardinal principles are reframed to provide twenty-eight premises to guide future developments in updating content, with increased use of the community, more personalization of education, and provisions for lifelong learning. A representative panel of experts was involved.

Tyler, Ralph W., ed. *Educational Evaluation: New Roles, New Means*. Sixty-eighth Yearbook of the National Society for the Study of Education, Part 2. Chicago: The University of Chicago Press, 1969.

See especially Chapter 7, "The Evaluation of Group Instruction"; Chapter 8, "The Role of Evaluation in Programs for Individualized Instruction"; and Chapter 12, "Appraising the Effects of Innovations in Local Schools."

Wilhelms, Fred T., ed. *Evaluation as Feedback and Guide*. 1967 Yearbook. Washington, D. C.: Association for Supervision and Curriculum Development, 1967, pp. 18–46 and 72–100.

Clifford F. S. Bebell discusses "The Evaluation We Have," emphasizing such factors as emotionality, grading system, tests and examinations, and the inertia that inhibits change. Doris May Lee writes about factors that inhibit realistic self-evaluation and urges important changes in teaching to improve evaluation.

Zais, Robert S. *Curriculum Principles and Foundations*. New York: Thomas Y. Crowell Company, 1976, pp. 369–392.

Zais emphasizes the necessary relationships between evaluation of pupil progress and total program evaluation.

33

Appraising and Reporting Student Growth

The preceding chapter emphasized reasons for changing the methods that many schools use in evaluating their total curricular programs. The philosophy and approaches presented there also apply to measuring what students know, can do, and outcomes in the affective areas of learning. The particular emphasis here is on results of their independent study. We propose comprehensive methods of appraising, recording, and reporting the progress of individual students. Combinations of these data also have relevance for evaluating the total program.

STUDENT SELF-APPRAISAL

Self-appraisal aims to enable each student to know continually what progress he or she is making. The test of the effectiveness of self-appraisal is the degree to which test taking on instruments prepared by teachers or external examiners ceases to become a traumatic experience for the learners. If their self-appraisal is well done, students know in advance how well they will do on tests prepared by others, assuming the tests are well devised.

Self-checking Exercises

Every classroom or independent study area needs a series of exercises prepared by teachers that will enable students to check individual progress. For example, in English, exercises on capitalization, punctuation, number and tense, sentence structure, paragraph structure, and the like are provided. These exercises are relatively brief, with the answer sheets immediately available so each student may know how well he or she has done and, especially, the kinds of mistakes that reveal need for further study. Reading tests of various sorts are also available for use at any time. Examples of comparable evaluative instruments in other subjects are typing exercises, rating skills to judge productions in art and music, self-testing exercises in foreign languages, and a wide variety of factual tests related to the various topics being studied in history, mathematics, sciences, and, in fact, all the school subjects. Students may work on these self-appraisal devices individually or with a partner. In any event, each one is encouraged to maintain personal records of what has been done.

Programmed Instruction

The school should provide each student with a textbook or technical device particularly planned to teach a given subject area without the constant supervision of a teacher. That idea is not new, but it certainly has received increased emphasis in recent times. The *programmed* materials may ask the students to fill in blanks, answer questions, select one of several multiple choice answers, solve a problem, find new ideas in science, or what not. Students engage in self-evaluation while working through a programmed textbook or teaching machine. The items are arranged in a sequential manner regardless of the type.

The program tells the student immediately whether his or her answer is right or wrong. No longer is it necessary to wait for a grade on a test or approval of an answer to a question in class. The point emphasized here is that besides having tremendous implications for curriculum development per se, programmed instruction serves an effective function in reporting to students, to teachers, and to others what the student knows. That reporting is done constantly, hour by hour, rather than at the end of six weeks or the established grading period. How-

ever, in many instances schools fail to take advantage of this opportunity. The progress of each learner through programmed instruction
materials should be recorded by the student and reported systematically to teachers and to parents.

Computer-assisted Instruction

The programmed instruction materials of today will doubtless constitute the museum pieces of tomorrow. What teaching machines do
today will be done more efficiently tomorrow by computer-assisted
instruction. Computer programs not only can monitor individualized
instruction, determining progress for each student according to personal talents and interests, but also may push the learner along more
efficiently than most teachers and most programmed instruction can.
Moreover, in addition to mediating instruction, the computer will produce individualized records of progress, so each person will know
much better how he or she is getting along. In turn, teachers, parents,
and other interested people also will know better what progress is
being made. Today's research and development programs will produce better and more economical computer-assisted instruction
tomorrow.

Self-appraisal Reports

The school should develop a system whereby each student can report
what she or he hopes to do in relation to strengths and weaknesses.
Personal descriptions will show plans for capitalizing on strengths and
overcoming or learning to live with weaknesses — and progress to
date. Such a program is essential for sound mental hygiene. It is also
important in any program of personal evaluation of progress.

Teachers in every subject should develop the appropriate forms for
self-appraisal and reporting. One column can list the goals of the subject, defined in terms of what students are expected to do and to become. A second column, to be filled out by the learners, can indicate
approximately how well each one believes it will be possible to accomplish the goals. A third column can indicate present progress as
defined by each one with respect to the various goals. To report to
parents and to the students, the teacher can then check, in the fourth
column, either agreement or disagreement with the self-appraisal made
by the student. A fifth column can be used for the student's final indication of agreement or disagreement with the teacher. Such a process
represents a tremendous move ahead in developing individual responsibility and understanding of the teaching-learning process.

The point is that teachers must give students much more responsibility to assess their own progress in learning. Teachers may waste much of their own time in grading papers; that time is spent better in improved planning and preparation. What may be even more important, when teachers grade too many papers, they deprive students of a significant learning activity and a sense of personal responsibility. Teachers must constantly push students to appraise their own productivity in the various curriculum areas.

WHAT STUDENTS KNOW

Students' self-appraisal should be complemented by systematic programs whereby examiners verify to the best of their ability what the students actually know at given intervals during the year. Standardized achievement tests and teacher-made tests provide this type of appraisal as a guide to students, parents, colleges, and employers.

Standardized Achievement Tests

A city, county, or state school system decides what students should know and employs experts to construct the most valid and reliable instruments possible to evaluate knowledge of that material. Here is where the government, through its experts, tells what historical facts, what mathematical problems, what spelling and grammar, what information about typewriters, what French vocabulary, what health rules, what scientific facts, what beliefs about social issues — what knowledge and skills in all areas of human activity represented by the several subject disciplines — are considered essential, desirable, and enriching. The information that the state expects everyone to know should be measured by tests prepared at the state level and standardized within that level so that each student and each school can determine how well the students are learning.

We recommended earlier that because of population mobility, such decisions should be national rather than local or regional. Does it follow then that assessment of student knowledge also be national? If curriculum experts determine, for example, the facts that everyone who is educable needs to know to be an effective, loyal citizen, then the assessment of student knowledge should be national in scope. Of course, regional and local differences in literacy, cultural goals, socioeconomic status, and the like affect scores on such tests, but the facts of such differences are known, and ameliorative steps can be taken.

Once more we should emphasize that we are discussing here only basic education, the aspect of total schooling that is the same everywhere. The evaluation of depth education is not a matter for state and national assessment in the same way that basic education is. It is possible, of course, for curriculum and evaluation experts to construct standardized tests that will help students know the progress they are making beyond the requirements of basic education, but such tests are not necessarily given in every school.

Teacher-made Tests

Because the curriculum of each school and of each class has certain elements uniquely necessary in the particular locale, teacher-made tests are needed to complement the standardized testing program. Moreover, standardized tests are given at major intervals of time whereas teacher-made tests are given much more frequently in order to provide guides for teachers and learners to plan future instructional activities.

The local tests need to evaluate knowledge not only of the subject disciplines but also of such matters as the library, the resource centers, and community learning opportunities. They also need to measure student knowledge of the availability and functions of various extra-class activities and the school's guidance services, which vary from one school to another.

The difficulties involved in teacher-made tests are well known. Many teachers have had little training for preparing tests that are valid, reliable, and useful. Even teachers who know how to prepare such tests often lack the necessary time and facilities to construct them. Therefore, the resultant testing is in many instances less valuable than it should be.

The bibliography at the end of this chapter suggests books that teachers may study in their efforts to improve the tests they make. Teachers need not feel insecure in the construction of objective, performance, and essay tests. The school's supervisory program can help them know how to score and grade such tests and analyze the test data statistically to arrive at sound conclusions. Teachers realize how these tests help them diagnose learning problems and suggest prescriptions to guide further assignments.

WHAT STUDENTS DO

This area of evaluation may be the most important of all. A student may *know* something, but inability to apply that knowledge through constructive action may leave her or his education relatively incomplete. An old cliché says that actions speak louder than words. Yet schools typically ignore or lightly treat this aspect of evaluation and fail to report behavioral outcomes to parents and others in a systematic manner, or else they cover them up in a multipurpose mark, as described in the preceding chapter. Constructive steps should be taken.

Probably no one group has done more to evaluate behavioral outcomes than Dr. Ralph Tyler and his colleagues during the Eight-Year Study of the Progressive Education Association in the 1930s. They described the procedures and developed instruments for measuring behavioral outcomes.

The teacher's first step is to define personal expectations of what students are to accomplish in measurable terms. Every teacher aim is quantifiable if stated properly. For example, if one of the teacher's goals for students is to appreciate literature better after having completed a given course in English, the teacher describes what persons who *appreciate* literature do differently from persons who *do not appreciate* literature. Do they read more books of higher quality? (And what is meant by "higher quality?") Do they buy books to establish a personal library? Can they read a page from each of two stories and determine that one of the stories is written better than the other? A similar procedure can be followed to determine behavioral outcomes in other subjects. In every case teachers must decide how to collect the data — through personal observation, through paper-and-pencil measuring instruments, through the application of scales, or by some other means.

Consider another illustration, this one from the area of small-group discussion as described in Chapter 22. Teachers hope that pupils in small-group discussion will express ideas clearly and persuasively, will listen effectively and understandingly to the oral statements of other members of the group, and will respect and appreciate each other in the process. Therefore, the teacher must keep an evaluative record of the discussion. For example, the teacher may record a tally each time a group member makes a substantive contribution, along with +, 0, or — to indicate the teacher's judgment of whether the statement was accurate, helpful, pertinent, or valuable according to whatever other criteria the teacher accepts for effective contributions.

Similarly, the teacher can appraise how good a listener each student is by tallying an indication of whether the student actually had listened to the contributions of other group members and how well they were understood. The evaluation may also include an appraisal of the positive contributions of each individual: how constructive, how creative, how enlarging. The teacher then combines tallies on quantity and quality of speaking and listening for a given grading period, comparing what the student did during that grading period with actions during a preceding one. To evaluate growth of the total group in discussion skills, the teacher may compare the average student scores for two different periods.

Sociometry may be used to determine changes in interpersonal relationships among students and, therefore, whether a given individual is progressing in personal relations with other students in the group. Such measurements become an essential ingredient of the evaluation of progress, or the lack of it, in programs of small-group discussion.

Another possible teacher goal is for students to read more books — and books of better quality. Teachers may evaluate that objective by asking their students to fill out a three-by-five-inch card each time they read a book or magazine. They list the name of the author, the title, and the name of the magazine or publisher of the book, plus a sentence recommending or not recommending the book or article to other young people; then they give the signed card to an assistant. The measurement involves counting the number of books read and evaluating the quality of each book on a predetermined scale. Periodically, the teacher has a private conference with each student, going over the cards to verify whether or not he or she has in fact understood the listed books. Then it is relatively simple for the professional teacher to evaluate the accomplishment of this reading objective for individuals or for a given group.

Some behavioral goals may be schoolwide, cutting across subject lines. For example, a faculty may wish to evaluate "ability to follow directions." During a given grading period, without publicity, individual teachers may be asked to report occasions when specific students followed directions very well or, conversely, failed to do so. Each example is recorded on a three-by-five card, which is then placed in an appropriate faculty box. The school assigns each faculty member the responsibility for accumulating cards for a given group of the students for whom he or she has responsibility as teacher-adviser. Thus the school evaluates each student on this particular objective, at the same time evaluating the total school. The project may be repeated periodically to judge other all-school objectives, such as good citizenship, punctuality, or ability to think creatively.

The foregoing examples obviously represent only a few of hundreds that might be given. The faculty, individually or as a group, needs to decide what behavioral goals are to be evaluated and then collect evidence to measure the extent to which the objectives are accomplished.

INDEPENDENT STUDY

Chapter 20 stressed independent study as the heart of the school program. We provide here a plan, developed by Dr. William M. Griffin of Boston College, for measuring the quality of independent study. Dr. Griffin used the following definitions and scale to evaluate special independent study projects in the Wayland, Massachusetts, High School.

A student performing effectively in independent study is one who —

Perceives things to do. *For example:* pursues instructional leads for further study, . . . compares various sources of information, . . . asks relationship-type questions, . . . integrates information from different subject-matter fields, . . . summarizes findings and places them in correct frame of reference.

Personalizes learning. *For example:* casts about for a project of real interest and value, . . . gives own unique reasons for doing what is done, . . . prepares a plan to structure the study, . . . distributes work schedule to allow for other commitments, . . . expresses satisfaction in a task of own selection and implementation.

Exercises self-discipline. *For example:* accepts limits of the school without denying self, . . . displays sustained and conscientious industry, . . . seeks procedural authority for own point of view and actions, . . . works in harmony with others in groups of two or three, . . . cooperates in maintaining climate for individual work.

Makes use of human resources. *For example:* initiates contacts with appropriate teachers and other persons, . . . shares interpretations, interests and ideas in good exchange, . . . comes prepared for conference discussions, . . . uses contacts to clarify thinking with pertinent and relevant questioning, . . . investigates suggestions which are offered.

Makes use of material resources. *For example:* broadens own knowledge through related readings, . . . makes use of tapes, records, and projectuals to expand knowledge, . . . displays deftness in locating library materials, . . . recognizes and uses the tools of the study area, . . . constructs special materials and devices for use in the work.

Produces results. *For example:* works at appropriate pace and follows through to completion, . . . plans projects which are subject to accomplishment, . . . states clear objectives, . . . displays habit of getting down to work, . . . finds applications for a creative idea.

Strives for improvement. *For example:* seeks advice from competent people, . . . corrects errors on one's own, . . . studies authoritative sources for best practices, . . . uses group sessions to test out ideas and clarify issues, . . . evaluates material in the light of personal experiences and first-hand knowledge.[1]

The independent study efforts of each student may be evaluated on a five-point scale. The school needs to decide which of the foregoing characteristics are to be judged. Although it is far better to evaluate a student on each characteristic, one generalized rating might be made to simplify the task for the teacher. In any event, the method of ap-

[1] William Maxwell Griffin, "A Study of the Relationship of Certain Characteristics of High School Seniors to Effectiveness in Independent Study" (doctoral dissertation, Syracuse University, 1964).

praisal should be explained to students, parents, and others who may see the record. The scaled judgment should be accompanied by a sentence comment illustrating the basis of the evaluation.

The scale might look like this:

(Statement of objective)   (Name of student)

1	2	3	4	5
		√		

Least			Most
Effective		Average	Effective

(Comment)

A check (√) is placed at the point along the line that best describes a student in a given quality, judging the individual's efforts in relation to the independent study efforts of all other students the teacher has ever known. The illustration shows a student who is somewhat better than average in effectiveness in the aspect of independent study being evaluated.

The important consideration is to accumulate a series of judgments and comments over a period of years so that changes in performance may be evaluated. A qualified person then might summarize the changes for reports to colleges, prospective employers, and any other interested people.

REPORTING STUDENT PROGRESS

The basic principle in reporting progress to students, to parents, to colleges, and to employers is to report each type of educational goal separately, even though the report is in a consolidated form. What a student *knows* and what he or she *does* should be listed in different sections. A third section should be devoted to independent study, using the scales described in the preceding section.

The written report provides information regarding specific achievements during each grading period. For example, it may include the percentage of right answers on teacher-made tests, standardized test scores, and number and quality of books read, the speed of typewriting — with the number of errors — and the like, listing comparable data for earlier marking periods.

The report should not include the student's standing in relation to other students. If a parent wants to know such data, the school should reveal it in a personal conference. When a student applies for college admission or a specific job, the school can present median and range figures for each of the subjects being reported so that the reader may know how the student compares to other students in the school.

What we are suggesting is a continuous progress reporting system instead of the production of letter grades every six weeks or twice a semester, a final course-end mark, or other conventional procedures. Evaluation thus becomes a regular part of the teaching-learning system constantly rather than periodically. The report does not reflect a pass/ fail situation. Some students simply progress faster than others.

Here is how such a program could work. The required portions of the curriculum areas are identified as segments, units, or portions distinctly separate from other parts that represent optional, additional creative or depth studies done by students who develop different goals beyond the required sector. Each of the required segments has a name and a number, identified on the report card. When the student completes a segment, the teacher or instructional assistant punches or marks the card. A qualitative indicator, such as above average, may be provided for the segments when appropriate. Otherwise, the indicator means satisfactory completion. The school mails these reports home periodically, once or twice a semester, with intervening reports only when requested or needed. The emphasis here is on the cognitive and skills areas.

The required content in all subjects would be listed, evaluated, and reported as illustrated here:

1. COMPLETION OF LEARNING SEQUENCES AND COMPARATIVE TESTS

SUBJECT: English

No. of Sequence	1	2	3	4	5	6	7	8	9	10	11	12	13	14	15	16	17	18	19	20	21
Above Average						●							●								
Completed	●	●	●				●			●	●	●				●					

COMPARATIVE TESTS:

Reading — California CTB

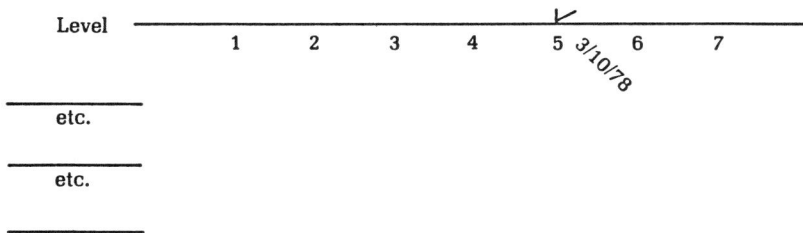

Level ——————————————————————
  1   2   3   4   5 3/10/78 6   7

——————
  etc.

——————
  etc.

——————

See the reverse side for the names of sequences by number and the nature of the tests.

A second report form describes periodically what each student accomplishes beyond the required segments in each subject. On each page of this report, the teacher in charge of a given project or activity records when a student reads more than is required, plays on the basketball team, produces an art work, develops a mathematics puzzle, or does any other special project. The report is simple: two or three descriptive phrases or sentences plus an indication of quality on such criteria as creativity, use of resources, self-discipline, and the like, as selected by each department. The emphasis here is on the affective domain.

The figure below illustrates how the form might be used for a special project in English.

This report emphasizes individual achievements with comparative judgments based on all students a teacher has ever worked with rather than on a particular class at a given time. Standardized instruments or district measures provide interested people with a basis for judging the relative quality of a student's performance in comparison with others.

Oral reports are also desirable. The point was made in Chapter 26, which concerned team teaching and staff utilization, that teachers should be scheduled with students fewer hours per week than is the case in the conventional school today. An important reason for freeing teachers from scheduled contacts with groups of students is to provide them with the time to confer with individual students and their parents regarding student progress. This conference is used to amplify the written reports and to suggest remedial and progressive steps to improve achievement. Variations in student needs prevent positive state-

2. SPECIAL PROJECTS COMPLETED

SUBJECT: English

DESCRIPTION	QUALITY		
	Superior	Average	Inferior
——————	Use Human Resources ⌞___|_✓_|____|____⌟		
——————	Use Materials ⌞___|___✓|____|____⌟		
——————	Creativity ⌞___|___|___✓|____⌟		
——————	Self-Discipline ⌞_✓_|___|____|____⌟		
——————	Value to Student ⌞_✓_|___|____|____⌟		
——————	Worth Doing ⌞___|___|__✓_|____⌟		
	Etc.		

ments on the frequency of these conferences. However, school policies might reasonably suggest a minimum of one student-teacher conference during each six-week grading period and one teacher-parent conference during each semester.

At least one teacher in the school must know every student as a total human being; therefore, one teacher should have the responsibility of accumulating the reports from all the other teachers and of consolidating the data into a report card. As indicated in Chapter 25, such an arrangement is basic to the guidance functions of the school. This teacher-adviser becomes a liaison between the parent wanting a comprehensive appraisal of his or her child's progress and needs and the different teachers that the child has. The arrangement saves both the parents and the teachers considerable time and systematizes the whole business of reporting progress. The teacher-adviser also provides information to colleges and to prospective employers. Obviously, the teacher needs time for these activities and must have clerical help.

The results of all the efforts described in this chapter and the preceding one are criterion-referenced and norm-based data for each student and for the school as a whole. Such data, pictorially presented, provide school personnel and others with more data of higher quality and usefulness than most schools possess today. Obviously, such efforts are crucial in secondary school curriculum improvement, the basic goal of this book.

TOPICS FOR STUDY AND DISCUSSION

1. Prepare for one topic in a subject you teach, or one you are preparing to teach, a self-checking test that will tell students what they already know and what they still need to study.
2. A colleague says, "I will not be replaced by a machine" (meaning a programmed textbook, a teaching machine, or computer-assisted instruction). Develop a series of reasons to support or reject your colleague's opinion in a group discussion.
3. What arguments will you use to defend or oppose a system of national assessment of learning? Include the relationships of such a system to curriculum planning and development.
4. Think of some purpose in your teaching that you are not measuring reliably at the present time (or if you are a university student, that your teachers are not measuring). Devise ways to quantify the objective. What does a student do who has accomplished the goal as opposed to what others do who have not achieved the aim? Then prepare a plan for collecting and interpreting the data and reporting your findings.
5. Discuss with colleagues who teach other subjects some common purpose you share, such as developing more responsibility for learning on

the part of students. Plan and carry through for one or two weeks a schoolwide system for collecting examples of situations in which students have or have not acted responsibly and for reporting that information to the students and their parents.

SELECTED REFERENCES

Bloom, Benjamin S., ed. *Taxonomy of Educational Objectives, Handbook I: Cognitive Domain.* New York: Longmans, Green & Co., 1956.
   This book presents a system for classifying educational goals related to the recognition and recall of knowledge and the development of intellectual abilities and skills. It provides illustrative test items.
French, Will, and Associates. *Behavioral Goals of General Education in High School.* New York: Russell Sage Foundation, 1957, pp. 85–230.
   Part III provides a basis for evaluation by listing a large number of performance outcomes under four general areas of competence: intellectual development, cultural orientation, health, and economic facility. It provides a table to help workers in any school develop evaluation priorities.
Krathwohl, David R., et al. *Taxonomy of Educational Objectives, Handbook II: Affective Domain.* New York: David McKay Company, 1956.
   Such affective goals as interests, attitudes, appreciations, values, and emotional sets are classified and illustrated under these categories: receiving (attending), responding, valuing, organizing, and internalizing.
Lange, Phil C., ed. *Programmed Instruction.* Sixty-sixth Yearbook of the National Society for the Study of Education, Part 2. Chicago: University of Chicago Press, 1967.
   This is an up-to-date analysis by eleven authors of the bases, developments, issues and problems, and future possibilities in programmed instruction. Chapters 3, 6, and 8 are especially significant for curriculum development.
Mager, Robert F. *Measuring Instructional Intent.* Belmont, Calif.: Fearon Publishers, 1973. 159 pp.
   This author, whose book about preparing behavioral objectives was widely used in the 1960s, has written a teaching book to help readers learn how to relate test items more closely to instructional goals.
———. *Preparing Instructional Objectives.* Palo Alto, Calif.: Fearon Publishers, 1962.
   This booklet is a self-teaching primer for teachers or anyone else who needs to learn how to express educational goals in behavioral terms — the first step in improving evaluation.
Popham, W. James, and Baker, Eva L. *Systematic Instruction.* Englewood Cliffs, N. J.: Prentice-Hall, 1970.
   This book provides a practical guide for goal-referenced instruction along with the techniques for evaluating the results and testing hypotheses.
Smith, Eugene R., and Tyler, Ralph W. *Appraising and Recording Student Progress.* New York: Harper & Brothers, 1942.
   The story of evaluation in the Eight-Year Study presents the philosophy

of appraisal that emphasized the development of performance objectives. Numerous examples of instruments and devices are included.

Wilhelms, Fred T., ed. *Evaluation as Feedback and Guide.* 1967 Yearbook. Washington: Association for Supervision and Curriculum Development, 1967, pp. 121–181.

Paul B. Diederich and Frances R. Link describe an innovative evaluation program that is generally conducted by groups of teachers rather than by individuals. The emphasis is on evaluating behavior goals. They also describe in detail a special project in English.

34

Curriculum Improvement and the Future

A major strength of the secondary school curriculum in the United States is that the schools literally belong to local citizens rather than to any central ministry of education. The country's founders decided to omit nationally organized education from the federal constitution, thus legally leaving the control of schools to the states. In practice, much freedom and responsibility for curriculum development are vested in persons who work in local schools.

The states urge local school districts to do research, to innovate, and in other ways to seek improvements in all aspects of curriculum content and the related methods of teaching and learning. Our personal experiences as elementary, secondary, and higher education teachers and administrators and as educational consultants underscore the importance of this concept. Those individuals and groups who oppose local and state control of schools usually have their own favorite projects they would like to install in all schools throughout the nation. Local control plus external stimuli have combined to encourage initiative and concerns for better schooling for all people.

Even when there have been massive, national programs to change the curriculum, as described in Parts II and III, these efforts have not forced all schools to conform. A good example was the development of new and expanded programs in mathematics, science, and foreign languages in the 1950s and 1960s under the guise of national defense, stimulated by the Soviet Union's space achievements. That influence soon lessened as the scientific and industrial expertise in this country provided a better image of achievements here. Local and state programs reaffirmed the concept that all subjects were important not for merely a few favorites, but for the individual youth and the national development.

WHERE THE ACTION IS

Efforts sponsored by foundations, state and national governments, and individuals and groups with specific ideas about improving schools, play an important part in motivating local groups to reexamine curriculum offerings and related program aspects. Although external motivation is an essential ingredient in the constant search for better programs, fortunately local school districts retain the power to decide whether to follow the proposals.

The diversity of populations in this country, coupled with this freedom from national requirements and specifications, provides stimulation for curriculum improvement. Tremendous differences exist between the needs of inner-city students and the needs of small-town students, and between various regions of the country. In general, the schools have never fallen prey to demands for uniformity even as increased population mobility developed.

The situation is further strengthened by the friendly competition that exists not only between school districts but also among schools in the same locale to develop new programs that proponents believe will better serve the interests and needs of the students there. Teachers and administrators need to feel this responsibility as well as the inherent opportunities.

There are diverse educational opportunities available for young adults as well as older people. Lifetime learning has become a possibility through the availability of mass media and the growing numbers of adult education programs that are offered at reasonable costs with few restrictions on age or previous education. Many employers also furnish training programs, either free or at minimal cost.

The foregoing practices contribute to the diversity in the secondary school curriculum because there is less need for students at that level to learn everything that they may need in later life. This situation has not prevented local school districts from providing adequate education for the young. Local control stimulates competition from one community to another. Business has seen that situation as a measure of community excellence and a good reason for people to want to locate in a particular area.

At the same time, increased state and federal contributions in funds and ideas to secondary schools in this country during the past half-century or so have enabled local schools to provide better programs. There have been few restrictions or strings attached to the various types of assistance. When controls are imposed in order for a district to receive funds, these controls have been mainly beneficial. Of course, the local district did not have to solicit or receive those grants. Much the same has been true with respect to moneys made available by foundations whose funds came from profits accumulated by various individuals and corporations.

Today, there is again emphasis on and debates over issues associated with the assessment of school quality. Should proficiency tests be administered to each student before a diploma is given? Should individual competences be measured periodically throughout the period of schooling? Are standardized tests reliable and valid? Can racial and economic biases be overcome or compensated for in such assessments? The answers to these questions often are unclear and cloud the resolution of the problems associated with present programs, evaluation procedures, and the granting of diplomas.

People from other countries sometimes find it difficult to understand how a major nation can operate successfully without national curriculum specifications. Mores vary from one nation to another, so there is little reason to argue one situation in comparison to another. The emphasis in this concluding chapter is simply that the secondary school curriculum in the United States, having resulted from relatively less influence at the national level, presents tremendous challenges and opportunities.

The frustrating aspect of local control of schools is that persons who would improve the curriculum have to develop imaginative ways to pursuade students, teachers, administrators, boards of control, and the public there to accept different programs. This condition accounts for the relatively slow spread of new practices, even when substantial evidence shows the need for and the possible benefits in the proposals for change. Obviously, it is easy to argue the benefits of both sides of this situation.

Possibly the future will bring basic changes as the mass media, especially television, tend to increase our knowledge but also to make us all more alike. For example, a recent nationally televised beauty contest revealed dramatically how the regional dialects are disappearing; the young people sounded much alike, regardless of what part of the country they came from. Drug use is almost as prevalent in small towns as it is in big cities. Crime waves spread quickly. What do all these developments mean for secondary school curriculum improvement in the future?

Another factor to consider is the effect of declining school enrollments on the curriculum. Empty spaces are found in many schools. Some schools are being abandoned entirely as students and teachers are transferred to other localities to make better use of the school district's facilities. A curriculum that was developed for the needs of one group may not exist in the new school. Will the new administration and teachers provide options?

In the meantime, the birth rate appears to be rising again slowly. Some experts predict major increases in the 1980s and booming school enrollments then and in the 1990s. Would curriculum improvements that attract more adults to the schools help cope with all these enrollment changes?

THE GENESIS FOR CURRICULUM IMPROVEMENT

Every teacher and administrator in every school has opportunities to improve the curriculum in all aspects relating to content, methods, and settings. Every problem that individual teachers face or local schools face in relation to total programs provides challenges to do so. Of course, some fail to act. However, our purpose is not to indicate blame for failure to exercise professional responsibilities, including curriculum revision. The point is that problems need to be viewed as opportunities to motivate program improvements.

Today's schools face challenges never experienced before, at least in the same degree. Organized teacher strikes and protests call for constantly higher salaries and improved working conditions. In many cases students, for a variety of reasons, are extremely difficult to manage. Violent acts against other students, teachers, and school administrators are unfortunately not uncommon. Drug sales and use by students in school buildings and grounds occur. Frustrated parents, taxpayers, and employers criticize the school programs for not dealing constructively with these difficulties. They also worry about increasing costs.

Interestingly enough, our experience is that schools that introduce more flexibility and less uniformity in their programs, along the lines suggested in earlier chapters of this book, experience both improved attendance and decreased discipline problems. Suspensions and other measures may be essential to cope with an immediate, violent action but in the long run those methods do not solve the problems. Imaginative teachers and administrators seek alternative solutions.

The genesis for secondary school curriculum improvement lies in constructive approaches as described in numerous places in this book. The combination of defensive and constructive approaches, with major emphasis on the constructive, is the positive approach.

THE FUTURE

Chapter 1 presented a number of issues that will be resolved one way or another in every local school and to some degree in state educational programs. Every teacher and school administrator may have an important role in resolving those issues.

Although it has always been fashionable to forecast what education will be like at some future date, we do not choose to join a particular cult of futurists. We doubt that our crystal ball is either more clear or more dull than the crystal balls of others who write about the future. Our belief is that the future will be influenced by more serious thinking and group actions by our readers and by university students preparing to join the profession.

The technology is available to make educational programs quite different and potentially better than they are today. Human knowledge has broken through many barriers to encompass ideas and concepts never experienced before. There exists in society an openness that no longer restricts education to a school building, to any particular age or group, or to any specialized content and methodology.

A basic question is, Where will this openness lead the secondary school curriculum? Both educators and lay citizens are suggesting that schools as they are known today will gradually — some say rapidly — disappear as they are replaced by a variety of alternative educational enterprises elsewhere in the community or area. Incidentally, the reasons and the proposals given are very similar to ones given in the late 1930s and early 1940s with respect to the federally supported National Youth Administration and Civilian Conservation Corps.

Those depression-based institutions provided training and work experience for youths who dropped out of school because of financial problems as well as irrelevant curricula and teaching methods. All over the country, these government agencies started a variety of programs to take the unemployed youths off the streets and keep them out of trouble. Many of the programs certainly provided work experience and other learning opportunities in ways that were absent in conventional schools. Students confronted realistic problems. The programs of work experience and conservation made more sense to many of them than the unrelated, sterile programs of schools that overemphasized college preparation for nonexistent work opportunities.

As soon as World War II started and the economy improved, young people were otherwise occupied. The NYA, CCC, and similar programs disappeared. The schools, however, kept programs basically the same as they had been before those competitors appeared on the scene. We remind our readers of these events not because history tends to repeat itself, but rather because such illustrations may stimulate thinking about future curricula.

Today a variety of alternative schools exist in various places, especially in larger cities. Most of these alternative schools are operated by boards of education within existing facilities, but sometimes they are located in abandoned warehouses, unused office spaces, and in other places away from school buildings. However, it would seem now that alternative schools *outside* the existing structure of schools will disappear. Schools with declining enrollments have space available. Also, different educational perspectives make optional or alternative schools possible within existing structures. No longer do such schools see the necessity of enforcing uniform rules of attendance, program selection, location of learning, and many other factors that characterize conventional operations. The curriculum in these alternative schools is necessarily more closely related to the present needs of youths than is the curriculum of the conventional school.

The major advantage of having centrally housed alternative programs is obvious. Students who accept one of these options, only later to find it undesirable, may readily transfer without major difficulties to another option within the same structure and under the same administration. Moreover, as the total curriculum moves toward better utilization of the community as a learning environment, the role of the school in relation to the other environments not only changes but does so on a more rational basis.

History tells us that the schools at any time reflect the current mores of the society in which they exist. Although some people hopefully claim that schools can change society, recorded history is not on their side. Schools may encourage the constructive criticism of social mores, but they do not in themselves change society.

Today's schools are closer to the centers of social action than any schools in the past. Violence and vandalism are rampant in communities and are prevalent in the mass media; hence they occur regularly in the schools. Police protection in schools is now welcomed in some places. As school programs deal more directly with these problems in ways suggested in this book and as school personnel become more effective in their constructive criticisms of the social mores, the future will find improved ways of dealing with these problems.

Back-to-the-basics advocates are urging schools to abandon all changes initiated since World War I and to reinstate the curriculum of the 1800s and early 1900s. Lacking both data and experience, they glibly point out that all the educational innovations of the 1920s and onward, which they term the products of "progressive education," have failed and are disappearing from the schools. Fortunately, they are mistaken.

The National Association of Secondary School Principals, in a program started by one of the authors of this book, for a number of years has surveyed annually its membership, which includes about 35,000 persons, mostly principals, who work in all kinds of schools scattered throughout the fifty states as well as in some countries abroad, to learn of efforts to improve schooling. The respondents describe programs in their schools that differ from conventional ones. They aim to arouse student interests, reduce suspensions and dropouts, and in general to meet student needs better. In the process, teachers are stimulated to perform better as their individual interests and competences are developed. The number of such programs constantly is increasing.

We have been involved for several years with a group of schools interested in broad-scale efforts to improve teaching and learning and the attitudes and interest of both teachers and students in the process. As indicated earlier, many of the revisions in this third edition have their genesis both in that project and in the many others that continue to be developed in this country and are reported to us.

The experiences thus far in this century have changed life and improved it in many ways. The same may be said with respect to the secondary school curriculum. You have read already in Parts II and III about improvements in the subject areas and in developments that cut across the conventional curriculum fields. You have learned in Part IV how options in the curriculum may help further to individualize learning and professionalize teaching. Part V cited ways to implement curriculum improvement, and this part of the book has indicated evaluation procedures.

We believe that people who analyze these changes and approach curriculum improvement constructively will have a beneficial effect on both the schools and society in the future. Organized education is here to stay, although we hope that the form and substance will continue to change.

A number of people who call themselves Futurists are trying to produce better schools by means of improved curricula and methods. We applaud their efforts while we concentrate more on seeking to implement in more schools what we already know to be useful and workable. This curriculum book can help you in the process.

The professionals who work in schools must help colleagues, students, and lay people to answer two simple and at the same time complex questions. Where are we today in curriculum development? Where would we like to be? The resultant assessment of needs provides a basis for curriculum improvement.

Yesterday's future is now. What of tomorrow? That question is answered best by the curriculum improvements of today. We refer you again to the issues in Chapter 1. How will you meet the challenges of the times?

TOPICS FOR STUDY AND DISCUSSION

1. What kinds of data do schools now possess that might be used more effectively in planning for future improvements in the curriculum?
2. What new and different data do schools need to collect? Their research and development programs are the lifelines both for present and future survival. Schools too frequently have not even caught up with present needs, at least in some curricular aspects. More data are needed as a basis for future planning.
3. Review the issues in Chapter 1. Have you changed your mind about any of them since you first read that chapter? If so, why? If not, why not? Summarize your answers in a personal statement and file it for future reference.
4. Use an approach similar to that in topic 3, only use the areas of consensus and disagreement of some group of which you are a part, for example, a university class or your colleagues in a school.

SELECTED REFERENCES

Clift, Virgil, and Shane, Harold G. *The Future, Social Decisions, and Educational Change in Secondary Schools.* Seventy-fifth Yearbook of the National Society for the Study of Education, Part 2. Chicago: The University of Chicago Press, 1976, pp. 295–315.
Ten questions are raised and four general answers provided to guide the thinking of the futurists. The authors suggest a list of additional readings.
Dickson, Paul. *The Future File.* New York: Rawson Associates, 1977.
The book assembles numerous proposals for changes in education at all levels.
Glines, Don E., *Educational Futures I,* Section D, "Modeling Future Learning Now," pp. D-1 to D-41 and D-54 to D-63. Millville, Minnesota: The Anvil Press, 1978.
The author gives transitional directions to achieving "Imagine High School" with detailed descriptions of living, learning centers and future curriculum experiences. A "futures glossary" is provided along with a bibliography and other resources.

Rubin, Louis, ed. *The Future of Education: Perspectives on Tomorrow's Schooling.* Boston: Allyn and Bacon, 1975.

> Another group of authors look into their respective crystal balls and suggest what is likely to happen.

Saylor, J. Galen, and Alexander, William M. *Planning Curriculum for Schools.* New York: Holt, Rinehart and Winston, 1974, pp. 348–387.

> The authors summarize numerous recommendations based on school situations and predict changes in American life. They list essential characteristics of future schools at all levels.

Shane, Harold G. *Curriculum Change Toward the 21st Century.* Washington, D. C.: National Education Association, 1977.

> The future is viewed by forty-six "noted persons" and ninety-six "young persons." The curriculum for that future reaffirms the seven principles of 1918 that have been the foundation of the twentieth century, then goes on to emphasize more personalization, more services to adult learners, mature past thirty and senior past sixty, and more emphasis on individual evaluation in an environment that will be increasingly urbanized and subject to even more rapid technological changes.

Toffler, Alvin, et al. *Learning for Tomorrow: The Role of the Future in Education.* New York: Random House, 1974.

> The author of *Future Shock* considers the psychology of the future and a group of other authors expound on the future in the curriculum and other influences on all levels of schooling. Some sample syllabi and future studies are described in the appendix.

Index